WITHDRAWN

ESSAYS ON
GOVERNMENT

ESSAYS ON GOVERNMENT

BY

ERNEST BARKER

Honorary Fellow of Merton College, Oxford
and of Peterhouse, Cambridge

SECOND EDITION

OXFORD
AT THE CLARENDON PRESS

Oxford University Press, Amen House, London E.C.4

GLASGOW NEW YORK TORONTO MELBOURNE WELLINGTON
BOMBAY CALCUTTA MADRAS KARACHI KUALA LUMPUR
CAPE TOWN IBADAN NAIROBI ACCRA

FIRST EDITION 1945
REPRINTED 1946
SECOND EDITION 1951

REPRINTED LITHOGRAPHICALLY IN GREAT BRITAIN
AT THE UNIVERSITY PRESS, OXFORD
FROM SHEETS OF THE SECOND EDITION
1956, 1960

PREFACE

IN this second and revised edition of *Essays on Government* one of the essays of the first edition has been omitted, and two new essays have been included. The essay omitted is an essay on the Government of the Third French Republic, which is now—at any rate in part—out of date. The new essays included are the essay on the theory of the Social Contract in Locke, Rousseau, and Hume, and that on St. Augustine's theory of society. The essay on British Constitutional Monarchy has been revised and expanded, and some changes have also been made in the essay on the Parliamentary System of Government: the other essays in this volume which appeared in the first edition (II, V, VI, VII, and IX) are reprinted in their original form. The omission of some of the old matter and the addition of two new essays have made it possible to divide the volume into three parts, each containing a number of connected and related essays.

The first Part is mainly concerned with political institutions. Two of the three essays which it contains—the first and the third—were originally written and published as pamphlets during the course of the War of 1939-45. One of these essays was intended to explain to readers in other countries the nature and the working of British Constitutional Monarchy; and it appeared originally not only in English, but also in other languages. The other, that on the Parliamentary System of Government, was intended to serve both French and English readers, and it therefore appeared originally both in an English and in a French version. The remaining essay in the first Part, on British Statesmen, first appeared as one of the volumes in the series *Britain in Pictures*, edited by the late W. J. Turner and published by the firm of Collins. The author is indebted to the editor and the publishers for permission to reprint the essay.

The second Part is concerned with some issues of political theory during the century which lies between the publication of Locke's *Two Treatises on Government* (1690) and the composition of Burke's *Reflections on the Revolution in France* (1790). One of the essays in this Part, that on Blackstone and the British Constitution, appeared for the first time in the first edition of this book.

The other three essays in the Part originally appeared in the form of pamphlets, articles, or introductions. The essay on the theory of the Social Contract was written in 1946 as an introduction to the volume *Social Contract* in the series of the World's Classics published by the Oxford University Press; and the author is indebted to Mr. Geoffrey Cumberlege for permission to reprint it here. The essay on Burke and his Bristol Constituency is the printed form of two lectures, the Lewis Fry Memorial Lectures, which were originally delivered in the University of Bristol in the autumn of 1930, and were afterwards printed as a pamphlet by the firm of Arrowsmith of Bristol. The essay entitled 'Burke on the French Revolution' was written in connexion with the 150th anniversary of the French Revolution, and it appeared originally, in French, in a number of the *Révue Philosophique* for the last quarter of 1939, which contained a series of essays, by different writers, under the general heading of 'La Révolution de 1789 et la pensée moderne'. In its English form it first appeared in the first edition of this book.

The third and last Part contains two essays dealing with the general problem of the relation of the Church to Society and the State. The first of these essays is an attempt to state the views of St. Augustine, as they were stated in the *De Civitate Dei* some fifteen centuries ago: the second is an attempt to state a contemporary view, as the matter appeared to the author *sub specie temporis sui*. The essay on St. Augustine's theory of Society was written as long ago as 1930: it first appeared as an introduction to a one-volume edition of *The City of God* published by Messrs. Dent & Sons in 1931, and it was afterwards reprinted, with some alterations, to serve as an introduction to the two-volume (and greatly improved) edition of St. Augustine's book in Everyman's Library (1945). Messrs. Dent & Sons have generously consented to its being reprinted here, in a context and connexion which may perhaps give it fresh significance. The other essay in the third Part, that on the Community and the Church, was written for the Conference on Church, Community, and State, which was held at Oxford in the summer of 1937, and attended by representatives of many churches from many parts of the world. It first appeared in a collective volume (one of a number prepared in connexion with the Conference), entitled *Church and Community*, and published by the firm of

PREFACE

Allen & Unwin: it is now reprinted here by permission of the original publishers.

Some of the essays in this volume—the third, the fourth, and the seventh—are concerned with France, and with the parallels, the differences, and the general relations between the institutions and political ideas of France and those of England. The writer cannot but think of a great French historian and thinker whose knowledge and insight and friendship bridged and spanned the Channel. He therefore desires to set here (as he did in the first edition) the inscription

TO THE MEMORY OF
ÉLIE HALÉVY

E. B.

CAMBRIDGE
6 *October* 1950

CONTENTS

Part I
ESSAYS ON GOVERNMENT

I. BRITISH CONSTITUTIONAL MONARCHY — 1
II. BRITISH STATESMEN — 23
III. THE PARLIAMENTARY SYSTEM OF GOVERNMENT — 56

Part II
ESSAYS ON THE THEORY OF GOVERNMENT
(1690–1790)

IV. THE THEORY OF THE SOCIAL CONTRACT IN LOCKE, ROUSSEAU, AND HUME — 86
V. BLACKSTONE ON THE BRITISH CONSTITUTION — 120
VI. BURKE AND HIS BRISTOL CONSTITUENCY, 1774–1780 — 154
VII. BURKE ON THE FRENCH REVOLUTION — 205

Part III
ESSAYS ON THE RELATION OF THE CHURCH TO SOCIETY AND THE STATE

VIII. ST. AUGUSTINE'S THEORY OF SOCIETY — 234
IX. THE COMMUNITY AND THE CHURCH — 270

INDEX

PART I

ESSAYS ON GOVERNMENT

Essay One

BRITISH CONSTITUTIONAL MONARCHY

I

OUR monarchy goes back, in a long continuous line, for more than one thousand one hundred years, to an ancient king called Egbert, who united all England under his sway as long ago as 829. For all that time—with only one brief interruption of eleven years, from 1649 to 1660, when we had a republic or 'Commonwealth'—there has been an unbroken line of kings. The monarchy is older than our Parliament, which goes back 700 years to the thirteenth century: it is older than our law courts, which go back 800 years to the twelfth century: it is older than our oldest universities. It is a remarkable illustration of this long continuity that King George VI can trace his descent straight back to King Egbert in the year 829. Sometimes the descent has gone in the female line; but it remains, none the less, a straight line of descent. The Papacy is the only institution existing today in Europe which is older than our monarchy.

The continuity of our monarchy inspires us with a sense of the continuity of our own national life through a long and storied past: it equally inspires us with a sure hope of the continuation of our national life through future centuries. It gives stability to our political forms and our social structure: it helps to prevent revolutionary dreams and sensational changes. But it is far—very far—from being a merely conservative institution. It does not prevent change. On the contrary, it has helped and fostered change; and it has changed itself in the process. This is the cause of its long survival. It has survived because it has changed, and because it has moved with the movement of time. It has survived because our kings, for the last 250 years—ever since the last internal disturbance of our affairs, a disturbance which we call 'the Revolution of 1688'—have been wise enough to forget past pretensions, to learn new lessons, to change their position with the changing times, and to join with their subjects in bringing about changes in other institutions. They changed their position, for example, in the course of the eighteenth century, to accord with the growth of a Cabinet system and the rise of the office of Prime Minister. They joined with their subjects in bringing about changes in other institutions during the nineteenth and twentieth centuries, when they helped in the passage of the Reform Bill of 1832, which made our House of Commons more democratic, and in the passage of the Parliament Act of 1911, which made our House of Lords less able to thwart or check the purposes of the House of Commons. Not that our kings became, either in 1832 or in 1911, political partisans, who espoused one of the contending sides. That would not have been a true way of helping to bring about change. They did something different and better. They simply acted in obedience to the unwritten rule of our national life which prescribes that the powers of the King shall be used in accordance with the will of the nation. They stood above party: they watched the nation; and they joined with their subjects in bringing about change when the will of the nation was set for change—and only when it was so set.

It is worth while to pause and consider the development of the British monarchy during the 250 years since the Revolution of 1688. It is a lesson in the art of preserving monarchy. At the beginning of the seventeenth century, our kings still governed as well as reigned. They had, it is true, advisers; but they did not necessarily take the advice which they were offered. They reserved the final decision for their own royal act of will. Now it is a law of life that the person who takes the final decision must, and will, be regarded as responsible. This responsibility will be enforced against any king who takes final decisions if, and as soon as, there is an effective national opinion which claims to judge and insists on judging. Such an effective national opinion had already been formed among us three centuries ago. But as long as the King still took the final decision, the only way in which that opinion could assert itself, when his decision was challenged and his policy was repudiated, was the way of rebellion or revolution. Those ways were tried in the seventeenth century. There was a rebellion in 1642, against Charles I: there was a revolution in 1688, against James II. By the revolution of 1688 the succession was changed. That was not all. A statute was also enacted—a specially solemn statute, which goes by the name of the Bill of Rights—to determine the limits within which the King could henceforth take decisions. We may call the monarchy henceforth a *limited* monarchy. Remembering that the limits were expressed in a constitutional document, we may also call it henceforth a *constitutional* monarchy.

We still attach great importance to this Revolution Settlement of 1688. But it was not a true solution, and it was not the final solution. A solution which left the monarchy with the power of decision within limits was a solution which still left room for disputes about the limits. There was something which had to be added before there could be any true or final solution of the problems which vexed the seventeenth century. This something was very simple, but it took a long time to discover. Final solutions are never found in a single year, or provided in a single document. They grow. In other words, and more accurate words, they are slowly found by tentative experiment. This was the case with the British solution of the problem of monarchy. It was slowly found in the course of the eighteenth century. It was eventually found when the younger Pitt became Prime Minister in 1783, and steadily remained Prime Minister, during the next eighteen years, through all the convulsions of the French Revolution.

What was the solution? It has already been stated by implication. It was, in a word, the consolidation of the office of Prime Minister—a Prime Minister acting at the head of a homogeneous Cabinet which he controls: taking decisions in that Cabinet; and responsible to national opinion, as that opinion is expressed in Parliament, for the decisions which he takes. What is the meaning of this solution? It is simple. It means that the Monarch henceforth ceases to take decisions, in any limits or under any conditions. He confines himself to taking the advice of his Prime Minister, tendered with the assent and backing of the Cabinet; and he always acts upon the advice so tendered. He ceases to decide for himself, and he therefore ceases to be responsible. He stands immune from criticism, from challenge, and from dispute—above the risk of rebellion, the threat of revolution, or the danger of dismissal. Responsibility, criticism, challenge, and the danger of dismissal are all transferred to the Prime Minister. The King remains. And, paradoxical as it may seem, he remains (as we shall presently see) in a position not only of dignity, but also of authority. In one sense he has abdicated. In another sense he has crowned himself with a new and brighter crown.

It will be seen that this modern system of constitutional monarchy may be called a system of dualism. Two figures occupy the stage. One of them is the head of the State: the other is the head of the government. One of them acts, in the formal sense of action, upon the advice he receives: the other offers the guiding advice on which the action is based. Why, we may ask, should there be this dualism? Would it not be simpler, and better, to follow the path of unity? There is a simple answer to that question. In our modern community, with its moving public opinion, the head of the government must be responsible, day by day, to that public opinion; and he must therefore be liable to dismissal, and supersession by another head, as soon as he loses its support. On the other hand it is also necessary, in any community and at any time, that there should be a head of the State—a permanent symbol of the community and a constant magnet for its loyalty—who represents permanently, and represents constantly, the continuity of the national life and the unity of the national purpose. There are thus *two* necessities; and these two necessities require two persons. They cannot both be satisfied by a single person. It may be a tempting thing to make one person both the head of the government and the head of the State. If it is tempting, it is also dangerous. Monarchy rises to a higher power when it resigns the conduct of day-to-day government, which it cannot combine with the representation of the unity and continuity of the State, and devotes itself to that one function of representation.

It may be urged, indeed, that the Monarch suffers when he becomes the symbol of the community and the formal representative of the State. It may be urged that he ceases to be a living and acting person, and becomes a magnificent cipher—a cipher who signs everything, but signs nothing except in obedience to advice; a cipher who acts everywhere, in the formal sense of action, but has nowhere the power of decision. If this were the case, and the constitutional Monarch were merely a cipher, it would be wrong to say, as has just been said, that the constitutional Monarch retains a position not only of dignity, but also of authority. But it is not wrong to use that phrase. He does retain, as we shall see when we come to examine the actual powers and the actual influence of British monarchy, a double position and a double role. He not only receives and follows the advice of his Ministers; he may also offer them advice and suggestions in the strength of his long tenure and his accumulated experience. He not only sits enthroned: he moves among his people, and he may move his people by his own motion. Meanwhile it is only just to add another observation. Even if the King were merely a symbol and merely a magnet, he would none the less be discharging a high and valuable function. We are easily apt to be too rational and too utilitarian. We forget the importance of emotion: we forget that sentiment matters as well as utility. To think about politics in terms of pure reason and cold utility is to think wrongly. There is a world of unbought and uncalculated sentiment which matters vitally in politics. Emotions, loyalties, feelings, chivalries—these are things that count, and count profoundly. The man who releases, the man who attracts, the man who expresses, this world of unbought and uncalculated sentiment is doing an incalculable service to the community. Reason has her sphere and her victories. Sentiment has also her triumphs; and they are not the least noble of triumphs.

Here we may end this brief summary of the development of British monarchy and the logic of that development. It is a summary which forms a preface—a natural and necessary preface—to any account of the present powers and prerogatives of our monarchy. It is a summary which shows that—stable itself, and yet changing—the monarchy has helped the whole of our national life to combine stability with change. Great Britain has been able—and will continue to be able—to adapt her existing institutions harmoniously to the changing requirements of time because she has the flag of monarchy at her mast-head and the ballast of monarchy in her hold. The flag may change its quarterings as the ship moves on its long voyage; but it always remains the same flag. The ballast may be shifted, this way or that, to suit the set of the currents and the roll of the ship. But the ballast is always there.

II

THERE are three different spheres in which the powers and prerogatives of the British monarchy, and its general operative influence, may be separately traced. The first is the sphere of internal life and domestic policy. The second is the sphere of foreign relations and foreign policy. The third is the sphere of the Commonwealth—the sphere of imperial policy.

1. The sphere of internal life and domestic policy has two different aspects. One of them is the ceremonial or formal side. The other is the practical. The monarchy is active on both sides, and it has to be considered in relation to both.

Of the ceremonial or formal side something has already been said in the preface of our argument. We have seen that the modern State—like all the States which have existed in history—requires a symbol of unity, a magnet of loyalty, and an apparatus of ceremony, which will serve to attract men's feelings and sentiments into the services of the community. We have also seen that the modern State—in this respect unlike previous forms of the State—has tended (at any rate in the Old World) to develop a formal head of the State, distinct from the acting head of the government, to serve in the particular capacity of a symbol of unity, a magnet of loyalty, and a centre of ceremony. If, as we have argued, a special organ is necessary for this high and valuable function, it is to be noted that a monarch has special qualifications for acting as this special organ. He is above the play of party. He does not owe his position to any act of election which may have been disputed between the different parties. This is not to decry party, or to deny the necessity of a system of political parties. Parties generate the steam which runs the machinery of government; and without parties we should not have political programmes, or members of parliaments representing those programmes, or Cabinets seeking to give them effect. But however valuable parties may be, a State needs something which has the quality of white light, and is free from the variegated colour of party. An hereditary monarchy supplies this something. An hereditary monarch owes his position to the simple and indisputable fact of birth. He is pledged to nothing except the discharge of his special function. His descent from his predecessors brings memories of the past to ennoble the duties of the present; and his children are the promise of a future continuous and congruous with both. The ceremony with which he is surrounded, whatever may be its cost (there were once critics of the cost among us, but their voices have long ceased to be heard), repays the cost in a rich return of the political sentiments and emotions which nerve and sustain a community. It is good to have a cheap administration—provided that it is also efficient. It would not be good to have a cheap or parsimonious system of monarchy. Life has its pomps and solemnities; and in politics, as well as in other matters, it is the better for having those pomps.

The British Monarch, on the formal or ceremonial side of our internal life, is the fountain of honours; and his court is the centre of 'Society', in that sense of the word in which it means *le grand monde*. Should there be a system of honours, fixed and conferred by the King, and should there be a high society of which his court is the centre? These are questions which may logically be asked in an age which is moving more and more towards equality. Yet there seems little disposition among us to quarrel with the system of honours, or to challenge the general idea of court and society. Even on the ground of logic, a system of honours is logically connected with the general appeal to sentiments and emotions which is now the basis of monarchy. If a man has responded to that appeal, by rendering military or political or other services, why (it seems natural to ask) should he not be honoured? All ranks and conditions among us may now win honours; and there are few who are not proud to receive them. The system of honours does not mean any privileged class. Honours are spread nation-wide. British trade unionists receive honours from their King; they even seek to return them. At the end of 1940, after the bombing of London, in which he had shared the dangers of his people, King George VI was presented by the president of the Trades Union Congress, in his own palace, with a specially struck gold badge of the Congress. And during the war of 1939–45, men and women of all ranks, from all the services and from civilian life, received honours equally and gladly.

There is still another thing to be said about the position of the British monarchy on the formal or ceremonial side of our domestic life and internal policy. In form, or ceremony, everything is done by the King. The courts of law act in his name: he enacts laws, by and with the assent of Parliament: he is the author of executive acts—issuing orders, making appointments to office, conducting international affairs, and commanding all the armed forces. This is all form or ceremony. The King lends his name: he lends his signature; but the decisions taken in his name, and the documents which he signs, proceed from officers of the community other than the King. This is an inheritance from the past—a past in which kings were active, and not only formal, agents. It is natural that in a conservative country the inheritance of the past should be treasured. Yet if it is natural, it may also seem curious and even questionable. Why, it may be asked, should an inheritance of so different a character be treasured in a present which has departed so far from the past? Does not this treasuring of a different past produce an unreal world, in which the forms of political life are totally different from the facts? Is it not all part of that British double-mindedness—or, as it is called by our critics, 'hypocrisy'—by virtue of which we *say* one thing, but actually *do* something different?

There is a good answer to these questions; and that answer takes us over the bridge from the formal or ceremonial side of the action of monarchy, in our internal life, to the practical or active side. The answer is a triple answer. In the first place it is a matter of practical importance—we may even say of profound practical importance—that British Ministers should be the King's ministers, and should carry the prestige of his name. It gives the ministers a far higher standing, and a much greater authority, that they should represent not only a party, and not only a parliament, but also the very symbol and the magnetic centre of the State. It is true that the ministers are responsible to Parliament, and not to the King. It is also true that their advice determines the action of the King, and that he cannot act except upon their advice. But it is also true that they are *his* ministers, and that they would not be what they are unless they had that dignity and style. The ministers who advise the King advise a man who is commander-in-chief of the armed forces; who is the enacter of laws and the author of executive acts; who is the fountain of honours and the source of appointments; who conducts international affairs and the issues of war and peace; who ramifies in every direction. The ministers who advise him share all his ramifications; and they share by reflection his dignity. The Prime Minister, the Cabinet, the judges, the civil service itself—none of these would be what they are unless they were the representatives and carried the prestige of the King. The King has an actual and practical importance in giving to the whole of government a prestige which it would not otherwise possess.

But the King has an actual and practical importance in a second way, which is more obvious, more direct, and more active. His name is not taken in vain; nor is his signature idly appended. He is regularly informed, and regularly consulted, day by day, and week by week. The Prime Minister is in constant touch with the King: he keeps him constantly in touch with the proceedings of Parliament, the deliberations of the Cabinet, the course of policy, the conduct of negotiations, and the whole range of executive action. The continuous tenure of a life-office makes a king, thus informed and consulted, a central source of long-time experience. Ministers come and go: the King remains. King George VI, in a reign which began at the end of 1936, has already been advised by four different Prime Ministers. Seated at the centre of affairs, and enjoying the benefit of time, the King has an unrivalled opportunity for acquiring a general sense of affairs which enables him to encourage or warn the ministers who offer the advice which he is necessarily bound to accept. It is particularly in this sense that he is an active part of the working of the British constitution. A head of the State who enjoys a life-office, and enjoys it by hereditary right, not only saves the State from the perturbations of periodical presidential elections: he can also give it the positive service of a ripe experience and a disinterested judgement of affairs. The curtain is seldom lifted on the rendering of this service. But the correspondence which passed between King George VI and Mr. Winston Churchill, his Prime Minister, in May 1943, showed a deep sense of mutual service.

There is still a third way in which the monarchy has an actual and practical importance in our internal life and the internal working of our constitution. In the constitution of every country there is always, and inevitably, some attempt to secure a balance of different factors. Where there is no such attempt, there can hardly be said to be a constitution. In the United States a balance is sought between the President, who (on a system peculiar to the New World) enjoys both the formal dignity and the actual authority of head of the executive, and the Congress, which represents and carries the legislative authority. In Great Britain balance is also sought; but it is sought in a different way. General authority, alike for the initiation of legislative measures and for the conduct of executive affairs, is vested in the Prime Minister and his Cabinet. But while we vest in one set of hands the general exercise of active authority, we also provide for balance. Here the King serves our purpose. His existence provides a cover, and a dignity, for an opposition to the government as well as for the government. We speak of His Majesty's Opposition, by which we mean an organized Parliamentary party which is opposed to the government and its policy. His Majesty's Opposition is a regular part of our system; and we have even gone to the length of assigning a regular salary, from the funds of the State, for the Leader of the Opposition who challenges the policy of the government of the State. This may seem paradoxical; but it works. In any case the existence of His Majesty's Opposition shows that the mantle of the King is a wide mantle, which can cover opposition as well as government. Indeed we may say that the King is doubly an organ of balance. He is not only an organ of balance by virtue of providing the cover and the sanction for an opposition which serves as a counterweight to the government. He is also an organ of balance in and by himself. He embodies—and it is his specific and separate function to embody—a fund of national political sentiment which is something separate from the fund of party feeling which supports both his government and his opposition. This is a real function —an active and practical function. It is not, after all, just a matter of form and ceremony, as distinct from actual fact and operative reality. We make that distinction in thought; but it is only a distinction in thought. In life itself the factors of form and ceremony—and the emotions, loyalties, feelings, chivalries, which are associated with them—are *themselves* an actual fact and an operative reality. It is in this deep sense that the King, in himself and by himself, is an organ of balance in the whole of our constitution. He acts by the advice of his Ministers, but he is something separate from his Ministers; and he represents real forces and sentiments in the national life which only he can represent.

2. The function of the King in the sphere of foreign relations and foreign policy is a function which may easily be exaggerated, as it has sometimes been exaggerated by continental observers. Edward VII, for example, was sometimes regarded as having pursued a personal policy, and as having swayed the direction and trend of British foreign relations at the beginning of this century. That is a thing impossible in a system of constitutional monarchy. In foreign affairs, no less than in national affairs, the King acts on the advice of his ministers. It is true—or rather it was once true, in the days when there were monarchies all over Europe, and those monarchies were connected by marriages—that the personal relations and connexions of the Monarch might be a factor in foreign policy. That might be an advantage, or it might be a handicap, to his ministers. On the whole, if it were allowed to count at all, it might be more of a handicap than an advantage. In this century, and in the present development of British monarchy, the personal relations and connexions of the Monarch may be eliminated from our consideration. It is not in that way, or by those means, that he can be of service in the conduct of foreign policy. Foreign policy is a matter of the whole State—of the welfare of the whole State and all the members of the State. It is no respecter of particular persons and personal connexions.

But if we put foreign relations on this plane—and it is the only plane on which they can be placed in our day and generation—there still remain a place and a function for monarchy in the conduct of foreign relations. It is the same place, and the same function, as in the conduct of domestic affairs. The King is the centre of that form and ceremony which is nowhere more important than in the solemn relations between one State and another. He is also the giver of informal advice—of quiet warning and quiet encouragement—based on his experience and on the tact for foreign affairs which he has acquired in its course. Perhaps it is in foreign affairs, even more than in domestic, that his influence is particularly felt. Here his knowledge is likely to be peculiarly extensive; here his criticisms and suggestions may carry peculiar weight. Domestic affairs belong largely to the sphere of party: they present tangled problems in novel forms, which demand immediate insight rather than long-time experience. Foreign affairs, in spite of all their vicissitudes, have a steadier trend; and it is here that a king's experience is likely to be of particular value. On the side of form and ceremony, too, as well as in giving practical advice, the King can render peculiar service in the realm of foreign affairs. The visits which he pays to other States along with his Queen (queens count as well as kings, and in the reigns of George V and George VI they have counted in a remarkable degree) may be important acts of policy, and valuable services to the comity and amity of States. The British Monarch is not a secluded monarch in the confines of his own country. He crosses the seas in peace, to visit the countries of the British Commonwealth and also to visit other States: he crosses the seas in war to visit his armies in the field. Our monarchy is, in this sense, a busy monarchy, which goes on its travels. As the King visits others, so he also receives their visits. He receives the credentials of foreign Ambassadors and Ministers; he receives and entertains the heads of other States: he is a general host and a general centre of hospitality. This is a function which can be discharged with a particular grace, and with a peculiar dignity, by a monarch trained to his office from youth, and imbued by birth and upbringing with the courtesies which it requires. Here again, as in our domestic life, the factor of form and ceremony becomes a matter of practical importance and active value in the actual conduct of affairs. There is a solemnity or pageantry of life which is part of its actual substance, and which gives, to performers and spectators alike, a sense of the significance—we may even say, a sense of the reality —of actions and events. There is not only a dramatic gain in maintaining this pageantry or solemnity. There is also an actual utility. The British people are not perhaps natural actors; and they would hardly maintain the pageantry of British life, which is so closely and essentially connected with the existence of the monarchy, merely on dramatic grounds. They maintain that pageantry because it pays—in dividends of the spirit.

3. The British monarchy is not confined to the United Kingdom and the British people. The King is also King through the whole of the range of the British Commonwealth and Empire, with all its nations and peoples. To understand, therefore, the full sweep and scope of British monarchy, we must study the meaning of the term 'Commonwealth' (whether with or without the adjective 'British') and the significance of the term 'Empire'.

BRITISH CONSTITUTIONAL MONARCHY 13

We may begin our study by adopting the image of two circles, side by side with one another, touching one another, and even intersecting one another.[1] One of these circles is the Commonwealth, or, more fully, the Commonwealth of Nations. This circle includes the eight autonomous or self-governing Commonwealth Countries of the United Kingdom, Canada, Australia, New Zealand, South Africa, India, Pakistan, and Ceylon. It was slowly formed, and gradually acquired a definite outline, by a long process of evolution, which began originally with British settlement overseas more than three centuries ago. Its form and outline became more precise after the jubilee of Queen Victoria, and the holding of the first 'imperial conference', in 1887: further precision was given by a statement issued during the Imperial Conference of 1926; a still further definition has lately been added by the declaration promulgated, by the representatives of the eight member countries, in April 1949. Since the promulgation of that declaration we may distinguish two 'rings' in this first circle—one ring of the Commonwealth Countries which acknowledge the King as not only the symbol of their association, but also the recipient of their allegiance; and another ring of those which acknowledge him simply as the symbol of their association in the Commonwealth.[2] But this distinction of 'rings' is perhaps in the nature of a subtlety; and we shall have reason to notice, in the course of our argument that the King is the acknowledged 'Head' of the whole of the Commonwealth, equally recognized as such by *all* the Commonwealth Countries.

The second circle, wide-spread in space, and of ancient origin in some of its parts (such, for example, as the British West Indian Islands) is 'the Empire', or, more exactly, 'the Colonial Empire', or again, as it is sometimes (but less happily) termed, 'the Dependent Empire'. This circle is one not so much of British settlement overseas as of British occupation of overseas territories

[1] They intersect in so far as countries included in the first circle (that of the Commonwealth)—not only Great Britain, but also Australia, New Zealand, and South Africa—are charged with the government of areas and territories included in the second (that of the Empire).

[2] At the present time India is the one Commonwealth Country included in this second ring, but the boundary between the two rings is fluid; and it is possible that Pakistan also may move from inclusion in the first to inclusion in the second ring.

by what the lawyers call cession or conquest.[1] It is an Empire, if one may still use that word (a word perhaps doomed to desuetude), composed in the main of colonies—but also of protectorates, and of what used to be called mandated territories and are now called trusteeships—which range in their systems of government, by infinite gradations, from the system of responsible parliamentary government in Southern Rhodesia to the system of tutelage in other areas. But however various this Empire may be, we may say of it that its parts are being educated, and are more and more educating themselves, to an ultimate consummation of responsible government in which they will one by one enter, as full members, the circle of the Commonwealth. Meanwhile, and as it stands, this second circle—the circle of the colonial or dependent empire—is the most remarkable of laboratories, full of tentative experiments in the great and difficult art of human government.

These two circles—the Commonwealth or British Commonwealth, and the British Colonial or Dependent empire—have both a common centre in the person of the King. They are united by a common connexion with the British monarchy. True, the King is King in different ways in the two different circles, and even within the two separate rings of the first of the circles. That is a matter which we must now proceed to study. But we must always remember, in the course of that study, that in spite of its differences of operation the one person of the King moves as a single animating force through the whole of the Commonwealth and Empire.

(a) It is natural to study first—because it is, in its ultimate origins, the oldest—the society or association of 'countries' or 'nations' (both of those terms are now commonly used, and the logic of our argument will show us that the term 'States' may also be used) which move in the orbit of the first circle, the circle of the Commonwealth. Here we may begin by describing first the position of the King in that primary nucleus of Commonwealth Countries in which he is recognized both as a recipient of allegiance and as a symbol of association. This primary nucleus, as it existed down to 1949 and as it still exists, is a

[1] The word 'conquest' is a legal term of art. It does not signify a military conquest of indigenous peoples. It means what a layman would call peaceful occupation of hitherto unoccupied (or very sparsely peopled) territories.

society of independent equals—'autonomous communities', as it was stated at the Imperial Conference of 1926, 'equal in status, in no way subordinate one to another in any aspect of their domestic or external affairs'. It is a society of which it was also said, at the same Conference, that 'free institutions are its life blood, and free co-operation its instrument'. It is a society which has already issued, during the course of its evolution, in a number of separate and autonomous communities, or States (for an 'autonomous community' is by its nature a 'State'), not only proclaimed as such in 1926 by the Conference of their own representatives, but recognized as such, at an even earlier date, in international law; and if any political prophecy is true, it will issue in many more. Yet though it contains, or consists of, separate and autonomous states, it is still a unity; and it has never been more of a unity than it showed itself to be in the course of the war of 1939-45. How shall we seek to explain this unity? We may say that it has deep underlying roots—a common belief in the practice of parliamentary government, and a common conviction of the value, and even the necessity, of co-operation between countries united by the similar practice of such government. But we have to find something more than roots of common belief and common conviction, which belong to the ground of intellect: we have also to find the flowers and fruits of common emotion and common feeling, which belong to the free and sustaining air of spontaneous sentiment. A tree is not only fed from its roots: it is also fed from the air and the light. Such reflections lead us to the conclusion that we can only fully explain the unity of the primary nucleus of the Commonwealth in terms of the unity of the monarchy, and of the emotion and feeling connected with the monarchy, which are common throughout its range. This is the truth expressed in the preamble to a great constitutional document—the Statute of Westminster (1931): 'The Crown is the symbol of the free association of the members of the British Commonwealth of Nations, and . . . they are united by a common allegiance to the Crown.' It is a truth which is brought home forcibly to our minds when we reflect on a simple fact. The British Prime Minister is the Prime Minister of the United Kingdom only. The British King is the Head of the whole of the Commonwealth.

There may seem to be a discrepancy, or an absence of logic,

in the fact which has just been mentioned—the fact that the British King has a wider range than the British Prime Minister. There is no discrepancy. The King, in his capacity of the common link of the different States united by a common allegiance to his person, can have no single Prime Minister: each State is a separate State, and each must have its own Prime Minister. The King has accordingly, in that capacity, a number of Prime Ministers: he has as many Prime Ministers as there are States of the primary nucleus of the Commonwealth. He is separately advised by each Prime Minister for the area of the State in which he is Prime Minister. It is theoretically possible that he might receive different and discrepant advices from his different Prime Ministers. It is theoretically arguable that he is not one, but many Kings; that he is as many Kings as he has Prime Ministers; that he is one King in the United Kingdom, another in Canada, and another in South Africa. Theoretical possibilities and theoretical arguments have not hitherto given us any great concern. He is one man, after all; and we see no sign of a division of personalities or of a struggle between different selves. We find ways and means of making the different advices tendered to him work together for his benefit—that is to say, for the benefit of all and each of the member States. The monarchy would be in a difficult position if such ways and means were not found, and if there did not exist a common interest, a common ground of belief and conviction, and a common air of emotion and feeling, which were the guarantees of their being found. But those ways and means are found; and those guarantees exist. On that basis the British monarchy can be the monarchy not only of Great Britain, but also of the British Commonwealth.

From what has been called the primary nucleus of the Commonwealth (and what may also be called, as indeed it has just been called, the British Commonwealth, or perhaps more exactly the British part of the Commonwealth) we may now turn to the Commonwealth at large, the Commonwealth *in toto*, the Commonwealth without adjective or qualification. This is a Commonwealth, newly defined, which is wide enough to include not only the States of the primary nucleus, which owe allegiance to the British King, but also the Republic of India, which owes no such allegiance. How has this expansion been achieved; how can a republic find its place by the side of monarchical States, and what position, if any, has the King in a Commonwealth which is a Commonwealth including a great republic in its membership? What, in the issue, has been the gain, and what the loss, to the significance of British monarchy?

The way in which the expansion has been achieved is as simple as it is subtle. The position of affairs in 1949 was that India wished at once to be a sovereign independent republic and to enjoy membership of the Commonwealth which had hitherto been termed the British Commonwealth. It was agreed by all that India, since she so wished, should be a republic. India had not been an area of British settlement, as the countries of the British Commonwealth (mainly or largely) had been[1]; and the people of India was an ancient and indigenous people of the East, which as such had its own tradition to cherish and its own future to determine. On the other hand it was also, and equally, agreed by all that India, since she so wished, should continue to be associated with the States of the British Commonwealth. Both she and those States stood to gain by the continuance of such association; and humanity at large would profit if a bridge remained between East and West to carry not only the commerce of commodities, but also (what is even more precious) the commerce of ideas and ideals. In such a conjuncture, and with such a basis of agreement, it only remained to find a method and a formula. To understand the formula which was found we must go back to the passage already quoted from the preamble to the Statute of Westminster. That passage contains two clauses. The first clause speaks of the Crown as a symbol of free association. The second clause speaks of the Crown as the centre and recipient of a common allegiance. The formula found, and the solution adopted, was that India should accept and endorse the first, but not the second, of these clauses. This was done by common agreement: on the one hand 'the Government of India . . . declared and affirmed India's desire to continue her full membership of the Commonwealth of Nations, and her acceptance of the King as the symbol of the free association of its independent member nations and as such the Head

[1] It must be remembered that South Africa was originally settled by the Dutch, and Canada by the French, and that (so far as the European population is concerned) South Africa is now mainly, and Canada still largely, peopled by the descendants of those original settlers.

of the Commonwealth'; on the other hand, 'the Governments of the other countries of the Commonwealth, the basis of whose membership of the Commonwealth is not hereby changed, accept and recognize India's continuing membership in accordance with the terms of this declaration'.

The result of this formula and solution is, in a sense, a distinction of two rings or aspects of the Commonwealth, and a corresponding distinction of two capacities of the British King. In the one capacity, and in the broad ring or aspect, he is just the symbol of association: in the other capacity, and in the other ring or aspect (the ring or aspect which we have called the 'primary nucleus' or 'British part' of the Commonwealth), he is not only that, but also the centre and recipient of common allegiance. But these are fine distinctions, which it would be a folly to press too logically or too far. We may distinguish the Commonwealth at large from the British part of the Commonwealth; but the fact remains that the declaration of April 1949 speaks of India *continuing* her *full* membership of the Commonwealth. We may distinguish the King as a symbol of association from the King as the centre and recipient of common allegiance; and on that basis we may argue that the King, while remaining a symbol of association for India, has lost the allegiance of India, and therefore suffers on the whole account. But is that true? Is it not rather true that, on the whole account, he has gained?

Here the crucial words are the words 'Head of the Commonwealth'. This is something new, and something which is so great a gain that it counterbalances any conceivable loss. Hitherto, in the British Commonwealth, as it existed down to 1949, it could be argued (as it was suggested above) that there were as many Kings as there were States of that Commonwealth, and that the King was a different King for each. Henceforth, in the Commonwealth as defined in 1949, there is a King who is 'the symbol of the free association of its independent member nations and *as such the Head of the Commonwealth*'.[1] It needs no subtlety to discover in these last words the unitary and uniting genius of the character of the King. He may be a symbol. But he is also,

[1] It is not suggested here that the argument mentioned in the previous sentence has ceased to be possible since the issue of the declaration of April 1949. That argument may still be advanced. All that is here suggested is that since the issue of that declaration the King has assumed a new position, not abrogating the old, but nevertheless new and important.

as such, the Head—the one and single Head—the Head of a body which is all the more united because it now has, and henceforth acknowledges, a Head.

It was said above, in the beginning of the argument, that the monarchy 'has survived because it has changed, and because it has moved with the movement of time'. It was also said that 'the monarchy, stable itself and yet changing, has helped the whole of our national life to combine stability with change'. Those words were used with reference to the internal life of Great Britain. But they may also be used with reference to the general life of the whole of the Commonwealth. If the statesmen of the Commonwealth had not been able to count on the idea and the instrument of monarchy, they would have lost that magic of flexibility which has enabled them to adapt existing institutions harmoniously to the requirements of time.

(*b*) It remains to examine the operation of monarchy in the circle of the Colonial or Dependent Empire. That empire, as has already been noted, has its technical divisions—its Crown Colonies; its various Protectorates and Protected States[1]; its different 'mandated' or 'trust' territories. It has also, in all these divisions—and this, too, has already been noted—its different stages of constitutional experiment, which vary with the *genius loci* from something in the nature of responsible government to a protecting and guiding tutelage. Further, besides these technical divisions and these various stages of constitutional growth, the Colonial Empire has also a wide geographical dispersion: it is scattered in different parts of Africa, in the Indian and Pacific Oceans, and in the Caribbean seas. All these scattered territories, in all their divisions and stages, are held together by a common King, who is the immediate King in the Crown Colonies (where the governors act in his name and by virtue of his general prerogative) and the protecting King of native sovereigns and chiefs in a number of other territories. The general scope of

---

[1] Protectorates are governed in the same way as Colonies, but have not been annexed. The practical difference between Colonies and Protectorates is now very small. The peoples of Protectorates are not British subjects, but British protected persons. Examples are Uganda, Zanzibar, and the Solomon Islands.

Protected States are countries which, while retaining their own sovereignty, have entered into treaties giving the British Government certain rights and responsibilities in them. Their peoples are British protected persons. Examples are Brunei, Tonga, and the nine States of the Federation of Malaya.

the Crown, and a common allegiance to the Crown, can unite in a common service, as the course of the war from 1939 to 1945 abundantly showed, soldiers drawn from the East and the West of the whole Colonial Empire. It can equally unite, as grades and stages in a single general system of growing liberty, all the constitutional varieties with which the Colonial Empire is studded. Under the one Crown can run systems of what used to be called 'indirect rule', through native councils (one of the most fruitful of colonial experiments), all the way from Nigeria to the Pacific; under the one Crown there can also run a variety of systems of colonial assemblies, calculated on a Western pattern, but in various stages of development, from the island of Jamaica in the West Indies to the islands of the Mediterranean and of the Eastern seas. The monarchy is the general shelter of the germination of political life and the proliferation of liberty.

We have spoken of the operation of monarchy in the circles which lie beyond the British Isles and the United Kingdom. In these broad circles, and in the whole general system of the Commonwealth and Empire, the monarchy is a symbol and an example of the art of keeping together and of the gift of human fellowship—of the art of tolerating differences, and of the gift of weaving differences together in a common agreement which is all the richer for all the differences. This is the greatest height of British constitutional monarchy; and this is the greatest and surest pledge of its continuance. A theorist in his study might conceivably suggest the possibility of substituting an elected president for the King in the British Isles. But the wildest of theorists would hardly suggest the possibility of making this hypothetical president of the British Isles the general president and Head of all the societies and circles which have rippled out from and still move round the British King. Only a man whose ancestors were Kings when the first British settlers, traders, navigators, and explorers went forth to lay the first foundations—only he can be the symbol, and as such the Head, of the great and general association which has been built on those first foundations.

III

IF the reader will pardon some personal words from the writer in conclusion of the argument, and will permit him to speak, for the sake of simplicity, in the first person, a personal confession of the growth and development of the writer's own attitude to monarchy may form a fitting conclusion.

I was born in the year 1874, a little after the middle of the reign of Queen Victoria. I have lived under Queen Victoria; under her son King Edward VII; under her grandson King George V; under her great-grandsons King Edward VIII and King George VI. I have watched the monarchy change and grow; and I have noted the growth and change of my own views of the monarchy.

My father was a Liberal working man; and as I grew to manhood, I naturally imbibed his opinions. He belonged to a wing or section of the Liberal party which inclined to republicanism —mainly on grounds of economy, and in the strength of a conviction that monarchy was an expensive institution, but perhaps partly on the ground that monarchy was connected with reaction, or at any rate inimical to progress. Queen Victoria had seemed to show a particular partiality for a Conservative Prime Minister; her numerous descendants were a charge on the revenue: my father was one of her critics. That was the original temper and frame of mind in which I began to think of monarchy. I have always kept the English form of Liberalism which I learned from my father, and I have come to believe in it still more deeply from my own experience of life and my own reading of history. But either my thoughts of monarchy have changed, or monarchy has changed, or both have changed together. Probably both have changed together. Experience of life has taught me that economy is not the only thing which has to be considered: it has equally taught me not to confuse the person of a particular occupant of an office with the office itself. I have watched, as we all have watched, the different sovereigns who have occupied the throne: and I have seen how they could adorn, and adorn in different ways, the throne which they occupied. Three things stand out particularly in my memory. They all belong to the last fifteen years. They all show how the cause of monarchy has been strengthened by the recent course of our national history.

The first of these three things was the Jubilee celebrations, in May 1935, of the twenty-fifth anniversary of the accession of George V. Those celebrations made us all aware—deeply and profoundly aware—how much we owed to a prudent and sagacious reign in which the King and the Queen (once more I must mention the Queen as well as the King) had endeared themselves to their people, and had drawn their people together into the unity and intimacy of a great family. The reign of George V is memorable in the history of British monarchy. The second thing was the brief reign and the rapid abdication of Edward VIII. That was the testing time of the hold of monarchy on the nation —a time which tried the mettle of the British people and the whole British Commonwealth—a time which confronted us suddenly with some of the gravest problems which monarchy can offer to a people. The test was met: monarchy survived: in the issue it was even strengthened. That brings me to the last of the three things which stand out particularly in my memory. This is the example of fortitude, in the face of a common danger shared day by day with their people, which was set by George VI and his Queen (once more the Queen as well as the King) during the Battle of Britain. They helped to rally and sustain their people; they made us feel, in the words of one of our admirals of the seventeenth century, 'We are all together, and behold one another's face with comfort'. Noble words. They helped to rouse us to that nobility.

One last word of explanation. This is a study of British monarchy—and of nothing but British monarchy. It is in no sense and in no way a plea for the general cause of monarchy. Each country follows its own way, in conformity with its own history and genius. In almost all the New World—apart from the territories of the British Commonwealth—and in a large part of the Old World, there is now no monarchy. Republics, in various forms, are the general order of the day. When nations have broken with their past, and set out on new voyages over new seas, they naturally fly republican flags. But there is no universal logic of republicanism—just as there is no universal logic of monarchy. When a nation has preserved continuity with its past, and continues to feel some piety towards its past, it will naturally fly the flag of monarchy which it has inherited from its past. But the monarchy which it preserves will be a changing and moving monarchy—changing and moving with the times, and actively helping the times to change and move. That, for the last 300 years, has been the nature of British monarchy. That is the secret of its survival, and that is the source of its strength.

Essay Two

BRITISH STATESMEN

I

WHAT is a statesman? The question is easily asked, but not so easily answered. Perhaps the best way of casting about for an answer is to attempt a distinction between the statesman and the politician. Etymologically, there is no great reason for separating the two terms. The one term came from the Latin language, the other from the Greek; and if either of them carried from its original fountain a purer significance than the other, it was the Greek term 'politician'. To Aristotle 'the politic man' was the highest type of statesman: a man with the power of directing public affairs in a 'polis' or city composed of free and equal members; a man who had been a subject before he became a ruler, and thus understood the art of being a subject as well as the art of ruling: a man, accordingly, who bore his high office with modesty and offered a shining foil to 'the despotic man' or dictator. But words suffer a change as they run through the generations; and the Greek word 'politician', beginning badly when it entered our language in the sixteenth century, was never able to recover from its beginning. Oblivious of the high Greek sense—connecting politician with policy, and connecting policy, in its turn, with an Italianate subtlety—Shakespeare makes one of his characters say, 'Policy I hate: I had as lief be a Brownist as a politician'; and even into the mouth of Hamlet, as he contemplates the skull thrown up by a grave-digger, he puts the soliloquy, 'It might be the pate of a politician . . . one that would circumvent God'. The fate of the word was sealed; and though it might occasionally emerge in a finer sense, to signify 'one that understands the art of governing', it came eventually to be associated with two other Ps—the P of party and the P of profession. A politician, in the language of the dictionary, is now 'one who engages in party politics, or who makes politics his profession'.

The Latin word 'statesman' was the beneficiary from the fall of the Greek word 'politician'. It was connected with the high

Roman notion of State and its associated notions of authority and sovereignty. They are notions less democratic than those which inhere in the original sense of the Greek word; but they are also more majestic. The statesman is the governor—the *gubernator* or steersman who guides the ship of State: he is the pilot who weathers storms and brings crew and passengers into the haven. He is a Henry VIII, the majestic lord who broke the bonds of Rome: he is the younger Pitt, the stately column that upheld his country when all Europe seemed to be cracking. This usage perhaps belongs to the nineteenth century, in which Goldwin Smith published his lectures on *Three English Statesmen* and there appeared a series of biographies of *Twelve English Statesmen* from William the Conqueror to Peel. Adam Smith, in the previous century, had a poorer idea of statesmen: in the spirit of Bentham, he pitted 'the science of a legislator' against 'the skill of that insidious and crafty animal vulgarly called a statesman or politician, whose councils are directed by the momentary fluctuations of affairs'. Here statesman and politician are still confounded. A little over a hundred years later, in the last decade of the last century, *The Times* could say of a contemporary that 'wide and varied training had made him not a politician, but a statesman able to take imperial views'. The word statesman had come into its own. It meant a man who transcended party and the profession of politics: a man who served the state and sought, with a single eye, to deserve well of the republic. But the disjunction between the statesman and the politician is perhaps unreal. Where shall statesmen be found, unless among politicians? And what is a statesman (at any rate in a democratic country) but a politician who, by the conjuncture of his genius with a tide in his country's affairs, has been carried on to high achievement and lasting fame? The great bulk of British statesmen have been politicians, and would never have become statesmen if they had not first been politicians. It is not ignoble, nor is it a disservice to the state, to serve a party. It is not ignoble, nor in any way mean, to embrace the profession of politics. The statesman, after all, is but a politician of a greater stature who has steered the ship of state on a more than ordinary voyage—happy in his own genius, but happy also in his opportunity.

II

From the beginning of modern history, with the accession of Henry VII, down to the present time, we may count nearly thirty persons (one of them a woman) in the roll of British statesmen. Some of these (Henry VIII, Elizabeth, and William III) were reigning sovereigns. We are left with twenty-five, from Wolsey and Burghley to Churchill and Smuts, who were subjects.

Before any attempt is made to estimate the qualities of these men, and the influence which they exercised in their own day and afterwards, two preliminary questions may be asked. What were the classes from which they were drawn? What was the training which they received?

It is not surprising, especially when we reflect that aristocracy was the precursor and (we may almost say) the parent of our modern British democracy, that the majority of British statesmen should be drawn from the landed interest and the aristocratic class. In our list of twenty-five we may count nearly three-fifths of the number whose roots were in the soil, and who came from the landed aristocracy or the landed gentry of the country-side. Three—Peel, Gladstone, and Joseph Chamberlain—drew their origins from the new world of industry and commerce which had begun, from the end of the eighteenth century, to impinge on the old world of the aristocracy and the gentry: others (eight others)—from Wolsey, through Burke and Canning, to some of the statesmen of our own day—came from the professional classes, and climbed to eminence either from the vicarage or on the ladders of letters and law. But no classification can be exclusive; and just as British classes have merged readily into one another, so British statesmen have sometimes combined in their persons the gifts and the attributes of different classes. Aristocratic descent was united with the profession of letters in Bolingbroke, as it has also been in other and more recent statesmen; and Rhodes, if he was a son of the vicarage, was also a magnate of the first order in the world of industry and commerce.

The training of British statesmen, or to speak more exactly their education (for the training of statesmen is a large matter which involves experience of life no less, and perhaps even more, than attendance on schoolmasters and tutors), has been varied and yet tolerably uniform. About half of the twenty-five began their training in public schools: Eton counts nine, and Harrow three; the remaining half were educated in their early days by tutors, or at some city or country school (such as the City of London School, or the Grammar School at Bishop's Stortford), or they have left no memorial of their early training on record. When we come to the later stages of the education of statesmen, we find a greater uniformity. The pattern now tends to follow the old scheme laid down, four centuries ago, by Sir Thomas Elyot in his *Book of the Governor*. There is a period of liberal training in the arts, generally at a university, often followed by a period of training in law, and sometimes by a period of training in arms. Oliver Cromwell *may* have combined all three—the university, law, and the army: he certainly spent a year at Sidney Sussex College, Cambridge: he *may* have spent a year at one of the Inns of Court: he had indubitably a large experience of arms. General Smuts combined in his person all three, but the more general experience has been a combination of two, and more particularly of the university and law: Burghley, Strafford, Burke, Canning, and Asquith all added the barrister's training to that of the university. But the elder Pitt, in the manner of Oliver Cromwell and General Smuts, was a cornet of horse as well as a student of Trinity College, Oxford; and two others of our statesmen, though they were denied the opportunity of the university, added the training of the military academy to the training of the public school—Wellington at Angers, and Churchill at Sandhurst. The five British statesmen who have added a military training to that of the university or the public school or both—Cromwell, the elder Pitt, Wellington, Churchill, and Smuts—have an honourable place in the record.

If we fix our attention purely on the university, we may notice that four-fifths of the statesmen included in our list had passed through a university. One of them, Burke, was a graduate of Trinity College, Dublin. Nine of them were members of the University of Cambridge: four of these Cambridge men (Burghley, Strafford, Castlereagh, and Palmerston) were all members of St. John's College: the other five (Oliver Cromwell, Walpole, the younger Pitt, Balfour, and Smuts) belonged to other and different colleges. Nine, and possibly ten (there is a doubt, and perhaps more than a doubt, whether Bolingbroke had any connexion with Oxford until he became an honorary doctor and was entered on the books of Christ Church in 1702), were members of the University of Oxford; four of these Oxford men (Canning, Peel, Gladstone, and Salisbury)—or, if Bolingbroke be added, five—were members of Christ Church: the other five (Wolsey, the elder Pitt, Charles James Fox, Rhodes, and Asquith) belonged to five other colleges. We are left with five statesmen who entered into politics without passing through the University—Wellington and Churchill, who went into politics by way of the army; Disraeli, who went by way of the bar and literature; Joseph Chamberlain and Lloyd George, who went by way of business and the profession of the solicitor.

Has the university training of the large majority of our statesmen affected their statesmanship? Those who believe in a classical education, and particularly in the form of that education which appears in the Oxford School of Literae Humaniores, may be inclined to make a large claim for the influence of the university on British statesmanship. The writer remembers a speech delivered by Asquith in the hall of one of the Oxford colleges, over thirty years ago, in which he said, 'It was here that I learned, from lectures on the *Republic* of Plato, such lessons of statesmanship as I have since sought to carry into effect'. Dr. Gilbert Murray has written, with the same reference to the Greek tradition of politics:

'If you take English political thought and action from Pitt and Fox onwards, it seems to me that you will always find present . . . strands of feeling which are due—of course among many other causes—to this germination of Greek influence; an unquestioning respect for freedom of life and thought, a mistrust of passion . . . a sure consciousness that the poor are the fellow citizens of the rich.'

It is certainly true that the Pitts and Fox, Canning and Peel, Gladstone and Asquith, were all nurtured in the classics: it is also true that Burke had been steeped in an Aristotelian tradition in Dublin, and that Rhodes continued to remember some of the lessons of Aristotle's *Ethics* which he had learned at Oxford: it is true, too, that philosophy as well as politics (but a philosophy not confined to the Greek tradition) engaged the mind of Balfour, and continued to engage the mind of Smuts. A broad general culture has attended the careers and affected the action of many of our statesmen. It has not always been due to a university training (Disraeli and Churchill may be cited in evidence); and even where it has begun in the university, it has been continued *proprio Marte* and developed by native vigour. But we may say of our universities that they have helped to imbue our statesmen with a liberal tradition of philosophy and humane letters, and that they have continued to inspire them, even when they had moved into a larger world of affairs, with an abiding loyalty to the spirit, and even to the society, of university life. Statesmanship has never been a specialized profession. It has been immersed in the general culture of the country. This is a fact which naturally consorts with a national tendency that runs in favour of the cultivated amateur, loving and following a profession without the professional spirit. But it is also a fact which equally consorts with the genius of democracy and with the Greek conception of the true nature of the statesman who serves a 'polis' composed of free and equal and like members.

III

FROM the theme of the recruitment and training of British statesmen we may now turn to consider the environment in which they have worked. Life is the interplay, and the mutual interaction, of man and environment. The life and activity of the statesman, during his tenure of office, is the interplay of his personality with the organized environment of contemporary society and the contemporary form of state. Society and the state act upon him, and he acts upon them in turn. The nature of his response, and the quality of his reaction, is the measure of his statesmanship.

The social environment of British statesmen, during the three centuries from the dissolution of the monasteries in 1536 to the Reform Bill of 1832 (and even after the Reform Bill), was a society of which the tone was set and the affairs were largely guided by a landed aristocracy and gentry. The landed interest ruled the counties through the Justices of the Peace: the landed interest filled the Parliament at Westminster, and entrenched itself on the steps of the throne. 'As is the proportion or balance of dominion or property in land', Harrington wrote in the introduction to *Oceana*, in 1656, 'such is the nature of the empire.' Government smelled of the honest soil: statesmen moved in a landed society where the talk was of bullocks and turnips, mixed with the classics, Italian architecture, the music of Gluck, and the general culture of the country-house. It was, in some ways, a dilettante and amateur society; but its members had (if only through the grand tour) European connexions and ramifications; and they took their politics *au grand sérieux*, with a dramatic zest. Disraeli spoke of the Venetian oligarchy which was enthroned (in company with Dutch finance and French wars) by the Revolution of 1688. It was older than the revolution; it was neither Venetian nor an oligarchy; it was essentially English and it was essentially an aristocracy—in living touch with the soil and all who lived on the soil. It was an *élite*; but it was an *élite* which recruited itself freely and struck its roots deep in the country. It had a sense of Europe and European affairs: it had a feeling (drawn from its new recruits and its own marriages) for commerce and commercial expansion: it was the nursing-mother of a cultured statesmanship, which treated high issues gravely, and could play—in the person of a Castlereagh, a Palmerston, or a Salisbury—a great European role.

Society began to change with the coming of the Industrial Revolution. Capital and Labour entered on the scene: 'the condition of England question' emerged, and transcended the powers of the old landed society: economics, in a graver form than the old issues of commerce and commercial expansion, began to dominate the general environment. Peel and Gladstone were both representatives of a changed or changing society; and in the careers of Cecil Rhodes and Joseph Chamberlain the change is still more evident. It is 'the proportion or balance of dominion or property' in industry and general business that now determines what Harrington called 'the nature of empire': it is the environment of great business to which statesmanship now tends to react and respond. 'For the last half-century or more', Lord Cecil has recently written, 'the landowners have been progressively ousted by the mercantile magnates.' The effect has been seen in domestic as well as external statesmanship; but it has perhaps been seen particularly in the sphere of external affairs. 'It is inevitable', as Lord Cecil notes, 'that the mercantile class, whose training must be to attribute the greatest importance to commercial and financial considerations, will bring the same point of view into the direction of external policy.' This is a particular crux of our times and a special problem of statesmanship. But if the new environment produces new problems, and creates new difficulties for statesmanship, it is also fruitful of new opportunities. If a new *élite* of mercantile and industrial magnates has emerged, there has also emerged a new *élite* of the leaders of Labour; and in the new mixed society of our times the old *élite* of the landed society still lives, and still seeks to serve the state. The future may show a richer and more varied statesmanship, responsive to a richer and more varied environment—if only (as our national history and our present temper may well encourage us to hope) the different elements of the environment can co-operate to form a single society with a single pulse and a common beat of life.

The political environment of British statesmanship, since the Restoration of 1660, has been the environment of an aristocratic government slowly but surely moving in the direction of democracy. Political form has corresponded to social structure; and political form, like social structure, and along with social structure, has affected the nature of statesmanship—as, indeed, the form of state in which he serves must always affect the action of the statesman. In the sixteenth and the first half of the seventeenth century, when the political form was still of the nature of monarchical absolutism, our statesmen—Wolsey, Burghley, and Strafford—were in fact as well as in name the servants of the Crown. They were of the type of a Richelieu, a Colbert, or a Bismarck—the type which lasted in France till 1789 and in Germany till 1918. The statesman under an aristocratic system of government is necessarily of a different pattern; and that pattern, though it acquires a new definition and accentuation under a democratic system, is not fundamentally changed by the coming of democracy. He is not so much concerned with the transaction of high affairs of state in the secrecy of the ruler's closet: he is rather concerned with keeping his fingers on the pulse of the people—immediately 'the people who count', but ultimately also the people at large, which 'the people who count' must carry with them if they are really to count themselves. This was the type of statesman that emerged in England after 1660. There is a passage in Burnet's *History of His Own Times*, descriptive of the first Earl of Shaftesbury, which may serve to describe the essence of British statesmanship since 1660. 'His strength lay in the knowledge of England, and of all the considerable men in it: he understood well the size of their understandings, and their tempers.' A feeling for England—for the state and condition of the English people, and for the trend of its opinion, rather than for matter and reason of state—was already a prime necessity of statesmanship in the first beginnings of aristocratic government; and that feeling has become still more necessary as aristocracy has widened into democracy.

An aristocratic system of government is generally, and perhaps logically, connected with the presence of party and the formation of a party system. There are different *salons*: there are rival hunts: there are different schools of opinion: in any case, and on a variety of grounds, there is a natural taking of sides. Burnet not only remarks on Shaftesbury's knowledge of England: he also remarks on his skill in the arts of party. 'I never knew any man equal to him in the art of governing parties.' The system of party has affected British statesmanship for the last three centuries. Beginning already with the Long Parliament (if not earlier), it has set the scene and largely formed the plot. We may deprecate some of the effects of party: we may say, as Bolingbroke has already begun to say when he writes his essay *On the Idea of a Patriot King*, that it substitutes *esprit de parti* for *esprit de patrie*: we may reflect that some of our greatest statesmen (for example, the elder Pitt and Sir Robert Peel) have sat uneasily to party. The fact remains that party has been, and is, an essential element of our general system of government; and it has affected our statesmen not only for evil, but also for good, and mainly for good. In the first place it has made them adepts in the grand dialectic of public debate, which is the sovereign method for the discovery of practical truth, as it is also the sovereign principle of all genuine democracy. Our statesmen have been compelled, by the very exigencies of their position, to be 'masters of the word'; and however much men may decry the word, in this age of the brutal act, the fact remains that the word—the word which expresses creative thought—is the ultimate master of the act. We never need deplore the part which parliamentary and party eloquence has played in the record of British statesmanship: we should rather give thanks for words which resound through the ages and shape the true life of the people, which is the life of the people's mind. Next, and of almost equal magnitude, there is a second effect of party. It has made our statesmen not lonely figures but the centres and inspirations of a loyal group of colleagues, who have thought that the finest flower of friendship was *idem velle, idem nolle, in republica*. England has not known the *prima donna assoluta* of statesmanship: it may almost be said, in a paradox, that the greatest statesmen in our history have not been men but groups. The Whig leaders after 1688, such as Somers and Montague, have left no great name behind them; but they, and the Whig philosophers in consultation with whom they acted, left their country endowed with a firm political and financial structure which weathered the movements of generations. We can count our great cabinets as well as our great statesmen, and perhaps even more. The Liberal cabinet, for example, which lasted from December 1905 to May 1915, was something greater than even the most eminent of its members.

The factor of party has not only inspired our statesmen with the great spirit of public debate and the unsolitary and unselfish temper of loyalty to a group: it has also furnished the nation, in virtue of the vicissitudes of party triumphs and party defeats at the polls, with a succession of contrasted and yet complementary statesmen who diversify and enrich the general national record. The Whig leaders after 1688 are ultimately succeeded by Harley and Bolingbroke: Harley and Bolingbroke are succeeded in turn, after an interval, by Walpole: Walpole is succeeded, after another interval, by the elder Pitt (a Whig of another stamp): and so the record runs—Disraeli succeeding to Gladstone and Gladstone again to Disraeli—down to the present time. It is curious to reflect that if we seek to distribute the British statesmen of the first eminence, since 1660, into the two categories of statesmen of the Right and statesmen of the Left, we shall find them almost equally balanced. But we shall sometimes be puzzled about the distribution. There are some who seem (like Burke) to belong to both sides: there are others (such as the elder Pitt) whose genius, or *daemon*, compels them to play a lonely hand. But the general run of British statesmanship is in the direction not of the solitary duellist, but of the team; and the general tradition has been the tradition of collegiate loyalty. We have tended to look askance at those who have changed their loyalty, and perhaps at some of those who have postponed the claims of party to the imperative commands of national exigency.

Even to-day the great Peel is perhaps undervalued in our general estimation.

The tenure of office which British statesmen have enjoyed has been generally brief. This has been partly due to the vicissitudes of party; but it has also perhaps been due to a national feeling that in great affairs the springs of initiative and the vigour of original influence may be exhausted within a *septennium*. If 'parliaments, like cats, grow cursed with age', the same is possibly true of administrations. Walpole had indeed a continuous tenure of twenty-one years: the younger Pitt of eighteen; and Lord Liverpool (if he may be counted, for the moment, among statesmen) held office for fifteen years. But a period of five years is more common: that was the length of Oliver Cromwell's protectorate, of the elder Pitt's Secretaryship of State during the Seven Years War, and of the ministry of Peel. Gladstone's first and greatest ministry lasted six years, as did the succeeding ministry of Disraeli: Asquith was the head of a Liberal ministry for seven; a general maximum of seven years, and an average of five, would appear to be the span of a British statesman. We may contrast the long tenures of Richelieu and Colbert, Napoleon and Bismarck, Metternich and many others: we may reflect that statesmanship, if it needs the fresh impulse of a vital initiative, is also 'a work of long breath', and that constructive effort must enjoy the benefit of time if it is to achieve a large and permanent result. But it is easy to exaggerate the value of the continuous influence of a single personality in the field of constructive creation. It is true that the holder of a great *titular* office acquires progressive prestige with the passage of years. It is otherwise with the creative and responsible statesman. Here the series matters more than any point or person in the series. Our system secures the series, and ensures that *uno avulso non deficit alter*. A series of new initiatives, continually renewed, is the best source of the permanent statesmanship of the nation.

There are two other general features of British statesmanship, both of them congruous with the features already described, and both of them springing naturally, in the same way as those features, from the general nature of our political environment. One of these features is the amateur quality, as it may not improperly be called, of most of our statesmen. They have not been professionals or professionally trained. Emerging first from an aristocratic, and then from a democratic society, they have had a general accomplishment, of which politics might indeed be the crown but was never the whole. They have combined letters or law or philosophy with their politics: they have added the social graces, and the general genius of contemporary culture, to the practice of statesmanship. This amateur quality has its defects as well as its attractive merits. Seeking to handle great affairs in the spirit which the Italians of the Renaissance called *sprezzatura*, 'with a certain disdain which conceals the art used', the amateur may fall into the slipshod; avoiding the pedantry of a plodding professionalism, he may also avoid, or elude, the necessity of application, and forget that garlands are won not without dust and heat and sweat. Yet perhaps there was wisdom, as perhaps there still is, in the instinct of our people which has remitted so much of central (and still more of local) government to the play of general intelligence. In the realm of policy that is the factor which counts; and in its strength a Palmerston may combine a jaunty air of *insouciance* with an essential statesmanship.

Another general feature of British statesmanship, not unconnected with its amateur quality, is the tentative method of its genius. It is essentially experimental: it deals with particular problems and actual situations: it proceeds from step to step, feeling the way as it goes. Long-range planning and premeditated design are alien to its instincts: it took us a century to develop the code of labour called the Factory Acts: it may take us long years to discover the *via media Anglica* between the claims of private enterprise and the claims of public control in the general sphere of economics. This method of the *interim* solution, and this policy of *pedetemptim*, are annoying to the ardent reformer in the world of domestic politics: they are no less annoying, in the world of external politics, to those who desire a planned design of international security. But the method and the policy naturally follow from the general nature of our political environment. The alternations of party, and the general length of the tenure of ministries, forbid the expectation of a long sequence of connected policies. Each statesman must plan his work for the life which he can reasonably expect; and each must also plan it on the assumption that he is likely to be succeeded by statesmen of a different type and party, who cannot take over and honour policies fundamentally different from their own. But it is not only the general nature of the political environment which imposes this general tactic on statesmen. It is also the general temper, and the general habit of life, in the nation at large. The experimental method is the general method of British conduct. It has not only been the method of the growth and activity of Parliament through the centuries; it has also been the method of business, the method of colonial enterprise, the method of the general activity of the British stock both at home and overseas. If it includes statesmen in its range, it equally includes the rest of the nation.

IV

Such, in its general lines, is the character of the social and political environment in which British statesmen have worked. We have now to consider the quality of their individual reaction, and the nature of the personal response which they have made to this environment.

When we seek to examine the impact of the statesman's personality on politics, the first question we shall do well to ask is a question which relates to what may be called the angle of his approach. What is the general point of view from which he regards matters of state? What is the dominant trend of the mind with which he seeks to bring into line the data and issues of politics? What are the 'hooks of apprehension' with which he seizes, and to which he seeks to attach, the floating stuff of current affairs?

One way of approach which has been followed, and followed with a deep sincerity, by a number of British statesmen, is the way of religion. Cromwell followed it in one century: Burke in another: Gladstone and Salisbury in a third. Without any hypocrisy (a charge readily brought by the facile mind against those who introduce thoughts of eternity into temporal affairs, but a charge which the reflective mind will no less readily repel), they accepted the primacy of religion and the ultimacy of obedience to its guidance. 'Sir', said Cromwell, 'you see the work is done by a Divine leading.' 'We know', wrote Burke, 'and it is our pride to know, that man is by his constitution a religious animal; . . . all persons possessing any portion of power ought to be strongly and awfully impressed with an idea that they act in trust, and that they are to account for their conduct in that trust to the one great Master, Author and Founder of society.' The same conception of a religious order of the world, and of the duty incumbent on states and statesmen to observe that order, inspired the policy of Gladstone, as it also inspired the policy of Salisbury. 'We are part of what has been well called the Federation of Mankind: we belong to a great community of nations, and we have no right to shrink from the duties which the community imposes on us.' The words are the words of Salisbury; but they might equally have been the words of Gladstone—as they might equally have been the words of Salisbury's son, Lord Cecil.

The religious approach to political issues, external as well as internal, is not peculiar to these statesmen, even if it is peculiarly marked in their statesmanship. It is a general trend of British statesmen. From the days of the Puritan Revolution onwards, religious issues have been great issues in our national life. It is not idly, or at random, that our political parties adopted, and long bore, designations—the designations of Whig and Tory— which had a religious origin. The tenets and temper of the Tories might be opposed to the tenets and temper of the Whigs; but the tenets and the temper of both were based on religious foundations, and even the struggle of parties was conducted within a framework of ideas which was built upon those foundations. In external expansion and foreign policy, as well as in the conduct of internal affairs, statesmen drew on the same inspiration. The growth of the British Empire, from the eighteenth century onwards, was conceived in those terms of trust which were first clearly enunciated by Burke. The direction of British foreign policy, in one of its best but too little regarded phases, was largely swayed by an evangelical inspiration which sought the abolition of the slave trade. If the influence of Wilberforce counted largely in this direction of policy, we should do wrong to forget the actual and active work (without which any mere influence would have run idly into the sands) of such statesmen as Castlereagh and Wellington. Castlereagh, in particular—a member of the same Cambridge college as Wilberforce, Clarkson, and Palmerston, who all laboured in the common cause—sought to make the abolition of the slave trade an article of the general policy of Europe.

Next to the religious approach, we may count the approach of political principle and conviction. We have already noticed the distribution of British statesmen into the two categories of statesmen of the Right and statesmen of the Left, and we have remarked on the even balance of that distribution. But the distribution, as we have also noticed, is by no means an easy matter. There is a sense in which it may be said that the personality of our statesmen, and the impetus of their personal convictions in the matter of politics, have generally been cast on the side of progress. This is perhaps particularly true of what may be called the aristocratic period of our history. Statesmen, because they were more far-sighted than the ordinary run of the aristocratic society in which they lived, and because they were able to rise above its rooted prejudices, could see the need of concession and could steer their course by tacking. They might simply feel, as Wellington felt, that the King's government must be carried on; or they might feel, as Peel felt when he was confronted by the argument of Cobden, that the case for concession and change was really an unanswerable case. Whatever their immediate reasons, it was largely this temper and feeling of statesmen, and particularly of the statesmen of the Right, which enabled the passage from aristocracy to democracy to be made without revolution. The 'country interest' and the landed society might be stirred to its depths—during the passage of the Reform Bill, during the repeal of the Corn Laws, or even as late as the passage of the Parliament Act—but the ultimate political conviction which prevailed among responsible statesmen, and which prevailed, through their influence, in the nation at large, was the conviction that the general welfare and the general will command the ultimate allegiance. The lesson was hard to learn; but it was a lesson which Disraeli himself, the violent opponent of Peel in 1846, accepted and practised afterwards.

We are thus led to the conclusion that, in the matter of political conviction and political principle, it is difficult to discover any clear antinomy—any absolute conservatism, or, for that matter, any absolute liberalism. This is not to say that our statesmen have been generally opportunists, or that they have tacked to the point of becoming trimmers, with no other end than that of 'keeping even the ship of State'. It is rather to say that they have not been doctrinaires, even if they genuinely professed a doctrine: it is to say, in the last resort, that the supreme doctrine on which they have acted has been that of discovering the general national will and of promoting, upon that basis, the general national interest. The necessity of tact in the discovery of social will has been the first principle of their tactic. The society which entertained that will might be conceived, as it was for long years, in narrow terms: even by Burke 'the British public' might be computed at no more than 400,000; but the conception widened with the generations, and the social will of a select society passed into the social will of the whole community. We live today among the play of that broader will. Yet we shall hardly be justified, if we look back at the past from the middle of the twentieth century, in condemning the statesmen of the past for a narrower vision. Few of them were obscurantists: few, if any, of them shut their eyes to the best thought of their times. Castlereagh was denounced by Shelley as an anarch; but Castlereagh also sought to proscribe the slave trade, in obedience to a mode of British thought which Shelley shared. Peel and Disraeli are not counted among Liberals; but the cause of social reform and the improvement of the conditions of labour was a cause which they too served. All in all, we may say of British statesmen at large—of Castlereagh and Peel as well as of Gladstone and Asquith—that the political principle which they brought to affairs was the principle of 'seeking', or, as the logicians call it, 'heuristic'. They might have a party creed: they had no total doctrine or 'general line'. They sought to discover the direction in which their countrymen's thought was moving; and the merit of their statesmanship was a merit of the discerning eye and the prescient instinct rather than of formed design or a settled rationalism.

Another approach to affairs of state, natural in a nation long concerned with commerce, and beginning, by the eighteenth century, to be also concerned with large-scale industry, was the economic. Many of our statesmen, whether or no they had been trained themselves in affairs of business, brought a business eye to the administration of national finance and the fostering of national commerce. They were political economists in the original sense of the term: they were students and practitioners of the art of 'State-housekeeping'. Here again they were responsive to the needs of the society in which they lived—a society in which, as early as the end of the seventeenth century, the landed class was dovetailed into the commercial, and the country interest was already combined with that of the city. The practical genius of English economic thinkers and writers, from the middle of the seventeenth to the middle of the nineteenth century, drew the attention of statesmen to their views, and encouraged an alliance of theory and practice. It was one of the greatest achievements of the Whig statesmen at the end of the seventeenth century, acting in consultation with Newton and Locke, to reform the currency, to establish a national bank and a funded national debt, and thus to institute a system of national finance which at once consolidated the nation at home and sustained its wars and expansion abroad. Walpole continued the tradition: the younger Pitt, with the wisdom of Adam Smith at his command, carried it to a still higher reach. In the nineteenth century the art of 'State-housekeeping' was illustrated by Gladstone and Peel; and whatever else may be said of the Victorian age, it may safely be said that no other age has excelled it in the prudent economy and careful husbandry of national resources.

But the economic aspect of statesmanship, or the economic approach to its problems, was not only concerned with the husbandry of national finance: it was also concerned with the policy of national trade (a matter, by its nature, closely linked with the husbandry of national finance), and with the general colonial and foreign policy which should accompany and support trade policy. One of the great issues which steadily confronted British statesmen was the issue of the marketing of British goods; and that issue in turn presented them, from the time of the younger Pitt onwards, with a choice between the conflicting ideals of Protection and Free Trade. They were compelled to be economists as well as financiers; and they obeyed the compulsion. A high debate was engaged on the proper system of the national economy—on corn laws, colonial preferences, the protection of shipping, and protection at large: it engaged the energies and taxed the abilities not only of Huskisson, Peel, and Gladstone, but also of private members such as Bright and Cobden: it made statesmen educate not only themselves, but also the general community, in the austerities of economic thought. Apparently closed, after the middle of the nineteenth century, by the victory of Free Trade, the debate was again reopened by

Chamberlain in the beginning of the twentieth; and it still proceeds. It has affected, and it affects, not only the policy of national trade, but also colonial policy, and, even beyond that, the general conduct of foreign affairs. We can hardly judge, even yet, whether the great debate has not been a distraction as well as an education; whether it has not diverted our minds, in our own internal affairs, from still deeper issues of the condition of our people and the relation of wealth to commonwealth; whether it has not also diverted them, in international affairs, from the more fundamental problem of a true public order, based upon public law, which is the supreme need and the supreme interest of all peoples and all states. But there is perhaps one thing to be said. The statesman who makes himself a business man, for the handling of the business side of affairs of state, is different from the business man who makes himself a statesman, and carries the temper and principles of private business into state policy. A state, or a commonwealth of states, is not a wealth-making concern. The wealth of the nation is indeed *a* concern of the national state. But *the* concern of concerns is the political concern of national well-being; and that, in its turn, is ultimately a matter of national ethics.

V

STATESMANSHIP has been so often concerned with foreign affairs and military action, in so many of the countries of Europe, that the statesman may almost seem, in the general course of European history, to be identical with the Foreign Minister. Our insular position has given us a more pacific tradition; and our statesmen have been as a rule Ministers of the Interior rather than Foreign Ministers. But the conduct of foreign affairs has always, and the conduct of war has often, attended the path of our statesmen. Both foreign affairs and war, but more especially war, impose new and more acid tests on statesmanship. The arena of domestic politics is indeed an area of struggle; but the struggle is conducted by the force of argument and the thrust of debate, it obeys a code of procedural rules, and it is engaged before a national body of spectators which mixes divided loyalties with some measure of common sympathy. In the conduct of foreign affairs the foils have a keener edge and less of a button on the point: the argument of force already begins to enter the foreground: the personality of the statesman has to be thrown with a more direct impact against rival personalities; and there are divided bodies of spectators. This is a ground on which it is difficult for the parliamentary tradition of statesmanship to move easily. It may be hampered, in the first place, by ingrained notions, derived from the domestic arena, of the courtesies of debate, the spirit of accommodation, and the value of compromise. In the next place, it will almost certainly be hampered, when it has to deal with governments based on a non-parliamentary tradition (the tradition of permanent power, able to act freely and *suo Marte*), by the defects of its own qualities. The statesman conducting foreign affairs under a parliamentary system knows that he has no abiding tenure: he knows, and his colleagues know, that 'we have a parliament and a public to which we are responsible'. He enters the arena with a handicap; and if the handicap may prove an ultimate strength, it is an immediate disability. When the clash of foreign policies passes into a clash of armies and fleets, the disability may be enhanced. In a parliamentary state, dominated by the civilian authority, the determination of higher strategy will tend to fall to the civilian statesman; and unless he himself possesses a strategic eye, or is happy in his choice of commanders and the confidence which he can repose, and inspire, in their judgement, he may forget the imperative military needs of a tense concentration of effort, and he may dissipate the national energy (as perhaps the younger Pitt did) by following the civilian habit of exploring a number of paths.

Before the Revolution of 1688 these difficulties had hardly arisen. The parliamentary system was still struggling into life: our statesmen in the sixteenth century were kings and their permanent advisers—Henry VIII and Wolsey, Elizabeth and Burghley: even in the seventeenth century Strafford was still a permanent minister (if only his wavering sovereign could have given him the honour of his trust), Cromwell had a virtual life-tenure and commanded the army as well as the civil administration, and William III, as long as he lived, was his own Foreign Minister. The testing-time came in the eighteenth century; it came, particularly and especially, with the period of revolution, restoration, and the growth of nationalities, which covered the end of the eighteenth and more than half of the nineteenth century. The astonishing thing, as one looks back on the roll of British statesmen who played a great part on the stage of foreign affairs during the testing-time, is the great names which it contains and the continuity by which they are linked. The eighteenth century produced a Walpole who could maintain peace tenaciously and a Chatham who could wage war gallantly; it also produced, in Chatham's son, the younger Pitt, a mixed and composite statesman who, for nearly one half of his career a greater edition of Walpole and for the other half a lesser edition of his father, epitomized in himself the merits and the defects of the statesmanship of his country. The nineteenth century added the names of Castlereagh, Wellington, and Canning, who all helped to steer their country, and Europe at large, with little essential divergence of view, through the perturbations of the period of revolution and restoration down to 1830; of Palmerston, who, inheriting the particular tradition of Canning, and alive to the growth of nationalities, was almost continuously the inspiring force of British policy (whether as Foreign Secretary or as Prime Minister) from 1830 to 1865; and of Salisbury, who brought to the conduct of foreign policy, in the last quarter of the nineteenth century, not only a sane and steady judgement, but also a profound devotion to the cause of public order and a deep sense of the duties incumbent upon all members of the community of nations. Two of the greatest of our statesmen of the nineteenth century, Peel and Gladstone, were essentially domestic statesmen; but both of them, and particularly Gladstone, deserve to be remembered in the record of foreign policy. It was said of Peel by a French statesman that he had no foreign policy but peace and goodwill among nations. Gladstone had a deep belief in the public law of Europe: he hated oppression even more fervently than Palmerston, and like Palmerston (and Canning before Palmerston) he wished to make the liberal tradition of Great Britain an influence and an aid in European development. The memory of Gladstone, in its turn, was still a living force with the British statesmen—Grey and Asquith—who were charged with the guidance of British foreign policy in the early years of the twentieth century.

When we reflect on these figures, and the links by which they are bound, we cannot but say that there was a steady course. *Quasi cursores . . . lampada tradiderunt*. The difficulties of accommodating the domestic tradition of a parliamentary system to the needs of a steady conduct of foreign policy were, after all, surmounted. A lasting tradition of policy was accumulated, like a coral reef, by a process of continuous accretion. In foreign affairs, as in domestic politics, the experimental genius of a historically minded people, tentatively creating a tradition which it seeks at once to maintain and to improve, is apparent. What Canning (not the greatest, but perhaps the most expressive of our foreign statesmen) wrote over a century ago might still be repeated in its essence today. The principles of British foreign policy were in his view 'respect for the faith of treaties, respect for the independence of nations, respect for that established line of policy known as the balance of power, and, last but not least, respect for the honour and interests of this country'. We might alter today the words 'balance of power', and seek to substitute other and more positive words which suggest the idea of a union of power, for the purpose of collective security, under a recognized and guaranteed system of international law: we might also interpret differently the words 'honour and interests of this country', giving them a wider scope, and admitting (or even contending) that the sovereign national interest, transcending and yet sustaining the nation, is the existence of an international order which shelters national development. But the general principles enunciated by Canning still stand in their main essentials.

If we take a summary view of the formation of our permanent tradition of foreign policy, we can see how our main statesmen have at once expressed and, in the act of expressing, ennobled a general feeling of the nation about the proper conduct of foreign affairs. A commercial people, anxious to spread our commerce and ready to embark, for commercial reasons, on wars and colonial expansion, we were also led by our commercial interests to desire a system of general and permanent peace as the system best calculated to secure and increase our commercial prosperity. Commerce was a two-edged influence: it could produce both war and peace; but its greater, or at any rate its more permanent influence, was an influence towards peace. Interpreting and expressing this trend, our statesmen also elevated it. Seeking to find a formula or method of peace, they advanced from balance to concert, and then from concert to League; or, as we may also say, seeking peace at first for the sake of commerce they came eventually to seek it for the sake of civilization. Statesmanship can not only express—it can also distil and purify—the feeling of a nation; and its function of distillation is also a function of national education. This was the work of Castlereagh and Canning, of Palmerston, of Gladstone and Salisbury; and it is the work which is still incumbent on the statesmen of our century. It is a work of guiding, in the act of following; of ennobling and sublimating, in the act of expressing; of always being a little ahead, in the act of marching together.

But British statesmen, in the realm of foreign affairs, have not only given something to their own country: they have also given something to Europe. It may have been something of a handicap to their foreign activity that they were predominantly imbued with the temper of domestic politics, and that they necessarily worked under the conditions imposed by a parliamentary state and its party system. But if it was a handicap, it was also a gain. Their sense of responsibility to the British public and Parliament was carried by them into Europe, and was made a gift to Europe. Like called to like, and nursed the embryonic like into consciousness and strength. If the people and its aspirations mattered in England, must they not also matter elsewhere? A liberal sense of 'respect for the independence of nations' was thus added as a leaven to the old European statesmanship which treated affairs of state as a dynastic mystery; and that sense, which had inspired Canning as it continued to inspire Palmerston and Gladstone, was a contribution of British statesmen to the society of European states.

There is one area of the exercise of statesmanship which has been peculiar to British statesmen. Besides handling questions of domestic and questions of foreign policy, they have also been called upon, by the growth and expansion of their people, to handle questions of imperial policy—questions which are at once domestic and, in a sense, foreign: questions which lie on the borderland between domestic and foreign. Their burden has been a triple burden; and it has not always been successfully sustained. There was failure during the eighteenth century, in the days of Lord North; and the failure resulted in the dissolution of the Empire. The failure was retrieved in the nineteenth century; and it is being more than retrieved in the twentieth.

We may thank British statesmen for some of the success. Lord Durham, a century ago, helped his country to make a momentous decision in favour of colonial self-government: Disraeli realized and preached the value of imperial cohesion: Rhodes, mixing business with politics, none the less left a great mark on the development of South Africa: Chamberlain made his tenure of the office of Colonial Secretary (1895-1903) a landmark and an inspiration. But the office of British statesmen, in the sphere of imperial affairs, has been less to guide and still less to control development, than to watch it at work, to register its trend with an observant and sympathetic eye, and, in a word, to ease its growth by making readily the accommodations which growth will always require. It was in the Dominions themselves that the idea and practice of Dominion status germinated and grew; and it was the merit, as it was also the duty, of British statesmen such as Balfour to register the germination and to ease the growth by the accommodations ultimately made in the Statute of Westminster. Similarly it was in the colonies of the dependent empire that the idea and practice of Indirect Rule, as a preparation for self-government, was developed by administrators, such as Lord Lugard, who were in living touch with native life and its living needs; and here again it was the merit, as it was also the duty, of the British statesmen of the Colonial Office to recognize the fact which was being accomplished. In both ways British statesmanship achieved one of its greatest triumphs—perhaps, indeed, the greatest of all. It showed itself a statesmanship which could welcome and accept the growth of a colleague-statesmanship, standing as an equal by its side, in the general width and range of the Empire. The figure of Smuts—great in war as well as in peace, and a thinker as well as a statesman—attests the height which such colleague-statesmanship can attain. It is a statesmanship which can co-operate not only in its own local range, but also in the centre and at the heart; which can act as co-adjutor not only in imperial, but also in European and world affairs.

VI

In the record of our own British statesmen two types of personality may be distinguished. One is the type of the creative or, as it may also be called, in the original sense of the word, the poetic personality. It has a dynamic quality: it is a mainspring of motion rather than a fly-wheel of administration. Though it is a type, it is not typical: it is a list of exceptions, and not a rule. Cromwell belongs to this category in the seventeenth century (and perhaps we may also add the name of Strafford): the elder Pitt belongs to it in the eighteenth: in the nineteenth century we may add the names of Disraeli, Rhodes, and Chamberlain: in the twentieth, those of Lloyd George and Churchill. The other type is that of the more prosaic and pedestrian personality which, ready in an emergency to measure itself against great issues, can bend with a sober patience to the long littleness of ordinary affairs. This is the type of Walpole, the younger Pitt, Castlereagh, Peel, and Asquith. It is a less fascinating subject of biography, which inclines more readily to Canning than to Castlereagh, and to Disraeli than to Peel. But the criterion of the biographer is not necessarily the true criterion for the appreciation of statesmanship. If we emphasize the individual genius and the peculiar idiosyncrasy of a particular statesman or a particular type of statesman, we may be led to neglect the individual and peculiar characteristic of statesmanship itself, as it has shown itself in our history. British statesmanship has been more a matter of a school, or schools, than of individual artists. Sometimes a personality may have inspired a school: we speak, for example, of Pittites, Canningites, Peelites, and again of Gladstonians. Sometimes, and perhaps even oftener, the reverse is the case: a school has flowered and expressed itself in a statesman, or in a succession of statesmen. In a society connected by a constant intercourse these connexions of the mind were natural: politics were combined with friendship, and friendship issued in the communication and transmission of lines of policy and thought. It is by this process of communication and transmission that the generations have been successively trained ('to his friendship and instruction I owe whatever I am', said the elder Pitt of Lord Carteret); that a school, or a number of schools, of statesmanship have been formed; and that the influence of individuals has been raised to the height of the influence of a group.

We are thus led to note once more a fact which we have already had occasion to note in treating of party—the fact of the group, and of group opinion and action, as the essential unit of

British statesmanship. Reflecting upon this fact, we may find ourselves tempted to doubt whether the single personality, with its own distinctive and separate genius, has ever played a foremost part in the guidance of our political development. We may feel drawn towards the view that it is the group, the school, the party, or the wing of a party, that has always mattered most; we may even feel drawn towards the paradox that the essential and most influential initiative of British statesmanship has proceeded not from genius of the first order, which has a solitary quality, but from the splendid second rate, which can co-operate readily with its like. We have had indeed emergent and dominant personalities, *felices opportunitate temporum suorum*—a Cromwell, a Chatham, and (posterity may yet say) a Churchill: men who have been or been felt to be like a Colossus, bestriding the narrow world with great steps. But just as the English voice is low, and the English singer has not the great volume of the continental—just as our choirs are greater than our soloists—so it would also seem to be in politics. Perhaps a general high level is the enemy of the highest; and where so many can do so well, there is little room for a single person to do supremely well. We have many leaders; but not, as a rule, *a* leader. Whether, in the final issue, we lose or gain may be a matter of opinion. Homer makes Agamemnon say, 'It is not good to have many masters: let there be one.' The writer remembers hearing a German Ambassador quote the Homeric saying at a dinner over forty years ago; and the Germans have generally followed its spirit. The British have generally held that there is greater safety, and even wisdom, in numbers.

Individuality is not extinguished—on the contrary, it may be said to be extended—when it acts in and through a group. Not only is it extended: it is also perpetuated, if it makes itself, as it may, a permanent part of the tradition of a continuous group. But we should be doing wrong to the national record, and committing a treason against its majesty, if we failed to appreciate the influence of the creative individual personality in the roll of British statesmen. Such figures stand by themselves, in solitude; and by virtue of their very solitude they have seldom left a line of successors. But their names are connected with great moments and great achievements; and when the great moment recurs, and the great achievement is again needed, their inspiration recurs. The war from which we have just emerged began on that day of September which was the great day of Cromwell's life—the day of the battle of Dunbar, the day of the battle of Worcester. In the course of the war Mr. Churchill became Prime Minister in the spirit, and almost in the circumstances, in which the elder Pitt became virtual Prime Minister during the Seven Years War. In time of war it is Cromwell and Chatham who wake again.

VII

It remains to consider finally the influence exercised by some of our leading statesmen on the general course of national development. We must come to particulars, and attempt to frame what Scott, in one of his novels, calls 'articles of condescendence', which will deal with the individual counts of statesmen.

But there is a caveat which must first be entered. When we are dealing with the State and statesmen, we have to remember that the State and its statesmen are not the only force which has been operative in the general course of our national development. Society as well as the State—society acting by the side of the State—has also been operative. This is true, in its measure, of all countries: it is perhaps particularly true of our own. Voluntary society, acting partly in the form of the religious congregation and partly in the form of the economic company, has been active in many fields of our national life. The voluntary principle, acting on the basis of the religious society, played a large part in the establishment of our national system of education; we have to remember the work of Bell and Lancaster, as well as the achievements of educational statesmen such as Forster and Fisher. The same principle, acting on the basis of the company, has played a large part in the history of our colonization and general imperial expansion, from the Virginia and Massachusetts Companies of the early seventeenth century to the Royal South African Company at the end of the nineteenth. It has even been said, by one of our economic historians, that 'the expansion of England in the seventeenth century was an expansion of society and not of the State'; and it may certainly be said that the general growth of the British Empire has been an achievement of society as well as of the State—if not more than of the State. But it is not always easy to draw a line of distinction.

Society and the State co-operate, and they interact as they co-operate. Was Rhodes, for example, a great figure in the history of British society, or a great figure in the history of British statesmanship? He was both in one; and his greatness, and the breadth of his vision, were intimately connected with his double capacity—as, it must also be confessed, were his difficulties. It was not easy to be simultaneously the manager of great companies and the Prime Minister of a State.

There is another caveat which must also be entered. If figures in the area of society matter as well as, and sometimes as much as, the figures of the statesmen who act in the area of the State, it is also true that among the figures of statesmen there are many that count whose names cannot be included in any 'articles of condescendence'. We may make a list of twenty-five statesmen; we may select the most eminent of them for a particular examination of the memory they left and the influence they bequeathed; but we perhaps omit in the process something that matters as much as all that we include. We omit Spencers and Montagus, Russells and Cavendishes and Bentincks, Pettys and Greys and Stanleys, who have counted in their generation and sometimes from generation to generation. We omit family tradition: we also omit what may be called the collective weight of the average, which determines so greatly the general standard and the general influence of statesmen. We omit too—necessarily, because our theme is the statesmen who have trodden the public stage; and yet statesmanship touches administration—the great anonymous administrators who have always helped, and sometimes inspired, the action of statesmanship. A French writer has said that the educational policy of the Third Republic was the work of 'M. Lebureau'. The 'bureau', from the time of Kay Shuttleworth, has also been closely connected with the development of British educational policy. Similarly colonial policy was for many years determined, in no small measure, by the Colonial Office; and Sir James Stephen, the Colonial Under-Secretary, whom wits called 'Mr. Over-Secretary Stephen', may be termed *the* colonial statesman of the first half of the nineteenth century.

Yet the great names shine, and because they shine they continue to light the national goings. It is curious, and yet explicable, that the greatest name—the name of the Englishman who, in the realm of action, is comparable to Shakespeare in the realm of thought—should shine with a cloudy light. Cromwell was a pillar of fire, but also a pillar of cloud. Great fiery sayings, and great fiery acts, came from the cloud; but his greatness has never been laid very closely to the general heart of his countrymen. His memory is encompassed by other memories—of civil war, of the execution of a king, of devotion to a sect, of a general partiality. His greatness remains. To read his speeches and letters, and to follow the working of his thought in the army debates recorded in the Clarke papers, is to see a seeking and questing mind, ready to 'put itself fairly' to others: it is to see the essential foundations of the British temper of debate. He had a deep patriotism, but it was qualified and ennobled by a religious fervour: he thought the English 'the best people in the world' but only if there was present in them, as their core, 'the people of God', ready to serve and follow the light of a divine leading. Both in the working of his thought and in the quality of his patriotism he left a permanent legacy; but it was a legacy to England rather than to Great Britain at large, and even in England it was a legacy to a part, a legacy to Nonconformity and the Free Churches, rather than to the general whole.

Chatham had a wider appeal, but he bequeathed a less permanent legacy. A great orator, and a great War Minister, he was also a great and unqualified patriot; and he could see by flashes deep into the heart of affairs. But he was unable to maintain a steady and sustained gaze; nor could he accommodate the fire of his patriotism to the fact of party and the need of sustained co-operation with a band of associates. He had essentially a solitary quality, and his spirit dwelt apart: his name still shines in the hour of danger, but he was a comet rather than a star. Burke, in one sense, was never a statesman: he was never charged with the responsible handling of great affairs. In another sense he has left a legacy of statesmanship which in its kind is unique. His mind soared high, with a steady beat, to the essential principles involved in the great issues of his time, internal, imperial, and foreign; and he expressed in imperishable English a fund of political wisdom directly drawn from experience. He belongs to the borderland between statesmanship and the philosophy of the state: he is a great figure in our literature as well as our politics. The dissemination of his writings has disseminated his influence not only in Britain, where he is still cited and will continue to be cited as the master of those who know in the sphere of politics, but also in the Empire at large, and not least in India. He was the first to enunciate a theory of party: he was the first to enunciate, in clear terms, the doctrine of trust on which our colonial policy has since been so largely based. The appeal to Burke is still an appeal which is made by statesmen of every party; and if the tradition he left is more a tradition of theory than of practice, the influence of that tradition only proves the importance of theory.

The younger Pitt was little of a theorist; and though he was counted among the great orators of his time, there are few who read his speeches today. Burke once called him 'the sublime of mediocrity', and there was some justice in the judgement. Yet his was an *aurea mediocritas*, so all-round that its cumulative effect touched the highest greatness. He had the economist's instinct for a prudent management of national finance and commerce: he combined it with a masterly skill in the art of parliamentary management; he combined both with a pure and sincere patriotism, undaunted and undefeated through long years of hazard, which steadily sustained the spirit of his country. He had indeed defects which almost matched his merits. Though he was the inspiration of Castlereagh and Canning, he was not himself a great foreign statesman: he was far from being a great War Minister: above all, he had no firm hold of ultimate political principles. He had not the passionate devotion of Fox to the cause of liberty and humanity: he postponed the cause of parliamentary reform, as he postponed the cause of the abolition of the slave trade, to the practical exigencies of the hour. He loved power, and he worked for the moment, or at any rate for the immediate future: Fox loved, or was forced to embrace, opposition, and he worked for a cause of reform which could only triumph long after his death. But whatever the defects of Pitt, he was utterly disinterested and indomitably resolute: confident in the exertions his countrymen could make and the example they could give: always endowed with the courage of hope, and able to communicate his courage to others. When all allowances are made for his weaknesses, the fact remains that if we were asked, as a nation, to submit one of our statesmen to the bar of judgement, as the shining type and example of their general character, Pitt would be the statesman whom we should generally unite in selecting.

It is no doubt an effect of our party system of politics that British statesmen have more than once stood in contrasting pairs. At the end of the eighteenth century Pitt and Fox formed the contrast: in the latter half of the nineteenth Gladstone and Disraeli formed a contrast of a different character. In one sense Gladstone stands in the line of succession from Fox, with the same devotion to ultimate political principles of liberty and humanity: in another sense he may be counted as a successor of Pitt, with the same instinct for sound national economy and the same passion for the House of Commons and the art of parliamentary management. But if he was both Fox and Pitt, he was fundamentally himself—at once of a subtle intellect and of a profound religious belief; at once a master of management and a man who could wake the sleeping fires of national conscience, at the call of justice and public law, to protest against wrong and oppression. Like Cromwell in one respect (though very unlike in most others) he appealed to a part rather than the whole; but on the part to which he appealed he left an abiding mark. Disraeli, in a varied and dazzling career, cast a wider net. He had more hooks of apprehension: he felt instinctively the magnitude of the 'condition of England question': he felt, with an instinctive prescience, the significance of the British Empire. Like Burke, he brought the imagination of an immigrant to the scene of British politics: like Burke, he belonged to the world of letters (though to another part of that world) as well as to the world of statesmanship. He professed fidelity to the tradition of the younger Pitt; but if he had any forerunner, it was Bolingbroke rather than Pitt. He was an electric shock to his times: it is more doubtful whether he has exercised an abiding influence. He served a great party with an adroit rapier; but it is not clear that he has become an integral part of the tradition of that party or of the nation.

Chamberlain and Asquith are not a contrasting pair in the sense of Pitt and Fox or of Disraeli and Gladstone. It was only in one brief period, during the renewal of the high debate on Protection and Free Trade at the beginning of the twentieth century, that they touched and clashed; nor was the varied career of Chamberlain, which mixed Radicalism with Liberalism and both with Conservatism as it moved through its orbit, consistent enough to present a foil to the unwavering and unbending tenacity of Asquith's political course. But a fundamental contrast none the less remains. Chamberlain is the greatest example of the incursions into the realm of politics which the stirring spirit of a new business age was now beginning to make. A moving and fermenting leaven, he brought the ideas of liquidation and reconstruction into the different conjunctures of affairs through which he passed; and while at one period of his career, from 1877 onwards, he was occupied with the remoulding of the organization and programme of the Liberal party, at another, a quarter of a century later, he was equally occupied with the remoulding of the Conservative party and with the reconstruction of the commercial policy of Great Britain and the British Empire. He had his *daemon*: he destroyed but he also renewed: he belonged to the creative and dynamic type; and the ultimate influence which he exercised, not only on economic issues but also on the broader issues of general imperial policy, may still be traced today. Asquith brought to politics the gifts of a trained Oxford scholar and the instincts of a great lawyer resolved to defend the brief of his party with a pure fidelity and a trenchant logic. He added no original ideas to his brief; but the period of his ascendancy none the less saw new ideas added—ideas of new social services and general social reform—which he accepted, and even welcomed, and which profoundly modified the old individualism of his party. In the style of Pitt and the tradition of Gladstone, he was a master of party and parliamentary management: he guided the nation steadily through the turmoil of a constitutional struggle, as he held it unfalteringly together in its entry into a great war; wherever he had tradition for guide and the rigour of a clear issue for stimulus, he could show a sturdy independence and an unfailing judgement. Like the younger Pitt, he failed to rise to the exigencies of war, but, unlike Pitt, he fell from power after two years of war and gave way to another statesman drawn from his own party; and in the issue he who in 1911 had seemed to stand at the zenith of his party and his party's cause was doomed to see it, before he died, disrupted and almost destroyed. The waves of war and the waves of a new social development which issued in the Labour party have both washed over his memory; and while the works of the peace period of his ministry survive, and the recollection of a loyal fidelity and a consummate ability remains, the words *pulvis et umbra* are written over his influence today. Yet he was, as it has been justly said, in the line of classical English statesmen: he acted in the high Roman manner, true to the ancient virtues

> Pudor, et iustitiae soror
> Incorrupta Fides, nudaque Veritas:

and if he fell with the fall of his party, the seven years which saw the collaboration under his guidance of men such as Grey, Haldane, Lloyd George, and Churchill form one of the greatest eras in the annals of British statesmanship.

It is too early to attempt any appreciation of the influence of the statesmen of the twentieth century, or to conjecture how statesmen such as Lloyd George and Smuts and Churchill will stand in the judgement and the tradition of our posterity. But there are some reflections which the present hour of British statesmanship suggests; and these reflections may bring the argument to a natural close.

One reflection which the name of Churchill suggests, as indeed it is also suggested by the names of the majority of our great statesmen, is that oratory is a great power; that it may attain, in a crucial hour, the dimensions of a great act; and that in any case, recorded for posterity and treasured by later ages, it perpetuates the memory and the influence of statesmen. Oratory is not to be despised: it may be the noblest of acts. Nor must we forget those sayings of statesmen—great sentences in orations, or sudden flashes in talk—which enter into the national memory and become 'as goads, and as nails fastened by the masters of assemblies'. The saying of Churchill, 'I have nothing to offer but blood, toil, tears, and sweat', goes back (but on a higher note) to the saying of the elder Pitt, who, in another dangerous hour when some were thinking that 'the time has come for England to slip her own cables and float away into some unknown ocean', was bold enough to proclaim, 'I am sure that I can save the country, and that no one else can'. It would almost be a measure of the influence of statesmen simply to record the sayings by which they live in the general memory.

Another reflection suggested by the present hour is that more than one of our British statesmen has counted in the world of letters as well as in the world of statesmanship, or has proved himself to be a thinker as well as a man of action. Churchill, writer as well as statesman, has his place in a gallery which includes Bolingbroke and Burke in one century, Disraeli in another, and Balfour and Smuts in a third. His name, like theirs, is a name of a double dimension.

But the last, and the greatest, of the reflections which our times may inspire turns on the emergence of statesmen drawn directly from the people at large and from the organizations of labour. The ministry of 1940-5 included, in a double team, on the one hand names such as Churchill and Eden and Lyttelton, and on the other hand such names as Bevin, Alexander, and Morrison. This may remind us again of a fact already noticed—that the social and political environment of British statesmanship has been an aristocracy passing gradually, but surely, into a democracy. There has long been an aristocratic strain in British statesmanship: it still survives; and it is still needed. It can still discharge a duty, perhaps the last but not the least in its record, by fusing its old tradition of service to the state with the emergence and aspirations of a new class of worker-statesmen, equally anxious to serve and ready now to learn, in comradeship and co-operation, the method and technique of service. There has emerged, as we have seen, a new fund of statesmanship in the British Empire to which the name of colleague-statesmanship may not improperly be given. It may be that in Great Britain too, but in another way and another sense, a similar fund of colleague-statesmanship also emerged in the war years. Labour, indeed, already provided its statesmen and its cabinets. But the purely Labour cabinets had been transient and embarrassed; and the co-operation of Labour in Coalition cabinets after 1931 was a small and partial thing. The co-operation of worker-statesmen in the ministry of 1940-5 was a full and equal co-operation. In this partnership they acquired a large and rich experience which they can transmit, as a tradition and inheritance, to the worker-statesmen who, in days to come, will independently steer the state on long voyages over new seas. If we may cherish that hope, we can see an assurance of the survival of tradition in the future, whether the old *élite* is still given some part in the service of the state, or the people prefers to give the duty and privilege of service entirely to a new *élite* drawn directly from its own mass.

Essay Three

THE PARLIAMENTARY SYSTEM OF GOVERNMENT

ONE of the great principles which the genius of France has contributed to civilization is the principle of national sovereignty. Every nation—so France has believed, and so France has taught the world—must be master of its own fate and arbiter of its own life. When France rejected the principle and practice of absolutism, in 1789, she installed in its place, for herself and the world, the principle and the practice of national sovereignty. She said to the Bourbons, 'You are wrong in proclaiming, "L'État, c'est moi" '; she said to herself, and she said to the world, 'Henceforth we proclaim, "L'État, c'est la nation"'. The self-moving and self-governing nation—not the nation moved by a single dominant person; not the nation governed, and drilled, by a single tyrannical party—this, it was then declared, is the unit of modern life.

This nation—this unit of millions and millions of members—needs an organ and agent through which it can act. It needs an organ and agent which represents and reflects its being, in all the facets and scintillations of its multitudinous life. That organ and agent is parliament. Parliament derives its authority from the nation, by an express derivation based on open and free election; and a parliament vested with such authority is the sovereign depository, for its term of office, of the sovereignty of the nation. It is the trustee which the nation has authorized to act on its behalf; and it exercises sovereign power, under the terms of its trust, for the nation which has given it the honour and the pledge of its confidence.

In proclaiming and establishing these principles France was true to the current of history, and faithful to the rolling movement of 'man's unconquerable mind' which determines the course of history. She was going back to an old tradition of freedom which had been impeded and clogged by the later development of her life under the *ancien régime*. She was putting away and casting aside the absolutism which had previously thwarted the free movement of her national life. She was enunciating new principles—but the new principles were also old. They were principles which had lived in her own medieval États Généraux and her own medieval free communes. They were principles which had lived among the mountains of Castile and Aragon. They were principles which were still living among the mountains and valleys of Switzerland; in the neighbouring island of Britain; among the dykes and canals of Holland; in the fjords and around the lakes of the Scandinavian north. There already existed, in 1789, a European tradition of self-government by assemblies: a sure and safe and sound tradition, deposited by the working of the human mind as it moved on its arduous way through time. It was the work of France to recover and revivify that tradition.

I. *History*

THE British speak of Westminster as 'the Mother of Parliaments'. But there is no one mother of parliaments; and in any case what the British mean is only that the Westminster Parliament has been the mother of other parliaments in the confines of the British Empire. The mind of man produces *similar* inventions—it even produces the *same* inventions—separately and independently at many different points. Feeling his way towards an ideal of self-government, which he can never abjure, man has invented various assemblies and parliaments, for the realization of his ideal, at many different periods and in many different countries. It is true that, as the anthropologists tell us, man's general inventions, in the ordinary sphere of the arts and crafts, are often diffused by a process of imitation; and it may also be true that, now and again, some invention, or some improvement, in the sphere of parliamentary institutions, has been diffused by a similar process. The example of French institutions was potent in nineteenth-century Europe: the example of the British Parliament was studied in the Europe of the eighteenth century; and the example of the institutions of the United States has been studied and adopted, during the last century and a half, not only in Latin America but also farther afield. But a sober review of history will convince the reflective historian— even while he is willing to allow the influence of imitation—that the invention of assemblies and parliaments has proceeded independently, like most of man's other inventions, in a number of different centres.

It is fascinating to record the number of centres. It is profitable as well as fascinating: for it proves, beyond any doubt, the natural movement of the mind of man—in different countries and under different auspices—towards one common method of government. The Swiss have an old and fine tradition of democracy—of popular self-government in cantons and groups of cantons—which is at least as old as the thirteenth century. Peasant democracies, with all the citizens assembling in their own direct assembly or 'folk-moot', still exist (and have existed continuously through the centuries) in some of the cantons of Switzerland: in the rest a single House or Chamber, elected by all the people of the canton, acts on behalf of the people. These are indigenous institutions, which an indigenous spirit of liberty has freely and independently created in each of the separate cantons of Switzerland. The old indigenous institutions of the separate cantons are matched by the newer but equally indigenous, if also more subtle and more complicated, institutions of the centre—the parliamentary institutions created by Swiss genius for the federal system which embraces all the cantons of Switzerland in a harmonious unity. Any man who seeks to study the height which democracy can attain will be well advised to fix his attention on the constitution of Switzerland. Here, in a native laboratory and under native inspiration, democracy has produced achievements which not only show its native strength upon its own soil and under its own conditions, but also afford suggestion and example to every country which seeks to tread the way of democracy.

Modern Spain, under its present rulers, is not enamoured of democracy or democratic systems. But if you go back to an older Spain, you will find a proud tradition of Spanish Cortes and Spanish liberties. The British are proud of the antiquity of their Parliament, which goes back to the thirteenth century. Cortes were already meeting in Spain in the twelfth century. The Castilian Cortes already contained representatives of towns in 1169; in Aragon representatives of towns and other districts attended even earlier, in 1162. No doubt the 'liberties' of medieval Spain were largely the liberties claimed by a privileged nobility; but the Spanish towns were also proud of their franchises and their charters, and as late as 1520 they challenged (though the event proved their challenge vain) the encroachments made on their liberties by the government of King Charles I (who, as emperor, was styled Charles V). The early dawn of Spanish parliamentarianism was clouded over; and a system of absolutism, aided by internal dissensions, was for centuries the fate of Spain —as it was also the fate of France before 1789. But those who seek to recall the origins of the parliamentary system in Europe will not forget the early contribution of Spain; and they may even remember that Spanish precedents, and Spanish influences, have been reckoned by some historians among the factors which contributed to the growth of the English Parliament during the thirteenth century. Men's minds early nourished the idea of parliament in Spain; and they will continue to nourish the idea.

From Switzerland and Spain let us turn to Scandinavia. Sweden is an ancient country, with an old and stirring history. Her constitution, like that of Switzerland, is native and indigenous: as a Swedish author has said, 'It is not modelled on the pattern of the political costumes which are *à la mode* in the rest of Europe, but rather after the lines of the old national costume of Sweden, with its peasant's jacket fitting the figure'. Early in the seventeenth century, in the great days of Gustavus Adolphus, Sweden began to turn an old Council of nobles into a new Diet of estates; and this new Diet, or Riksdag, contained not only the three estates of the nobility, the clergy, and the bourgeoisie, but also a fourth estate of the peasantry. This Diet was a genuine parliament, which waged a long and vigorous struggle against the monarchy; and by the constitution of 1809 it was firmly established as an equal partner in the Swedish State. The subsequent course of history has steadily strengthened the Swedish assembly in an uninterrupted progression of power. In 1866 the old Diet of four estates became a parliament of two houses; and that parliament, reforming and broadening its own composition, and gaining control of the Royal ministers on the lines of a cabinet system, has established a pattern of progressive democracy, and inaugurated an epoch of social reform, which have renewed, on a higher plane, the ancient glories of Swedish achievement.

In the great region of culture and civilization which lies

between Scandinavia and Spain—the region of France herself: the region of Belgium and the Netherlands—the tradition of an assembly of estates runs back to the middle of the Middle Ages. The États Généraux of France are as old as the year 1302: they contained, from their first beginning, elected representatives of the towns; and their activity in the fourteenth century was vigorous and salutary. The continental position of France and the long wars on which her monarchs embarked led eventually to the desuetude of the États Généraux; and few as their meetings had been in the fifteenth and sixteenth centuries, they were discontinued entirely between 1614 and 1789. But their fire, if repressed, was still smouldering; and it burst into a triumphant flame with the coming of the Revolution. France recovered her heritage; and through all the vicissitudes of her life she has maintained it ever since. *Fluctuat, nec mergitur.* The heritage of France is too precious—too precious for herself, and too precious for the world—ever to be submerged.

The struggle for liberty of the local estates in the countries which now are Belgium and the Netherlands is as old as the days of the Burgundian Dukes of the later Middle Ages. It was a struggle which rose to a noble height when they challenged the authority of Philip of Spain at the close of the sixteenth century. The Netherlands won: their liberty was acknowledged in 1648 by the public law of Europe; and the people of the Netherlands, with a grave and sober tenacity, built for themselves a house of constitutional liberty, and a home of toleration and of the free printing-press, which were the glory of the seventeenth century. That house and that home still endure: widened, strengthened, and deepened, they are still the abode of a people which has never abandoned the cause of parliamentary liberty. Belgium was forced to sail stormier seas; but even under a foreign yoke the men of Brabant were still proud to remember their own *joyeuse entrée*. In the liberal days of the early nineteenth century—days since overcast by the storms and thunder-clouds which have again and again rolled westwards from Prussia, but days which the spirit of man will inevitably renew—in those days Belgium too recovered her heritage (as nations always will when the heritage is in their heart's blood); and the Belgian Constitution of 1830, one of the great documents of liberty, is the century-old testimony of its recovery.

We are sometimes apt to forget how widespread parliaments are over all the civilized world. We are ourselves Europeans: we look at our own European continent: we see the menace which has threatened the parliaments of our continent; and we fail to remember that there are four other continents—and that the sun shines there if it is darkened for us. Parliaments have grown in Asia; and they will grow in Asia still further. The new Indian constitution of November 1949 adopts expressly and fully the parliamentary system of government. The whole new world of America—both in the north and the south—is a world of various forms of parliamentary liberty. In the continent of Africa there are parliaments today in Algiers, in Cairo, and in Cape Town; and as Africa grows in its stature, and develops its mental resources, the 'dark continent', as men have called it, will increasingly enter into the light of parliamentary liberty and parliamentary discussion. Finally, there are parliaments, and a vigorous parliamentary system, in the continent of Australia. No believer in the authority of the general judgement of man can doubt the value of a system which is endorsed so widely, and in so many continents, by the authority of that judgement. Parliaments are common over the whole of the civilized world. If some of the States of a single continent have turned non-parliamentary in the course of the present century, is it logical to salute them as heralds of the future? Should we not rather say that they have turned their faces away from the parliament of man, and that they have made their motion a foiled and circuitous wandering among the backwaters of history?

Wide in its general diffusion, the institution of parliament also runs back, for centuries and even millennia, in the record and annals of time. History, as well as geography, is eloquent of its achievement. Three thousand years ago, as early as the days of Homer, or even earlier, the tribesmen of early Greece met and debated in what they called the 'agora'—the gathering or the assembly. It was not a habit confined to the Greeks. The Latins of ancient Italy equally assembled in their 'comitia'; the Celts of Gaul had their gatherings; and the very Teutons of Germany (whose descendants lately professed to prefer the inspired voice of the leader to the national debate of the assembly) had what they called their 'folk-moots'. Indeed it is one of the ironies of history that German historians—only a century ago—

were apt to claim as specifically Teutonic, and as the special glory of the German genius, this general habit of the 'folk-moot'. It was a claim which raised the just indignation of the historians of France; and no sober historian today would admit that the German tribesmen of the woods possessed a monopoly of what may be called 'the democracy of the tribe'. It was a common inheritance of the tribal age—an inheritance shared by Germany (all the more sad that its memory should lately have been rejected in Germany), but an inheritance equally shared by the Celts, the Slavs, and the other peoples of early tribal Europe.

What was the subsequent history of this early tribal assembly —the 'agora', or 'comitia', or 'moot', or whatever it might be called—in which the tribesmen all met (not through their representatives, but in person and face to face) for the purpose of common debate and common deliberation? To answer that question we may take one instance, and consider what happened in England. Here, over a thousand years ago (let us say by the year A.D. 900), the different tribes of the land were beginning to be united in one Kingdom of England. It was impossible to have a folk-moot of all England—geography was an insuperable barrier—and there was accordingly instituted a chosen assembly of the wise, the 'Witan', which consisted of nobles, high officials, and the leading clergy. It was a small assembly, which perhaps never numbered more than 100; and it was not an elected assembly. But it was none the less, in some sort of sense, an assembly which represented the nation; and it stood by the side of the King, with its own claims to some right of counsel and consent, as the representative of the nation. The old folk-moot had thus become the new Witan. The new Witan was in its turn to change; and it changed with the coming of feudalism, which may be dated, in England, from the Norman Conquest of 1066. It changed into a body called the Great Council, or *magnum concilium*, which was composed, and composed entirely, of the great feudatories, lay and ecclesiastical, who held land and rights over land by the direct grant of the King. This was a body, larger than the Witan (it may have included some hundreds of members), which equally claimed, and sought to exercise, a right of counsel and consent; and it could equally claim to exercise that right by virtue of being, in some sort of sense, representative of the kingdom. But it was only the land and the great landed proprietors that it represented: it was, we may say, a body which smelled of the land; and its natural tendency was a tendency to defend the claims and privileges of owners of land. Its limitations were the source and cause of the next advance—the crucial and final advance—in the history of the growth of an English Parliament.

During the thirteenth century, and in the first half of the fourteenth, the feudal Great Council was gradually turned into two Houses of Parliament. The Great Council became one of the Houses—the House which is henceforth called the House of Lords; the other House was the House which is henceforth known to history as the House of Commons. It was, in the main, the action of the King—eager to escape from the sole and undivided presence of a single body of feudal magnates—which was responsible for this great change. He called into alliance the people: he summoned to a new House of Commons representatives elected by the people—two representatives from each of the counties or shires, of which there were nearly forty, and two representatives from each of the towns or boroughs, of which there were nearly 100. (The whole House of Commons was thus, by the fourteenth century, a body of nearly 300 members.) The important thing to be noticed here is that the new House of Commons was based on local communities. The county members represented the *community* of the county; the borough members represented the *community* of the borough. The appearance of the House of Commons is thus, as it were, the reappearance of the old local or tribal folk-moots—folk-moots now gathered together, by means of representatives elected by them and sent by them to the capital, in a central assembly where they are all united. We have to remember that each of the counties, in the medieval system of life, had its own county court or moot. We have equally to remember that each of the boroughs had its own borough court or moot. That is why we may call the House of Commons a gathering of the moots. That is why we may say that it is a return, in a new form and on a higher level, of the old principle and practice of the folk-moot. The King added the old principle and practice of the folk-moot to the feudal principle and practice of a Great Council of great landowners. In doing so, he made the Parliament we still know.

The Parliament which was thus gradually created in the

thirteenth century and the first half of the fourteenth has had a continuous life ever since. There have indeed been one or two slight intermissions of the regular meeting of Parliament in England. The longest was the eleven years intermission between 1629 and 1640; but that ended with a civil war between King and Parliament, and its eventual result was the establishment of Parliament not only as a regular and indispensable part of the system of government, but also (and this was a result which was endorsed and sealed by the English Revolution of 1688) as the major and sovereign part. Maintaining a continuous life, and growing in strength from stage to stage of its life, the English Parliament since the seventeenth century (the century when Englishmen first began to settle in numbers overseas) has germinated or proliferated into a number of parliaments. Wherever Englishmen have gone to settle, they have carried with them the idea that they ought to have, and that, by the law and custom of their country, they actually had, a right to a parliament of their own in the place of their settlement. When they settled in Massachusetts and the other territories which are now the United States of America, they took parliaments with them as part of their equipment; and that is the ultimate origin of the State Legislatures and the Federal Congress of the United States. The same process has been repeated in Canada, South Africa, Australia, and New Zealand. There can be no body of settled Englishmen, of any size, without a parliament. It is in that sense —but only in that sense—that Westminster is 'the Mother of Parliaments'.

England has had no monopoly of parliaments; but she has had a remarkable continuity, and she has achieved a remarkable diffusion, of the parliamentary system. Is it her merit, and does it proceed from any peculiar genius of Englishmen? No! There are indeed some peculiar qualities of Englishmen—and, equally, some peculiar defects—which make it easy for them to work a parliamentary system. They have generally the quality of being tolerant: they have generally the defect of being empirical and illogical: and both the quality and the defect enable them to work a system of parliamentary debate and deliberation, which demands the gift of tolerance for opponents, and requires the empiric habit of plodding along with makeshifts and compromises. (One can be logical in the solitude of the study: one had better be illogical, or at any rate empirical, on the crowded floor of a public chamber.) But it is not on the basis of their peculiar qualities—or even of their peculiar defects—that the English have managed to make so much of parliaments. It is good fortune rather than their own genius that they have to thank. They have been trebly fortunate. In the first place, they have had the good fortune of their insular position. The people of an island (at any rate before the days of air power) can better afford the struggles of parliamentary debate, because they are less vexed by the struggle of the frontiers, and less kept on a constant alert by the needs of national defence. In the second place, the English have had the good fortune of their social and economic development. Already in the fourteenth century, in the days of the great English wool trade with the Continent, the nobility and gentry were acting with the bourgeoisie and men of business, and conversely the bourgeoisie and men of business were becoming allied with them by marriage, and might even hope, by being ennobled, to enter their ranks. A tradition of social homogeneity, based on the peculiar conditions of English economic life, enabled the aristocratic class to co-operate with the other classes, and made it possible for the 'Notables' to join with the *tiers état* in working a parliamentary system to which they could both contribute. Finally, the English have had the good fortune which springs from the peculiar character of the development of their religious life. They have been divided, since the seventeenth century (indeed they were already beginning to be so divided in the sixteenth century), into two different bodies of reformed Christianity—the Anglicans, and the adherents of the Free Churches (who are generally called Nonconformists). These two different bodies were in one sense united: they both accepted the principle of religious reformation. In another sense they were divided, and even deeply divided: the one body wanted a greater amount of reformation than the other, and it wanted (in order to get that greater amount) to be more free from the State, and from State control in religious matters, than the other body wanted to be. The two bodies were thus united, and yet divided. They were at once united enough to agree, and divided enough to dispute. Now this is the temper of mind which the working of a parliamentary system requires. Here, too, there must be union on fundamentals (above all on the fundamental value of maintaining democracy and the democratic policy of progressive reform); but there must also be disagreement on non-fundamentals—disagreement between those who want more reform and more democracy, and those who want less. May it not therefore be said that the English 'climate of religion' was also a climate singularly suited to the development of a parliamentary system? And was not this a good fortune of the English?

But if the English have had good fortune, and if the high development of a parliamentary system in England is mainly based on this good fortune, it does not follow that a parliamentary system cannot exist without good fortune. It can exist, and it should exist—just because it is simply a duty incumbent on the free spirit of man—even under arduous conditions. Some men find it easy to be good, because good fortune gives them easy conditions. Some men find it hard to be good, because life has confronted them with hard conditions. But goodness is still a duty whatever the conditions of our life may be; and the man who rises to goodness under harder conditions will rise to a greater height. France has had hard conditions in her long struggle through the centuries to build herself a good system of political life. She has had the hard conditions imposed by her frontiers. She has had—at any rate till the days of her Revolution, if not afterwards—the harsh conditions imposed by the social cleavage of her ancient regime. She has had less favourable conditions than England in the climate of religion. Still she has struggled on—and not only struggled, but achieved. The record of French democracy since 1789, and not least since 1870, has its own shining pages. France may be trusted to struggle on still in spite of her difficulties, taking her stand by the banner of freedom, even when the banner

> '... torn, but flying,
> Streams like the thunder-storm *against* the wind'.

It may be that conditions will smile more propitiously in the latter half of this century. It may be that frontiers will be more safely secured under a new system of Europe. It may be that a new age of plenty, and of social reform and social security, will provide an easier social ground, and a firmer basis of social unity, for systems of parliamentary liberty. It may be that, in a securer world, men will find it more easy to agree to differ, and to differ without ceasing to agree. But whatever comes, and whatever goes, the system of parliamentary liberty—achieved by some with the aid of favourable conditions: sought by others, but sought among troubles and setbacks, under harsher and sterner conditions—will remain a 'good' which, just because it is a 'good', is a *duty*.

It is better, and nobler, to speak of it in that way—as a duty, and not as a benefit. It is, indeed, a benefit. There is no greater benefit a man can have than to know and to do his duty. But duty is duty, apart from benefits, and the height of our argument will be concerned with this matter of duty. Parliamentary liberty may be a benefit. It may be an old and historic inheritance, as we have sought to suggest. It may be a general and widely diffused system, which ranges from continent to continent, as we have also sought to show. But its great and sovereign defence is that it is the duty of man—the duty of political man— the duty of man as a maker and member of organized societies. Man, as a member of an organized society, *must* control his life by his thought and the motion of his mind. Otherwise, he is not man.

II. *Theory*

MAN, in his essence, is a rational being. His freedom consists in the exercise of his reason. He is himself, and free, when he is exercising his reason. What, then, is the reasonable method— the method according to reason; the method of freedom, since reason and freedom are like the two sides of a coin—for the conduct of the affairs of men in a human society?

How do men act—or rather, how do they plan and determine their action—when they are an organised body, forming some sort of group, and bound to act as a group? The answer is that they 'get together'. They pool their minds: each puts forward his point of view, and all discuss and compare their different points of view. That is what happens in a family council: that is what happens in a meeting of the members of a company: that is what happens everywhere, in any living, reasoning, free society. It happened in tribal gatherings and folk-moots, thousands of years ago; and it happens still today. That is parliament, or 'parley': that is the use of 'the Word', which, as the Evangelist tells us, 'was in the beginning', and which, we know for ourselves, will be with us to all eternity. But no parley, or use of the Word, stops short at mere parley or words. If it did, we should not be men, but apes; and our action would stop at chattering. We are men, and not apes; and since we are men, and reasoning beings, we use our talk, our discussion, our comparison of points of view, in the service of reasonable action, which is the aim and object of all our discussion. We seek by all our talk, and by all our comparison of points of view, to discover a common point of view which will satisfy us all, and on which we can all agree to act. We seek to distil an elixir of unity: we seek to crystallize a concord of minds. Our search is a search for the common—for a *modus convivendi*—for what the politicians call a 'compromise'. You will notice in all these words one little syllable, 'con' or 'com'. It comes from a Latin word which signifies 'together'. That shows, or suggests, the ultimate thing which we are trying to do. We are trying to get together into the common light of a common reason pervading and illuminating the whole of our society, and making the whole society reasonable. We are burning, as it were on an altar, our individual reasons, in order to kindle the common flame of a common reason—a reason of the whole society in which we can all partake. It is not an easy thing to do. Individual reason, partial views, and sectional interests, are all very obstinate things. The common reason which is the common freedom of the whole society may be a fine elixir and a precious concord of minds: but it is not easily distilled, or readily crystallized. Yet the common reason has to be found, however difficult the finding may be, and it has to be found by a process of common thought. Either that—or you submit yourself, passive and unreasoning, to the dominion of a single section or the dictatorship of a single man. There is no other way. And if you submit yourself, passive and unreasoning, your society ceases to be a free society. It even ceases to be a society. Any society, to be worthy of the name, must consist of *partners*, who enjoy a say in the affairs of the society. When a society ceases to be that, it ceases to be a society. It becomes a mere heap of the leader and his followers—followers strung together, like so many dead birds on a string, by the compulsion of leadership.

We have been speaking hitherto of a society whose members can all meet together, immediately and in person—a society such as a family or a company, or the tribal group of early times. What is to be done with the great society, where an immediate meeting of the members, in presence and in person, is impossible? The answer to that question is, in brief, a system of representation. The members of a great society must elect representatives who will meet on their behalf, debate on their behalf, and find on their behalf the elixir of a common reason. This was an answer which began to be given, as we have already had reason to notice, during the Middle Ages. In the twelfth, thirteenth, and fourteenth centuries—in Spain, in England, in France—representation began to flourish. The answer was thus beginning to be given. But it was only beginning to be given. It has taken centuries to work out the answer fully. Indeed it cannot be said to be worked out fully even yet—even now, in the twentieth century.

Representation is a very great thing. It is, in fact, a multiple thing. You may think it a simple thing that a great society should elect representatives to deliberate and decide on its behalf. In fact, it is far from simple. Four things are involved, as men have slowly and gradually discovered during the centuries, whenever you embrace the idea of a system of representation. The first of the four is an electorate—an electorate organized in constituencies, with regular methods of voting—which will duly, carefully and wisely elect its representatives. The second is a system of parties—*national* parties, each reflecting some *general* trend of thought pervading all the society—which will submit to the electorate a number of candidates for its choice; and not only so, but will also submit, along with the candidates, the programmes of policy for which the candidates stand. Such a system of national parties is a necessary part of any system of representation: it provides the electorate with the organized data of choice—alike in candidates and programmes—without which it would choose in the void. Granted an organized electorate and a system of national parties, the third of the four things involved in the idea of representation—the central and cardinal thing—will naturally follow. This third and cardinal thing is the parliament of the elected candidates, the parliament of the Word, which debates and discusses the alternative programmes of policy reflected in the nature of its own membership and seeks to discover the elixir of a common policy true to the thought of the whole society. But even that is not the whole of the matter. There is still a fourth thing which is necessary—as necessary as any of the other three—so necessary, indeed, that the other three may labour in vain if it is not present. This fourth and vitally necessary thing is a guiding cabinet—a cabinet guiding parliament, and yet at the same time guided by parliament (so fine and delicate is the adjustment of the whole machinery of the representative system of government)—which adds the final touch to the representative system. The cabinet was the last of the four elements of representation to be added, in the course of its slow and gradual development. It began to be added in the eighteenth century; it was finally added in the nineteenth. With its addition the system of representation—the system of parliamentary government—may be said to have assumed its final form.

But only its final *form*. Not its final *balance*, or the final *spirit* of its operation. That is a task which is still with us, and is likely still to be with us for many centuries to come. No human institution can ever assume a static form, or attain a state of stationary perfection. It would be death to the progress of the human spirit if any of the institutions in which it expresses itself could ever become static, or ever attain a stationary state. So it is with parliament and the system of parliamentary government. We may have attained the four things needful. We have still to attain their proper balance, and to discover the proper spirit of their operation—or, if that word may be used, their 'inter-operation'. There is a malady, or a maladjustment, to which the four organs of parliamentary government—the electorate, the system of party, the parliament, the cabinet—are all subject. Each of the four has to fit into the other three: each of the four has to play its part—and to be content with its part. But it is not an easy thing for any of the four to be so content. Every human institution tends naturally to institutionalism. It exaggerates itself. Not content with discharging its specific function, it readily seeks to encroach. This is a tendency shown by each and all of the four institutions of representation—by the electorate; by the system of party; by the parliament; by the cabinet. All are necessary: all are equally necessary; but each is apt to think that it is specially necessary, and each is apt to claim predominance over the others. The electorate may wish to exaggerate its right of election, and may seek to impose a *mandat impératif* on the members whom it elects, or to control them by the methods of referendum or recall. The system of party may exaggerate itself into the mastodon of a single totalitarian party. Parliament may seek to vindicate its unique position as the sole depository of national sovereignty, and, exalted by a sense of its own importance, it may refuse to recognize—or at any rate to recognize adequately—the guiding function of cabinet. Cabinet, not content with guiding, may wish to control and command: it may seek to elide, instead of recognizing, the high and solemn function of parliament, and it may cultivate an immediate *rapport* with the electorate, instead of maintaining that intimate *rapport* with parliament which is the essence of its own function.

These are all maladies of maladjustment. They arise because each institution indulges in institutionalism. Instead of seeing itself as a part, which must play its function as such, and claim no more than that, each institution is prone to see itself as a whole, to regard itself as a rounded O, and to claim a total sovereignty. That is an aberration. There is no sovereignty of the electorate. There is no sovereignty of party. There is not even a sovereignty of parliament—at any rate, no such sovereignty as can either flout the electorate or hold the cabinet dangling at the end of a rope. There is no sovereignty of cabinet. No part is sovereign. The one thing sovereign is the whole—the whole system of representation—the whole system of reasoning debate, which runs through all the parts; which needs *each* part and *every* part; which needs, above all, the inter-adjustment and balance of all the parts. That, and that only, is the miracle of reasoning self-government, which is the highest reach of the practical reason of man.

No nation has yet perfected this miracle of reason. Consider, for example, England. She has, as we have seen, been fortunate. She has a Parliament which has had a continuous history since the thirteenth century. She has a party system which began to be formed in the seventeenth century. She has a Cabinet which runs back to the end of the eighteenth century. Even so, she has still to achieve the right and proper balance of the four parts or organs of representation. Perhaps she has allowed her Cabinet to gain unduly on her Parliament. That, at any rate, is a complaint which is often heard in England. She has not yet organized her electorate even to her own satisfaction, or adjusted it properly to its function of producing a Parliament which mirrors the nation. She has never settled, to her own satisfaction, the nature of her party system, or properly adjusted the power of party to the rights of the electorate and the privileges of Parliament. She has her problems still to solve. Consider, next, the example of France. Without the good fortune and the historic inheritance of England—walking, as it were, through fires that burned beneath the crust of the ground, and walking through country largely unknown and uncharted—she had to face in the eighty years after 1870 all the problems of adjustment (between electorate, party, parliament, and cabinet) which are involved in a system of representative government. She faced them with a troubled tenacity; and her achievement is one of the brightest pages in the history of the French genius. But it is a page which has imperfections as well as achievement. Perhaps the guiding Cabinet never achieved its full and true position in the general balance of the State. Perhaps it was subject to too much tutelage from committees of the Chambers. Perhaps it was not armed with sufficient power of dissolving the Chamber of Deputies and appealing to the verdict of the electorate. Nor was the system or party so organized, either in the Chambers or in the country, that France could count on the presence of *national* parties, each reflecting some *general* trend of thought pervading the whole of the nation. France was still struggling with the problems of representation when the brute blow of foreign force fell upon her in 1940. But England, too, was struggling; and so were all parliamentary States. The problem of human government is a problem never solved. There is no Nirvana—no paradise of absorption in the nursing arms of perfection—as long as man retains the dignity of man.

The reflective reader may murmur, at this stage of the argument, 'The writer has proved too much. He has proved that representative self-government, based on the reasoning thought of a community, is a matter of such delicate adjustment, and so difficult of attainment, that it is really beyond human compass'. But is that really the upshot? The writer has simply sought to be honest, and to tell the honest truth. The honest truth is that representative self-government is a high and noble endeavour—an endeavour, rather than an achievement; a duty, rather than a right—which may well inspire free spirits to give everything for its sake. An endeavour: an unceasing endeavour. How can the application of man's free reason to this arduous problem of government be anything but an endeavour? To say that the task is hard is simply to prove it worth while. It is easy—tragically easy—to fall into the nursing arms of dictatorship. One only need throw up the arms—and fall. When you are confronted with the choice of Hercules—on the one side of you the arbitrary tyranny of one leader and one party: on the other side a method of rational self-government, by the assembled and voluntary thought of a people, acting through all its organs on a due system of balance and adjustment—when you are so confronted, will *ease* be your best criterion? The use of reason is never easy. It is a matter of sweat and pain. The sweat and the pain are never greater than they are when all of us as a community—not you or I in our studies, but all of us in the hurly-burly of Press and platform, party and parliament—are attempting to use our common reason for the conduct of our common affairs. But that is not an argument against making the attempt. A system of government which depends on the use of reason is never easy. How can it be? It is a difficult system, a delicate system, a subtle system, a system requiring the nicest of balance among all the organs by which it acts. But what man who believes in himself and his stars and the guiding power of the mind would reject it because it is difficult, or delicate, or subtle, or a matter of nice balance?

'The miracle of reasoning self-government.' That was a phrase which we used at an earlier stage of the argument. Make some approach to that miracle, and in what a world you are living! You have armed yourself with the four organs which you need for the play of the common reason—electorate, party, parliament, cabinet. You have done your best so to adjust the organs that none of them encroaches: that each discharges its own special function, and is content with its discharge: that each contributes to the other what the other needs, and none of them takes from another what the other ought to have. You have in your hands a most remarkable instrument of government—a thinking community duly equipped with the system of organs required for its thinking. What other instrument of social reform and social security could you desire? If the community cannot think out its social policy, who can? What other instrument of international understanding and the collective security of nations could you desire? If thinking nations, expressing their thought by public debate, cannot understand one another, who can? A national society which is thinking its way in the world is a reasonable society, a fine society, and a supple society—supple, because its mind is not cast in the mould of a dogma: supple, because it meets the demands of life with its own fresh reaction of thought; supple, always supple . . . but, above all, reasonable and, because it is reasonable, free.

III. *Practice*

It is said that an ounce of practice is worth a pound of theory. It has also been said, 'By their fruits ye shall know them'. We have spoken of the theory of representation and parliamentary self-government. What is to be said of its practice? We have spoken of the digging and trenching of the parliamentary field: what is to be said of its fruit? Faith is a good thing; but there are also works. What are the works of parliaments in history—alike in war and in peace?

In this present conjuncture of the world's affairs, with war an ever present threat, we tend to judge all institutions by their military value, and by their achievements in war. If we made that our *sole* criterion, we might achieve curious results. We might, for instance, come to the conclusion that of all the institutions recorded in history the German General Staff was the greatest. Did it not plan wars and conduct campaigns, for nearly eighty years, with an unparalleled efficiency? If war be the sole criterion, was it not therefore the best of all possible institutions? There are few of us who would accept that conclusion. War, and success in war, are not everything; and even the German General Staff, judged by its own chosen standard, was not always justified. It failed, and it threw in its hand, in 1918 and again in 1945. Yet success in the ordeal of war, if it be not the whole of the picture, will always stand in the foreground. What then is the record of parliaments in facing the ordeal of war?

The parliaments of France have been vexed, from first to last, by war and the threat of war. The National Assembly of 1871 not only took over from Napoleon III a legacy of military defeat (for which no parliament could be blamed): it was also confronted, in its first beginnings, by civil war. It rescued and reorganized France. It negotiated peace: it paid a war indemnity, in full, two years before the final date fixed for its payment: it gave France a parliamentary constitution which enjoyed a far longer continuous life than any other constitution since 1789. In the strength of this parliamentary constitution France conducted, for the next forty years, a tenacious foreign policy; she consolidated and expanded her empire; she reformed her internal life. A sharp and searching test was imposed by the war of 1914–18. German armies encamped for four years on the soil of France. The French Parliament faced the German armies. Parliament never, for a moment, abdicated. It was in constant session: it steadily surveyed and directed the life and effort of France, and at the end of fifty-one months it stood erect and triumphant. It is only fair to remember the events of 1914–18 when one turns to the event of 1940. In that terrible year a Parliament which had weathered fifty-one months under an earlier trial fell at the end of less than two months of invasion and occupation. Was that the fault of the parliamentary system of France? What a rash and precipitate verdict it would be to return the answer 'Yes'! A hammer-blow fell upon France, beyond comparison and beyond calculation. France reeled. The German mechanics of mass production of war machines and munitions had smashed, for the moment, a Nation. Of course they smashed Parliament with the Nation. They would equally have smashed an Empire (they did, in 1870), or any other form of government. The event of 1940 is not an indictment of parliament, either in France or elsewhere. If it is an indictment of anything, it is an indictment of that peace-loving habit of mind (most human, most understandable, but in its consequences most terribly tragic) which made so many nations, in the years before 1939, ingeminate 'Peace' when there was no peace, and prevented them from arming against the storm when they saw the thunder-clouds lowering. The peace-loving habit of mind is something different from parliamentarianism, though it is easy to confuse it with parliamentarianism. A parliamentary State, as the record of history shows, may face a just war with a stout heart. The clinging to peace, in the years before the war of 1939–45, cannot be fairly regarded as due to parliamentarianism or as peculiar to parliamentary States. It was a general phenomenon and a general feeling in different States of different types—a phenomenon and a feeling which the memories of the horrors of 1914–18, and the expectations of still worse horrors in a new world war, were amply sufficient to explain.

It has just been said that the record of history shows that parliaments can wage wars stoutly. The example of English history, during the last three centuries, may here be called in evidence. The English Long Parliament, which sat from 1640 to 1653, was able to conduct even a civil war with tenacity and vigour: it was equally able, when the civil war was over, to defend the national interest, by land and sea, with resolution and success. There was a restoration of the Monarchy in 1660, but Parliament was at least an equal partner with the restored Monarchy; and the power of Parliament grew so steadily that by the Revolution of 1688 England finally and unquestionably became a parliamentary State. That parliamentary State was almost immediately plunged in war; and indeed for over a century, down to the year 1815, war—and war on a great and serious scale—was a recurrent feature of its life. The English parliamentary State played its part in the War of the Spanish Succession from 1701 to 1713; and it was not an inglorious part. It played its part again in the Seven Years War from 1756 to 1763; and under a great War Minister, William Pitt the elder, it achieved some of the greatest glories recorded in English annals. Not long afterwards it was engaged once more in another seven years war —the War of American Independence, which raged from 1775 to 1782: and here, if it was defeated by its own American colonists, and forced to acknowledge their independence as the United States of America, it held its ground on terms of equality with its European foes, and made with them terms of peace which generally maintained the *status quo ante bellum*. The final and most searching test of the parliamentary State by the ordeal of war came in the twenty years of hostilities (from 1793 to 1815, with one brief intermission in 1802) which followed on the French Revolution. These years were a test of endurance and grit; and under the guidance of the younger Pitt and his successors the test was successfully faced. By 1815 it might safely be said that the English parliamentary State had shown, in the course of over a century of recurrent hostilities, that a system of parliamentary government was at least as adequate to face the test of war as any other system.

That lesson has been reinforced in the twentieth century. For almost exactly a hundred years after 1815 England enjoyed, with only brief interruptions, a period of peace and prosperity. A new epoch began in 1914, when she had to face the menace of German militarism which France had already had to face in 1870. Side by side with France, in an equal and close alliance of two parliamentary States, she faced and repelled the menace —aided, sustained, and carried to final victory by the adhesion of a third great parliamentary State, the United States of America. The menace recurred again in 1939. Once more the two great parliamentary States of western Europe faced it together, side by side. Once more, when France rose again from defeat, they finally repelled and expelled it—aided and sustained once more, but in a far greater measure than before, by the giant strength of the great parliamentary State of the western hemisphere. The end of the war of 1939–45 has shown that parliamentary States—the small as well as the great (who can forget the tenacity of the smallest of all of them, Norway?)—are justified of their faith in their system of government. The parliamentary State may have defects in war, but it has at least one merit which must overbalance every defect. When it goes to war, it carries with it the free spirit of a free people.

There is little need to speak of the achievement of parliamentary governments in peace. Yet it would be a treason to peace, which

'... hath her victories
No less renowned than war',

as a war-time English poet wrote—it would be a treason to peace if we said nothing of the victories which peace too has won under the system of parliamentary government. It is true that a parliamentary State may show defects in peace, as it may also show them in war. Faction, or the irreconcilable conflict of parties (for the party system is perhaps the most difficult of all the elements of a parliamentary system)—this is one of the saddest defects of a parliamentary State. But if it can fall into faction, the parliamentary State can also summon the solidarity of a free and voluntary community for great efforts of national reform and national reconstruction. The achievement of the first thirty years of the third Republic—say from the constitutional laws of 1875 to the law of Separation of 1905—was a large achievement of general reform in every sphere of the life of France. The historian, too often, turns the limelight on the ferment, the factions, the scandals, the froth and bubble, which occupy the surface of life. It is the quiet depths which matter most. A study of the legislation and administration of France, during the thirty years we have mentioned, will put the froth and bubble in a due perspective. Laws on the Press, such as the great law of 1885; laws on education; laws on trade unions and their position; laws on the liberty of associations; the quiet working of the *conseil d'État*, and the defence of civil liberty under the developing system of *droit administratif*—these are the things that form the true history of parliamentary France, the France which, in the words of an American scholar, 'maintained domestic tranquillity, developed a fine system of public education, attained a high and well-distributed economic prosperity, and enlarged her Colonial Empire'. That was the true and real France of the Third Republic; and that was the real fruit of her parliamentary government.

England, too, has known her periods of peaceful reform and reconstruction under her system of parliamentary government. In England, just as in France, these periods have been periods of steady and agreed development—not the sweeping and feverish reconstruction, once dear to Nazi Germany and to Fascist Italy, of a band of revolutionaries eager to shatter the whole existing scheme and to remould it in the image of their own peculiar doctrine. There are two periods of such development which may be noted in England. The first was the period which followed on the reform of Parliament by the Reform Bill of 1832, when a new and broader Parliament immediately set to work to make a new and better country. The reform of municipalities: the reform of the system of poor relief: the first beginnings of national provision for education: the first effective act for improving conditions in factories: an act for the emancipation of slaves in all the British dominions—these were some of the fruits of the reform of parliament and of a stronger and better system of parliamentary government. The second period came in the beginning of the twentieth century, when a new wave of liberal sentiment filled the House of Commons with a large majority of members eagerly devoted to a liberal policy of reform. After the year 1906, and down to the year 1914—mainly in the ministry and on the initiative of Asquith, and with the aid of Lloyd George and Churchill—a policy of social reform was inaugurated, and a system of social services was instituted, which altered the general conditions of life for the vast bulk of Englishmen. Old age pensions were instituted; employment exchanges were opened; trade boards were set up to improve conditions and wages in the weaker and poorer industries; a system of national insurance against ill-health, and a similar system of national insurance against the risk of unemployment, were both introduced. The movement thus begun has continued and gained momentum down to the present time, through all the struggles and all the vicissitudes of party politics. The system of social services, and the general policy of social security, were not forgotten even in the stress of war. The English Parliament showed itself adequate, in the years between 1939 and 1945, not only to cope with the problems of war, and to nerve and strengthen the Government for a total effort of war, but also to face the problems of peace and reconstruction. War failed to distract Parliament from the problems of social life, and even in the course of war new legislation was passed, in 1940 and 1941, to extend the scope of pensions and to ease the conditions under which assistance could be given to the unemployed. If the English Parliament, like other Parliaments, can be censured for having failed to prepare in advance for war, it may also be praised for its efforts, and its behaviour, in the period when war was raging. And any praise which is given it should be given equally, and even more, to 'the Parliaments in exile' (if that term may be used), which upheld the banner of parliamentary liberty on other soils than their own even in the turmoil of war.

Judged by their fruits, and by their works in war and in peace, the parliamentary States stand secure before the bar of the world. Judged by the men they produce, and the type of statesmen they breed, they may equally stand secure. True, a non-parliamentary State provides, as it were, a great vacuum, in which some single solitary figure may seem to attain an eminence which can never be reached by parliamentary statesmen. But the eminence of the unchallenged—the 'leaders' or the dictators —who stand above competition, and need not meet rivals in debate, is perhaps a fallacious eminence. In any case they are sparse and scattered in the annals of time; and they seem dependent for their emergence on the play of chance or even the elemental insurgence of force. The great merit of the parliamentary system is that it provides, by its very nature, a constant training ground for the production of statesmen, with an arena of peaceful competition in which they can test and measure their powers before a watching and judging world. This is a priceless benefit. The doctrine of leadership lies at the mercy of the leader's chance emergence. The system of parliamentary government is a calculated and reasonable system, which makes a reasonable provision, by its competition of parties and by its parliamentary debates, for the selection of a constant succession of parliamentary leaders trained and approved in its processes.

Parliaments, therefore, are not in their nature incompatible with statesmanlike leadership: on the contrary, they provide a scientific method for the eliciting of leadership. It is true, indeed, that parliaments may not always throw up great statesmen. The great statesman requires, to nerve and inspire his efforts, the backing of a great and loyal party. If parties are small, and not only small but jealous, statesmanship is deprived of its primary requisite. Great minds will hardly thrive in an atmosphere of petty jealousy. Parliaments and parties must be worthy of themselves in order to be worthy of good leaders. This is the task and problem of parliaments; and the just historian is bound to admit that they have not always risen to the measure of their task. But he will also admit, and indeed contend, that parliaments must not be judged by their temporary aberrations. They must be judged and measured by their general genius and the general nature of their long-time effort. Judged by that standard, he will add, the parliaments of the French Republic have left to France a legacy of shining names. There were Thiers and Gambetta in the beginning: there was Waldeck-Rousseau in the middle course: there were Clémenceau, Poincaré, and Briand in the days which are only just gone. These are names which will stand, at the last account, in the general great roll-call of France.

An Englishman may be pardoned if he recalls some names in the English roll. Oliver Cromwell is often counted a dictator, and remembered as a general of cavalry and the eventual leader of a stern Puritan Army. But Cromwell was trained in Parliament: he sat in the Long Parliament, for thirteen years, as a member for the borough of Cambridge; and no man who has read his speeches—particularly his speeches in the Army debates (for the Army itself, in his days, debated the Word of God and discussed the affairs of the nation)—can doubt that the spirit of parliament, and the instinct for reasonable debate of differences, were deeply ingrained in the spirit of his mind. It is no paradox to count Cromwell in the ranks of parliamentary statesmen. Leap a century, from 1650 to 1750 (not that there were not shining names in the interval), and you come to the 'Great Commoner', William Pitt the elder, afterwards the Earl of Chatham, who not only nerved his country to the height of naval and military effort during the Seven Years War, but also stood for the cause of liberty, and defended the rights of the American colonists, in the early stages of the troubles which led to the War of American Independence. He was a 'parliament man', a man thrown up by the system of parliamentary government; and even more of a 'parliament man' was his second son, the younger William Pitt, who established (if any one man did) the position of Cabinet in the system of parliamentary government, and served as 'the pilot who weathered the storm' of long and arduous wars till his death in 1806. He was followed by a long line of successors in the nineteenth century, and the succession has not failed in the twentieth. It is like the tree with golden branches which the Sibyl describes to the hero of Virgil's *Aeneid*. 'Pluck one,' she says, 'and there is still another, and another—all of gold.' Two of the golden branches on the tree of English parliamentarianism deserve to be mentioned in conclusion. One is the name of Gladstone—orator, financier, lover of liberty, lover of peace and reform—who sat continuously in Parliament from 1832 to 1894, a record unequalled in English annals. The other is the name of Winston Churchill—orator, historian, soldier, statesman, versed in the arts of both peace and war—who has sat in Parliament continuously (but for the briefest of interruptions) from 1900 to the present year. Surely, if the example of England proves anything, it proves that parliament can throw up leaders, and that—once it has thrown them up, tested them, and found that they are not wanting—it is ready to give them, without any grudging, the honour of its trust.

IV. *The Seed and its Harvest*

PERHAPS too much has been said of England. If it be so, the author throws himself humbly on the mercy of his readers—only pleading that England is an old laboratory of parliamentary experiment, and that the antiquity of the laboratory may perhaps serve as some excuse for seeking to elicit some of the lessons of its experience.

There is a still further lesson of English experience which it would be wrong not to mention, the lesson that a parliament, once it is rooted in a country's soil, may proliferate or germinate. The tree of parliament grows seed; the seed is carried by those who emigrate and settle in new-found lands; and lo! the seed is planted, and new parliaments grow, in those new-found lands. This has happened with the English, as we have already had reason to notice, ever since the early years of the seventeenth century. The English settlers claimed—and they did not claim in vain—that they carried with them, as a right which was theirs by the common law of England, the right to have a representative body. There were already parliaments in the English North American colonies, and in the English West Indian islands, over 300 years ago. These were the early germs of the Commonwealth Parliaments of today, which are now the equal and associated partners of the Parliament at Westminster. Such is the infectiousness of parliaments: such is their spreading contagion. But that is not the whole of the matter. Parliaments have not only gone to new lands where Englishmen have settled, as a right of Englishmen under the common law of England. They have also gone to old lands, inhabited by native populations, which have come into English hands by what we call conquest or cession; and they have there become a right of the native population under the policy of England. This is a different matter from the right of Englishmen who have settled in a new and empty territory to enjoy a parliament of their own in the territory of their settlement. It is a matter of the expansion of parliaments to non-English populations. On the whole, it must be confessed, this is a recent development—a development of the latter half of the nineteenth and of the twentieth century. Moreover, it must also be confessed, the development of parliament among native populations has not generally gone so far as the development of

PARLIAMENTARY SYSTEM OF GOVERNMENT 83

parliament has gone in territories settled by emigrants of English stock. But it has gone a long way, and it is going farther.

The English territories overseas, other than the territories settled by English emigrants, could down to 1947 be divided into two parts. The first part—a part unique and majestic—was the Indian Empire. The second part—a part scattered far and wide—was, and still is, the Colonial Empire. The Indian Empire has now disappeared, in virtue of a voluntary renunciation of power by England, in the year 1947, which is one of the landmarks in human history. It has now become the two self-governing Commonwealth countries of India and Pakistan, the former predominantly Hindu, the latter predominantly Moslem; and India has become an independent sovereign Republic, though by her own wish she remains a member of the Commonwealth.[1] But even while India was still tied to England by the bonds of Empire, parliaments had already begun to grow, partly in the several Indian provinces, and partly in the form of a central assembly, of a federal pattern, representative of all the provinces. Legislative assemblies for the provinces of India were first instituted in 1861. At first these provincial assemblies were composed of nominated members; gradually they became elected; in process of time, by an Act of 1919, part of a cabinet system was added; finally, in 1935, the whole of a cabinet system was added to the elected assemblies or parliaments of the eleven provinces of India. A central assembly representative of all the provinces was also first instituted in 1861. By successive developments, and in virtue of Acts of the Westminster Parliament passed in 1892, in 1909, in 1919, and in 1935, this central assembly acquired a broader composition and a greater measure of powers; and in particular, by a provision of the Act of 1935, a partial cabinet system, such as had been added to the provincial legislative assemblies in 1919, was grafted on the central assembly. This provision, however, owing to internal difficulties, never came into operation; and finally the Westminster Parliament, which

[1] The new constitution of India, adopted and enacted in the Indian Constituent Assembly on 26 Nov. 1949, is a document which richly deserves study. It contains a notable declaration of Fundamental Rights (Part III) and of Directive Principles of State Policy (Part V): it also contains a statement and enactment of the institutions and methods of the parliamentary system of government on the British model (in Part V, Chapter II, for the whole of the Union, and in Part VI, Chapter II, for the States of the Union).

since 1861 had been gradually giving parliamentary liberty to the peoples of India, took the great and final step of complete renunciation of power, and voluntarily acknowledged the sovereign independence of the two parts of India (the Hindu and the Moslem), their right to determine their own constitutions and frame their own parliaments, and their freedom to decide whether or no they wished to retain any bonds of connexion with England.

Meanwhile, in the Colonial Empire, legislative assemblies of every sort and pattern (here one pattern to suit one set of local conditions, and here another to suit another) have been, and are being, instituted. In many of the African territories, and in some territories in the Far East, a development of what was called 'indirect rule' has left authority in the hands of traditional rulers, under English supervision; and here local native councils, which have their own treasuries and law-courts, are admitting an increasing representation of the general public. Often, too, a proportion of the members of the Colonies' central legislatures are elected from among those of the local councils, while others are directly elected by the people of the towns, where no traditional rule exists and local government is in the hands of municipal councils.

This growth of experience, which has diffused and is diffusing the parliamentary spirit in an Empire, as well as broadening and deepening it at home, is not peculiar to England. It has, indeed, assumed a peculiarly large scale in English history; but France has also shown that parliamentary liberty is compatible with imperial expansion, and that the growth of an empire can also be the growth of parliaments. Indeed, there is one respect in which France has gone beyond England. The Third Republic had already begun to summon representatives from *some* of the French overseas territories to the metropolitan parliament in Paris; and today, under the new constitution of 1946, 78 of the 622 members of the Parisian *assemblé nationale* are drawn from *all* the overseas territories which are organized as 'departments' or 'colonies'. This has no parallel in the British system: the idea of colonial representation in the British Parliament, canvassed as long ago as 1776, has never been adopted. But France has gone still farther under her new constitution. She has now established a French Union, joining together in one not only metropolitan France and the overseas departments and colonies, but also the 'associated territories and states'—in Morocco, for example, and Tunis and elsewhere—which are connected with metropolitan France by separate bilateral agreements, and are thus distinct in their nature from overseas departments and colonies. This Union has its own separate assembly, meeting in Versailles and not in Paris, with members half drawn from one of its sides and half from the other; and this assembly is empowered not indeed to initiate or pass legislation, but to consider and give its advice on legislation proposed by the government which affects the members of the Union. The half of its members drawn from the overseas part of the Union are elected by local assemblies, themselves elected by the local inhabitants, in the several divisions of that part; and there is thus the germ—if only at present the germ (for the union assembly is only a consultative body, and the local assemblies are little more)—of a federal parliamentary system. Here again Great Britain offers no parallel or analogy: the idea of an imperial federal parliament for the whole of the British Commonwealth has indeed been canvassed, but has never gone any farther. It has thus been the policy of Great Britain to follow the line of devolution, and to encourage separate and sovereign parliaments in Commonwealth countries beyond the seas: it has been the tendency of France to follow the line of attraction, and to encourage representatives from her overseas territories to attend a central assembly, or assemblies, meeting in the mother country.

In different ways, but side by side, France and England have together shown that the spirit of parliament is a marching and spreading spirit, which goes with them wherever they go—a spirit not confined to their national boundaries, but diffused as widely and broadly as they are diffused themselves. This is the role appointed by history, and by their own genius, to the collaboration of our two nations. France has steadily been, ever since her Revolution, a generous apostle of the rights of men and citizens wherever her influence has spread. England, too, to the best of her ability has carried a torch of civil and political liberty in all her goings about the world. The collaboration of France and England—aided and sustained by all their allies—is the way of ways to the general diffusion of that rational system of parliamentary government which is demanded by the dignity of human reason and the freedom of the human spirit. Freedom is our joint duty: and we can best do our duty together.

PART II
ESSAYS ON THE THEORY OF GOVERNMENT (1690–1790)

Essay Four

THE THEORY OF THE SOCIAL CONTRACT IN LOCKE, ROUSSEAU AND HUME

I

THE general idea of the Social Contract, which has haunted the generations (it was current in the days of Plato, during the fourth century B.C., and it still flutters in the pages of Herbert Spencer's *The Man versus the State* at the end of the nineteenth century of our era), may be criticized on various grounds. The critic may urge that it was mechanical, and not organic, in its interpretation of political life; juristic, and not ethical, in its rationale of political obligation; *a priori*, and not historical, in its explanation of political society and political authority. The criticisms have their justice. The theory of the Social Contract could flourish only in an age, or 'climate', of thought in which the historical sense (the legacy left by the Romantic movement to the historians of the nineteenth century) was still imperfect and undeveloped. But if it was unhistorical, the theory was still historic—and historic in more than one sense. Not only could it show a long and continuous history, from the days of the struggles of Popes and Emperors at the end of the eleventh century: it had also been a factor in the process of historic causation—a factor making for freedom, whether it was applied, as it was by the Huguenots after 1570, to defend the cause of religious liberty, or employed, as it was by the English Whigs in 1688 and afterwards, to buttress the cause of civil liberty. Historic continuity, religious belief, and legal argument, could all be pleaded in its favour; and if it were judged by its fruits, on a pragmatic test of truth, it could bring to the bar of judgement a record of rich achievement. Even if there had never been a contract, men actually behaved 'as if' there had been such a thing; and behaving and acting in terms of quasi-contract—or what the lawyers call 'contract implied in law', an idea which may be extended to cover the case of 'contract implied in government' —they made those terms of quasi-contract serve good and admirable purposes. The theory of the Social Contract might be mechanical, juristic, and *a priori*. But it was none the less a way of expressing two fundamental ideas or values to which the human mind will always cling—the value of Liberty, or the idea that will, not force, is the basis of government, and the value of Justice, or the idea that right, not might, is the basis of all political society and of every system of political order.[1]

Sir Robert Filmer, in his *Patriarcha*, speaks of the theory of contract as 'first hatched in the schools, and fostered by all succeeding papists for good divinity'. There is warrant for his view. Manegold, a papalist pamphleteer who wrote about A.D. 1080, already held that 'if in any wise the king transgresses the contract by virtue of which he is chosen, he absolves the people from the obligation of submission'. But it is in the writings of St. Thomas Aquinas that the theory of contract is finally hatched (*circa* A.D. 1250). 'St. Thomas', Lord Acton once wrote, 'had a very large element of political liberalism.' That very large element of political liberalism was based on a conflation of three sources—the teaching of the Bible, the doctrines of Roman Law, and the principles of Aristotle's *Politics*. The Bible taught that the powers that be are ordained of God; but it also taught that David made a covenant with his people. It was the doctrine of Roman Law that *quod principi placuit legis habet vigorem*; but it was also the doctrine of Roman Law that the reason why this was so was that 'the people, by the *Lex Regia* passed in regard to his authority, confers upon him and into his hands all *its* authority and power'.[2] The principles of Aristotle's *Politics* might seem to favour a monarchy of the one best man; but they also favoured a clear distinction between the king and the tyrant, and they endorsed the right of the masses not only to elect the

[1] The writer would refer, in this connexion, to the argument in his *Political Thought in England from 1848 to 1914* (pp. 165-6), and to Professor Buckland's criticism of that argument in *Some Reflections on Jurisprudence* (pp. 63-6).

[2] We have to remember that in the theory of Roman Law any *lex* must proceed from the people: *lex est quod populus Romanus . . . constituebat*.

magistrate but also to call him to account. Here was material for a balanced view; and the view of St. Thomas is balanced accordingly. He draws a distinction between three ideas of authority—the idea of its *principium*; the idea of its *modus*; and the idea of its *exercitium*. On the basis of this distinction he argues (1) that the *principium* or essential substance of authority is ordained of God, but (2) that its *modus* or constitutional form (be it monarchy, aristocracy, democracy, or a mixed form) is determined by the people, and (3) that its *exercitium* or actual enjoyment is conferred—and as it is conferred may also be withdrawn—by the people. Developing the third proposition he writes, in the *De Regimine Principum*, that government is instituted by the community, and may be revoked or limited by the community if it be tyrannical; and he even adds that a tyrannical ruler *meruit . . . quod ei* pactum *a subditis non reservetur*.

This general view became the general property of the Middle Ages; and it descended from the Middle Ages to Hooker, and through Hooker to Locke. (It is for this reason that 'the identity of the first Whig' has been discovered in St. Thomas.) The view accorded well with the conditions and sentiments of the Middle Ages. On the one hand it suited the temper, and the general system of ideas, of feudal society. Feudalism generally was a system of contract, under which each man could say to his lord, 'I will be to you faithful and true . . . *on condition that* you keep me as I am willing to deserve, and all that fulfil that our *agreement* was, when I to you submitted and chose your will'.[1] It was part of this general system of contract that the feudal king, at his coronation, entered into an implicit contract with his feudatories, when he exchanged a coronation oath, pledging him on his side to good government, for their reciprocal oath of homage and fealty. On the other hand, the contractual view also suited the temper and the system of ideas of the medieval clergy. It imposed a limit on secular government: it was a guarantee of the rights of the clergy and of *libertas ecclesiae*; and the right of the people to deprive the king of authority for breach of contract could supplement (as it could also be supplemented by) the right of the Pope to deprive the king, by excommunication, of the divinely given *principium* of authority for offences against its

[1] From a Wessex document 'Of Oaths' (*circa* A.D. 920) in Stubbs, *Select Charters*, 9th edition, p. 74.

Giver. We may add that a prevalent belief in the ultimate sovereignty of Natural Law formed an atmosphere of ideas favourable to the contractual view. If there was Natural Law, there must also be natural rights; if there were any limitations imposed on natural rights, those limitations must be due to a voluntary contract made by the possessors of such rights; and if the question were raised, 'What is the sanction of such a contract?', the answer could readily be given, 'The sanction is Natural Law'. There was always a close and intimate connexion between the idea of Social Contract and the idea of Natural Law; and the connexion is particularly evident in the theory of Locke.

When it passed from the Middle Ages into the thought of the sixteenth century (and of the first half of the seventeenth), the theory of the Social Contract continued to show a large clerical tinge. In an age of religious struggles it became the theory of minority confessions, serving to justify their resistance against any government which sought to impose the religion of the majority. In this way it could equally serve the cause of minority Calvinism or the cause of minority Romanism, and indeed it was equally adopted by both. Sir Robert Filmer noted, in a pithy apophthegm, that 'Cardinal Bellarmine and Calvin both look asquint this way'. Either side, it is true, professed to be primarily and essentially a believer in the divine ordainment of the powers that be; and either side sought to attribute to the other, and to disclaim for itself, the audacious radicalism of championing resistance and buttressing it by a doctrine of contract. But both sides, in the last resort, and when it came to the pinch of oppression, were equally contractarian. On the Calvinist side there is Languet, defending the cause of the French Huguenots in the *Vindiciae contra Tyrannos* of 1581 (a work translated and printed in English in the significant year 1648, and afterwards reprinted in the no less significant year 1689); and there is also the German Althusius, expounding the genius of Dutch Calvinism—and, with it, a theory of contract—in his *Politica methodice digesta* of 1605. On the Catholic side there is the Jesuit Suarez, developing a subtle and scholarly theory of contract in his *Tractatus de Legibus* of 1611; there is the Jesuit Mariana, a more radical contractarian (who was ready to allow to the individual the right of tyrannicide), in his *De Rege et Regis Institutione* of 1599; and still more radical, and even more ready to allow the right of tyrannicide, there are the French Catholic theorists of the League which opposed the right of succession of the Protestant Henry of Navarre. In the age of the Wars of Religion and down to the Peace of Westphalia in 1648, the Social Contract was a weapon of religion—religion, it is true, which was mixed and confused with politics, but which was essentially struggling, in the midst of all the confusion, to vindicate the cardinal rights of religious liberty.

A new age ensued in the century which lies between the publication of Hobbes's *Leviathan* in 1651 and the publication of Rousseau's *Du Contrat Social* in 1762. This is the great age of the doctrine of the Social Contract; the age of a purer and less turbulent philosophy of political principles, expressed by thinkers of the order of Hobbes, Spinoza, Locke, and Rousseau; the age in which the general background of Natural Law (which always stands behind the doctrine of the Social Contract) is firmly constructed and systematically illuminated by the thinkers of the great School of Natural Law, which runs from Grotius and Pufendorf to Fichte and Kant.[1] Here, and before we turn to the specific theories of the Social Contract advanced by Locke and Rousseau, we may pause to consider the general nature and the general implications of the doctrine. Hitherto we have been concerned with the genesis of the idea. We must now consider it analytically, resolving it into its elements, and noticing, as we do so, that the elements are mixed.

In effect, the idea of the Social Contract is composed of two ideas, which, if they are closely connected, must also be distinguished. There is the idea of the contract of government, the *pacte de gouvernement*, the *Herrschaftsvertrag*. There is the idea of the contract of society, the *pacte d'association*, the *Gesellschaftsvertrag*. The theory of a contract of government is a theory that the State, *in the sense of the government*, is based on a contract between ruler and subjects. It is possible to stop at this point, as many thinkers did; but if we continue to reflect, we shall begin to see that though we have come to a stopping-point we have not yet reached the stopping-place. The theory of a con-

---

[1] The writer would refer to his translation of Gierke's *Natural Law and the Theory of Society*, and to pp. xli–l of the translator's introduction. Space here forbids any attempt to give an account of the School of Natural Law; but the proper understanding of Locke and Rousseau demands a knowledge of the theory of that School.

tract of government really postulates, as a prior condition, the theory of a contract of society. There must already be something in the nature of an organized community—in other words, a potential body of subjects, already cohering in virtue of a common social will, as well as a potential ruler, ready to assume the burden of government in agreement with that will—before there can be any contract between ruler and subjects. We must therefore hold, if we are thinking in terms of contract, that besides the contract of government, and prior to the contract of government, there is also a contract of society, a social contract proper (in the strict sense of the word 'social'); and we must conclude that the State, *in the sense of a political community, and as an organized society*, is based on a social contract—or rather on myriads of such contracts—between each and every member of that community or society. We shall therefore say that the contract of government creates *potestas*, but only *potestas*; we shall say that the contract of society creates *societas* itself; and we shall recognize that *societas* is greater than *potestas*, or at any rate prior to *potestas*.

It is on the contract of government that the medieval schoolmen, and most of the Catholic and Calvinist theorists of the latter half of the sixteenth and the early years of the seventeenth century (not all—Althusius and Suarez both went deeper, and they both recognized that the idea of contract was double), laid an exclusive emphasis. It is on the contract of society that Locke and Rousseau, like Hobbes, laid all their emphasis; and we may even say that none of the three (though there are peculiarities in the theory of Hobbes which may qualify the statement) was concerned with the contract of government. Indeed, it is obvious that while we can hardly believe in a contract of government without believing, at any rate implicitly, in a contract of society, it is possible to believe in the second without believing in the first. The community once formed by a contract of society may be self-governing, without any distinction of rulers and subject, and therefore without any possibility of their making a contract with one another. This was the theory of Rousseau. Again the community, once it is formed, may appoint a 'fiduciary' or trustee government with which it makes no contract, but which it may dismiss for breach of trust on its own interpretation of the nature of the trust. This was the theory of Locke. Finally, the community, once it is formed, may empty itself of every right and every power into a sovereign Leviathan, which makes no contract with it and is therefore subject to none of the limits of a contract of government. This, we may say, was the theory of Hobbes.[1]

Some few words may be added, in conclusion of this section of the argument, about the present bearing and contemporary value of the idea of contract. (1) *Society* is not constituted, and never was constituted, on any basis of contract. Society is an all-purposes association—'in all science . . . in all art . . . in every virtue and in all perfection'—which transcends the notion of law, and has grown and exists of itself. In the strict sense of the word 'social', there is not, and never has been, a social contract. (2) On the other hand, *the State*, as distinct from society, may fairly be conceived in terms of contract; and we may regard it as constituted on the basis of contract—though seldom (except after revolutions, or, again, in the case of federations) created by an act of contract. The State, as such, is a legal association, constituted by the action of its members in making a constitution (such action sometimes, as in Great Britain, being along a line of time, rather than at a point of time) and therein and thereby contracting themselves into a body politic. The constitution of a State is the articles of a contract which constitutes the State. From this point of view we may speak, if not of a social, at any rate of a 'political contract', expressed in the articles of the constitution, whether those articles have been gradually formed or have been precipitated in a single act. But (3) there is no need in our time to invoke or apply the idea of a 'governmental contract', by which one part of the State, called the ruler or rulers, has covenanted with another, called the subjects. The one political contract—which unites us all (rulers and subjects alike) in terms of the constitution, and under the constitution, according to our respective capacities as defined in the

[1] On the other hand we have to notice (1) that in the theory of Hobbes every subject covenants with every other, in one and the same act, to form a society *and a obey a government*, and a subject will therefore break a sort of contract of government (not with the ruler, but with other subjects) if he refuses to obey; (2) that in the theory of Hobbes, as it eventually develops, the ruler is bound to give protection to the lives of his subjects, and if he fails to do so they may rebel—so that after all there *is* an implicit contract between ruler and subjects, which the ruler himself may break. (These are the peculiarities in the theory of Hobbes which qualify the statement that he was not concerned with the idea of a contract of government.)

constitution—this one contract is enough, and it is the only contract. In days when government was still held to be *sui generis*, and to stand over against subjects as something of a separate order, it was natural to think that there was, or should be, a contract between them which fixed their mutual limits. Today the government is not *sui generis*; it is just a part of the legal association, as the body of general citizens is equally a part; and its rights and duties are fixed, like those of the citizens generally, under and by the one and only contract of the constitution.[1]

II

'SOMERSET is one of the old and essential English counties; and the clothing industry of Somerset is an old and honourable industry. It was in Somerset, and from a family engaged in the cloth trade, that John Locke was born, three hundred years ago to-day.[2] He began his life about the time when John Hampden was contesting the legitimacy of ship-money; he ended it in the year in which John Churchill was winning the battle of Blenheim, when the Bill of Rights and the Act of Settlement had been securely written in our Statute-book. It was the good but well-deserved fortune of this modest Englishman, one of the incarnations of the judgematical good sense of his country, to become the accredited prophet of a not ignoble cause—the cause of Civil and Religious Liberty, to which many a good glass of port was drunk in the course of the eighteenth century. It was a cause which Milton and Sidney had preached before him; but the perspicacity of his thought, and the appeal of a style which was all the more convincing because it was unpretending and unadorned, combined with the circumstances of his life and the conjuncture of the times to give him finally the national ear. For fifteen years he lived in close association with Shaftesbury, the fiery founder of the Whig Party; for another five, which were spent in voluntary exile, he lived in Holland, among the liberal or "Remonstrant" Dutch Calvinists, and in the company of Huguenot refugees who had fled there from France in 1685. When William of Orange landed in England, in November, 1688, Locke soon followed; and in the course of 1690 there appeared from his pen three works which have become a part of the English heritage. One was a *Letter on Toleration*, which

---

[1] The ideas here summarily stated have since been developed and explained by the writer in his *Principles of Social and Political Theory* (1951).
[2] The first two paragraphs of this section are reprinted from an article contributed by the writer to *The Times* on 29 Aug. 1932—the tercentenary of Locke's birth.

had, indeed, appeared in Latin a year before from a Dutch printing press; another was the *Two Treatises on Government*; a third was the *Essay on the Human Understanding*. Add to these two other works, which appeared during the next few years—one on *Education*, and another on the *Reasonableness of Christianity*—and the bequest of Locke to English thought has been enumerated. It was a rich and various bequest. It touched religion, both in its practice and in its principles; it touched, and perhaps it touched most particularly, politics; it touched the theory of knowledge and the principles of metaphysics; it touched, and it affected for long years to come, the methods of instruction of the young.

'It was the political theory of Locke which affected the nation at large most deeply. Nor did it only affect England. It penetrated into France, and passed through Rousseau into the French Revolution; it penetrated into the North American Colonies, and passed through Samuel Adams and Thomas Jefferson into the American Declaration of Independence. We are generally prone to think of Locke as the exponent of the Social Contract. It would be more just to think of him as the exponent of the sovereignty of Natural Law. He put into plain English, and he dressed in an English dress of sober grey cloth, doctrines which ultimately go back to the Porch and the Stoic teachers of antiquity. There is, he taught, a Natural Law rooted and grounded in the reasonable nature of man; there are Natural Rights, existing in virtue of such law, among which the right of property in things with which men have mixed their labour is cardinal; and finally there is a natural system of government, under which all political power is a trust for the benefit of the people (to ensure their living by natural law, and in the enjoyment of natural rights), and the people themselves are at once the creators and the beneficiaries of that trust. These may sound abstract doctrines; but abstract doctrines can form a creed, and a political creed can fire and inspire a political party. The doctrines of Locke became the creed of a great party, and of a succession of great statesmen (for the Whigs, with all their defects, deserve that appellation) who between 1688 and 1832 worked out a system of Parliamentary Government that may justly be called the great contribution of England to Europe, and, beyond Europe, to other continents.'

The beginning of the reflections on government which eventually appeared in the *Two Treatises* of 1690 may be dated as early as 1667, when Locke, who was a physician as well as a philosopher, and a physician before he became a philosopher, was first associated through his profession with the Earl of Shaftesbury. It was in this way that he acquired some practical experience of politics and a sense of political realities. He served under his patron as secretary of the Board or Council of Trade (1673-5), and was thus immersed in problems of colonial administration; and he drafted a constitution for Carolina (of which Shaftesbury was one of the 'lords proprietors') which combined the fine principle of toleration with an express acquiescence in negro slavery. But the period of the definite germination of the *Two Treatises* may be said to begin about 1679. Locke was still associated with Shaftesbury, and lived occasionally with him at Thanet House, in Aldersgate, where he had made his headquarters in order to keep in touch with his Whig friends in the City of London. But it was a troubled time—the time of the agitation for the Exclusion Bill, of Petitioners and Abhorrers, and of generally inflamed tempers—and Shaftesbury had become 'a daring pilot in extremity'. Locke thought it wise to spend most of his time in Oxford, where he had long been a senior student of Christ Church. (He had been educated at Westminster, destined to become the great Whig school, and he had followed the natural course—still followed by Westminster scholars today—which led from Westminster to Christ Church.) The Oxford of those days, like England generally, was much agitated by political problems which ran up into high questions of theory; and indeed the University, in July 1683, solemnly burned in the Bodleian quadrangle a number of books on political theory. It was at this time that Locke may have studied Hooker's *Ecclesiastical Polity* and thus begun to follow the line of thought which runs back to St. Thomas Aquinas, and beyond him to Aristotle.

'But two books had recently appeared in 1680 which would whet reflections on politics. One was a reprint of Philip Hunton's *Treatise of Monarchy*, which had originally appeared in 1643. Some scholars have thought that Locke's opinions were largely formed by this *Treatise*; and in any case Hunton (a member of Wadham College) had been considered by Sir Robert Filmer as worthy of being bracketed for attack with Hobbes and Milton and Grotius in his *Observations concerning the Original of Government*, first published in 1652. The other book which appeared in 1680 was a posthumous work of Filmer himself—the famous *Patriarcha*, to which Locke afterwards devoted the first of the

Two Treatises of Government which were germinating during this period of his life.'[1]

At this point, in 1684, Locke was deprived of his senior studentship by the Dean of Christ Church, Dr. Fell, acting under pressure from Lord Sunderland, one of Charles II's Secretaries of State. He retired to Holland, the home of toleration and the free printing press; and there, as has already been noticed, he forgathered with the more liberal of the Dutch Calvinists and with the Huguenots who flocked into the country after the Revocation of the Edict of Nantes. In this company he could steep his mind again in the great traditions of Puritanism—natural law; individual rights; the State limited by fundamentals; toleration for the conscience of man. He had been bred in Puritanism (a strong force in the county of Somerset); and while he was living in Holland (1684-9) *antiquam exquisivit matrem*. When he wrote the *Two Treatises*, finished the long-meditated *Essay on the Human Understanding*, and composed the first *Letter on Toleration* (to which others were subsequently added)—all during his period of residence in Holland—

'he had in him the great Puritan sense of the supreme importance of the individual soul; the Puritan feeling for the soul's right to determine its own relations to God, and to enjoy, at the least, toleration from the State and from all authority in so doing; the Puritan instinct for setting bounds to the State—"thus far, and no farther"; the Puritan echo of the plea of Antigone when she cites the higher law, which is the law of Nature and God, against the edicts of Creon. True, these nobler elements were mixed in Locke, as they were mixed in the nonconformity of the English middle class, with ignobler things. The sacred right of property was somehow included among the sanctities; and an individualism based on religion was made to trail clouds of ingloriousness. That is the penalty of making the solitary individual the pivot of all your thought. It was a penalty paid not only in England, but also in America. The Declaration of Independence, with its initial appeal to "the Laws of Nature and of Nature's God", shows one side of Locke, who lived in American thought in 1776 even more than he lived in England. The deep sense

[1] Quoted from an article by the writer in *The Times Literary Supplement* of 25 Aug. 1932. It may be added here that the First Treatise, 'in which the false principles and foundation of Sir Robert Filmer and his followers are detected and overthrown', is not discussed in this essay. The essay deals only with the Second Treatise, entitled 'an Essay concerning the true original, extent, and end of Civil Government'.

of property evident in American thought, including even property in the person of others, showed another. The two sides had already been conjoined in Locke's draft of a constitution, for Carolina. The figure of the Individual—seated on his desert pillar—this, in brief, is the symbol with which we are left, alike by the *Essay* and the *Two Treatises*. In the *Essay*, as Professor Alexander has said, "knowledge, as Locke conceives it, is part of the life-history of an individual". In the *Treatises*, as he has also said, "the body politic is an aggregate of consenting individuals". Thought, in its march, has now left behind the Individual on his desert pillar. But it is perhaps not amiss to look back. There is no peril of our being turned into a pillar of salt if we do so, and we need not fear. On the contrary we may even hope. In these crowded and gregarious days of community we may recover by such retrospect something of the salt savour of life—some sense that individual personality is after all the unique intrinsic value we know upon this earth. It may be that there is too much salt in Locke's philosophy. If it be so, the centuries have added their qualifications and antidotes.'[1]

In building his political philosophy Locke starts, like Hobbes, from the conception of a state of nature, in which men are living as equal and separate units. But whereas in Hobbes each unit claims a natural right (which is more properly a natural power or *potentia*) to do as he likes irrespective of others, in Locke each unit recognizes limitations on his own will, especially the two limitations of a right of property, vested in his fellow-units, and of a right of punishment of transgressors of natural law, vested in each and all (§ 7). There is a right of property, because each man has property in his person, and therefore in his labour, and therefore in the things with which he has inextricably mixed his labour (§ 27). Thus Locke placates the propertied classes among the Whigs, arguing for a natural and inherent right of property, not created by the recognition and guarantee of a community, but existing before the community; whereas Hobbes—really more radical (and similar, in this respect, to Rousseau)—holds that property, like all other rights of the subject, is the creation of government, and subject, as such, to the control of its creator. Again there is also a right of punishment—indeed there is a double right: 'there are two distinct rights, the one of punishing the crime, for restraint and preventing the like offence, which ... is in everybody, the other of taking reparation, which belongs

[1] Quoted from the same article.

only to the injured party' (§ 11). Such a right of punishment is the necessary corollary of the right of property; but the difficulty of such a pre-political condition as Locke describes is that it is really political. Locke's state of nature, with its régime of recognized rights, is already a political society.

He seeks to meet this difficulty, and to distinguish the state of nature from a state of organized society, by noting the imperfections present in a state of nature. When men are judges in their own case, as in such a state they are, three imperfections ensue—partial judgements; inadequate force for the execution of judgements; and variety in the judgements passed by different men in similar cases. There are therefore three things needed to remedy these imperfections—a judicature to administer law impartially; an executive to enforce the decisions of the judicature; and a legislature to lay down a uniform rule of judgement (§§ 124–6). In order to secure these remedies, men 'give up every one his single power of punishing [not, as Hobbes argued, *all* their powers, and certainly not their power over property] to be exercised by such alone as shall be appointed to it amongst them [that is to say, an executive], and by such rules as the community, or those authorized by them to that purpose, shall agree on [in other words, a legislature, composed either of the people itself or of its representatives]' (§ 127). But while Hobbes had conceived of the contract of surrender, by which a society is formed, as one with the institution of government, Locke distinguishes two separate acts. By the first, men having 'consented to make one community or government, they are thereby presently incorporated, and make one body politic, wherein the majority have a right to act and conclude the rest' (§ 95).[1] By the second, 'the majority' resolve 'upon the placing of the supreme power, which is the legislative' (§ 132); and here we may note Locke's exaltation—somewhat qualified, as will presently appear, in his later argument—of the supremacy of the legislative power. But from the first he regards the legislative, even if it be the supreme power, as 'limited to the public good of the society' (§ 132). It is 'only a *fiduciary* power to act for certain ends', and 'there remains still in the people a supreme power [another and higher 'supreme power'] to remove or alter

---

[1] Locke's enunciation of the majority principle and his defence of that principle in §§ 96–9 is a notable, if imperfect, study of a fundamental problem.

the legislative, when they find the legislative act contrary to the *trust* reposed in them' (§ 149).

Here, in the conception of trust, Locke is drawing on the English law of equity, as he had previously drawn (and generally draws) on the different and yet cognate idea of a general Law of Nature. But before we pursue the idea of trust, there is something to be said about Locke's general conception of the powers of government—not only the legislative, but also the other powers. We have seen that his account of the imperfections of the state of nature suggests three remedies for those imperfections, and that these three remedies would appear to be an executive, a judicial, and a legislative power. Actually, however, he proceeds to argue in terms of *two* powers rather than three. These two are (1) the legislative, and (2) the executive, which would seem to include the judicial and to be mainly concerned with the internal problem of dispensing justice under the laws promulgated by the legislative. He notes of the former that 'there is no need that the legislative should be always in being', and of the latter that 'it is necessary there should be a power always in being which should see to the execution of the laws'; and he concludes that on this ground—the discontinuity of the one, and the continuity of the other—'the legislative and the executive power come often to be separated' (§§ 143-4).[1] But Locke has a third power still to produce (so that, in the event, he speaks after all in terms of *three* powers); and he calls this power by the name of the 'federative'—in other words the power that makes *foedera*, or treaties, and is thus concerned with external relations. We must not, however, lay too much stress on this new distinction which produces a 'federative' power in addition to the executive. These two powers, 'though . . . really distinct in themselves . . . are hardly to be separated', and 'are almost always united'. We may thus come to two conclusions about Locke's conception of the powers of governments. The first is that though, like Montesquieu, he speaks of three powers, his three powers (the legislative, executive, and 'federative') are different from the three powers distinguished by Montesquieu; and it was Montesquieu who first established the executive, legislative, and judicial powers as the current classification. The

[1] This would appear to be as far as Locke goes in the direction of any doctrine 'of separation of powers'.

second is that though Locke incidentally speaks of the legislative and the executive as 'coming often to be separated', he does not emphasize their separation (and still less that of the judicial power); and he generally seems to regard sovereignty—so far as he has any theory of sovereignty (a problem still to be discussed)—as something unitary.

We may now return to the conception of trust, and to its bearing on Locke's general theory of contract. Early in 1689—the year before the publication of the *Two Treatises*—even the House of Lords, as a part of the Convention Parliament, had agreed by 55 votes to 46 that there was an original contract between the king and the people; and the practical consequences drawn from that premiss had been (1) the parliamentary deposition (euphemistically termed 'abdication') of the king, (2) a vacancy of the throne, and (3) the parliamentary institution of a new king—or, more exactly, of a new king and queen (William and Mary) reigning conjointly. Locke accepted and justified the consequences; but he did not accept the premiss. He did not, like Parliament, think in terms of a contract of government: he thought in terms of a contract of society, followed by the creation of a fiduciary sovereign under and by a trust-deed. It may be argued that the notion of trust implies a contract; and it may be urged in support of the argument that trust is the *mandatum* of Roman law, and that *mandatum*, in Roman law, is a form of consensual contract. If this argument were accepted, there would be two contracts in Locke—a formal contract of society and a later consensual contract of government. But this is not really Locke's view; nor is it a view which can be properly drawn from the English conception of trust, which may be like, but is not the same as, the Roman conception of *mandatum*. Trust implies three parties—the creator of the trust, or trustor; the trustee; and the beneficiary of the trust. *Vis-à-vis* the trustor, a trustee may be said to enter into a contract that he will undertake an obligation towards a third party; but *vis-à-vis* that third party (the beneficiary of the trust) the trustee does not enter into a contract—he simply accepts an obligation, and accepts it unilaterally. If we now apply the conception of trust to politics and political theory, we must notice that here there are only two parties—the community, which is both trustor and beneficiary of the trust; and the government, which is trustee. As trustor, the community may be said to enter into a contract with the trustee—that is to say, with the government; as beneficiary—*and Locke regards it principally as beneficiary*—it enters into no contract. From this point of view, the government makes no contract with the community for which it is trustee; it accepts an obligation, and it accepts it unilaterally, knowing the bounds set by the trust and by the law of God and Nature which stands behind the trust (§ 142).

Political trusteeship accordingly means a burden of obligation; its most prominent aspect is liability for abuse, or even neglect, of the powers held in trust—a liability which extends to removal for action contrary to the trust (§ 149). The trust-conception of government—not only adopted in Locke's theory, but also accepted in parliamentary practice afterwards ('in the course of the eighteenth century it became a parliamentary commonplace that all political power is a trust')[1]—is thus more unfavourable to government than the conception of an original contract between government and the people. Contract implies an agreement between two independent parties, each of which has rights of its own, and each of which surrenders some of those rights for a consideration received. The trustee, in regard to the beneficiary, is not such an independent party. There is no mutual surrender of rights for mutual receipt of consideration. The trustee has duties and not rights as against the beneficiary; the beneficiary has rights and not duties as regards the trustee. We may thus conclude that Locke dismisses the notion of a contract of government because it is too favourable to government, which would thereby be recognized as an independent party confronting the community—whereas, in his view, it only exists in, through, and for the community. Hobbes, on the other hand, though he too dismisses the notion of a contract of government, does so for an opposite reason: because it is too favourable to the community, which would thereby be recognized as an independent party confronting Leviathan, whereas, in his view, it only exists in and through Leviathan. (Even Hobbes, however, could hardly say that the community existed *for* Leviathan—on the

---

[1] Maitland, Introduction to Gierke's *Political Theories of the Middle Age*, p. xxxvi. The reader is referred to the general argument of pp. xxviii–xxxvii of Maitland's Introduction, and to the essay on 'Trust and Corporation' in the volume of his *Selected Essays*.

contrary he said, or implied, the opposite—and here his argument begins to swirl among rapids.)[1]

Three other elements in the theory of Locke may be noted in conclusion of the argument.

1. He believes that the people become a corporate body through their own associations, and of themselves: 'when any number of men have so consented to make one community or government, they are thereby presently incorporated', and can thenceforth act by the majority principle (§ 95). Hobbes, on the contrary, holds that a corporate body can only be formed in the person of the sovereign, who, by receiving into his person all the persons (that is to say the rights, or rather the powers) of his subjects, first makes them one person or body politic in himself. Locke regards the incorporation of a society as something internal, and as consisting in the voluntary coherence of its members; Hobbes regards it as something external, and as consisting in the cohesive force applied by the head to the members. For Hobbes, there can be no corporation apart from the head; for Locke, there can be a corporate society even without a trustee. There is some warrant in the statute book after 1689 for Locke's view. 'The Public', apart from the king and without the king, is treated in law as a corporate body responsible for the national debt. The king, as Charles II had shown at the time of the Stop of the Exchequer (1672), was not a punctual debtor; and though he might be trustee for the community, the community itself commended itself most as a responsible body to anxious creditors. The community, under the style of 'the Public', accordingly becomes enough of a corporation to borrow from its members and pay them their interest: it even enters into financial transactions with the East India Company.[2]

2. On the other hand, Locke has no clear view of the nature or residence of sovereignty. He speaks at one time of the supreme power of the people, or in other words the community; he speaks at another of the supreme power of the legislative— which may, it is true, be the community, but may also be a body of representatives appointed by the community; and in still another context he remarks that 'where . . . the executive is vested in a single person who has also a share in the legislative, then that

[1] See above, p. 92, note 1.
[2] Maitland, Introduction to Gierke's *Political Theories of the Middle Age*, p. xxxvi.

single person, in a very tolerable sense, may also be called the supreme power' (§ 151). 'Under *which* king, Bezonian', one is tempted to ask—community; legislative; or single person? Locke has no certain answer. His thought turns less on sovereignty than on the rights of the individual and the limits set by those rights to the sovereign, whoever he may be. Behind these rights, as their stay and pillar, stands the majesty of Natural Law; and we may almost say that the ultimate control, or final sovereign, is neither the legislative nor even the community behind the legislative, but a system of Natural Law upholding natural rights. When the community acts, in the last resort, in some rare and great event of oppression, as master of its own fate, it acts in the name, and on behalf, of this final majesty.

3. There is, however, an anticipation in Locke's *Second Treatise* of Rousseau's idea of the permanent and permanently acting sovereignty of the community. In one passage, already quoted, he speaks of the rules of law agreed on *either* by the community *or* by those authorized by them to that purpose (§ 127); and in another and more explicit passage he suggests that 'the majority having ... the whole power of the community naturally in them, may employ all that power in making laws for the community ... and executing those laws by officers of their own appointing; and then the form of the government is a perfect democracy' (§ 132). But though he attains the idea of the permanent and permanently acting sovereignty of the community, Locke does not press the idea. He stands on the whole for the Whig grandees, entrenched in the House of Lords and influencing the House of Commons. He leaves the supreme power in the hands of the king in parliament (but it is to be a reformed parliament, and in §§ 157-8 he has a notable passage on the crying need of parliamentary reform); and he conceives the ultimate power of the community (or shall we say 'penultimate', remembering that Natural Law is the last and farthest ultimate?) as only emerging when the legislative has to be removed or altered for acting contrary to the trust (§ 149)—when government is dissolved, and the people are at liberty to provide for themselves (§ 220)—when supreme power 'upon the forfeiture of their rulers ... reverts to the society, and the people have a right to act as supreme' (§ 243). It is 'rarely, rarely' that the will of the community acts—only on those rare occasions when govern-

ment is dissolved and revolution requires its remedy. Bosanquet has justly argued in his *Philosophical Theory of the State*,[1] that though Locke attains the conception of the sovereignty of a general will, the will is general, but not actual. Similarly—but also conversely—though Hobbes attains the conception for a moment (in his version of the original contract of society), he throws it overboard as soon as it is attained, and plumps for a will—the will of Leviathan—which is actual, but not general. Rousseau may be said to attempt a reconciliation, by arguing for a general will which is as actual as the will of Leviathan is for Hobbes, and as general as the will of the community is for Locke. But did he succeed in his attempt?

III

ROUSSEAU was not a philosopher—at any rate in the sense in which Hobbes, Locke, and Hume were philosophers. He was rather a *littérateur* of genius and an acute sensibility, who drew ideas from the surrounding air by the magnet of his intuition, and proceeded to make himself their incomparable exponent. Nor had he acquired, as Locke had acquired through his association with Shaftesbury, any practical experience of political affairs, except what he drew from his observation of the affairs of Geneva. He was an *a priori* theorist, and belonging to the age of the *Encyclopédie* he could theorize readily in many fields. He adorned and illuminated (or dazzled) the field of political theory with a large number of writings. The greatest was the *Du Contrat Social* of 1762; but it had been preceded by the *Discours sur l'Égalité* of 1755, by the 'Économie politique' (an article in the *Encyclopédie*) of the same year, and by two brief treatises of the year 1756 which analyse and criticize the international schemes of the Abbé de Saint-Pierre; and as it had had three predecessors, so it was followed by three successors—the last four of the *Lettres Écrites de la Montagne* (dealing partly with criticisms of the *Contrat Social*, but mainly with the constitutional problems raised by the action of the Genevan Government against himself and his writings), which appeared in 1764, the *Projet de Constitution pour la Corse* of 1765, and the *Considérations sur le Gouvernement de Pologne* published posthumously in 1782 but written some ten years earlier.[2]

[1] pp. 104–6.
[2] *The Political Writings of Jean-Jacques Rousseau*, by C. E. Vaughan (Cambridge

In the volume of his writings, and still more in the appeal of his style, Rousseau transcended Locke. Writing in French, the universal language of the eighteenth century, he appealed, as Locke never did, to a European public. In independence of thought, in power of philosophic reflection, and in maturity of judgement, he was inferior to Locke. He drew, in the main, on the current theory of the School of Natural Law, as it had been expounded in the seventeenth century by Grotius and Pufendorf, and as it was being expounded, in his own time, by two Swiss writers—Jacques Jean Burlamaqui (sometime member of the Council of State at Geneva) who published in 1747 his *Principes du Droit Naturel* and whose *Principes du Droit Politique* was published posthumously in 1751, and Emmerich de Vattel, of Neuchâtel, who published in 1758 his *Le Droit des gens, ou Principes de la Loi Naturelle*. It is in terms of the current theory of the School of Natural Law that Rousseau should properly be interpreted. It is true that at points—and those of the first importance —he departed from that theory. But it is also true that he was, in the main, its literary exponent; and it is also true that his very language and terminology are those of the School of Natural Law. When he writes, for instance, of the contract of society as producing *un corps moral et collectif*, he is reproducing the *corpus morale collectivum* of the Latin original from the authors of the School of Natural Law who wrote in Latin.[1]

The authors of the School of Natural Law had made their subject include three several branches of theory—a theory of society; a theory of the State; and a theory of the relations of States, or, in other words, a theory of international law and relations. Generally, it was the last of these branches of theory which principally engaged their attention. But Vattel, if he devoted three of the four books of his treatise to 'the nation considered in its relation to others', devoted the first of the four to 'the nation considered in itself', by which he meant a theory of the State and of society generally. Rousseau would appear to have intended to follow the same design. The four books which now form the *Du Contrat Social* were intended, like Vattel's first book,

---

University Press, 1915), is a full edition of all the works mentioned, with introductions and notes.
[1] See the writer's translation of Gierke's *Natural Law and the Theory of Society*, p. 324, n. 197, and also the Introduction, pp. xliii–xlvi.

to contain an account of 'the nation considered in itself'; but they were to be followed, as we learn from a concluding sentence, by an account of 'the nation considered in its relation to others', or, in other words, by a theory of *le droit des gens*. 'After laying down the true principles of *droit politique*', Rousseau wrote, 'and attempting to establish the State on its basis, it will remain for us to consolidate it by its external relations, and that will comprise *le droit des gens*.' But he found the theme too vast; and his treatise *Du Contrat Social* is a propylaeum which leads into nothing further.[1]

We may thus attach Rousseau to the School of Natural Law; but we must also dissociate him from it. It is a significant thing that the first draft of the *Contrat Social* contained a long chapter, originally entitled 'Du droit naturel et de la Société générale', which was meant to refute the idea of natural law. It is also a significant thing, and suggestive of an oscillating mind, that the whole of this chapter is omitted in the final draft and the printed version. Where did Rousseau actually stand in regard to the idea of natural law? He hardly knew. On the one hand he needed it—for how could there be a legal thing like a contract of society unless there were a natural law in terms and under the sanction of which a contract could be made?—and he also found it in his authorities. On the other hand he disliked it; and he felt in his bones that the nation made law, and not law the nation. How can we solve the antinomy?

The truth is that Rousseau was a romantic caught in the toils of a classical conception (if the idea of natural law may be called classical), in which he had dressed himself but in which he did not believe. He is two things in one, and he may be said both to belong and not to belong to the School of Natural Law.

'On the one hand he has the individualism of that school, and he has also its universalism. He believes in the free individual, who is everywhere born free; he believes in a universal system of *droit politique*, which rests on a ubiquitous basis of individual liberty. If he had followed this line of belief to its ultimate conclusion, he would have been a votary of the natural rights of man and an apostle of undiluted

---

[1] In his *Confessions* Rousseau speaks of having conceived the design of a general work on *Institutions politiques* (external as well as internal?) as early as 1744, when he was a secretary to the French Ambassador in Venice, and of having detached the *Contrat Social* from what he had written of this work and 'resolved to burn all the rest'. See C. E. Vaughan's edition, vol. ii, pp. 1-2, and vol. i, p. 438, n. 1.

liberalism. But there is another side to his teaching—a side which is at once very different, and, in its ultimate influence, far more important. The final sovereign of Rousseau is not an individual or a body of individuals. The final norm of social life is not a body of Natural Law, issuing in a system of natural rights, which proceeds from the reason of the individual, and is everywhere the same because that reason is everywhere identical. The sovereign of which he speaks is a "moral person", and the final norm is the "general will" of that person. Now it is true that *persona moralis* was a term of art in the School of Natural Law, by which it was used to signify the nature of a corporate body as a "person" which was something other than a physical person; and it is also true that the idea of the will of *omnes ut universi*, as distinct from the will of *omnes ut singuli*, was an idea also current in that school.[1] But it is equally true that the "moral person" and "general will" of Rousseau are ideas which transcend the limits of natural-law thought. Rousseau was a romantic before Romanticism; and he prepared the way for the new style of German thought which was to divinize the Folk-person and to historicize law as the expression in time of the general will or consciousness of right which proceeds from that person. Hegelianism and the Historical School of Law can find their nutriment in him, as he himself found his nutriment in the School of Natural Law; and while the springs of the past flow into his teaching, the springs of the future also issue from it.'[2]

This was the general setting, and the general influence, of the *Contrat Social*. A book so Janus-like can easily be interpreted in opposite senses. For a long time, and by most thinkers (as well as by the general public), it was interpreted as a paean on individualism. Its first sentence was a sufficient cue: 'man was born free, and everywhere he is in chains.' (But read only a few pages farther, and you will find, at the end of the first paragraph of the eighth chapter, that 'man ought to bless without ceasing the happy moment'—the moment of the social contract—which snatched him for ever from the state of nature in which he was born, and 'turned a stupid and limited animal into an intelligent being and a man'. The pendulum swings rapidly.) But there were other excuses than a cursory reading of the opening words of the *Contrat Social* to justify this line of interpretation.

---

[1] Here again, in the distinction of *volonté de tous* and *volonté générale*, as well as in the use of the term *corps moral et collectif*, Rousseau reproduces in French what had been said in Latin before him.

[2] Quoted from the writer's introduction to his translation of Gierke, op. cit., p. xlv.

Though the argument of the *Contrat Social*, if studied more closely, shows a rapid transition from an initial individualism towards collectivism, the earlier discourse on the *Origin and Foundations of Inequality*, which was written for, but failed to win, a prize offered by the Academy of Dijon, was more of a single piece, more purely a gospel of return to nature, and more of a paean on individualism. But it is not what Rousseau wrote before the *Contrat Social*—it is rather what followed after, in the days of the French Revolution—which explains the individualistic and emotional explanation of the philosophy of the *Contrat Social*, as a gospel of return to nature and the natural rights of man. It was easy to interpret the revolutionary *Déclaration des Droits de l'Homme et du Citoyen*, first drafted in 1789, as a doctrine suckled on the milk of Rousseau; and when that was once done, it was easy to take the converse step, and to interpret Rousseau in the light of the *Déclaration*, on the principle that he could best be known by the fruits supposed to be his. Actually, the influence of Rousseau's teaching on the French Revolution was far less than it has been supposed to be. Actually, too, his philosophy is far less a philosophy congenial to the France of 1789, and far more a philosophy congenial to the Germany of twenty and thirty years later (the Germany of Fichte and Hegel), than its individualist interpreters guessed. In effect, the philosophy of the *Contrat Social* is a 'philosophy of the bridge'. It marks the transition from natural law to an idealization of the national state. It may begin with Locke. But it ends by going back to the idealization of the Polis proclaimed in Plato's *Republic* (that, and not 'a return to nature', is the real return of Rousseau), and in that act of going back to Plato it also goes forward into the future and becomes the *praeparatio evangelii Hegeliani*.

Three propositions may be advanced about the theory implicit in Rousseau's *Contrat Social*. In the first place, he regards the State as a progressive force which lifts man gradually upward from his primitive condition. Far from suggesting any return to a state of nature, he holds that the state of nature was unstable and became intolerable. The need of self-preservation dictated a contract, formed by the free will of all; and the society so created resulted in the establishment of justice and the attainment of a higher (because rational and self-conscious) morality. He believes in the miracle of the true State, rationally constructed and continuing to act by rational self-control—the miracle that turns a stupid and limited animal into an intelligent being. The State which he attacks—and he does attack the State—is only the perverted or despotic State, irrational because it is not the expression and organ of a free rational will.

The second proposition, which follows on the first, is that Rousseau is not a sentimentalist of nature, but the austere rationalist of political society. He objects to a patriarchal theory of the State, as he objects to a theory which bases it on force, because neither supplies a rational basis for political obligation. The only basis of the State which he will admit is the rational basis of a reasonable will. So far we may applaud his theory; but we may add that he would have escaped from a mist of confusion, and avoided the inexplicable miracle of a sudden contractual emergence from a primitive and stupid condition into a civilized blaze of enlightenment, if he had stopped to draw a distinction between society and the State. The society of the nation is a given fact of historical evolution, not created by any contract of society, but simply there. The State based on that society may be, or may become at a given moment of time (as France sought to do in 1789), the result of a creative act performed by the members of the society, acting through some assembly or convention for the purpose of making a constitution under which, and in terms of which, they are resolved to live for the future as a legal association.[1] In that case, and in that sense, a sort of contract may be said to underlie the State; but there is none which underlies the nation or the fact of national society.

The third proposition, which supplements and elucidates the second, is that Rousseau refuses to base the State on mere will, and insists that it must be based on a will of a particular quality —a general will directed to the attainment of the general good. When he speaks of this general will, or *volonté générale*, he uses the adjective to indicate the *quality* of the 'object' sought, and not the *quantity* of the 'subjects' or persons by whom it is sought. He rejects the mere will of all (*omnes ut singuli*); he argues for a will of a general intention (the will of *omnes ut universi*), which, far from being felt or expressed by all, may have to be expressed by a single man—the 'legislator'—who grasps its demand. The distinction here drawn between the will of all and the general

[1] See above, p. 92.

will is, as we have already noticed, a distinction current among the writers of the School of Natural Law. But it receives a new edge in the theory of Rousseau; and it becomes in his hand a keen two-edged sword which seems to defend democracy (and primary democracy at that), but ends by arming Leviathan. Was not the Napoleon of the Code an admirable 'legislator'?

We touch at this point on a cardinal difficulty in Rousseau's thought. He wants to use his two-edged sword in defence of *primary* democracy, with no representatives, without any parties, and within the confines of the small State which primary democracy demands. He rejects representative government, or *parliamentary* democracy. But he only does so to find in the issue that he has rejected democracy itself. The unguided democracy of a primary assembly without any parties is a *souverain fainéant*. A 'mayor of the palace' must be provided; and we are left in the issue with Pepin of Héristal acting as 'legislator' for the *souverain*.

Rousseau belonged by origin to the city-state of Geneva, to whose 'magnificent, most honoured, and sovereign seigneurs' he dedicated his *Discours sur l'Égalité*. The free institutions and the civic life of Geneva affected his thought. We may almost say that they Hellenized his views into a belief in primary democracy, making him at once the votary of the contemporary Swiss canton and the apostle of the ancient civic republics of Athens and Sparta. We may also say, in another phrase, that they hypostatized his abstract idea of a sovereign general will, and turned it into a mundane matter of government by a primary assembly. There is much to be said in favour of the idea of the general will, taken in and by itself. The problem is the translation of the idea; its application in actual life; the discovery of the organ through which it acts. It is here that Rousseau sails into troubled waters; and it is here that we have to study the tacks and shifts of his thought.

We must begin our study with his version of the contract. He is like Hobbes in that he postulates the entire surrender of himself by each individual in the moment of the contract: he is unlike in that he regards each individual as surrendering himself to no man, but 'alienating himself with all his rights to the whole community' (I, c. 6). All, in the sense of all the individuals surrendering, form the *état*; all, in the sense of the community to which surrender is made, form the *souverain*; and all are thus, at one and the same time, a passive body of subjects and an active body of sovereigns. Here Rousseau enunciates his famous paradox, 'Each, giving himself to all, gives himself to nobody': in other words, each gives himself to himself, and each is still his own master. The paradox conceals a paralogism. I surrender all myself—and I surrender it all to 999 others as well as myself: I only receive a fraction of the sovereignty of the community; and ultimately I must reflect that if I am the thousandth part of a tyrant, I am also the whole of a slave. Leviathan is still Leviathan, even when he is corporate.

There is a further difference, however, between the Leviathan of Hobbes and the Leviathan of Rousseau, over and above the difference that the one Leviathan is a sole person and the other a community of persons. The Leviathan of Hobbes is at once a legislative and an executive, uniting all the powers. The community which forms Rousseau's Leviathan is purely a legislative, confining itself to the generalities of legislation. For particular acts of authority the community institutes a *gouvernement*, an intermediary body for the execution of the laws which it makes, standing between itself as *souverain* and itself in its capacity of *état* (III, c. 1). This government, however, is only a temporary and limited commission: while the sovereign community exists of itself, and its sovereignty is inalienable and indivisible, the government exists by grace of the sovereign, and its power can be resumed or divided at will by the sovereign. There is thus no contract of government for Rousseau; he will only recognize the one contract of society: 'there is only one contract in the State, that of association, and it excludes all others' (III, c. 16).

But though the community may thus alienate executive power to a commission (temporarily, and subject to the resumption or division of such power as it may will), it never alienates legislative power to representatives. That would be to alienate sovereignty, which is impossible. Here Rousseau differs fundamentally from Locke, who, if he had envisaged the possibility of the community acting itself as legislative, had also assumed that it would normally act through its representatives. Rousseau dismisses with a cavalier gesture any idea of parliamentary democracy: representation is derived from the iniquitous and absurd system of feudal government; representatives in counsel are like mercenaries in war; the English people thinks it is free, and deceives itself greatly—it is only free during a general election (III, c. 15).[1] Banishing parliamentary democracy, he accordingly preaches the doctrine of a primary legislative, sovereign over an executive which serves as its *commissaire*.

There is an old lesson of politics—the principle of balance (John Stuart Mill could even call it the principle of antagonism) —which teaches us that, in actual life, States need a strong executive as well as a strong legislative. There is also another lesson of politics—perhaps more recent, but certainly no less important—which teaches us that a strong executive and a strong legislative must not simply confront one another, on a system of division of powers, but must also co-operate with one another, in a system of reciprocity and mutual confidence. Rousseau paid little heed to the first of these lessons; and we can hardly blame him (after all he was writing in 1762, and a developed cabinet system of reciprocity between the executive and the legislative power still lay in the future) for not thinking of the second. He was hardly concerned with practical necessities: he was hot in pursuit of the logical symmetry of an ideal scheme of popular sovereignty. We may therefore limit our criticism to an inquiry into its logic. Was it, after all, symmetrical; and was it a consistent scheme?

On his scheme the generality was to be the sovereign body, in the capacity of a legislative; and the reason was that the generality, and only the generality, could be trusted to will a general will, and to rise superior to particular and sectional interests. Was this a well-founded trust? Hardly; for when his journey begins the traveller finds that he has to traverse ranges —and they are somewhat mountainous ranges—of logical difficulty. In the first place he has to distinguish a real general will from a mere will of all—the will of a true collectivity from a mere aggregate of wills. How is this to be done? Rousseau answers, 'By the presence or absence of party-lines in voting' (II. c. 3). If party is present, and a great clique carries the day,

---

[1] This attitude to English parliamentarianism was inherited, or at any rate shared, by Kant and Hegel. Kant regarded the English constitution as an oligarchy, with parliament acting not only as legislative but also, through its ministers, as executive—and that in the interests of a party, or even of individuals. Hegel regarded parliament as an institution of *die bürgerliche Gesellschaft*—bourgeois or tradesmen society—concerned to advance particular interests, and therefore inferior to a monarch who stood above the play of society.

the general good will be sacrificed; if there are no parties, and each individual votes individually, the individual selfishnesses in voting will cancel one another, and the general good will be the residuum. In an age which still interpreted party as faction (the age, for example, of Bolingbroke and the theory of the superiority of *la patrie* to *le parti*) this was perhaps a natural view; and yet it is hardly logical to argue that individualism in voting is the royal road which leads to collectivism in decision. Party, after all, is a necessary means of precipitating in a set form a programme of the general good, and of realizing that programme in the strength of concerted action; and Burke was wiser than Rousseau when he argued at the end of his pamphlet on *The Present Discontents* (published eight years after the *Contrat Social*) that party was 'a body of men united for promoting ... the *national* interest upon some particular principle'. The true freedom of the citizen consists in the citizen's choice; and where is the citizen's choice unless there are alternative programmes, presented by different parties, between which choice can be made? It is not the absence, but the presence, of party—if party is only organized as a body of opinion about the national interest and the general good, and not corrupted into a sum of personal interests—which is the true criterion of the existence of a general will.

In the second place—and here we reach another range of logical difficulty—the question arises whether the whole people, if it be set to legislate for itself, can ever discover for itself the general good which, *ex hypothesi*, it really wishes to enact. To distil the requirements of the general good in an actual measure of legislation is something which requires both an intellectual effort of sustained reflection (or, better, sustained discussion) and a moral effort of abstinence from private and sinister interests: it will not come of itself, through the automatic cancellation of private interests by one another. Rousseau himself is aware of the necessity of distillation; but he will not trust representatives to do this necessary work. He accordingly introduces a wise legislator—antique in idea, but contemporary history has shown us that he may be terribly modern in practice—as a *deus ex machina* to tell the people what they ought to will. 'Of itself, the people always wishes the good; of itself, it does not always see it' (II, c. 6). Here emerges the 'leader' and 'guide'. Here too, as we have already noticed, the sword of Rousseau turns round in his hand, and shows its other edge.

In effect, and in the last resort, Rousseau is a totalitarian. We need not exaggerate the importance of the 'legislator' to arrive at this result. Omit the legislator altogether: the result is still there. Imagine Rousseau a perfect democrat: his perfect democracy is still a multiple autocrat. He leaves no safeguard against the omnipotence of the *souverain*. It is significant that the *Contrat Social* ends with the suggestion of religious persecution. The man who has publicly acknowledged the articles of the civil faith, which it belongs to the sovereign to determine, and who has then acted as if he did not believe in those articles—*qu'il soit puni de mort*. Rousseau was so far from believing in *les droits de l'homme* that he went to the other extreme. He was so convinced that it was enough for the individual to enjoy political rights (as a fraction of the collectivity) that he forgot the necessity of his enjoying the rights of 'civil and religious liberty'. The English Whigs and their philosopher Locke, with all their faults, were wiser in their generation.

There is still a third range of logical difficulty, less terrible than the second, but still sufficiently formidable. How can the great state of modern times reconcile its size to a primary legislative? Rousseau himself realized that his theory suited only the small community, such as Greece had known and Switzerland still knew; and he would have reconciled it to the greater size of the modern state either by advocating a movable metropolis, if a state had many towns, or by suggesting some system of federalism. The suggestion of federalism remained merely a suggestion:[1] the advocacy of a movable metropolis may remind us of an early phase in the history of Trade Unionism (described in the first chapter, entitled 'Primitive Democracy', of the Webbs' book on *Industrial Democracy*), when trade union branches in different towns were made in rotation the 'governing branch' of the whole of that union for a fixed period. The phase soon passed; and the later development of Trade Unionism admirably shows (though sometimes with lapses back to 'the primitive')

[1] Federalism is only mentioned in a single sentence of the *Contrat Social*; but there is a story that Rousseau wrote sixteen chapters on the subject, which he entrusted in manuscript to a friend who destroyed them at the beginning of the French Revolution. See Vaughan's edition of *The Political Writings of Rousseau*, vol. i, pp. 95-102, and vol. ii, pp. 135-6.

the impracticability of Rousseauism, and the need of representative institutions in any large society which seeks to follow the arduous path of true self-government.

Here we may leave the *Contrat Social*. One may say of it, in an old medieval distich,

> Hic liber est in quo quaerit sua dogmata quisque,
> Invenit et pariter dogmata quisque sua.

You can find your own dogmas in Rousseau, whether you belong to the Left (and especially to the left of the Left) or whether you belong to the Right (and especially to the right of the Right). The only dogmas which it is difficult to find are those of the Centre—the Centre to which the English Whigs, whom a later generation called Liberals, have really always belonged, though they have always professed to belong to the Left. There is no comfort for the Centre in all the shot fabric of Rousseau's book. That is why it is natural, and even permissible, to prefer the hodden grey of Locke's cloth to the brilliant but parti-coloured silk of Rousseau. . . . Yet what a magic has style—above all when the language is French. It makes the tour of the world, and it carries with it everywhere the ideas which it has adorned. It is curious to reflect what would have happened to Rousseau's ideas if they had been given, about 1760, to an English writer in Cambridge, or a German writer in the University of Halle, and he had been told to express them to the best of his ability. Would the English writer have set the Cam on fire—let alone the Thames? Or the German the Saale—let alone the Rhine?

IV

LOCKE and Rousseau, if in different ways and different degrees, accepted the idea of the social contract: Hume, more historically minded, and more conservative in his convictions, was its critic. His sceptical intellect led him to approach political theories—the theory of divine right as well as the theory of social contract, but more especially the latter—with a touch of acid realism, which was mingled with a half-ironical suavity. 'There is something,' he seems to say, 'in your different theories; but less, much less, than you think.'

The essay 'Of the original contract' was first published (along with an essay 'Of passive obedience' and a suggestive essay 'Of national characters') in the new edition of *Essays Moral and Political* which appeared in 1748. It starts from the proposition that the theory of divine right and that of original contract are both the constructions of a party—a proposition which implies that they were built by the English Whigs and Tories, and built in the course of the last hundred years. The proposition may be disputed. Both theories have a wider range than England; and both go back to the Middle Ages, or even earlier. When Hume ends his essay by noting that 'scarce any man, till very lately, ever imagined that government was founded on compact', and makes this an argument for concluding that 'it is certain that it cannot, in general, have any such foundation', he is on erroneous ground.

Leaving this error on one side, we may proceed to ask what sort of contract Hume has in his mind. It would appear to be the contract of government, and not the contract of society—the original contract between the king and the people which had been approved by the Convention Parliament in 1689. It is a contract 'by which the subjects have tacitly reserved the power of resisting their sovereign, whenever they find themselves aggrieved by that authority with which they have, for certain purposes, voluntarily entrusted him'. This theory of contract stands opposed to the other theory which makes authority a divine commission—not a popular trust—and, as such, sacred and inviolate. Both theories, to Hume, have some truth; but neither is wholly true. He has little to say of the theory of divine right, except that, by the same logic by which it covers the sovereign power, it must equally cover every petty jurisdiction, and 'a constable, therefore, no less than a king, acts by a divine commission'. His real theme is the theory of original contract; and here he allows that government, 'if we trace it to its first origin in the woods and deserts', certainly *originated* in consent—but he equally denies that in the world of today it *exists* by consent. The original contract has long been obliterated by a thousand changes of government: almost all governments now existing are founded on usurpation, or conquest, or both. There may still be some rare disorderly popular elections of government; if there are, they are to be deprecated; and in any case the English Revolution of 1688 was not one of them—'it was only the majority of seven hundred who determined that change [in

Hume's view, merely a change of the succession] for near ten millions'. The most that can be allowed is that the consent of the people is *one* just foundation of government; but 'it has very seldom had place in any degree, and never almost in its full extent'. To suppose *all* government based on consent is to suppose 'all men possessed of so perfect an understanding as always to know their own interests'—'but this state of perfection is likewise much superior to human nature'. And if you take refuge in the argument that at any rate there is tacit consent, or implied consent, and support your argument by saying that a man gives such consent merely by staying in a country when he could leave it if he so desired—well, the answer is that there is no consent, of any sort, unless there is freedom of choice, and there is actually no such freedom. Why, you cannot even emigrate without permission if the prince chooses so to ordain.

Hitherto the argument of Hume has rested on an appeal to the evidence of history and the observation of facts. In the second part of the essay he attempts a more philosophical refutation of the idea of contract. Distinguishing the moral duties to which we are instinctively impelled (such as pity for the unfortunate) from those to which we are impelled by a sense of obligation 'when we consider the necessities of human society', he proceeds to consider three duties which belong to the latter category. There is justice, or a regard to the property of others; there is fidelity, or the observance of promises; there is the political or civil duty of allegiance. These duties flow, he argues, *and flow independently*, from the sense of obligation imposed by the necessities of human society. Why base allegiance on fidelity, as the contractarians do when they refer the duties of subjects (and with them the duties of sovereigns) to the foundation of observance of promises supposed to be expressed in a contract? We must keep allegiance and fidelity separate. 'The obligation to allegiance being of like force and authority with the obligation to fidelity, we gain nothing by resolving the one into the other. The general interests or necessities of society are sufficient to establish both.'

The answer which Hume thus gives to the problem of political obligation may be briefly summarized. 'Obey the powers that be. It is true that they are ordained by usurpation, or force, or both; but you must none the less pay them obedience for the simple reason that society could not otherwise subsist.' It is hardly a satisfactory answer. There is something, after all, in the idea of fidelity which goes deeper than the idea of allegiance, and which is really the basis of allegiance. There is such a thing (to use Burke's phrase) as an 'engagement or pact of the constitution',[1] which demands the fidelity both of rulers and subjects; under which both equally stand; and to which both are equally bound. What is the proof of this engagement or pact? Well, there is one sort of proof which Hume himself is bound, upon his own showing, to admit. He ends the essay 'Of original contract' by 'an appeal to general opinion'. 'In all questions with regard to morals', he writes, 'there is really no other standard by which any controversy can be decided.' What, then, was the general opinion of Hume's own country (if, like him, we may confine our view within the four seas) about the problem of political obligation? Surely it was in his day, as it had been before his day and continued to be after his day, an opinion that obligation was not unilateral; that it embraced both sovereign and subject in a common pact or engagement; that both, in a word, were equally bound by the law of the constitution. The opinion is as old as Magna Carta: it is also as recent as the most recent theory of the sovereignty of the constitution—the constitution which, in its essence, may be called the political contract.

Here we may leave the idea of contract. Historians have not loved the idea; they know the records of history, and they do not believe that there ever was such a thing. Lawyers have not loved the idea: they know what actual contracts are, how lawyers draft them and courts enforce them, and they do not believe that the social contract is anything more than a sham—a '*quasi*' or an '*als ob*'. Where historians and lawyers are agreed, a mere layman may think it wise to be silent. And yet there must be some 'soul of truth' in so old and inveterate an idea,

> Would men observingly distil it out.

Perhaps enough has already been said, in the course of the argument, to suggest where this soul of truth may be sought. Meanwhile it is not inapposite—though it may also be a mere offering

---

[1] The reader is referred to the argument at the end of the first section, p. 92.

on the altar of pragmatism—to end by recurring to the good service which the doctrine of contract (and the doctrine of natural law which is behind it, or above it) has rendered to the cause of liberty, and to the general cause of political progress. Its fruits do not prove its truth. But they deserve to be remembered. The English Revolution of 1688 was cradled in contract, and the American Revolution of 1776 had the same ancestry. In both the idea of contract can plead some title to have contributed to the cause of liberty. It may seem more paradoxical—perhaps purely paradoxical—to argue that the idea of contract has contributed to the cause of political progress. Is not a deed of contract a dead hand on political development, and is not a belief in 'historical growth' the true philosophy for the progressive? Perhaps we may answer that things are not always what they seem. A deed, if we conceive it broadly enough, may be a beckoning hand to progress rather than a dead hand on development. The idea of an original contract and a deed of political association may have its restrictive side. This was the argument of Tom Paine when he opened the *Rights of Man* by denouncing Burke for seeking to lay the dead hand of 1689 on the living present of 1791, and for saying as it were to the Convention Parliament and its antique notion of contract, 'O Parliament, live for ever.' But the idea of contract and the deed has also its constructive side. It implies that political development is not an automatic growth; that it springs from human will, and the act and deed of men; and that it must continue to spring from, and must even be accelerated by, the same creative force. It may be a paradox, but it is also a truth, that those who cling to the idea of growth may sometimes oppose a new growth, having only too much of the historic sense—and equally that those who cling to the idea of an original deed of creation may often encourage reform and progress, even though (or perhaps because) they have little of the sense of historic growth.

Essay Five

BLACKSTONE ON THE BRITISH CONSTITUTION

I

THE quarter of a century which spans the years between 1763, when the Seven Years War was ended by the Peace of Paris, and 1788, when the constitution of the United States of America was ratified by eleven of the thirteen original states, may not improperly be called the period of the American Revolution. It was a lively and exciting period of progressive hope and creative thought. Young Jeremy Bentham (if indeed he was ever young) struck its keynote in the opening sentences of his *Fragment on Government*, published when he had just attained the age of 28. 'The age we live in is a busy age, in which knowledge is rapidly advancing towards perfection. In the natural world, in particular, everything teems with discovery and with improvement.' Citing as examples of man's conquest of the natural world the recent explorations of the most distant and recondite regions, and the new analysis of the subtle element of the air,[1] he turns, with an even greater zest, to the moral world. 'Correspondent to *discovery* and *improvement* in the natural world', he remarks, 'is *reformation* in the moral'; and with these sanguine words he embarked on that career of reforming the moral world —particularly its states, and more particularly their laws— which lasted until he died, an old man of 84, in the year of the passing of the Reform Bill, 1832.

It was indeed an age of hope, averting its face from the Gothic obscurities and barbarities of the past ('before Montesquieu all was unmixed barbarism'), and turning, with a resolute but elegant composure, towards a new age of enlightened control of nature and human life. What it achieved in the world of nature

[1] Bougainville had begun his voyage round the world in 1766, and Cook had made his famous voyages in 1768 and 1772. In 1766 Cavendish had discovered hydrogen, or 'inflammable air': in 1774 Priestley had discovered oxygen, and named it 'dephlogisticated air'. The brothers Montgolfier were using hot air to raise balloons in 1773.

is a matter outside our scope. In the moral world it laboured, with an impeccable loyalty of logic, to establish the grand principles of enlightenment; but its achievements were less fortunate, or at any rate more catastrophic, than the hopes which it fondly nursed. The ray of enlightenment, turned on the dark and tangled mass of problems which an age-long growth had accumulated, proved unexpectedly explosive. It produced not reformation, but revolution; not one revolution, but two—the American and the French.

A rich harvest of political ideas was garnered, on both sides of the Atlantic, during the period of the American Revolution. The quarter of a century from 1763 to 1788 was fertile in notable writings on the British or Eastern side; and it equally produced, on the American or Western side, a harvest of pamphlets, state papers, and political documents, which must be ranked among the permanent classics of political theory and invention. On both sides the year 1776—the central year of the period—may be called an *annus mirabilis*. On the American side it was the year of the Declaration of Independence; of the Virginia Bill of Rights and the Virginia Constitution; of the Pennsylvania Constitution, with its initial 'declaration of rights' and its subsequent 'plan or frame of government'; and of Thomas Paine's *Common Sense*. On the British side it was the year of Adam Smith's *Wealth of Nations*; of Bentham's *Fragment on Government*; and of the first volume of Gibbon's *Decline and Fall of the Roman Empire*. The one side was innovating and inventing: the other was reflecting critically on the policy and legacy of the past.

If we consider the whole quarter of a century in which the year 1776 is at once the middle and the zenith, we may note, on the British side, the simultaneous pursuit of three main lines of inquiry. In the first place, and in the domain of legal study, the general knowledge of the common law was given a new and firm basis by the publication of Blackstone's *Commentaries on the Laws of England* (1765–9); and a little later, under the impulse or provocation of the *Commentaries*, the foundations of a science of jurisprudence were laid by Bentham in his *Fragment on Government*. In the second place, and in the domain of the study of politics, the field of political theory was illuminated by Burke, both in profound pamphlets (such as the *Thoughts on the Cause of the Present Discontents* of 1770, and the *Letter to the Sheriffs of*

Bristol of 1777) and in great speeches such as that on American taxation in 1774 and that on conciliation with the colonies in 1775; and it was also elucidated by Paley, on a more academic plane, in the *Principles of Moral and Political Philosophy*, based on his Cambridge lectures (as Blackstone's *Commentaries* were similarly based on his Oxford lectures) and published in 1785. Finally, and in the domain of economics, the study of political economy was made an independent and influential science—and a science for statesmen as well as for men of business—by Adam Smith's *Wealth of Nations*.

These remarkable achievements (some of them almost of the nature of codes of knowledge), in the three domains of law, politics, and economics, were the achievements of three Englishmen, an Irishman, and a Scotsman; and from that point of view they may be said to belong to the British side of the Atlantic. But there is also a sense in which they belonged to the American side as well as the British. For one thing they dealt with American issues as well as the issues of British life. Even the sober Paley had his eyes fixed on American problems: Burke, the agent of the colony of New York, and conjoined in the representation of his Bristol constituency (from 1774 to 1780) with a Mr. Cruger of New York,[1] was steadily intent on American affairs: Adam Smith was not only the critic of the mercantilist policy which determined the economic relations of Great Britain and the American colonies, but also a philosopher of imperial policy and the author—in the last chapter of his *Wealth of Nations*—of a 'project of empire' for the better government of the overseas British dominions. For another thing, and whether or no they dealt with American issues, British writers had a public in the American colonies and were read by American readers. The *Commentaries* of Blackstone were one of the best British exports; and they reposed on the shelves of American libraries by the side of Locke's *Treatises on Civil Government*.

Meanwhile there was also a busy ferment of political thinking, and no little publishing, on the American side of the Atlantic. It is curious to find an Englishman, Paine, who had crossed to

---

[1] Cruger was a merchant with large interests both in Bristol and New York. He represented Bristol from 1774 to 1780, and again, after an interval, from 1784 onwards. He returned to New York, his native city, about 1790, and died there in 1827.

Philadelphia in 1774 and immediately embarked on journalism, conspicuous in the American field. He had a lively mind and an attractive style; but we must not exaggerate the importance of his *Common Sense*, published in the January of 1776, or of the thirteen numbers of his *American Crisis* which appeared between the December of that year and the April of 1783. There were profounder minds and firmer pens, steeped in a far more durable ink, to argue the American cause. The American genius ran to the pamphlet, the periodical, and the political document. Some of the pamphleteers were men of British education and training. Such, for example, was Daniel Dulany of Maryland, who had been educated at Eton, Clare College, and the Middle Temple, and whose pamphlet of 1765 ('Considerations on the Propriety of imposing Taxes in the British Colonies') was reprinted in London in 1766, and produced by the elder Pitt in the House when he was arguing for the repeal of the Stamp Act. Such again was James Wilson, a graduate of Edinburgh, who published in 1774 a legal and constitutional argument under the title of *Considerations on the Authority of Parliament*. Others, of a greater calibre and a deeper influence, were thinkers purely of the American soil and of a native American genius. There was Benjamin Franklin of Philadelphia: there were James Otis and John Adams of Boston, both steeped in the law and both tenacious defenders of the legal rights of the colonists: there was Thomas Jefferson of Virginia, democrat, scholar, and architect, 'author', as he himself wrote in the epitaph for his own tomb, 'of the Declaration of American Independence and the Statute of Virginia for Religious Freedom'; and finally, at the close of the account, and in the consummation of American political philosophy, there were the authors of the eighty-five papers of the *Federalist* of 1788—Alexander Hamilton of New York, and James Madison and John Jay of Virginia. It is a great gallery of striking figures; and if none of the figures in the gallery carries a book in his hand (a book of close argument and 'long breath', such as the British figures carry), some of them, none the less, are of the first order of majesty, and the pamphlets and documents which they hold in their hands have made world history. The 'author of the Declaration of American Independence and the Statute of Virginia for Religious Freedom' was a great author.

Looking at both sides of the Atlantic, and scanning the achievements of British and American thought, in this period of what Bentham called 'reformation' but history has preferred to style by the name of revolution, we are naturally led to inquire, 'what were the common elements, and what were the grounds of division?' A study of the political theory embedded in the *Commentaries* of William Blackstone may serve to explain both the current trend of orthodox political opinion and the nature of the dissent which was already beginning to challenge orthodoxy. Among all the exponents of British ideas during this period Blackstone comes naturally first. Not only was he the senior among the British writers who handled themes of law and politics during the period between 1763 and 1788; and not only were his writings the first to be published. He was also the least original, and the most systematic, of the publicists of his period; and it is the merit of his writings, and their just title to consideration, that they state in an unexceptionable style, with an unexceptionable orthodoxy, the views on law and politics which were generally current in England on the eve of the American Revolution.

II

WILLIAM BLACKSTONE (1723–80) was the son of a London merchant in the silk trade. After the usual English education of his time, he was elected to a fellowship at All Souls College, Oxford, and during the tenure of his fellowship he read for the bar and became a barrister. Not succeeding at first at the bar, he condescended in 1753 upon lecturing on law at Oxford—a condescension which others, in the like case, have similarly practised since his time. His lectures were so successful that a certain Mr. Viner (who had already entertained the notion even before he began to lecture) was led to found the Vinerian Chair of English Law in the University.[1] Blackstone became the first of a long line of Vinerian professors; and he held the chair from 1758 to 1766. Once more his lectures, now delivered *ex cathedra*, were singularly successful—so successful, that they brought him

[1] This was the first Chair of English Law to be founded in the old Universities. There had been Regius Professorships of Civil (or Roman) Law since the time of Henry VIII; but the laws of England had not hitherto been the subject of a chair, nor, indeed, had any lectures on English law been delivered in a university until Blackstone began to lecture in 1753.

a good practice at the bar and ultimately (in 1770) a judgeship; so successful, that he was led to publish them *in extenso* and to make a profit of £14,000 (or so it was said) by their publication. Transcripts, he found, had been made of the lectures and lent from hand to hand (one of these transcripts is said to have been used in the education of George III): some of the transcripts, as Blackstone explains in the preface to his published *Commentaries*, had been 'imperfect, if not erroneous'; others had 'fallen into mercenary hands and became the object of clandestine sale'. The lecturer naturally wished to be judged by his authentic text, and—still more naturally—to enjoy the benefits of an open and public sale.

Such was the origin of the four volumes of *Commentaries on the Laws of England*, which appeared during the four years 1765-9. (During the course of their publication Blackstone left Oxford and his chair; and with a seat in the House of Commons, which he had held since 1761,[1] he devoted himself to law and politics in London.) The success of his four volumes was enormous; and they took their place in English libraries, during the last quarter of the eighteenth century, by the side of Gibbon's *Decline and Fall* (1776-88) and Adam Smith's *Wealth of Nations* (1776). If Macaulay, at a later date, was to introduce history into ladies' drawing rooms, Blackstone had already—and that nearly a century earlier—carried law into gentlemen's studies. A classical scholar and an elegant English versifier, he adorned law no less by the grace of his style than by the perspicuity of his arrangement: he made it generally readable and generally interesting.[2] Eight editions were published in England during his lifetime, before the year 1780: Gibbon made 'a copious and critical abstract' of the first volume, adorned with remarks or criticisms of his own, which, as he notes in his autobiography, 'was my first serious production in my native language':[3] above all, Jeremy Bentham was moved to write a *Comment on the Commentaries*, and to print, in 1776, a part of the *Comment* anonymously

[1] He was first member for Hindon, Wiltshire, and then (from 1768 to 1770) for Westbury, in the same county.
[2] I would cite, as examples of the interest of the *Commentaries* to the pure layman, Blackstone's treatment of suicide (iv. 189-90); his account of deodands (i. 300-2); and his remarks on 'petit treason' (iv. 203-4).
[3] For an account of Gibbon's abstract and remarks, see Sir William Holdsworth, *A History of English Law*, vol. xii, pp. 750-4.

under the title of *A Fragment on Government*. A French translation was published between 1774 and 1776, which has been described as neither accurate nor French; and Catharine II is reported to have had the *Commentaries* translated into Russian. More important than its vogue in France or Russia was its vogue in North America. A reprint appeared in Philadelphia in 1771; and attacks having been made on the treatment of Dissent in the *Commentaries* by two dissenting ministers in England, Dr. Priestley and Dr. Furneaux, and Blackstone having made a reply, the attacks and the reply were published in Philadelphia, in 1773, in a little volume entitled *An Interesting Appendix to Sir William Blackstone's Commentaries*, with the sub-title of *Palladium of Conscience*. There were also subsequent American editions of Blackstone's work, which are said to be nearly equal in number to the English editions.

We are here concerned with Blackstone not as a lawyer, or as an interpreter of English law, but rather as a political thinker and an exponent of English political ideas—and that at a crucial period of incipient dissension in the British Commonwealth, when the clear and important exposition of ideas was a matter of crucial importance. He had singular qualities of exposition; but he had also some defects. In himself he was a good old-fashioned conservatively minded Whig, or in other words (which may be applied to many of the Whigs) a liberal of that conservative type of liberalism which suffers from hardening of the mental arteries. He sat in Parliament for a rotten borough: he required a bottle of port before him when he was writing (so the story runs) 'that he might be invigorated and supported in the fatigue of his great work': he had a corpulency of body, accentuated by an unhappy aversion from exercise; and his belief, as one might expect on the basis of such data, was a happy but heavy belief in the divine right of whatever is. But his conservatism was due to something more than port, corpulence, and a rotten borough. He had a genuine passion of admiration for English law—not so much statute or enacted law as the common law, or, in other words, the law depending partly on the tradition of ancient custom and partly on the wisdom of judicial decision. He found English law reposing in the great age of settlement which preceded the tumultuous age of reform and revolution: he studied and expounded it in the age of the happy lull, the period of charmed quiescence, which made Talleyrand say in retrospect, 'He who did not live before 1789 never knew the charm of life'. Blackstone had the temper *del tempo felice*; and having that temper, he regarded the law of contemporary England almost in the light of a very peculiar gift of God to Englishmen.[1] He thought it had almost attained perfection; and like Sir Edward Coke in the seventeenth century, he approached it almost with veneration. He was content to be its expositor; and he was its born expositor.

In the first place he had a naturally tidy and systematic mind. As bursar of his college, he had arranged the documents relating to its property; as a delegate of the Press of his university, he had done his best to systematize its affairs; as Professor of English Law, he sought, in the same spirit and with equal industry, to arrange and systematize the law on which he lectured. In the second place, he had that gift of lucid and fluent prose which marks the age of Dr. Johnson, and shines in the writings of Burke and Adam Smith, and of Paley and Paine, as it does in those of Hamilton and Madison. A systematizer, with a gift of style, he produced a classic book of exposition, which influenced thought all the more because it was *not* original, and because it was simply a statement of current ideas and practice. Like the Institutes of Justinian in Roman law, it became, and still in some measure is, a basis of legal education. Nor was that all. It also became, and still in some measure is, a basis of decision in the courts, where his name may still be heard and judges may still fortify their decisions by his authority.[2] It is a curious testimony to his contemporary vogue that one Sir J. Eardley-Wilmot, anticipating the spirit of Mr. Bernard Shaw's *The Intelligent Woman's Guide to Socialism*, should have used the *Commentaries* as the basis of what we may call the intelligent woman's guide to law, in the form of 'an Abridgment intended for the use of young persons and comprised in a series of letters from a father to his daughter'.

We must remember—for it is a fact of cardinal importance—that the vogue of the *Commentaries* was common to both sides of

---

[1] See below, pp. 133-4.
[2] Holdsworth (*The History of English Law*, xii. 716-17) speaks of 'the respect shown to the book by Blackstone's successors on the bench', and cites two cases of the year 1935 which testify to the authority of the *Commentaries*.

the Atlantic. Burke, in his speech of 1775 on Conciliation with America, remarking that 'in no country perhaps in the world is the law so general a study', and adding that 'the greater number of the deputies sent to the [continental] congress were lawyers', told the House of Commons, 'I hear that they have sold nearly as many of Blackstone's *Commentaries* in America as in England'.[1] The influence of Blackstone in America was an abiding influence. His book suggested to the American jurist Kent the idea of his *Commentaries in American Law* (1826-30). In America as in England—but in America even more than in England—it helped to shape the course of legal education and to encourage the university teaching of English law. This was an influence which was all to the good—an influence which, as it has been justly said, helped to maintain connexion between England and America.[2] But there is another and a more immediate aspect of Blackstone's influence on Anglo-American relations; and when we look at this aspect, it is natural to feel some qualms about the effects of his influence. His *Commentaries* were a contribution (unintended, indeed, but none the less actual and real) to the great debate which was just beginning to be engaged between the mother country and the North American colonists. We have to remember that Blackstone's first volume was published in 1765, just at the moment when troubles were beginning to rise: we have to remember that all the four volumes were reprinted in Philadelphia in 1771, when the troubles were coming to a head. James Otis, Samuel Adams, and John Adams all knew Blackstone's work: it gave to the American lawyers, who were the backbone of resistance and the core of the colonial assemblies, their general idea of the English point of view, in matters political and legal, at the crucial hour of the struggle. Unfortunately, and in spite of all his merits, Blackstone sometimes nodded; and his book was hardly an ideal exposition of English political ideas in the particular contingency, and for the peculiar conjunction of affairs, in which it was actually used.

We are thus led to consider the defects of the *Commentaries* at the particular time at which they appeared, and in terms of the

---

[1] Holdsworth (op. cit. xii. 712 n. 5) quotes an estimate, from the introduction to Hammond's American edition of the *Commentaries*, that nearly 2,500 copies had been sold in the thirteen colonies before the Declaration of Independence.

[2] Holdsworth, op. cit. xii. 726.

contribution they made (or failed to make) to Anglo-American understanding at that particular time. There are reasons why we may regret that Blackstone should have been the spokesman of English law, and therein and thereby of the English constitution, at such a crucial hour. Law is a great and sovereign study; but it is necessarily limited in scope, and necessarily litigious in temper. (*Lex* and *Lis* are always yokefellows.) It was perhaps a pity, in any case, that lawyers should have been so largely and deeply concerned, on both sides, in the struggle between Great Britain and the American colonies; but it was almost certainly a pity that a lawyer of Blackstone's character should have been the voice of England to American lawyers at that time. It did not matter that he had not a great or creative mind. A more original thinker might well have been a worse expositor. It did matter that he was unphilosophical, and that, in more than one passage, he showed himself also illiberal.

His want of philosophical grasp is apparent in the second section of his Introduction, which bears the title 'Of the Nature of Laws in General'. It is a confused mish-mash of Locke and Montesquieu with writers of the school of natural law such as Pufendorf and Burlamaqui.[1] It contradicted, as we shall have reason to notice presently, his own general theory; it helped to furnish American lawyers with natural-law arguments for resistance; and its chief merit is the negative merit of having produced, by way of reaction, the analytical school of English jurisprudence represented by Bentham and Austin.[2] But it is Blackstone's lack of liberalism which matters more than his lack of philosophy. In part his illiberalism—or what seemed to Americans to be his illiberalism—was inevitable and involuntary. He was a lawyer. He was stating the legal theory of the constitution. This is the purpose of the third and fourth sections

---

[1] Van Tyne, *The Causes of the War of Independence*, p. 237, asks with some surprise, 'What did Christopher Gadsden [of South Carolina] mean by allusion to those "latent though inherent rights of society, which no climate, no time, no constitution, no contract, can ever destroy or diminish"? To a mind that venerated the Constitution such ideas were poisonous.' The answer is that Gadsden was quoting Blackstone, or rather paraphrasing Blackstone (i. 54, and i. 245), in that part of his book where, as we shall see later, Blackstone himself was quoting, or rather paraphrasing, Burlamaqui: see below, p. 137, n. 4.

[2] The foundation of that school may be said to be Bentham's *Fragment on Government*. This is a searching analysis of seven pages—out of a total of twenty-four—in the peccant second section of Blackstone's Introduction (pp. 47–53 inclusive).

of his introduction, which deal with 'the Laws of England and the Countries subject to the Laws of England'; it is the purpose of the various chapters of his first book which deal with Parliament, the King, 'the civil State', and 'the military and maritime States'. The legal theory which he was stating vested the King with powers which he did not exercise in fact, but which had none the less to be stated as facts of English law. It is the penalty of a progressive constitution that legal facts do not square with political realities; and Dicey remarked long ago, in the first chapter of his *Law of the Constitution*, that 'the terms used by the commentator were, when he used them, unreal, and known to be so'. But if their unreality was known in England, the case was different in America; and Americans, with Blackstone's book before them, might be pardoned if they failed to see that its statement of legal facts was an unreal picture of political realities. The involuntary illiberalism of Blackstone was an unintended disservice to Anglo-American understanding.

But his illiberalism was also in some measure voluntary. A member of the established Church, and a beneficiary of the established political system of rotten boroughs, he did not escape partiality. Two examples may suffice to show his lapses. The first concerns his attitude to Dissent. In the first edition of his *Commentaries* he had spoken of it in terms which he was forced by the criticisms of Priestley and Furneaux to modify in later editions; but even his modification could still be criticized as failing to give a wholly correct account of the nature and the position of dissenting bodies.[1] The second example, which concerns his attitude to parliamentary representation, is in one respect the converse of the first. It shows Blackstone more of a liberal in his first edition than he was in the later editions. In his first edition, treating of the incapacities which disabled men from sitting in Parliament, he had mentioned only three. Men must not be minors; they must not be persons unwilling to take the oaths of allegiance, supremacy, and abjuration, and to subscribe the declaration against transubstantiation; they must not be aliens. A few years after the publication of the first volume of the *Commentaries*, events occurred, in the course of 1769, which induced Blackstone to extend his conception of these incapacities, and to add a new sentence to his text. The history of these

[1] Holdsworth, op. cit. xii. 713-14.

events is curious. In 1764 John Wilkes, being then member for Aylesbury, had been expelled from the House of Commons for the 'scandalous and seditious libel' of a violent attack on the King's speech, contained in No. 45 of his periodical *The North Briton*. In March 1768 he stood again as a candidate for the county of Middlesex, and was elected. The shadow of his previous offences[1] and expulsion hung over him; but, undaunted, he challenged the government in a violent letter, published in the *St. James's Chronicle* at the end of 1768, in which he charged the ministers with responsibility for bloodshed in the riots which had followed his election. The result was that, in February 1769, a motion was brought before the House for the expulsion of Wilkes for his previous offences and for the new offence of his recent letter. During the debate on the motion, George Grenville cited the authority of Blackstone in favour of Wilkes, arguing that the only incapacities which disabled a man from sitting in Parliament were the three which had been stated in his *Commentaries*, and that none of them affected Wilkes. Blackstone was sitting in his place during Grenville's speech: there was a pause of some moments when Grenville sat down, in the expectation that he would speak; he was silent. But in later editions of the *Commentaries* a new sentence was added, after the statement of the three incapacities which alone had been stated in the early editions: 'And there are not only these standing incapacities; but if any person is made a peer by the King, or elected to serve in the House of Commons by the people, yet may the respective Houses upon complaint of any person, and proof thereof, adjudge him disabled and incapable to sit as a member; and this by the law and custom of parliament.' Blackstone's view of 'the law and custom' had evidently grown. No wonder that the more liberal Whigs afterwards made 'The first edition of Dr. Blackstone's *Commentaries* on the Laws of England' one of their toasts.

But it would be unjust to depict Blackstone as wholly conservative, or to pay an exclusive attention to the illiberalism which he occasionally showed. A man who was influenced and stimulated by the great Lord Mansfield, as he was, could not

[1] Besides the offence of 'sedition' held to be involved in the matter published in No. 45 of *The North Briton*, Wilkes had also been charged with the offence of 'blasphemy' (accompanied by obscenity) in *An Essay on Women* which parodied Pope's famous *Essay on Man*—and parodied also, in its notes, Bishop Warburton's notes on Pope's *Essay*.

be wholly conservative. A man who could champion, as he did, the cause of the University teaching of law—in itself a reform, and its consequences likely to liberalize and even revolutionize the law[1]—could not be altogether illiberal. In a number of respects he showed himself zealous, and in some he was even active, for the reform of the law. He criticizes in his *Commentaries* the severity of English criminal law and the excessive frequency of capital punishment: he regarded the barbarities of his own day as inferior to the method of imprisonment in penitentiary houses; and he helped Lord Auckland (the author of *Principles of Penal Law*) in the passage of an Act introducing reforms in the system of punishment, in the year 1779.[2] He criticized the game laws, 'which have raised a little Nimrod in every manor': he criticized also the poor laws, as 'very imperfect, and inadequate to the purposes they are designed for'. But Blackstone may also be defended upon a more general ground, which he has himself suggested.

In a notable passage of the second chapter of his first book[3] he deals with the qualifications of electors and the state of the suffrage. He suggests that the constitution steers between the two extremes of 'numbers' and 'property'. On the one hand 'there is hardly a free agent to be found, but what is entitled to a vote in some place or other'. On the other hand, 'though the richest man has only one vote at one place, yet, if his property be at all diffused, he has probably a right to vote at more places than one'. All would thus seem to be for the best; but he proceeds to add a qualification. 'This is the spirit of our constitution: not that I assert it is in fact quite so perfect as I have here endeavoured to describe it; for, if any alteration might be wished or suggested in the present frame of parliament, it should be in

[1] Blackstone himself makes this point in the first section of his Introduction, 'On the Study of Law' (i. p. 30).

[2] See iv. 371–3 in the later editions. The effect of the reforms introduced by the Act was that offenders liable to transportation might in lieu thereof, at the discretion of the judges, (1) be employed, if males, in hard labour for the benefit of some public navigation, or (2) be confined, whether males or females, to hard labour in certain penitentiary houses, where proper care might be taken both of their health and their morals. 'And if the whole of this plan be properly executed', Blackstone suggests, 'there is reason to hope that such a reformation may be effected in the lower classes of mankind . . . as may in time supersede the necessity of capital punishment, except for very serious crimes.' It may be said that the Act of 1779 entitles Blackstone to rank as one of the forerunners of Romilly.

[3] i. 171–2.

favour of a more complete representation of the people.' Here Blackstone stopped in the earlier editions. But in the later editions he adds a curious and characteristic footnote, explaining and developing the first part of the sentence which has just been quoted:

'The candid and intelligent reader will apply this observation [that the suffrage is less perfect than it is described as being] to many other parts of the work before him, wherein the constitution of our laws and government is represented as nearly approaching perfection, without descending to the invidious task of pointing out such deviations and corruptions as length of time, and a loose state of national morals, have too great a tendency to produce. The incurvations of practice are then the most notorious, when compared with the rectitude of the rule; and to elucidate the clearness of the spring conveys the strongest satire upon those who have polluted or disturbed it.'

Were Blackstone's *Commentaries* intended, then, as a 'satire'? Hardly. This is an *ex post facto* justification, which must not be taken too seriously. The truth is that Blackstone was in a dilemma. As a lawyer, he felt bound to think English law and the English constitution perfect. As a man, he knew that they were not. He wrote as a lawyer in his text: he hedged as a man in a footnote, and that in a later edition. The lawyer triumphed over the man. There are, indeed, some occasional signs of struggle; but on the whole the perfection which is the ideal of English law is for Blackstone also its actual and living reality. Under English law, he remarks (at the end of the first chapter of his first book), 'all of us have it in our choice to do everything that a good man would desire to do, and are restrained from nothing, but what would be pernicious either to ourselves or our fellow-citizens';[1] and he is moved to echo 'the expiring wish of the famous father Paul to his country, Esto Perpetua'. Nor was it only the law of his own time, and of the year 1765 (the year of the publication of his first volume), which he was ready to idealize. He went even further: he was inclined to believe that English law had attained its zenith a century before his time.

[1] Blackstone is here referring to Montesquieu: 'Dans un état, c'est-à-dire dans une société où il y a des lois, la liberté ne peut consister qu'à pouvoir faire ce que l'on doit vouloir, et à n'être point contraint de faire ce que l'on ne doit pas vouloir' (*L'Esprit des Lois*, xi. 3). Father Paul is Paolo Sarpi, the Venetian patriot, who died in 1623.

Perfection came in the reign of Charles II: it came in the year 1679. This may seem a curious reign and a curious date to choose. An ardent Whig might naturally interject, 'But what of the year 1688?'—which, by the way, would be for him, too, a date of perfection; but then a good deal had happened, as a Whig might naturally urge, between 1679 and 1688. Blackstone had an answer ready for any ardent Whig 'You are forgetting, Sir,' he would say (if one may paraphrase his argument, as it is advanced in the last chapter of his *Commentaries*)—'you are forgetting the great reforms which were quietly achieved by the lawyers in the reign of Charles II'. For 'though the monarch'—and here Blackstone himself is speaking in his own opulent style—'deserves no commendation from posterity, yet in his reign (wicked, sanguinary, and turbulent as it was) the concurrence of happy circumstances was such that from thence we may date ... the complete restitution of English liberty, for the first time, since its total abolition at the conquest'. The slavery of military tenures was abolished, and 'that great bulwark of our constitution', the Habeas Corpus Act, was passed. Add the statute for holding triennial Parliaments: add the abolition of the writ *de haeretico comburendo*: add the statute of frauds, 'a great and necessary security to private property'—'and the whole, when we likewise consider the freedom from taxes and armies which the subject then enjoyed, will be sufficient to demonstrate this truth', that

'the constitution of England had arrived to its full vigour, and the true balance between liberty and prerogative was happily established by *law*; in the reign of King Charles the Second'.

The merry monarch who 'deserves no commendation from posterity', but whose reign receives so warm a eulogy at Blackstone's hands, would perhaps have smiled, in his 'wicked' way, and might even have bowed, in polite acknowledgement of this celebration of the perfections of 1679.[1]

[1] One word in italics, in a footnote (iv. 432), might perhaps have been displeasing to Charles II: 'The point of time at which I would choose to fix this *theoretical* perfection of our public law, is the year 1679; after the Habeas Corpus Act was passed, and that for licensing the press had expired.' (Incidentally, the licensing act was indeed allowed to expire in 1679, but was renewed in 1685 and only finally expired in 1695.) The whole argument is expounded in iv. 431-2; cf. also iv. 49.

III

FROM the method and spirit of Blackstone's exposition we may now turn to consider its substance. What is his general conception of the nature of law? What is his view of the nature of public or constitutional law? Finally, what is his conception of the constitutional relations between Great Britain and the British colonies?

1. The propositions enunciated by Blackstone 'on the nature of laws in general' in the second section of his introduction need little examination. They made Bentham fret and fume, and they produced his *Fragment on Government*. But were they worth his powder and shot? They certainly suffered from three defects. In the first place, they were not original. They were borrowed from continental jurists of the school of natural law, and particularly from Burlamaqui, a Swiss scholar who had published his *Principes du Droit Naturel* in 1747, and whose book had been translated into English in 1748.[1] Secondly, his propositions are confused and contradictory, considered in themselves. Thirdly, they do not square with the rules and principles of English law which he states in the subsequent text of the *Commentaries*. One example may suffice to show both the internal contradiction of the propositions which Blackstone enunciates in this second section, and their contradiction by the subsequent text of the *Commentaries*.

In the course of his argument 'on the nature of laws in general' Blackstone enunciates the proposition that 'there is and must be in all [forms of government] a supreme, irresistible, absolute, uncontrolled authority, in which the *jura summi imperii*, or the

[1] Blackstone, lecturing at Oxford as Professor from 1758 to 1766, might have used Wolff's *Jus naturae* (Frankfort, 1740-8), or Vattel's *Le Droit des gens ou principes de la loi naturelle*, a work interpreting and adapting Wolff's *Jus naturae*, which was published in London and Leyden in 1758, and appeared in an English translation in London in 1759. Actually, he used the earlier and inferior work of Burlamaqui, and that in an English translation. The fact was noted by G. P. Macdonell, in his article on Blackstone in the *Dictionary of National Biography*. It is curious that Blackstone makes no acknowledgement of his debt, and that Bentham, his critic, should have been unaware that he was really criticizing an unacknowledged original. But the duty of acknowledgement was less keenly felt in Blackstone's day than it is now; and while he gives three references to Pufendorf, two to Locke, and one to Grotius, he mentions no other modern authority in the second section of his introduction.

There is a curious sentence, by the way, about Burlamaqui's *Principes du Droit Naturel* in the *Biographie Universelle*. 'Cet ouvrage a longtemps servi de texte aux leçons des professeurs de Cambridge.' Remembering Blackstone's use of the work, one is tempted to substitute 'Oxford' for 'Cambridge'.

rights of sovereignty, reside'.[1] This is a drastic proposition. But it has just been preceded, and it is almost immediately succeeded, by a proposition as drastic, but exactly contradictory. The preceding proposition declares that there is a 'law of nature, coeval with mankind', which 'is of course superior in obligation to any other: . . . no human laws are of any validity if contrary to this; and such of them as are valid derive all their force and their authority . . . from this original'.[2] The succeeding proposition states that there are natural rights, such as life and liberty, which 'need not the aid of human laws to be more effectually in every man than they are', and which 'no human legislature has power to abridge or destroy'.[3] It would pass the wit of any philosopher to reconcile a supreme, irresistible, absolute, and uncontrolled sovereignty with a controlling system of natural law and an absolute system of natural rights. In this second section of his introduction Blackstone succeeds in enunciating diametrically opposite propositions; and the reader may, at his choice, take either the doctrine of sovereignty which was pressed by George III and the British Parliament against the cause of the American colonists, or the doctrine of natural law, and of natural rights to life, liberty, and happiness, which was pressed by Jefferson against Great Britain in the Declaration of Independence.

If we had only the second section of the introduction on which to go, we should be left wandering in chaos and dark night. Fortunately, Blackstone sheds some new light on the issues he has here raised in a later section of the introduction to the *Commentaries*, where he is discussing the laws of England. It is a light which is fatal to any idea of a controlling system of natural law or an absolute system of natural rights. Any such idea, we now discover, is contradicted not only by the general doctrine of sovereignty, but also by the rules and practice of English law.

---

[1] i. 49.

[2] i. 41. This natural law is identified by Blackstone with ethics; and 'the foundation of what we call ethics, or natural law', is declared to be the one precept 'that man should pursue his own happiness'. He thus combines an unreflective system of utilitarian ethics with an unreflective devotion to a system of natural law. Bentham, who dismissed natural law (along with natural rights and the original contract) as a fiction and a rattle for the amusement of children, and concentrated his efforts on building a reflective system of utilitarian ethics, was naturally disgusted by Blackstone's easy-going philosophy, which muddled what he distinguished and confounded shadow with substance.

[3] i. 54.

When Blackstone leaves the *apices juris naturalis* (which are only, after all, in the nature of a theatrical background to his real argument), and gets down to the sober business of the laws of England, he does plain homage to the sovereignty of the British parliament. 'I know it is generally laid down that acts of parliament contrary to reason are void. But if the parliament will positively enact a thing to be done which is unreasonable, I know of no power that can control it.' He can find no example in English law which proves that the judges are able to reject a statute of which the main object is unreasonable: 'that were to set the judicial power above that of the legislature, which would be subversive of all government'.[1] There is thus no power of judicial review which can enforce 'the eternal, immutable laws . . . which the creator has enabled human reason to discover';[2] and though 'no human laws are of any validity if contrary to these',[3] no human power can disallow the validity of human laws which are actually contrary. The theatrical background remains a mere background.[4]

2. Blackstone's view of the nature of public or constitutional law is to be found in the third and fourth sections of his introduction, and, more particularly, in the first book of his *Commentaries*. It starts (and this is singularly English, and illustrative of the genius of English law) from the conception of rights—individual rights—the rights of individual Englishmen. Public law is simply and naturally regarded as a system or series of rights belonging to individual men, or bodies of individual men, when they act in a political capacity; and it merges easily and

---

[1] i. 91. [2] i. 40. [3] i. 41.
[4] It is, of course, possible that though there cannot be judicial review or judicial disallowance of unreasonable laws, there may be another way—the way of civic resistance. That way had been taken in 1688; and Blackstone, in a cautious passage (i. 245), alludes to the experience of 1688. 'So far as this precedent leads, and no farther, we may now be allowed to lay down the law of redress against public oppression.' The law which Blackstone lays down is that if all the three circumstances of 1688 recur—a subversion of the constitution by breach of the original contract; a violation of the fundamental laws; and a withdrawing of the King out of the kingdom—this conjunction of the three circumstances would amount to an abdication. But what if all three are not present? Then, Blackstone replies, 'since both law and history are silent, it becomes us to be silent too, leaving to future generations . . . the exertion of those inherent (though latent) powers of society, which no climate, no time, no constitution, no contract, can ever destroy or diminish'. Civic resistance is not here absolutely dismissed; but it is left—except in one particular conjunction of circumstances—'to future generations'.

readily (indeed, there can hardly be said to be any difference between the one and the other) into the private law which forms the system or series of rights belonging to individuals, or bodies of individuals, when they act in a private capacity. The arrangement of the first book of the *Commentaries* is significant. It is entitled, 'Of the Rights of Persons'. It begins with a first chapter, 'Of the Absolute Rights of Individuals'. It proceeds with thirteen chapters (II–XIV) which deal, first with the Parliament; next with the King, his family, his councils, his duties, his prerogatives, his revenue, and his subordinate magistrates; and after that with the People, both as divided into aliens and natural born subjects, and as divided into clergy, civilians, soldiers, and sailors. To these thirteen chapters—which may be styled, though they are not so styled by Blackstone, the chapters of public law— there succeed immediately, and with no mark of distinction or division, five final chapters of private law (master and servant, husband and wife, parent and child, guardian and ward, and corporations) which complete the book. It is all a matter of rights, and of the rights of persons; and it all starts with 'the absolute rights of individuals'.

This line of approach, or scheme of arrangement, was natural to a lawyer of Blackstone's time. Blackstone himself combined it, as we have already had reason to notice, with some measure of illiberalism. But in itself, and in its own nature, it is fundamentally liberal. Rights of nature may not be in question: indeed, they cease to be mentioned when Blackstone warms to his work. The rights of Englishmen, however, are always and everywhere present. They are not only the foundation: they are the very stones of the building. We can understand, as we reflect on this fact, why Blackstone, in his inaugural lecture of 1758, had spoken of 'a land, perhaps the only one in the universe, in which political or civil liberty is the very end and scope of the constitution'.[1] We can understand why he should repeat, in the first chapter of his first book, when it was published in 1765, that 'the idea and practice of this political or civil liberty flourish in their highest vigour in those kingdoms, where it falls little short of perfection ... the legislature, and of course the laws, of England being peculiarly adapted to the preservation of this inestimable blessing even in the meanest subject'.[2] We can understand,

[1] i. 6. [2] i. 126–7.

finally, why he should hold that these rights and liberties 'were formerly ... the rights of all mankind, but, in most countries of the world being now more or less debased or destroyed, they at present may be said to remain, in a peculiar and emphatical manner, the rights of the people of England'.[1]

The rights which constitute 'political or civil liberty' may be reduced, in Blackstone's view, 'to three principal or primary articles: the right of personal security, the right of personal liberty, and the right of private property'.[2] These rights are English birthrights, enshrined in English law. There is thus no contrast for Blackstone between liberty and law. They are related to one another as the hand is to the glove. 'The first and primary end of human laws is to maintain and regulate these absolute rights of individuals.'[3] By regulating rights law is already 'introductive of liberty'. But rights have to be maintained, as well as regulated; and liberty has to be preserved, as well as introduced. We have thus to remember that '*that* constitution or frame of government, *that* system of laws, is alone calculated to maintain civil liberty, which leaves the subject entire master of his own conduct, except in those points wherein the public good requires some direction or restraint'.[4] A particular system of laws, a peculiar constitution or frame of government, is therefore essential to the preservation of liberty and the maintenance of rights. Blackstone's general argument is directed to prove that England possesses this particular system, this peculiar constitution or frame, and possesses it in three ways.

The first way is that of declarations of rights. 'Fundamental articles'—the three principal or primary articles of personal security, personal liberty, and private property—'have been from time to time asserted in parliament, as often as they were thought to be in danger.' When the Virginia Convention issued the Virginia Bill of Rights on 12 June 1776, and the thirteen United States of America issued their unanimous declaration of

---

[1] i. 129.
[2] In the Declaration of Independence these become the rights of life, liberty, and the pursuit of happiness.
[3] i. 124.
[4] i. 126. It is to be noticed that Blackstone, true to the genius of English law, makes no distinction between 'the constitution or frame of government' and 'the system of laws'. In America, beginning with the colonial constitution of 1776, that distinction is always drawn.

independence on 4 July of the same year, they were following an old way already described by Blackstone. He recites, in the first chapter of his first book, 'the great charter of liberties . . . for the most part *declaratory* of the principal grounds of the fundamental laws of England'; he recites 'the petition of right . . . a parliamentary *declaration* of the liberties of the people'; he recites 'the bill of rights, or *declaration*', with its claim of 'undoubted rights and liberties'; he recites 'the act of settlement, whereby . . . some new provisions were added . . . for better securing our religion, laws, and liberties, which the statute *declares* to be "the birthright of the people of England", according to the antient doctrine of the common law'.[1] The American declarations of 1776 were thus calculated on a precedent, and based on an ancient doctrine, which Blackstone himself had just described eleven years earlier. Not to make the new, but to declare the old, and to corroborate it by such declaration—this has been the general method of English-speaking peoples.

The second way is that of the common law, regarded as the product of custom and immemorial tradition. This whole body of law protects by its action, and defends by its remedies, the rights and liberties inherent in itself, and rooted in its own customary nature—rights and liberties which have indeed been declared in Parliament, and fortified by such declaration, but which are anterior, because they are birthrights, to any act of declaration. It is perhaps upon this account, Blackstone suggests, that in the course of time 'the free constitution of England has been rather improved than debased': it is perhaps on the opposite account, and owing to the victory of Roman law, that 'states on the continent . . . have lost . . . their political liberties'.[2] Depending as it does on custom, common law 'carries this internal evidence of freedom along with it, that it probably was introduced by the voluntary consent of the people'.[3] The people thus made it; and they naturally made it for the protection of their own birthright. It is the true safeguard of their rights. Statutes, or enacted laws, are in comparison of less importance. A fate of imperfection and inadequacy 'has generally attended most of our statute laws, when they have not the foundation of the common law to build on'.[4] The poor-laws are cited by

[1] i. 127–8.
[2] i. 67 (the third section of the introduction).
[3] i. 74.
[4] i. 365.

Blackstone as an example of this fate. But he makes a further and still more sweeping criticism of statute law. Imperfect as it is when it builds without any foundation of common law, it is even more imperfect when it innovates rashly upon that foundation. 'To say the truth, almost all the perplexed questions, almost all the niceties, intricacies, and delays (which have sometimes disgraced the English, as well as other courts of justice) owe their origin not to the common law itself, but to innovations that have been made in it by acts of parliament.'[1] Here speaks Blackstone the common lawyer, and here he speaks from the heart. It was here, in particular, that he was challenged by Bentham as the would-be legislator or censor, who desired a code of enacted law to introduce lucidity and the light of a principle into what he regarded as the dark jungle of the common law.

The third way in which England may be said to possess a particular system and a peculiar frame is the way of the rules of the constitution. These rules are enshrined in, and are part of, the common law; and therefore, though we may describe it separately, the way of the rules of the constitution is only a part, or example, of the general way of the common law. The logic of Blackstone's method in describing the rules of the constitution is significant. Having declared the three principal or primary rights of security, liberty, and property, he proceeds to declare 'certain other auxiliary subordinate rights of the subject, which serve principally as barriers to protect and maintain inviolate the three great and primary rights'. These auxiliary, subordinate rights of the subject are five in number. The first is the constitution of Parliament, and its powers and privileges, which thus appear as a right of the subject, and not as an organ or as powers of the state. The second is the limitation of the King's prerogative; and here again, by virtue of the word 'limitation', the executive itself appears in the guise of a right of the subject. The third is the right of applying to the courts of justice for redress of injuries—a right which makes the judicature, like the Parliament and the executive, a right enjoyed by the subject. The fourth is the right of every individual to petition the King, or either House of Parliament, for redress of grievances in any matter which the ordinary course of the law is too defective to reach. Here, and in this right of petition, the people enters in

[1] i. 10.

person, by the side of Parliament, the executive, and the judicature. It enters again in the fifth and last right, 'that of having arms for their defence, suitable to their condition and degree, and such as are allowed by law . . ., a publick allowance, under due restrictions, of the natural right of resistance . . .'.[1]

It is these five auxiliary subordinate rights which essentially form the English constitution; and it is in describing them in detail that Blackstone describes that constitution. The constitution is for him a body of rights belonging to the subject, and vested in the subject. Its 'fundamental articles' are recited in a chapter which is headed 'Of the absolute rights of individuals'. Its animating spirit is that of 'the antient doctrine' of the common law about the rights of the subject. It is not the state, or the sovereignty of the state, or the rights and duties of the state, which make the constitution, form its articles, and determine its spirit. It is the subject and his liberties—more especially those 'auxiliary subordinate' liberties which serve as barriers to protect the original and principal reservoir of his three primary liberties. In the whole of this general approach Blackstone is fundamentally true to the English genius; and the lawyers of our century still echo the lawyer of the eighteenth. Dicey may criticize Blackstone; but he also repeats his teaching. 'In England the so-called principles of the constitution are inductions or generalisations based upon particular decisions pronounced by the Courts as to the rights of given individuals.' Or again, 'With us the law of the constitution . . . is not the source, but the consequence, of the rights of individuals, as defined by the Courts; . . . in short, the principles of private law have with us been, by the action of the Courts and Parliament, so extended as to determine the action of the Crown and its servants; thus the constitution is the result of the ordinary law of the land.'[2]

We may now turn from this summary of Blackstone's general view of the constitution, as a body or sum of the rights of the subject, to the account which he gives of the mutual relations of Parliament, the King, and the courts of justice—the three institutions which form the bases, as we have already seen, of the first three 'auxiliary subordinate rights of the subject'. Speaking in the terms generally current in his century, he enunciates two

---

[1] i. 140–5. On 'the natural right of resistance' see above, p. 137, n. 4.
[2] Dicey, *Law of the Constitution*, c. iv, pp. 193, 199 (8th edition).

propositions. The first proposition—which relates, in the main, to Parliament—is that the British constitution is singular, and a standing exception, in being a mixed constitution, which combines the three types of monarchy, aristocracy, and democracy. The executive power of the law is lodged in the single person of a monarch, who is also a part of the legislature; the lords spiritual and temporal are an aristocratic assembly; the House of Commons, 'freely chosen by the people from among themselves', is a kind of democracy. This monarch, these lords, and this House of Commons, form one aggregate body, composing the British Parliament; and 'here there is lodged the sovereignty of the British constitution, and lodged as beneficially as is possible for society'.[1] The second proposition—which relates to all the three institutions—is that the British constitution is marked by a separation of powers. The legislative power is vested in the aggregate body of Parliament: the executive power is vested independently in the King (Blackstone, writing in formal terms, has naturally nothing to say of the informal institution of the cabinet, which was already beginning to make the executive power of the King's ministers actually dependent on Parliament): the judicial power has a distinct and separate existence, and 'the administration of common justice is in some degree separated both from the legislative and also from the executive power'.[2]

These two propositions were the commonplaces of Blackstone's age. But their enunciation, and more especially the enunciation of the second, involves him in difficulties, and even in contradictions. One may speak of separation, but it is also necessary to speak of sovereignty; and if one has started from the doctrine of separation of powers, it will not be easy to reconcile that doctrine of separation with any doctrine of sovereignty which may subsequently be stated. Blackstone can hardly be said to make the attempt. He leaves separation of powers and the sovereignty of Parliament in two watertight compartments. The two doctrines are not only left unreconciled: they are also left unrelated. Nor is his doctrine of sovereignty, taken by itself, consistent with itself.[3] On the one hand, he lodges sovereignty

---

[1] i. 50–1. [2] i. 269.
[3] See above, pp. 135–6, on the inconsistency which may also be traced between his general doctrine of sovereignty (in the second section of his introduction) and his general view of natural law.

in the hands of Parliament. 'It hath sovereign and uncontrollable authority in making ... of laws concerning matters of all possible denominations ... this being the place where that absolute despotic power, which must in all governments reside somewhere, is entrusted by the constitution of these kingdoms.'[1] On the other hand, he also lodges sovereignty in the hands of the King. This he does in the course of his chapter 'Of the King's Prerogative'. Distinguishing the three various kinds of prerogative, he notices principally two—the royal character, or prerogative considered as dignity, and the royal authority, or prerogative considered as power. (The third kind, which is the royal income, or prerogative considered as revenue, he leaves to a later chapter.) Both of these kinds of prerogative—both dignity and power—are connected by Blackstone with sovereignty. In virtue of his dignity, 'the law ascribes to the king the attribute of sovereignty'.[2] In virtue of his power, 'I lay it down as a principle that, in the exertion of lawful prerogative, the king is and ought to be absolute; ... in the exertion, therefore, of those prerogatives which the law has given him, the king is irresistible and absolute, according to the forms of the constitution'.[3] This is a notable proposition. It is true that it is qualified. This absolute power is a matter of 'the forms of the constitution': and beyond those forms there are 'extraordinary recourses to first principles', on the model of the Revolution of 1688. And yet, 'obedience cannot be maintained ... without obedience to some sovereign power', and 'the absolute sovereignty and transcendent dominion of the Crown' is certainly 'laid down ... most strongly and emphatically in our law-books'.[4]

How can the sovereign and uncontrollable authority of Parliament be reconciled with the irresistible and absolute exertion of prerogative? That is a question which Blackstone hardly stays to answer; and indeed it was a question which, if he was content to write purely as a lawyer, and with a strict respect to 'the forms of the constitution', he was hardly able to answer. He might have replied that the sovereignty of Parliament was exerted only in the making of laws, and that the sovereignty of the prerogative—the lawful prerogative, as defined in and by the common law and the great declarations which he had previously recited—was a matter only of what he calls 'the executive

[1] i. 169.   [2] i. 241.   [3] i. 250, 251.   [4] i. 251.

power of the law'. But the distinction or separation involved in such a reply is a distinction which collapses in the very act of being stated. The prerogative, as it is expounded by Blackstone, is not merely an executive power. It is also legislative; indeed, it is also judicial. Separation is overwhelmed by the general and inclusive sovereignty of the prerogative. In the legislative sphere, we are told, the King, as a constituent part of the supreme legislative power, 'has the prerogative of rejecting such provisions in parliament as he judges improper to be passed'.[1] In the judicial sphere, it is part of the prerogative that 'he . . . has alone the right of erecting courts of judicature'.[2] Indeed, the power of the prerogative bulks so largely, when Blackstone proceeds to state its specific attributes, that it seems to bestride the world. It has five principal attributes in the regulation of intercourse with foreign nations: it has as many as six in the conduct of domestic affairs—and these six include commerce and religion as well as the rejection of 'provisions in parliament' and the erection of courts of judicature. Blackstone's American readers, already imbued in the years before 1770 with ideas of separation rather than of sovereignty, and destined to push such ideas to further and larger consequences in 1787, may well have felt that he harped too much on sovereignties, supremacies, and prerogatives. He may have been only displaying the somewhat antiquated treasures of the museum of English law. But how were they to know that that was all he was doing? And did he know it himself? Or did he think that he was explaining the actual practice of his own day? If he did, he was sadly mistaken. Practice—the practice, for example, of the King's ministers in their relations to Parliament, or the practice of Parliament itself, as expressed in its standing orders[3]—is left all too little regarded.

But it would be an error, and an injustice, to depict Blackstone as a votary of the prerogative of the Crown. (He was a votary of confusion of ideas rather than of one idea.) At least three passages in his *Commentaries* may be cited to the contrary.

---

[1] i. 261. Actually, the royal 'veto' had not been used for sixty years when Blackstone wrote.

[2] Here Blackstone, as Holdsworth notes (xi. 265), was hardly correct.

[3] The standing orders of the House of Commons, of which Blackstone was a member, may well be argued to be an important part of the constitution. Three of the most vital standing orders relative to public business date back to the years 1707, 1713, and 1715.

In the chapter 'Of the King's Duties', which precedes the chapter 'Of the King's Prerogative', he argues that the king is limited by the terms of his contract with the people—terms 'now couched in the Coronation oath', as settled in 1689, and forming 'most indisputably a fundamental and original express contract'.[1] In another passage, which comes in the beginning of his chapter on the prerogative, and serves to qualify the sovereignty assigned to the king in virtue of the dignity of his royal character, he argues, as has already been noted,[2] in favour of a right of civic resistance to 'such public oppressions as tend to dissolve the constitution and subvert the fundamentals of government'. In developing this argument he contends that the precedent of 1688 supplies 'a law of redress', and proves a legal right of resistance, in any future conjuncture of circumstances which is exactly parallel; but for the rest, and in any different conjuncture, he would seem to hold that the right of resistance is an *extra-legal* right ('the exertion of . . . inherent though latent powers of society'), and he declines, as a lawyer naturally would, to say what sort of conjuncture may justify in the future the assertion of such a right. Finally, in the chapter 'Of the King's Revenue', which succeeds his chapter on the prerogative, he condescends upon some important particulars of recent constitutional development which seem to him dubious. He suggests that the Crown has latterly gained an adventitious power through the great increase of taxation, the consequent rise of a multitude of new officers concerned with the collection and management of the revenue, and the consequent extension of the influence or 'persuasive energy' of the executive power to every corner of the nation.[3] He speaks of the matter with a guarded restraint; but even in his discreet pages a hope is expressed that with the gradual reduction of taxes 'this adventitious power of the Crown will slowly and imperceptibly diminish'. Reflecting that issues of taxation were already beginning to divide Great Britain from North America, we can readily guess how any American, reading these pages, might inquire, 'Why should we give taxes to the Crown to increase its adventitious power, to extend its patronage, and to enable it to bring both the British parliament and our own assemblies more under the sway of its persuasive energy?'

[1] i. 234, 236.   [2] *Supra*, p. 137, n. 4.   [3] i. 334–7.

3. We are thus brought, in conclusion, to a consideration of Blackstone's view of the constitutional relations between Great Britain and the American colonies. He does not use the word, or entertain the idea, of Empire, as Burke in his speeches is already beginning to do. He has no conception of an imperial commonwealth. It is significant that he states his view of the relations between Great Britain and the American colonies in a section of his introduction (and only there) which is entitled 'Of the Countries subject to the laws of England'. He is concerned only to examine how far the laws of England—the laws of 'the Kingdom of England itself', which is their 'original and proper subject'—have effect and application outside the kingdom. From this point of view it would appear that there is an interior and intimate concern or estate of England, where the laws of England are in perfect vigour, and perfect rights are enjoyed; and that round this interior concern there is an outer ring, or rather a series of rings, at once connected and distinct. Wales and Scotland were once such rings; but Wales was taken into partnership in the interior concern, under an Act of 1536, by 'the generous method of triumph' once practised by the republic of Rome, and Scotland was united with England (though still retaining its separate municipal laws) by the Act of 1707. There remain three rings—three exterior (or, as Blackstone remarks in one context, 'inferior') dominions. The first is the 'dependent subordinate kingdom' of Ireland. The second includes some 'other adjacent islands', among them, down to 1765 (when the Crown completed its purchase of the previous interest of the proprietors), the Isle of Man, but since that year—which was also the year of the publication of Blackstone's first volume—only the islands of Jersey, Guernsey, Sark, Alderney, and their appendages. The third ring includes, outside these adjacent islands, 'our most distant plantations in America, and elsewhere'.

This is the setting in which the North American colonies appear. Without remarking on that setting, or upon its implications, we may turn to Blackstone's account of the legal position of the colonies. They may be classified, he remarks, from two points of view—according to the method of their acquisition, or according to their interior polity. From the first point of view, he draws a distinction, cardinal in our law, between colonies acquired by settlement ('where the lands are claimed by right of occupancy only, or by finding them desart and uncultivated, and peopling them from the mother country') and colonies acquired by conquest or cession. In colonies by settlement, he notes that it has been held that the settlers carry with them all the English laws in being at the time of the settlement, and thus enjoy the benefit of the laws of England. This involves the conclusion that they enjoy those three principal or primary rights, and those five auxiliary subordinate rights (including the right to a parliament or assembly of their own, and the right to a limitation of the prerogative), which he subsequently states, as we have seen,[1] to be the absolute rights of individuals under the laws of England. Blackstone, however, does not draw that conclusion in the passage[2] in which he describes the constitutional position of the colonies. At the best he leaves it implicit; and he explicitly makes two statements which have almost an opposite effect. The first is that, in his view, settlers in colonies by settlement carry with them not all the English laws then in being, but 'only so much of the English law as is applicable to their own situation and the condition of an infant colony'. The second is that the extent of what they carry, 'what shall be admitted and what rejected', is a matter 'to be decided, in the first instance, by their own provincial judicature, subject to the reversion and control of the king in council, the whole of their constitution being also liable to be new-modelled and reformed by the general superintending power of the legislature of the mother-country'.[3] In these two statements—but particularly in the latter, and more particularly in the concluding phrase of the latter—Blackstone seems somewhat harsh. Not only does he fail to state explicitly the conclusions to be drawn from the legal idea that settlers in colonies by settlement carry with them the English laws in being at the time of settlement. He also seems to go out of his way in order to state definitely and forcibly the overriding rights of the legislature of the mother country—rights which enable it to modify, by statute, the common-law rights carried with them by settlers. His general description of colonies by settlement may be correct—so far as it goes. But does it go far enough in stating the common-law rights of settlers? And does it not, perhaps, go too far in emphasizing the right of the British

---

[1] *Supra*, pp. 141–2.   [2] i. 106–9.
[3] i. 107.

Parliament to new-model and reform the whole of the constitution of a colony by settlement?

We have still, however, to consider his account of colonies acquired by the other mode—the mode of conquest or cession. In these colonies by conquest or cession, he tells us, 'that have already laws of their own' before the time of conquest or cession, 'the King may indeed alter and change those laws; but, till he does actually change them, the antient laws of the country remain'. Here, then, the English laws, and the common-law rights of Englishmen, are not carried; and here the three principal and the five subordinate rights are not introduced or established. 'The common law of England, as such, has no allowance or authority there; they being no part of the mother-country, but distinct (though dependent) dominions. They are subject however to the control of the parliament.'[1] All this may seem innocent enough, and true enough, when it is considered *in vacuo*. But Blackstone proceeds to fill up the vacuum by a most surprising remark. 'Our American plantations', he remarks, 'are principally of this sort, being obtained in the last century either by right of conquest and driving out the natives ... or by treaties.' What follows? A simple conclusion. The American colonies are not, 'principally', colonies by settlement. They do not therefore enjoy the laws of England, or the common-law rights of Englishmen. They are, 'principally', colonies by conquest or cession. They are thus no part of the mother country, but distinct (though dependent) dominions; yet, however distinct, they are still subject to the British Parliament.[2] This is what Blackstone says, and it is surely not unjust to describe it as most surprising. It is surprising in what it implies and in what it wholly omits. It implies that the bulk of the colonies were not colonies by settlement, and therefore that the common law, as such, had no allowance or authority there. It wholly omits the fact that whatever they were, and whether they were colonies by settlement or no, 'the main principles of the common law had been generally introduced'.[3]

[1] i. 107.
[2] Blackstone thus cuts out the American colonies, at any rate 'principally', from the mother country, but still keeps them under its Parliament as much as if they were parts of the mother country by virtue of their being colonies by settlement from it.
[3] Holdsworth, op. cit. xi. 236, n. 6: cf. also 83, 242, 247. Blackstone himself

It remains to consider Blackstone's classification of the colonies from the second point of view, which is concerned with their interior polity as distinct from the mode of their acquisition. From this point of view he distinguishes three sorts of colonies—those with provincial establishments, or constitutions depending on the commissions and instructions issued to the provincial governor; those with proprietary governments, 'in the nature of feudatory principalities'; and those with charter governments, 'in the nature of civil corporations'. The third sort of colony (which included, for instance, Massachusetts) was of particular and peculiar importance; and since Blackstone applies to this sort the notion of the civil corporation, we are naturally led to inquire what is involved in that notion. The answer may be found in the last chapter of Blackstone's first volume, which treats of corporations. A colony which is in the nature of a civil corporation will be analogous to an English municipality, or to the trading companies of London, or to the Universities of Oxford and Cambridge. It will be the creation of the King, in virtue of his royal prerogative. It will have the power of making by-laws for its own better government, 'unless contrary to the laws of the land, and then they are void'. It will be liable to the visitation of the King, which will be exercised in the court of King's Bench, where all its misbehaviours may be redressed and all its controversies decided. It will also be liable to dissolution, by forfeiture of its charter, through negligence or abuse of its franchises. Such are the consequences which follow on the notion of the civil corporation, which thus assimilates the chartered colonies, as Burke noted in his *Letter to the Sheriffs of Bristol*, to 'the municipal corporations within this island, to which some at present love to compare them'. It was a notion which did not altogether square with Blackstone's other notion of the absolute rights of individuals, under the common law, to enjoy a parliament and a system of limitation of the King's prerogative wherever the common law ran. But Blackstone is hardly to be blamed if the legal notion of the civil corporation did not altogether square, in its application to colonies, with other and deeper legal notions which he had himself described as inherent in the common law. He is the less to be blamed, because he did not press

admits (i. 109), 'Most of them have probably copied the spirit of their own law from this original'.

the notion of the civil corporation to any consequences, but contented himself simply with stating it, and with adding that it vested the colonies to which it applied with such rights and authorities as were specifically given them in their charters of incorporation.[1]

Such, in the main, are Blackstone's views of the nature of laws in general; of the public or constitutional law of England; and of the relations existing, under that law, between England and her colonies. They are by no means altogether illiberal; and perhaps it would be wrong to expect any different views from a lawyer writing a legal treatise, and seeking to explain the actual forms and principles of the English law of the eighteenth century. If, none the less, we attempt to advance any criticisms, there are three things which may be said of Blackstone. First, he deals too largely, and also too indiscriminately, with 'sovereignties' and 'absolute powers'—sovereignties and powers now vested in Parliament, and now in the King, but always resident in England. Secondly, he is too full of the idea of the concern or estate of England, which rides majestic among 'inferior' or 'dependent' dominions. Thirdly, he is generally complacent, and sometimes irritatingly complacent, about the perfection of English law as it stands, alike in Church and in State. ('Everything is now as it should be', he remarks in regard to freedom of religious opinion; and the remark, though made in that one connexion, strikes a note which vibrates through his book.) It is true that he speaks of an original contract and a right of civic resistance; it is true that he speaks of the fundamental articles asserted by parliamentary declarations; it is true that he describes the English constitution under the head of auxiliary rights of the subject, buttressing the three principal rights of his civil liberty, and that he includes the limitation of prerogative under those auxiliary rights; it is true that he sees something wrong in the poor laws, the game laws, the methods of criminal punishment, the increase of the taxes, and the extent of the influence, or adventitious power, which this increase has brought to the executive. But his

[1] It is at this point that the notion of the civil corporation, which assigns to a colony only the rights specifically given, quarrels with the notion that settlers in a colony by settlement carried with them, apart from gift and without any gift, the laws of England, and the rights thereunder, which existed at the time of the settlement.

general verdict is couched in terms of pure panegyric. On the last page of his *Commentaries* he writes: 'Of a constitution so wisely contrived, so strongly raised, and so highly finished, it is hard to speak with that praise which is justly and severely its due.' If it was hard, Blackstone conquered the difficulty. Indeed, he conquered it only too successfully.

But if there are thus some things which may be said in criticism of Blackstone, there are also some which must be equally said in his praise. The first is a matter of his long-time influence in America. Immediately, and on a short-time view, he may have helped to loosen the bonds between Great Britain and America. Ultimately, as it has been justly said, he helped to draw the bonds tighter. 'The immense popularity of the *Commentaries* in America . . . has helped to add to the link of a common language that other link of common legal principles.'[1] Nor was it only his book that counted. It was also the example of what he had done to establish the teaching of English law in a great English university. On the basis of that example chairs of English law were established in American universities such as Columbia and Harvard; and the liberal influence of the university on legal studies, the literature of law, and the theory of law, flourished even more generously on American soil than it did on the English soil from which it had been imported.[2] A second thing which must be said in Blackstone's honour is a matter of his permanent influence in his own country. This was a double influence. It was partly an influence which made, in England as in America, for the introduction of legal studies into the university, and thereby for a more liberal handling of legal education. Slower in England than in America, this was an influence which none the less worked; which gradually liberalized legal training; and which brought the legal thinking of university professors and teachers into a living and stimulating connexion with the legal work of the courts and the bar. Partly, again, his influence was an influence which made, in the long run, for the reform of English law, and thus aided the practical efforts of Romilly and his successors in the first half of the nineteenth

---

[1] Holdsworth, op. cit. xii. 726.
[2] Kent, whose *Commentaries* have already been mentioned (*supra*, p. 128), became professor in King's College (Columbia) in 1793. Story, another great jurist, became a professor at Harvard in 1830. Both of them were holders of high judicial office.

century. It may seem curious that Blackstone also should thus be numbered among the reformers—the more curious because his own genius can hardly be styled a reforming genius. But perhaps we may say that he aided reform, without any design or intention, by stating the *status quo* so admirably that his statement became a sign-post pointing to a better future. At any rate a recent holder of the Vinerian chair, which he first adorned, has said of him words with which we may end: 'I think that it is true to say that his summary of the main principles of English law was of great assistance to the lawyers of the nineteenth century, because it gave them a clear view of the law which they proposed to reform.'[1]

[1] Holdsworth, op. cit. xii. 726.

Essay Six

BURKE AND HIS BRISTOL CONSTITUENCY, 1774-1780

I

My theme covers the six years from 1774 to 1780. The scene of the action is Bristol. The dramatis persona is an Irishman—about 5 feet 10 inches in height and fifty years of age; wearing a tight brown coat and a little bob-wig with curls; near-sighted, so that, as he spoke, you might mark an occasional working of the brow, as you would also notice a beaky nose and a tight-pursed mouth; often harsh in tone and violent in gesticulation, and always speaking with much of the Irish accent and 'an habitual undulating motion of the head ... which had the appearance of indicating something of a self-confident or intractable spirit'—an Irishman you might have thought to be a schoolmaster if you had not known in advance that he was the Chrysostom of English politics; an Irishman called Edmund Burke.

The six years from 1774 to 1780, during which Burke was Member for Bristol, were stirring years in the world's affairs. America was in revolt, and the British Commonwealth was cracking and rending; Poland was at death's door, and the first partition of the Polish kingdom had taken place in 1772. England watched the one and the other with an obtuse placidity: 'the disorder and discontent of all America', Burke wrote to Rockingham, 'operate as little as the division of Poland.' In Sweden, in the year of the Polish partition, the young Gustavus III had vaulted to an absolute throne by a bloodless *coup d'état*; and the Duke of Richmond, supping in Paris at the Swedish Ambassador's in 1776, and noticing a piece of plate 'representing the glorious revolution of Sweden', reflected that George III had it in his power 'with the greatest ease and quiet to imitate the King of Sweden', and that the English might 'at last own themselves, like the Swedes, unworthy to be free'. The prescient eye of Burke detected, in the far distance, still another cloud, more terrible than those which lowered over the British Commonwealth, more menacing than that which obscured the future of British liberty. He had visited Paris in 1773: he had met the *philosophes*; he had seen, in its own home, the spirit of political rationalism and the zeal of religious agnosticism. He returned home pensive and brooding. In a speech of the same year, on religious toleration, he proclaimed the need for a union of all Christian sects in an 'alliance, offensive and defensive, against those great ministers of darkness in the world, who are endeavouring to shake all the works of God established in order and beauty'. It is a first faint shadow of the coming French Revolution: it is the first hint of Burke's *Reflections* on that Revolution.

But it would be an error to think that, in those years, men stood shivering in the cold and gloomy dawn of an impending day of ruin. Politicians might ingeminate their gloomy vaticinations: society at large moved in a spirit of hope through a morning of sunny promise. 'He who did not live before 1789', Talleyrand once observed, 'never knew the charm of life.' 'The age we live in', wrote the young Jeremy Bentham in 1776, in the preface to his first work, 'is a busy age, in which knowledge is rapidly advancing towards perfection.' In 1773 the brothers Montgolfier were raising balloons by hot air: in 1774 Dr. Priestley, a dissenting minister, who was at the same time a master both of political and of physical science, discovered oxygen, some eight years after Cavendish, a millionaire member of Peterhouse, Cambridge, had discovered hydrogen: in 1772 Captain Cook sailed in the *Resolution*, and for the next seven years was busy in discovering new secrets of the Southern Seas. Bentham could well boast that 'in the natural world . . . everything teems with discovery and with improvement'; and caught by the contagion of sympathy, he could very naturally proclaim that, 'correspondent to *discovery* and *improvement* in the natural world, is *reformation* in the moral'. Never, indeed, was there greater zest for the reformation of the moral world. Not to speak of the labours of Voltaire and Rousseau, or of Helvetius and Beccaria, on the Continent, we may celebrate even in our own sleepy country an eager body of pioneers and road-makers into a better future. There was Bentham himself, already proclaiming, at the age of 28, the need for developing, in our law and our politics, the fundamental axiom that *'it is the greatest happiness of the greatest number that is the measure of right and wrong'*. There was Thomas Spence, bookseller and revolutionary, who preached to the Literary and Philosophical Society of Newcastle in 1775, at the age of 25, the gospel of land-nationalization; there was John Cartwright, Lieutenant in the Navy and a Major of the Militia, who in 1776, at the age of 36, began the battle of a long lifetime by publishing a pamphlet, *Take Your Choice*, in favour of annual Parliaments and equal representation; there was John Howard, who visited prisoners in their affliction when he was High Sheriff of Bedfordshire, and published his *State of the Prisons* in 1777; there were the Quakers, who, as early as 1761, were protesting against the slave trade, and there was the general sentiment against the trade—a sentiment felt by no man more deeply than it was by Burke—which induced even Parliament, as early as 1776, to pass a resolution against it.

I have now, I think, said enough to show the wonders of these six years—or, if you will, of the eighth decade of the eighteenth century in general. I will only remark, as I leave them, that I have often thought that the year 1776 is the very pivot and hinge of the period—a genuine *annus mirabilis* of English thought and life. It was the year of the American Declaration of Independence; it was the year of the appearance of *Common Sense*, a pamphlet by a wandering English stay-maker and exciseman, called Thomas Paine, at this time living in Philadelphia, which helped to produce the Declaration; it was the year of the publication of Bentham's *Fragment on Government*, from which I have already quoted, and which started Utilitarianism on its long and beneficent career: it was the year of the publication of Adam Smith's *Wealth of Nations*, which founded the great and peculiarly English science of political economy; it was the year of the publication of the first volume of Gibbon's *Decline and Fall*, which marks an epoch in English historiography; and finally, as I have already said—if there be any 'finally' in a watershed so fertile of running springs—it was the year of *Take Your Choice*, and of the first resolution of a British Parliament against the slave trade.

Bristol, in the eighteenth century, was still a walled city; and Bristol Bridge, like London Bridge, still carried a row of houses on either side. The streets were narrow, twenty feet wide on the level, and less at the height of the first floor, where the houses, built in the old way of timber and plaster, overhung towards one another. In the middle of the city, shops and workshops were casually intermixed; now, as you passed, you would hear the clang of a hammer or the whirring of a loom, and now again you would catch the chaffering and the laughter of the shop. Above the shops hung signs of the most various, from Lions and Spread Eagles to gaudy figures of Turkish Bashaws and Golden Boys; for advertisement has always been with us. The streets themselves craved wary walking. They were paved with rough blocks of stone along which you slithered, and in the middle ran a gutter for the gathering of garbage. Matthew Brickdale, when he was a wool-draper's apprentice, and before he became the candidate for Parliament who was defeated by Burke in 1774, was accustomed to use the obscurity of the night for sweeping the garbage of the High Street into a narrow passage, where it would trip and souse the nocturnal wayfarer. The pigs of the citizens, as well as their apprentices, had a use for garbage: they rooted and grunted in the gutters; and a scandalized corporation paid fees to an officer for cutting off their tails in vindication of its by-laws. '*Summa rusticitas*', as I remember hearing Maitland say some fifty years ago, in a lecture on the medieval borough, '*Summa rusticitas*—the pig was ubiquitous.' Not that the *rusticitas* of Bristol was confined to the pig. In summer days it had a sweeter smell, when the meadows at the back of the citizens' houses had just been cut, and the hay-carts went about the streets.

In population and in wealth Bristol had outstripped Norwich in the course of the eighteenth century, and was generally accounted to be the second city in the kingdom. We may estimate the number of its inhabitants at something under 25,000 at the beginning of the century, and something over 40,000 by the middle. Their wealth was due to the predominant share which they enjoyed, in virtue both of historical connexions and geographical advantages, in the colonial trade with North America and the West Indies—a trade which was the most flourishing, because under the mercantile system it was the most favoured, of all the branches of English economy. Adam Smith, in a great chapter of the *Wealth of Nations*, was to deal a fatal blow at the logic of the system under which Bristol flourished. It was a system which made the colonists, in the main, a people of customers, producers of raw material for the industries of England, and therein especially of Bristol, and consumers of the manufactured commodities of England, and therein not least of Bristol. Upon this system Smith remarked, in his dry way: 'To found a great empire for the sole purpose of raising up a people of customers may at first sight appear a project fit only for a nation of shopkeepers. It is, however, a project altogether unfit for a nation of shopkeepers, but extremely fit for a nation *whose Government is influenced by shopkeepers.*' In other words, as he proved in detail, the system was bad for the nation at large, because it encouraged and enriched the section engaged in colonial trade at the expense of the rest of the nation; and it could only exist because, and so long as, that section could influence the government to tilt the balance in its own favour. When we remember that Adam Smith was a friend of Burke, and that he said of him that he was 'the only man I ever knew who thinks on economic subjects exactly as I do without any previous communication having passed between us'—when we remember this, we can only say that it was a sad and paradoxical chance which made Burke, with his way of thinking, the Member for Bristol, with its way of living.

Unconscious of the coming doom of its protected American connexion—a doom doubly pronounced in the same year, 1776, by the political principles of the American Declaration of Independence and the economic arguments of the *Wealth of Nations*—Bristol was busily and happily engaged in commerce during the first three-quarters of the eighteenth century. A cast of commerce tinged all its life. 'The very parsons of Bristol', it was said in 1724, 'talk of nothing but trade, and how to turn the penny.' The Rector of St. Stephen's himself, the great Josiah Tucker, who crossed swords with Burke and wrote shrewdly, if not always sagely, about politics and economics, seemed more at home in the counting-house than the temple; and he was called by his adversaries Josiah ben Tucker ben Judas Iscariot. In their wealth the citizens generally were proud, 'very proud, not affable to strangers, but rather much admiring themselves, so that an ordinary fellow who is but a freeman of Bristol conceits himself to be as great as a senator of Rome, and very sparing of his hat'. Their critics said that they had less culture than pride; a vast majority, it was wittily if irreverently remarked, were 'as illiterate as the back of a tombstone'.

But Bristol had a good deal of style and even of grandeur in its social life. Negro slaves, vivid (as one imagines) in their red coats as they went about the streets, were kept as personal servants till far into the eighteenth century. A certain 'rich brewage', as Macaulay termed it, was current in Bristol: it was called Bristol Milk, 'not only', says a writer of 1727, 'because it is as common here as milk in other places, but because they esteem it as pleasant, wholesome and nourishing'. According to Fuller, it was the first 'moisture' given to babies in the city; according to a Bristol *Guide*, only sleds, or sledges, 'which they call gee hoes', were permitted in the streets, 'lest the shake occasioned by carts on the pavement should affect the Bristol Milk in the vaults'. These are perhaps jesting slanders; but it is certain that Bristol was a fine city, and enjoyed a good deal of high living and almost metropolitan style. Pepys, in 1668, had already noticed that the city 'is in every respect another London'; and, meeting there his maid Deb. Willett's uncle (poor Deb., who had to be dismissed to satisfy Mrs. Pepys's not unjustifiable jealousy), he had recorded of the sober merchant: 'Very good company, and so like one of our sober, wealthy, London merchants as pleased me mightily.' Bristol, indeed, clung close to London; and its well-to-do citizens were often overcome by a feeling that they must 'run up to London' on some alleged business. Already, in 1775, you could do the 120 miles in 16 hours at the rate of 3*d.* a mile.

But the city was connected with Newfoundland, the Carolinas, and Antigua almost as closely as it was with London. Not to mention John Cabot, or his sailing from Bristol, we may remember that James I had granted a charter to a company of adventurers from Bristol and London to settle in Newfoundland. Bristol still retained an interest in this grant; and it was Bristol oil, extracted from Newfoundland fishes, which still lit thousands of lamps in England in the eighteenth century. Farther to the south, Bristol men had helped to colonize Massachusetts; the old and honourable family of the Lowells, in Boston, who, according to the local rhyme, speak only to the Boston Cabots, 'as the Cabots speak only to God', refers its origin to Bristol. But the great interests of the city lay still farther to the south.

Bristol merchants were the owners, or mortgagees, of tobacco and sugar plantations in Virginia and the Carolinas, from which they drew supplies for their local industries; and others, again, were interested deeply in the West Indies. It was no uncommon thing for one partner of a Bristol firm to be living across the Atlantic while another conducted the business at home; or, at any rate, a firm would keep a resident agent across the seas. Cruger, who was Member for Bristol along with Burke from 1774 to 1780, belonged to the local firm of Cruger and Mallard (and was also son-in-law to a Bristol man called Peach, who had some interest in the slave trade), but he was himself a citizen of New York; and Richard Champion, who was Burke's great supporter and friend in the city, had interests and connexions in South Carolina, where, indeed, he eventually settled and died. These amphibious Bristol merchants exported serges and pipes (the city was a great maker of pipes) to the colonies; they imported tobacco and sugar for their factories and refineries. They managed the passage of emigrants, and some of the Bristol aldermen were even accused of aiding emigration artificially, in order to get labour for their estates, by frightening petty rogues into begging for transportation, by conniving at 'man-stealing' and even at 'kidnapping' (the 'nabbing' or seizure of children), and by forwarding the recruitment of indentured servants for a period of servitude in the plantations. Saddest of all, to our modern way of thinking, was the slave trade. It was not indeed condemned by the general morality of the age: good men engaged in it, and even Quakers are said to have invested in the traffic; nor can we, who have heard in our time the cry of Chinese slavery, who know the urgency of the problem of labour in newly developed countries, who are aware of the existence today of slavery, or quasi-slavery, in tropical and semi-tropical countries, afford to cast many stones at our ancestors. It is sufficient simply to record the facts, and to let the facts speak for themselves. There was a slave trade in the eighteenth century which was of the nature of what Adam Smith calls 'a roundabout trade'. It consisted in exporting goods to West Africa in the Guinea ships, of which forty belonged to the port of Bristol, and exchanging them there for slaves; in transporting slaves from West Africa to the West Indies and the Southern Colonies, and exchanging them there for sugar; and in bringing the sugar to the English refineries for manufacture and sale. The African company engaged in the trade consisted of merchants in London, Bristol, and Liverpool. Of 473 members of the company recorded in 1759, 242 came from Bristol and 231 from the other two ports. Of 60,000 negroes transported in one year, the Bristol vessels are said to have carried 30,000. Here, once more, we cannot but feel that the trade of Bristol had a dubious and uncertain foundation; here, once more, we cannot but say that it was a sad and paradoxical chance which made Burke (the eager humanitarian, who drafted about 1780 the Sketch of a Negro Code) the representative of a city which had come to be identified with negro slavery.

There were two Bristols in the eighteenth century, and they were divided from one another. There was the Bristol of the Port and the City; and there was the Bristol of Clifton and the Hot Wells. The first of the two Bristols was not only a city of trade and industry: it had a religious life of its own; and however illiterate the bulk of its citizens may have been, there were some lights of literature which shone brightly in the city and attained a national fame. With its many churches the city was, in the main, an Anglican community; and in the early part of the eighteenth century the members of the Establishment had persecuted and proscribed the Dissenters. The latter half of the century showed a different quality. The Bristol Quakers, reformed by the zeal of Joseph Fry, were an influence in the city. They were one of Burke's *points d'appui*: he had himself been educated in his youth at a Quaker school, kept by the family of the Shackletons: he maintained a lifelong friendship with the family; and when he stood for Bristol in 1774 there came a letter from one of the Shackletons to the Bristol Quakers: 'I think then thou mayst with great truth assure our friends there . . . that Edmund Burke is a man of the strictest honour and integrity; a firm and staunch Protestant; a zealous advocate... for liberty.' The Methodists, too, had come to be a power in the city after the early beginnings of 1739, when George Whitefield had induced John Wesley to join him in preaching in the open air to the colliers of Kingswood, and had seen 'the white gutters made by their tears, which plentifully fell down their black cheeks' as he preached. They, too, were supporters of Burke in 1774; but their support declined when John Wesley, in 1775, declared against the American cause, and this was one of the first causes of Burke's gradual loss of his hold upon his constituency.

Among the literary lights which shone in Bristol about this time there was one which had just been quenched by an early and self-inflicted death in 1770. This was Thomas Chatterton, whose precocious genius has only been equalled by that of Rimbaud; the poet-fabricator of the pseudo-medieval Rowley poems, whose production rivalled, and indeed outvied, the 'Ossian' of his contemporary, James Macpherson, and presented to scholars a problem almost equally annoying and equally attractive. Samuel Johnson, who had attacked Macpherson in 1775, visited Bristol in the next year, accompanied by Boswell, to inspect the Rowley manuscripts, and perhaps to see his friend Burke's constituency with his own eyes; but he went away as unbelieving as he had come, only saying: 'It is wonderful how the whelp has written such things.' More prosaic, but more steady, was the light of the Rector of St. Stephen's, Josiah Tucker, who became Dean of Gloucester in 1758, but retained his rectory and remained one of the foremost figures in Bristol until his death in 1799. He had written an *Essay on Trade* in 1750, which proclaimed the principles of Free Trade a quarter of a century before the *Wealth of Nations*; he had written in 1752 *Elements of Commerce and Theory of Taxes* for the instruction of the future George III; and indeed he was so much of an economist that when he was being considered in 1757 for the Deanery of Bristol, which he failed to get, the Bishop wrote of him, in comparing him with another and successful candidate, that the one had made religion his trade and the other trade his religion. He was a vigorous and independent thinker, who rushed into most frays with gusto; he was burned in effigy in 1751 for championing a bill in favour of the naturalization of foreign Protestant refugees, the people of Bristol thinking that it would throw English labour out of employment; he was one of the few residents who aided Clarkson when, in 1787, he rode down to Bristol on his crusade against the slave trade. He took an independent line on the American question, maintaining that the American colonies were not worth the cost of retention, and that they had better be left to go their own way. His pugnacious genius naturally led him into conflict with Burke. However lightly he might think of the American connexion, Tucker was too solid an Englishman not to support an English government when it was engaged in war; and Burke's speech on American Conciliation moved him to publish a critical letter in which he designated the Member for Bristol as 'an artful more than a solid reasoner, and a determined partizan of the rebels'. Burke, who was generous, and who seems besides to have had an amused respect for the Dean, remarked on the criticism, in a letter to a Bristol friend: 'There is wit at the end of the pamphlet, and it made me laugh heartily. The rest did not alter any of my opinions.'

Burke had another critic, a feminine critic, not indeed in Bristol, but at any rate in close proximity at Bath. This was Mrs. Catharine Macaulay, pre-ordained by the fate of her name to the writing of history, and authoress of a *History of England from the Accession of James I to the Elevation of the House of Hanover*, which ran to eight volumes. She had published in 1770 *Observations on a Pamphlet entitled 'Thoughts on the Cause of the Present Discontents'*; she was to publish, twenty years later, one of the thirty-eight or more 'replies' to the *Reflections on the Revolution in France*. She settled in Bath in 1774, and here she established connexions with Bristol. More closely connected with Burke is the figure of Hannah More, dramatist and poetess, founder of Sunday Schools and authoress of tracts, who lived in Park Street, but had already visited London and met Burke and his circle early in 1774. She played her part in Burke's election later in the year. When he lost his voice through his many speeches she sent him a wreath with the inscription:

> Great Edmund's hoarse, they say. The reason's clear:
> Could Attic lungs respire Boeotian air?

and when he was declared elected it was she and her sisters who made the cockade of myrtle, bay, and laurel, trimmed with silver tassels, which he wore at his chairing. The friendship begun in 1774 lasted until Burke's death. Hannah had been charmed when in 1774 she was 'introduced by Miss Reynolds to Edmund Burke (the sublime and beautiful Edmund Burke!)'; she was still charmed in 1790, when she wrote: 'I met Mr. Burke and a pleasant party: indeed, he is a sufficiently pleasant party of himself.' One cannot but think, as one reads her words and reflects on her compliment, of another scene, an unforgettable scene, in 1784. Dr. Johnson lay dying, and Burke and four or five others were sitting with him. Burke said to him: 'I am afraid, sir, such a number of us may be oppressive to you.' 'No, sir,' said Johnson, 'it is not so; and I must be in a wretched state indeed when your company would not be a delight to me.' Burke, in a tremulous voice, replied: 'My dear sir, you have always been too good to me,' and very soon after he went away. I should always love Burke, and Johnson too, if that were my only warrant.

You will pardon the digression. I must return to Bristol, the other Bristol, the Bristol of Clifton and the Hot Wells. You will remember the vogue of the inland spa in the eighteenth century, until sea-bathing came into fashion when George III set his heart on Weymouth, and 'the new Bristol and Weymouth Diligence, in one day' began to run twice a week in 1779. Next to Bath, Bristol was the inland spa of chief celebrity. The *Thermologia Bristoliensis* of 1703 had trumpeted its praises, announcing the virtues of its waters, and recording, among other cases, how 'William Beckford, Esquire, His Majesty's Slopster, was cured of the diabetes in thirteen weeks'. There was a pump-room on the bank of the Avon, through which the foot-way ran; it was picturesquely overhung, to suit the new Gothic taste of the age, by horrid and frowning rocks. Visitors resided on College Green, and went out to Clifton to take the waters. Nor were they confined to taking the waters. There were musical breakfasts and evening balls in the New Vauxhall Gardens, close at hand; there was riding on Durdham Down, 'and the best lady attending the Hot Well will not refuse riding behind a man, for such is the custom of the country'. All this attracted a gay and aristocratic, or at any rate wealthy, company; but it was a company distinct from the residents of the Port and the City. 'The popularity of Clifton in fashionable circles', writes the historian of Bristol, 'deterred rather than encouraged the migration of Bristolians.' None the less, it was sometimes Clifton and the Hot Wells which brought visitors to Bristol who afterwards found close ties with the Port and the City. Such a visitor was Edmund Burke.

I have set the scene, and now I must introduce the actor, who, indeed, has already peeped through the curtains again and again. Edmund Burke was the son of a Dublin lawyer, and he was born on the New Year's Day of 1729. His school was the Quaker school of the Shackletons, which left a lifelong impression and affection in his vivid and sensitive mind; his college was Trinity College, Dublin, where he spent five or six crowded years of rapid development from 1744 to the end of 1749. It is a college which has shown itself able to produce polymaths, who are not seldom tinctured by some degree of genius; in Burke it produced a genius, pure and absolute, who was tinctured by a more than respectable polymathy. Nothing came amiss to the universal hunger of his eager mind. He read the romances of *Palmerin* and *Don Bellianis of Greece*; he wrote poetry in the style of Spenser and Lovelace and Waller; he mastered the Latin classics; he studied the logic of Burgersdicius and the metaphysics of the Schoolmen; in a word, he passed, as he told a friend, through the four *furores*—the mathematical, the logical, the historical, and the poetical. He throve in his studies; he won a scholarship in 1746; he proceeded to his Bachelor's degree in 1748. He throve even more, as perhaps the mind of the student always does (and, indeed, the mind of man in general), in the spaces of leisure which he filled for himself outside the area of work. At the age of fifteen he was already writing noble prose; and suddenly kindling, in a casual letter to a friend, he could glow, merely upon the provocation of a mention of astronomy, into a passage such as this:

'Let us cast our eyes up to the spangled canopy of heaven, where innumerable luminaries at such an immense distance from us cover the face of the skies—all suns as great as that which illumines us—surrounded with earths perhaps no way inferior to the ball which we inhabit—and no part of the amazing whole unfilled; systems running into systems, and worlds bordering on worlds.'

In his fourth year, at the age of 18, he founded a club which still survives as the Trinity College Historical Society: anticipating, in a student apprenticeship, the solemn occupations of his later life, he learned in it to debate, to orate, and to write trenchant minutes; and he was already being accused by a fellow-member, as he was afterwards accused by his political adversaries, of being 'damned absolute'. But it was in the two years after he had taken his degree (the years 1748–9), when he still kept his rooms in Trinity College but had time on his hands, that his ardent activities—journalistic, political, and literary—were most remarkable. Early in 1748 he published thirteen numbers of a paper called the *Reformer*. The numbers dealt largely with the stage, in which he had come to be deeply interested by frequenting a Dublin theatre managed by Sheridan's father; but one of them spoke, in accents which are already prophetic of the later man, of the sad social condition of Ireland, and another, in the same accents, of Christianity and the Christian spirit of toleration. Still more striking than the thirteen numbers of the *Reformer* are the dozen or so pamphlets and articles which (it has been contended in a recent work, by Mr. Samuels of Dublin, on *The Early Life, Correspondence and Writings of Burke*) were written by him in the course of the Lucas controversy of 1748 and 1749. The Lucas controversy raised a number of political issues of primary importance—the issue of the rights of the Dublin freemen in parliamentary elections; the issue of the rights, and the limits to the rights, of the Dublin House of Commons in dealing with disputed elections; the issue of the political and economic dependence of Ireland on England under the system of Poynings' laws and the Irish commercial code. On all these issues the twelve pamphlets and articles express the Whig or Liberal side. Their style is that of Burke: their argument is that of Burke: they anticipate, in dealing with the theory of popular election, the line which he afterwards took in his speeches for Wilkes and his *Thoughts on the Cause of the Present Discontents*: they anticipate, in dealing with the commercial code, the advocacy of Irish free trade which he was to pursue in 1778 and afterwards, and which was to alienate his Bristol constituents. Most astonishing of all these pieces is the *Second Letter to the Citizens of Dublin*, at the end of 1749, which, in its references to Bolingbroke, its conception of a 'Patriot Commonalty' (rather than a patriot King), and its theory of a 'Patriot Parliament' holding its power 'in trust for the people', moves the reader involuntarily to exclaim: 'Aut Burke aut diabolus.' Our wonder grows the more when we reflect that it was also in these last two years at Trinity College, according to tradition and Burke's own indications, that there was written the draft of an essay in aesthetics—that *Essay on the Sublime and Beautiful* which, afterwards published in 1756, so impressed the great German Lessing that he set about translating it and was helped by it to produce the theory of his *Laokoon*.

It was an Irishman with a full and brimming mind—with a practised pen, and with a tongue already practised in debate—

who came over to England in the spring of 1750 to read for the bar at the Middle Temple. What might not be anticipated from such a mind, a pen, a tongue? But Burke was an Irishman in a strange land; his only resource was a small allowance from a critical and irritable father; his health was so far from established (there was a taint of tuberculosis in his family, and he suffered from an affection of the hip which always affected his gait, and gave to Sir Joshua Reynolds, with the observant eye of a painter, the idea of his having two left legs) that he perhaps lacked the necessary vigour for an immediate assault upon a career. Genius which has flourished apace at a university may flag for some time afterwards: genius without means or patronage is in any case handicapped; and it would seem that there is a rhythm in the development of great talents which, if they do not get off the mark at once with every favouring breeze, as was the good fortune both of the younger Fox and the younger Pitt, delays their starting on the great circle of their voyage until the tide or climacteric which comes about the age of 37. Certainly it was not until 1766 that Burke's sails were finally filled by the breeze; nor was it until he was 37 that he found a seat in Parliament and began that career of parliamentary debate and oratory to which he had seemed predestined by his activities in the club at Trinity College nearly twenty years before. Much of the record of his first sixteen years in England has perished. He was never called to the bar: there was something in him which could not stomach the profession of the law, of which he often spoke critically in later years; and on this issue he became estranged from a father with whom he had never stood in easy or intimate relations. For a time he fell into straits. There is a story of his meeting in St. James's Park, somewhere about 1755, an Eastern wanderer, called Yusuf Emin, who, like himself, was astray in London. They fell into conversation. Emin asked his name. 'Sir, it is Edmund Burke. I am a runaway son from a father, as you are.' Burke then presented him (he was always generous—and always, it must be added, till the end of his life, in involved circumstances) with half a guinea, saying: 'Upon my honour this is what I have at present—please to accept of it.' But this was not all, and Burke had something more for Emin. He took him home to his rooms over a bookseller's shop near the Temple, and he made him his amanuensis in transcribing two works on which he was busy. Here, in the mention of these two works, we touch something of an epoch in the waiting period of Burke's life between 1750 and 1766; and here, in his writings, we can catch the first signs of the tide which was to lead him on to fortune.

The two works were *A Vindication of Natural Society*, a political work in the style of Bolingbroke (who had recently died in 1751), and the *Essay on the Sublime and Beautiful*, which has already been mentioned. They both appeared in 1756; they gave him vogue, and the entry into those literary circles which bordered close, if only in the relation of client to patron, upon the aristocratic circle of politics; they also brought him fresh literary work, of a political nature, which brought him in turn still nearer to the door of St. Stephen's. In 1757 he published, perhaps in co-operation with one or more members of his family, an *Account of the European Settlements in America*, which is the first sign of the constant interest he was to devote, for nearly thirty years, to American affairs. In 1759 he published, for Dodsley the printer, the first number of an *Annual Register* which has continued to appear year by year ever since. For many years, even while he was in the thick of politics, he continued his connexion with it: the yearly summaries, or Historical Articles, which he wrote are among our authorities for the history of this period; and this annual habit of reviewing the world's politics and the world's affairs must have enriched his mind and kept his eyes steadily fixed on the political horizon and its constellations. Established in these ways, and by these testimonies of his genius, as a polite writer and rising publicist, he naturally offered himself as the ideal secretary for an aspiring member of the charmed and noble ring of parliamentary politicians. The connexion between the politician and the indefatigable secretary who conducts his correspondence, manages his affairs, prepares his speeches, and even (it may be) composes his books, is a connexion which is still with us, and it was a connexion even better known to the eighteenth century. The first employer of Burke's great gifts was a member for Petersfield, known to history (not altogether justly) as single-speech Hamilton. Burke worked for him between 1759 and 1764; he was with him in Ireland, when he went there as Chief Secretary in 1761; he perhaps manipulated for him the Irish House of Commons; and he must have been his general adviser on the state and posture of Irish politics and Irish politicians, perhaps little altered since he had known them and written about them in his last two years at Trinity College. But the connexion ended, after some years, in an angry rupture. Hamilton, polite and selfish, tried to drive a generous but passionate and wayward genius in blinkers: he demanded from him the whole of his time and the sacrifice of any independent life of the mind; and Burke rebelled and resigned. He was once more on the world, but, fortunately for him and fortunately for England, there was another and nobler politician who desired a private secretary. This was the Marquis of Rockingham, the leader of the finest and the most distinguished, if not the most active or the most successful, of the various sections of the Whigs. In July 1765, a week after Rockingham had become Prime Minister, Burke became his secretary; and soon, his nature working powerfully on Rockingham's affection, he became his right hand, his goad to action, his trumpeter, his manager, his plague, his inspiration. A seat in Parliament was immediately found for him, by the influence of Lord Verney, at the foot of the Chilterns, in the borough of Wendover. He was in his native element at last; fortune, for years still and silent, had now sent him a favourable breeze; and his ship bounded forward on its long voyage, through sunshine and storm, over the waters of English politics.

He had never dropped his old undergraduate passion for public speaking and the happy clash of debate. In his early days in London he had frequented the actor Macklin's School of Oratory, and practised himself in public elocution; later he had attended the 'Robin Hood' Debating Society, where he encountered the pertinacity of a baker 'whom', says his biographer, 'nobody else could overcome, or at least silence'. In 1764 he had joined in founding the Club—the Literary Club: Dr. Johnson's Club—where he could cross swords with Johnson and Garrick and Goldsmith. He had also followed another way of preparation for oratory. The stage was the fashion of the age: it set the tone of parliamentary oratory; and Burke, from his Dublin days, had always frequented the theatre. He was the friend of Peg Woffington and of Garrick, and when we read of him in his later days, 'moving into the middle of the House, contrary to the usual practice . . . with the most natural air imaginable, with seeming humility, and with folded arms, beginning his speech in a low tone of voice . . . soon after, however, becoming animated by degrees', we cannot but think of the well-graced actor coming on the stage. With all this preparation, but above all with his natural ardour of springing thought and bubbling imagery, he came at once to the front at the beginning of his first session, in 1766, 'filling the town with wonder', as Dr. Johnson said, by the speeches he made on the American troubles.

There is a great and homogeneous period of Burke's life which runs from the year 1765, in which he became Rockingham's secretary, to the year 1782, in which Rockingham died. It is perhaps the greatest in his career. The period which immediately followed, from 1782 to 1790, was one of partial eclipse; the period which followed that, from the appearance of the *Reflections* in 1790 until his death in 1797, was splendid with a gorgeous and many-coloured sunset, but it was also darkened by passionate political forebodings and the premature death of an only and dearly-loved son. In the long years of his association with Rockingham, between his thirty-seventh and his fifty-third year, he stood in the masculine and sober hey-day of his best powers. They were not, indeed, years of political success in the terms in which the world calculates. They began with a Rockingham ministry which, served by Burke, repealed the Stamp Act (as Bristol, by the way, petitioned it to do and thanked it for doing), but which only lasted for 'one year and twenty days'; they ended with a Rockingham ministry which, moved by Burke, carried a number of measures of economical reform (moving Bristol, in turn, once more to a vote of thanks), but which lasted only from the end of one March to the beginning of the next June. With the exception of these two brief ministries, the Rockingham connexion, for more than a decade and a half, was condemned to labour in opposition; and the fate of his connexion was necessarily also the fate of Burke. But if the tide was adverse, he took *Nitor in adversum* for his motto. The passion for liberty and the zeal of the Whig tradition were upon him; and whether it were a matter of the rights of the electorate, as in the Wilkes case, or of the liberty of Parliament from the corrupting influence of the Court—whether it were the issue of American freedom from compulsory taxes, or of Irish freedom from commercial restrictions—whether it was toleration for Roman Catholics, or toleration for Nonconformists, that was at stake—he was consistent in the line which he took, and indefatigable in the ardour which he expended. If we had only his writings and speeches of this period: the *Thoughts on the Cause of the Present Discontents* of 1770, the two American speeches of 1774 and 1775, and the letter to the Sheriffs of Bristol of 1777; the fine speeches he made when he came to Bristol in 1774, and the still finer speeches which he made when he departed from Bristol in 1780; the great speech on economical reform of 1780—if we had only these, and nothing more, we should miss, indeed, the burning passion of his Indian speeches, as we should miss, even more, the volcanic splendour of his writings on the French Revolution, but we should have more than enough for establishing a great and luminous reputation.

His ardour and activity are the more remarkable when we reflect upon the party with which he had identified his fortunes. It was a party which may remind us of a stately fleet of Spanish galleons, solemn and splendid as they rode at anchor, but singularly apt to remain in their anchorage, and sadly immobile when action was urgent and the trumpet was sounding. They had great names: there was Rockingham himself, of the great Yorkshire house of Wentworth; there was the Duke of Portland and the Duke of Richmond; when he was not busy in fox-hunting, there was also Lord John Cavendish. Wentworth and Bentinck, Lennox and Cavendish—the names shine in our English skies: could anything more be desired? Nothing, perhaps, except this (so Burke might have answered, and indeed actually answers if we read between the lines of his *Correspondence*), that the bearers of these honoured names would realize the nature of a time 'which calls for the whole of the best of us'; that they would not stay immured in their castles, on the plea of health or foxes or private affairs; that they would come to London before the session began in order to concert a policy; that they would brave the Court and the crowd for the sake of their policy; in a word, that they would work for their party, live for their party, and, if necessary, die for their party, in the grand old manner of the seventeenth century. A passion of activity is natural to a zealous party organizer, and Burke, if we may use a modern name, was the Rockingham party organizer. He suggested policies, drafted petitions, arranged for meetings, looked after elections, arranged everything and goaded everybody. He had something of a didactic habit, and he became something of the professor in politics. We can almost see him, spectacles on nose (he began to use 'a glass' as early as 1766), with lips tightly pursed and ferule in hand, lecturing his placid fine-featured aristocratic pupils. They listened with admiration; they corresponded affectionately with their dear Burke, and begged him to sit for his picture; he dined at their tables and stayed at their houses; but he could never fire them with the passion of action which burned in himself. Perhaps he suffered a little from the company he kept and the rubs he endured. As he grew older he was apt to fret and fume, and his Irish temper sometimes flared and exploded. There was also another influence to which he perhaps succumbed. Living in close touch with the grand seigneurs of England, he fell into a sort of contagious or induced temper of aristocratic thought. It was for the leaders of the people, he felt, to guide the people by their knowledge; it was for the people to find their leaders and to accept their guidance, imposing no mandates and giving no instructions, but leaving free course to a wisdom which was sovereignly conversant with matters of state. We may applaud the constitutional doctrine of the free representative which Burke preached to the people of Bristol; but as we read his correspondence we cannot but feel that he preached it with something of a mixture of professorial pride and aristocratic aloofness.

Light and shadow were mixed in Burke, as they are for us all, but the spaces of light in the canvas of his life are richly and generously diffused. Gossips and critics have counted his faults, and they are undoubtedly there, but to count them heavily is to 'scour a narrow chamber' with a disproportionate (and an unrewarded) zeal. I have already spoken of a pedantic tinge; I have already spoken of an aristocratic contagion. His finances, as I have already said, were always uncertain, and it must be confessed that he lived and died in debt; but I would also confess that I firmly believe that they were almost as honest as they were improvident (which is saying a good deal), and that no taint of unclean speculation or stock-jobbing scandals can justly soil his memory. He was surrounded, in the country house at Beaconsfield, which he had bought in 1768 and in which he lived for the rest of his life, by an Irish circle of relatives and connexions at which society was inclined to look askance; but if a sort of loyal clannishness, natural to an Irish temper, was stamped on his life and perhaps hindered his political advancement, it is no blot on his character. He had, however, other and more inherent marks of an Irish temper which hampered his genius more seriously. Passion was his enemy, as it was also his friend and the nerve of his power and vitality. He knew it, and he confessed it. In a letter to Fox, in 1777, making one of those resolutions which are so impossible of execution because they are so contrary to the set and the bent of a whole character, he says that he is thoroughly resolved to abate a habit of urging matters 'with an earnestness so extreme, and so much approaching to passion', that it was apt to be interpreted as indicating 'some latent private interest'. But he had to be himself, and sometimes he sank into a worse self. He had the great sarcastic and satiric gift of the Celtic genius: he could fall into an Irish passion of railing and invective; and he could not always keep his gift within the bounds of wisdom, or even of decency. He was capable of great lapses of tact and taste in moods of excitement; and even in his quieter hours he lacked those subtle filaments, those delicate tentacles of social apprehension, which keep a man in sympathetic touch with his associates and his auditors. His oratory itself, with all its magnificence, suffered from this defect. Forgetting his hearers, and following only the electric suggestions of a rapid and winged intelligence, he would soar from some issue into skyey worlds of general principles, or he would dart away from it down illustrative by-paths which his eye had detected, until he fell into that fault of 'copiousness beyond measure' which Horace Walpole remarked, and at which the country gentlemen of the House fretted and fumed— 'we rustics', as one of them said, showing that he was a rustic who knew his Horace, 'waiting and waiting for the stream to flow past, while it rolls and will roll unexhausted to all eternity'.

These are some of Burke's shadows. I cannot count the lights; but I can say some two or three things which any student of Burke may fairly and truly say. He was an unselfish man, who worked hard and unceasingly, with little regard to personal advancement, and with a large devotion to the party he had espoused and the causes he cherished. If he had only had a larger measure of the one fault of selfishness he could easily, in spite of his other faults, have made a far greater material success of his life than he did. He might have engineered or forced his way into cabinets; he might even have acquired a fortune. He did neither; but with 'a kind of earnest and anxious perseverance of mind', as he said of himself, he worked for two causes—the cause of liberty, as he understood it; the cause of humanity, as he conceived it. His understanding of the cause of liberty was that of his age and his own temperament, and it had the limitations of both. He never understood why the people of England should be free to elect its members by general suffrage in equal constituencies; he never understood why the people of France should be free to break with its past and to make a new future. But he understood why America should be free from English taxes and English interference; he understood why Ireland should be free from religious and economic oppression; and wherever he understood the cause of freedom he was ready, beyond most of his contemporaries, to implement his belief, to stake himself upon his faith, and to give the whole of the best of himself to making the cause prevail. His understanding of the cause of humanity was perhaps more comprehensive than his understanding of the cause of liberty. He was a man of a 'long-sighted and strong-nerved humanity' (the phrase is his own, but I need not say that he did not use it of himself), who laboured on behalf of negroes, on behalf of debtors, on behalf of the misguided fanatics of the Gordon Riots, on behalf of the wretched victims of the English criminal law; in a word, for the relief of any sufferings that a quick eye could detect or a warm heart could feel. Nor did he only labour; he also gave, whatever his own straits might be, to all whom he found in distress—the wandering Oriental Emin, the destitute poet Crabbe, the struggling painter Barry. If he was passionate, he was also generous; and his passion and his generosity were both the fruits of the same warm-hearted zest.

There is a sort of vitality—an ebullience of mental activity backed by physical vigour and spirits—which is one of the secrets of the success of great teachers, great orators, and great statesmen. Burke, at any rate in his middle years, had a large vitality, but he never had, in the fullest sense, the success of his vitality. We cannot wholly attribute the comparative failure of his political career either to his social and temperamental defects, or to the unselfish quality of his personal character. To blame entirely his defects would be unfair to the intelligence of his colleagues, who were certainly capable of pardoning even worse defects (if it had been necessary, and if their possessor had really 'imposed' himself) to a man of his oratory, his grasp of affairs, his diligence of application. To allege his unselfishness solely in excuse is to make him a little more than human, and to forget that he showed himself as anxious as most of his contemporaries for the advancement of his family and his friends. Perhaps we touch the truth if we say that he suffered from being, at one and the same time, neither tactful enough nor pushing enough for his age and his circumstances. And if we ask the reason for the latter of these disabilities, it would seem to be that he was so enamoured of his party, and so much under the glamour of his great and aristocratic connexion, that he failed to put a proper value upon himself, and so made himself too cheap when it came to the making of those party arrangements which determine the allocation of office. Even without rank and fortune he could have been *faber fortunae suae*, as Jenkinson was in his own day and others have been since, if he had stood more boldly for his own interests. His colleagues were so used to his serving them and the party, that they were content for him to go on serving; and even while they admired him and wished him thoroughly well, they left him out in the cold. In a sense Oliver Goldsmith was right when he laid his finger on party; but we may alter the famous line in the *Retaliation* and say of Burke that he was one who to party gave up not only what was meant for mankind, but also what was meant for himself. He did not show himself made of that iron and iron-hearted stuff which crushes the earthen vessels in the turbulent political stream; and his colleagues allowed him to float in the figure, and at the valuation, of an elegant jar of the finest oratorical porcelain, which was somehow also useful for all sorts of domestic functions of party and political management.

There is a passage in the diary of Charles Greville, the grandson of Burke's Duke of Portland, which is of no little interest. Why had his grandfather, a man of very second-rate abilities and no power of speaking, succeeded Rockingham as leader of the party in 1782? Was it because the party was so thoroughly aristocratic? He had talked over the matter one night in 1848, at Holland House, with old Sir Robert Adair, then a man of 85.

'Adair told me that old Lord George Cavendish expressed the greatest indignation at their party being led by Burke in the House of Commons, and it was the prevalent feeling, together with the extraordinary modesty of Burke, who had no vanity for himself, though a great deal for his son, which accounts for the fact, so extraordinary according to our ideas and practice, that though Burke led the Whig Party in the House of Commons for four or five years, when that party came into power he was not offered a place in the cabinet, but put in a subordinate office, which he condescended to accept, seeing men so immeasurably inferior to himself occupying the highest posts.'

II

SOON after he came to London in 1750 Burke began to be drawn, by the vogue of hydropathy and the tide of fashion, down the Great West Road which led to Bath and the Hot Wells of Bristol. In 1751 he is writing to his old friend and schoolfellow, the Quaker Shackleton, from Monmouth, to which he has just proceeded by way of Bath and Bristol; and at the end of September, 1752, he is telling him how, 'about the beginning of summer, finding myself attacked with my old complaints, I went once more to Bristol, and found the same benefit: I thank God for it'. He seems to have fixed his affections on the West Country—a country, he writes, 'extremely pleasant; sweetly diversified with hills and woods intermixed with villages; very populous . . . we have one point of view from which we can count six steeples'. It was in the West Country, at Bath, that in 1757 he found his wife, the daughter of an Irish doctor who practised there, the Jane of whom he wrote, in a little essay entitled *The Idea of a Wife*, which he gave her once on the anniversary of their wedding-day, 'Her gravity is a gentle thoughtfulness; . . . her smiles are inexpressible . . . her voice is a low soft music.' A soft Irish voice, grown softer still in the air of the West Country, a voice that comforted and sustained for forty years the earnest and anxious perseverance of a mind not seldom overwrought—that is the gentle memory, the faint, sweet echo, of Jane Burke.

Burke and the West Country had thus met early and happily; but there is a long gap, and many blank pages, in the history of their connexion between his marriage at Bath in 1757 and his election for Bristol in 1774. The first sign of the new connexion is a letter from a Rev. Dr. Wilson, dated from the Hot Wells, Bristol, on 28 June 1774. This Dr. Wilson was a divine, the son of a bishop, who, falling in love with Mrs. Macaulay, erected within the altar-rails of his church a statue which represented her in the guise of History—pen in hand, and her left arm propped on a pile of volumes of her historical writings—but who afterwards, losing his passion upon her marriage to a young Scotsman, removed the statue and utterly erased *veteris vestigia flammae*. An habitué of the Hot Wells, where he had been lately residing for the benefit of his health, Dr. Wilson had been conversing 'with a few friends at Bristol, merchants of fortune and character', and 'desired by two or three' he writes to Burke to ask whether 'if they find themselves strong enough, you will be ready to serve them, if they put you up as a candidate to represent them'. A crisis, we perceive, was beginning to arise in the political affairs of Bristol. It happened to coincide with a crisis in Burke's own political career. The coincidence of the two crises made Burke, by the end of the year, the junior Member for Bristol.

The crisis in Burke's political career was simple; nor was it really serious. For the last eight years he had enjoyed the interest of Lord Verney, and he had sat for the Borough of Wendover without any charge in nursing his constituency or in meeting the expenses of his election. By 1774 Lord Verney was in financial straits; and, as Burke wrote to Rockingham, 'he will, indeed he must, have those to stand for Wendover who can bear the charge'. A General Election was approaching, a new seat had to be found, and here Burke was in a dilemma. He must have known that Rockingham would readily provide a *pied-à-terre* for his secretary and mentor; that a quiet borough in Yorkshire, where the Rockingham interest was strong, would at once be his for the asking, or even without the asking. This was the way of ease, but it was not the way of pride or of policy. Burke was the virtual leader of a party; he stood in the forefront of the Whigs; he was the man with whom North corresponded on the business of the House, as a Prime Minister corresponds today with the Leader of the Opposition. In such a position it was not indeed necessary, but it would be singularly advantageous, if he could sit for one of the great popular constituencies, which would lend authority to his protests and weight to his policies. There was Westminster, with its 9,000 electors; the City of London, with its 6,000; Bristol, with 5,000; Norwich, with nearly 3,000; any one of these would be a basis, a platform, a pedestal. It was true that such a constituency would certainly need 'nursing', and might even need cosseting; but that could somehow be managed. What was more serious was the expense of any contested election to a man of slender means and ever-leaking purse. Could that obstacle be faced? Was there any way of leaping it, or was it insuperable? We can imagine the conflict of thoughts in Burke's mind; we can understand how his answer to Dr. Wilson's letter contained a mention of 'difficulties', which are not explained, but which we can easily guess to have been financial; we can readily comprehend how, when that mention seemed to put a stop to the Bristol parleys, he darted, perhaps a little wildly, after the illusory hope (suggested by the mercurial Wilkes, who, however, instantly forgot his own suggestion) of standing for Westminster; finally, we can conceive how, after all, he began to let his thoughts settle down quietly, if a little dully, on the prospect of sitting for the little Borough of Malton, in the far East Riding. But Bristol had not said its last word; and this bring us to the history of the crisis in Bristol politics, the issue of which was to settle the crisis in Burke's own political affairs.

Bristol, resolved to be a quiet city, free from the perturbations of parliamentary elections, had made a polite arrangement, towards the end of the reign of George II, under which Whigs and Tories were to share its two seats for the next three Parliaments. But quiet is always difficult to find, more especially in politics, and most of all when it is based on a gentleman's agreement between opposite parties; nor is it a matter of surprise that in 1774 the City of Bristol was far from quiet. The sitting Tory member, Matthew Brickdale, had been less erratic and less troublesome as a member than he had been in his early youth as a woollen draper's apprentice, but he had voted steadily in Parliament for an anti-American policy which irked the trade and the traders of the City. The sitting Whig member, Lord Clare, was an abler and a more influential man, but an even more questionable member: Whig as he was, he had joined the Court interest and supported the ministry in all its measures against America. Both Brickdale and Clare were standing again for election. The Whigs were perturbed; indeed, the whole mercantile class was perturbed. The policy of Lord North had hit the trade of Bristol between wind and water. A house which had previously exported 3,000 pieces of stuff to the Colonies was in 1774 exporting 200. The Bristol pipe-makers, who had previously exported 500 or 600 boxes of pipes, were now exporting none. The Whigs saw their opportunity. They resolved to run at the approaching election a Mr. Cruger, a merchant who had considerable interests both in New York and in Bristol. Some of the finer and more adventurous spirits desired to go farther, and to run a second Whig candidate. Prominent among them were two Quakers—Richard Champion, a merchant with interests in the Carolinas, who had started a china factory in Bristol in 1768, and Joseph Harford, an iron merchant, who had invested capital in Champion's factory. The second candidate whom they had in mind was Burke. Perhaps they knew something of his Quaker schooling and his Quaker connexions; certainly they knew that he was the virtual leader of the Rockingham group, which, from their point of view, was eminently sound on American questions; and they would know, too, about his great April speech on American Taxation, which had just been printed by Dodsley and largely circulated in Bristol, as they would also know about the votes of thanks he had just received from the Manchester Committee of Trade, and from the African Company of Liverpool, London, and Bristol merchants, for his exertions in the cause of commerce. Here was a candidate ready to their hand, if only they could over-leap or break through the obstacles which stood in the way. The obstacles were serious. There was a tangle of party and personal difficulties, not the least of which was the disposition of the Cruger connexion to act in a splendid but selfish isolation; there was the problem of finding a new and separate election fund for a candidate who could bring only himself and his own native talents into the fray. Dr. Wilson had written to Burke on 28 June, but it was not until Saturday, 8 October, that his friends were able at last to put his name before the electors. By that time the election had already begun, and the first day of the poll elapsed; Burke himself, disappointed of Westminster and despairing of Bristol, had gone northward, by way of Doncaster, to his Yorkshire Borough of Malton. It was at Malton, on the afternoon of Tuesday, 11 October, that he received the news from Bristol. He took a post-chaise that evening, and travelling 270 miles in forty-four and a half hours, he was in Bristol at half-past two on the afternoon of Thursday, 13 October, the sixth day of the poll. 'He drove directly to the mayor's house, who not being at home he proceeded to the Guildhall, where he ascended the hustings, and having saluted the electors, the sheriffs and the two candidates (Lord Clare had by this time disappeared, and Brickdale and Cruger alone were left), he reposed himself for a few minutes, and then addressed the electors.' He was late in entering the fray, but he flung himself into it with a gay Irish ardour. You may read the whole story—the polling day by day, the skits, the squibs, the pamphlets, some of them so true to Burke's style that they must have come from Burke's pen—in an admirable little work by Mr. G. E. Weare, the bearer of a name already well known in the City in 1774, on *Edmund Burke's Connection with Bristol*. In spite of some fluctuations at the polls, the issue was never seriously in doubt; and after nearly a month of voting and treating and canvassing and pamphleteering, the sheriffs, at 12 o'clock on Thursday, 3 November, declared Henry Cruger and Edmund Burke the Members for Bristol. It was almost to a day the anniversary of the landing of William of Orange and the glorious Whig revolution of 1688. Enthusiasm ran high: the victors were 'chaired . . . amid the acclamations of an innumerable concourse of people . . . and the ladies, from the crowded windows of the houses in the different streets, were not wanting in testifying their joy'. Burke rode resplendent over his difficulties, and as he rode and waved his hat we can imagine Hannah More shedding some delicious tears to see her nodding cockade of 'myrtle, bay and laurel, trimmed with silver tassels'.

These were indeed happy days for a man of Burke's temperament—perhaps the happiest days of his life. A round of dinners followed the victory; he was admitted a freeman of Bristol; all the world was gay. 'This is the second city in the kingdom,' he wrote to his sister in Ireland, 'and to be invited and chosen for it, without any request of mine, at no expense to myself, but with much charge and trouble to every public-spirited gentleman, is an honour to which we ought not to be insensible.' Jane Burke had stayed in their London house, which had been burgled during the election (but she had not been seriously frightened, thinking that the alarm in the house was only an express from Bristol), and Jane in London received news from her husband about 'a very handsome dinner' and 'a good entertainment' and his entertaining 'some glimpse of hope that I shall see you shortly'. Perhaps he himself was happiest when on 18 November, on his way home to Beaconsfield, he stopped at Oxford, where his only son had just come into residence at Christ Church, and 'drank a glass of wine with him and some of his young friends' to the toast of Bristol and the health of Richard Champion. For Jane Burke there was destined another and more placid but more abiding joy. Richard Champion and his wife gave her a wonderfully decorated tea-service of Bristol China, with every piece inscribed *Optimae Britannicarum Matronarum*—'to the best of British wives'. We can imagine her, with her inexpressible smile and a low, soft voice of inquiry about the tastes and needs of her guests, presiding over the tea-table and its service, and still remembering Bristol and Richard Champion, even when Bristol had been parted from her husband, and even perhaps, during the long fifteen years of her widowhood, when her husband had been parted from her.

In the speech which he had made when he was declared member Burke had spoken with a sublime disregard of the raucous clamour of party rage and petulence. 'We hear them, and we look upon them, just as you, gentlemen, when you enjoy the serene air on your lofty rocks, look down upon the gulls that skim the mud of your river, when it is exhausted of its tide.' But the gulls never desert the Avon, and the clamour of trouble never ceased to fly round the head of Burke so long as he was Member for Bristol. It was perhaps a little thing that he was abhorred by the Tories; that the clergy had walked in procession to the polls to vote against him; that on the day of his election all the bells were obstinately silent in the church towers and steeples. It was a more serious thing that he and his Whig colleague never saw eye to eye. The partnership of 'Doodle Doo' from New York and 'the Hibernian Demosthenes', as they were irreverently called by their adversaries, was uneasy from the first. They had contested the election separately, with separate funds and platforms. Cruger had preached short Parliaments and a place bill for disabling members from holding public offices; Burke, six years before, in the *Thoughts on the Cause of the Present Discontents*, had sought to prove the futility of both policies, and he had seen no reason to alter his views. Cruger, when he returned thanks for his election, descanted on 'the legality and propriety of the people's instructing their representatives in Parliament', and termed himself 'the servant of my constituents, not their master, subservient to their will, not superior to it'. Burke on the same occasion, boldly contradicting the fashionable and popular doctrine of his own colleague, had declared, in a great and classical passage, that 'authoritative instructions and mandates issued ... are things utterly unknown to the laws of this land', and that a member of Parliament, representing the whole commons of all the realm, owed only the free devotion of his own unbiased opinion and judgement to the discovery and advocacy of the general good. 'You choose a Member indeed; but when you have chosen him, he is not Member of Bristol, but he is a Member of *Parliament*.' Here we touch the most serious and the noblest trouble which lay before Burke—a trouble far greater than that with the Tories; a trouble far deeper than that with Mr. Cruger, however deeply 'the absurd and petty behaviour of my foolish colleague' might rankle; a trouble with his whole constituency; a trouble which went to the roots of the theory and practice of parliamentary representation.

I have already spoken, in other connexions, of the sad and paradoxical chance which made Burke, with his ways of thinking, the Member for Bristol, with its ways of living. There were faults on both sides, and the failure of Burke to agree with Bristol was by no means entirely due to Bristol. The election of 1774 was like a sudden love-match, based on an ardent but ignorant affection, and divergences of views and of temper began to appear as soon as the marriage was celebrated. Even during the election a writer with the pseudonym of 'Bristol' had urged, 'it is plain that ye have greatly mistaken one another, and the best thing that can now be done is to make explanations and apologies on all sides and part'. 'Bristol' was only anticipating, by six years, what was destined to happen in 1780. In truth Burke, in the circumstances of the case, and even apart from his expressed views on the nature of parliamentary representation, was hardly fitted, under eighteenth-century conditions, to sit for a great popular constituency. He was poor, and he was in opposition. The two together were fatal. A rich man might have succeeded, even though he was in opposition, because he could have used his wealth to conciliate the support of his constituency. A poor man might have succeeded, provided that he belonged to the side of the government, because he could have induced the government to grant favours and places to his constituency. A man who was both poor and in opposition was already condemned in advance. There was some justice in the contention of another of the many election pamphleteers, who called himself 'Senex', that 'a superior fortune in these corrupt times is a necessary qualification'. There was less justice, however, in the reason which the writer gave for his view. He urged that a superior fortune was necessary in order to prevent a member from being corrupted by government. He might have urged more truly that it was necessary in order to enable a member to corrupt—or, as the wise would call it, to conciliate—his own constituents.

But even if he had been rich Burke might still, with his previous training, his temperament and his views, have failed to keep the affections of Bristol. He came from a pocket borough, in which he had enjoyed eight years of peaceful inattention from his constituents. He came with something of a didactic habit of mind, which made him a noble lecturer, but a poor winner of popularity. He came from the Rockingham connexion of grand seigneurs, anxious to do good to the people, but expecting the people to receive with a ready confidence and gratitude the good they were anxious to do. Another of those Bristol election pamphleteers (he called himself 'Caution', but he may well have been the same as 'Bristol' or 'Senex') had put a pertinent question. 'Do you know that he is the agent and instrument of the Rockingham party? Do you know he has written a book recommending the principles of that party? That they amount to this . . . that they will invest themselves with the people's rights, who shall be free in their power but not otherwise, for that *they* shall have virtue and ability enough for you all?' This was a shrewd thrust. It becomes all the shrewder when we reflect that Burke, with that generalizing tendency which was strong upon him in spite of all his denunciations of metaphysical abstractions, had elevated the tendency of his party into a principle of politics. He had preached, in the very instant and article of his election, the doctrine of the free member, representing the whole of the nation, who admits no tie on his judgement and sits loose to local instructions. In its essence it was an admirably true doctrine. But as Burke himself taught, the point about political doctrines is less their internal and inherent truth than their external and actual application. 'The majors make a pompous figure in the battle,' he once wrote, 'but the victory of truth depends upon the little minor of circumstances.' In this sense he had contended, in all his speeches on American affairs, that the doctrine of parliamentary sovereignty was indeed true, but you got only a little way with its assertion; the essential thing, the real crux, was the method and mode of its application, the understanding of the minor of circumstances, in a word, the policy in the given case. This was the crux which arose for Burke himself in Bristol, when it came to the actual practice of his doctrine of representation. Would he listen to the little minor of circumstances? Would he act *suaviter in modo*? Could he attune himself to a great popular constituency? That is the essence of our inquiry.

Before we turn to that inquiry, it is only fair to Burke to observe that he had to put his doctrine to the proof in a sea of stormy circumstance. He had been returned for Bristol on the wave of a Whig revolution in its party politics. But would that revolution endure? We can see in the light of after-events, and on a view of all the Bristol elections of the eighteenth century as they are recorded in Latimer's *Annals of Bristol*, that the answer was inevitably bound to be in the negative. Down to 1754 Bristol was a Tory constituency. From 1754 to 1774 it was represented by a declared Tory and by a Whig who was really a Tory. In the reaction of 1774 two Whigs were returned. In 1780 a natural reaction to the other extreme resulted in the return of two Tories. In the three elections of the rest of the eighteenth century Bristol returned to its old equilibrium before 1774, and was represented by a declared Tory and by a Whig who, on two of the three occasions, was really a Tory.[1] The rhythm of the century ran against Burke. The immediate tide of the times was no less adverse. If Burke had been returned on any single issue, it was the issue of America. In 1774 the country

---

[1] Cruger, who was a genuine, if not exactly a representative Whig, was elected in 1784 by a small majority on the strength of his local connexions. On the two other occasions a conventional Whig of good connexions was imported from outside.

was drifting into war with the Colonies, and the Bristol merchants, heavily hit in their colonial trade, wanted peace. Burke was the great exponent of peace and conciliation; he had been the agent of New York in England since 1771, and was versed in American conditions: the merchants turned to him to save their trade—and, incidentally, to save America. By 1775 war had come, and the change which always comes in any country with the coming of war was already at work. The nation rallied to the national standard: to be pro-American in 1775 was equivalent to being pro-Boer in 1900; and, anyhow, there were contracts for the supply of the troops to be got by the merchants, who were already, as Burke said in one of his violent phrases, 'sniffing the cadaverous *haut goût* of lucrative war'. Burke and his party persevered in their old policy, and they became unpopular because they were naturally, if unjustly, conceived to be unpatriotic; Bristol rallied round the flag. By the beginning of 1777 the Common Council was congratulating George III on the success of his arms, and hoping that 'the seeds of rebellion would speedily be eradicated'. By 1778 troops of volunteers were being raised and subscriptions started in aid of the national cause. The Tories of Bristol subscribed a fund of £21,000: it hardly mattered that only £4,500 was actually paid, for, as Burke sarcastically said, the government wanted 'names' and credit even more than cash; and, in any case, the Whigs, led by Harford, were only able to subscribe £363 to their own particular cause of aiding American prisoners of war. Burke fretted and fumed; he suggested to his friends in Bristol a policy of public petitions against the policy of the Government, petitions followed up 'by a regular solicitation, pursued through all the modes of civil resistance and legal opposition'; he even suggested the possibility of a sort of Whig counter-troop of volunteers, 'under the guidance of those who will not betray you to the enemy abroad or at home'. But these were idle arms against a sea of troubles, and if it comforted him a little personally, it profited him nothing with the bulk of his constituents that, as Franklin wrote to him, his 'health was among the foremost' at the dinners of the American Congress in Philadelphia.

There were other issues which arose during the war, or out of the war (as indeed all issues, in the course of an engulfing war, seem to spring from its ramifying operation and influence), that raised fresh storms on the troubled waters of the years in which Burke was Member for Bristol. One of the greatest of those issues was the economic, or, as it may also be called from the particular quarter in which it arose, the Irish issue. In 1774 Burke and his constituents had seemed to be in agreement on economic questions. They both desired an open trade with America; and indeed that was the issue which had drawn them together. But there was a fundamental divergence of views behind their apparent agreement. Burke's constituents believed in an open trade so far as it suited their view of their interests. If they thought that a close or restricted trade was better suited to those interests in any quarter—and in nearly every quarter they thought that this was the case—they reverted to their normal belief in a system of rigid protection. Burke, a disciple or an anticipator of Adam Smith, had a natural belief in a system of open trade, under which every part of the Empire freely used its natural advantages to the general benefit (as he was convinced) of the whole. 'That to which I attached myself the more particularly', he wrote to an Irish correspondent on the New Year's Day of 1780, 'was to fix the principle of a free trade in all parts of these islands, as founded in justice and beneficial to the whole, but principally to this, the seat of the supreme power.' The divergence came to a head in regard to the economic affairs of Ireland. Ever since the Revolution of 1688, and indeed ever since the Restoration of 1660, Ireland had lain under a system of economic restriction designed for the benefit of English agriculture, English manufacturing towns, and English ports. By 1778 the course of the war had raised the question of its modification or abolition. It was argued in public that Ireland had contributed to the war, and she deserved her recompense; it was felt in secret that Ireland was beginning to be restive, and she needed some inducement to remain quiet. Paradoxically enough it was Lord Clare (now Earl Nugent), the Whig who was really a Tory and had disappeared from Bristol in 1774, by whom the issue was raised; but whatever else Nugent was he was Irish, and that fact explains the paradox. As an Irishman also, no less than as a believer in open imperial trade inspired by the conviction that a benefit to the trade of Ireland would be a benefit to England and the Empire, Burke supported the action of Nugent, and even proposed an extension of the concessions for which Nugent had moved. A storm arose in Bristol and the English commercial world, which blindly saw ruin in such a policy; for 'these things', said Burke, 'are hid from their eyes'. Burke persevered in spite of the storm, and in spite of positive orders from some of his constituents to vote against any and every concession of free trade to Ireland. The weak North, who had at first favoured the proposals of Nugent and Burke, bowed to the storm of opposition in 1778, and again, when the proposals were renewed, in the early part of 1779. North bowed again before another storm, a storm of a very different order, at the end of 1779, when in the face of muttering Irish discontent and the menace of the Irish volunteers, who were ready to extort by force what had not been conceded by grace, he granted to Irish trade a fuller measure of freedom than Burke had ever demanded. It was a paradox of this new situation that Burke, who had been eager in activity before, was now silent and inert, unable to speak against a ministry which had adopted and extended his own policy, but equally unable to speak for a ministry which had adopted the policy precipitately in obedience to *force majeure*. The Irish noticed and censured his silence, and the man who had been thoroughly unpopular in Bristol, in the beginning of 1778, for supporting the cause of Irish free trade, became almost as unpopular in Dublin, by the beginning of 1780, for failing to support the cause openly and actively—and that without ceasing to suffer from unpopularity in Bristol. The sea of economics—the sea on which the contending winds of Free Trade and Protection blow against one another—was indeed a stormy sea for Burke, as it has been for many another statesman since his time.

The other main issue besides the economic which arose out of the war, or was at any rate connected with the war, was the religious issue. We had stood together in war; why should we be divided, either in war or in peace, by a system of measures of repression, or at any rate of inequality of treatment, which divided the privileged Anglican sharply from members of other confessions? Burke was a convinced Anglican, in spite of the lying rumours which made him a crypto-Jesuit educated at St. Omer; but his mother was a Catholic, his wife's father was a Catholic, some of his best friends were Quakers, and he had always, from his Trinity College days, believed in the principle and the cause of toleration, whether for Catholics or for Nonconformists. Already in 1773, in a speech in favour of the relaxation of penal laws against Dissenting preachers and teachers, he had spoken of such laws as nets, that entangled only 'the poor fluttering silken wings of a tender conscience'. When, therefore, a Catholic Relief Bill was proposed in the English Parliament in 1778, and a similar bill was at the same time proposed in the Irish Parliament, he gave a quiet but effective support to both. Both bills were successful; Burke received the warm thanks of the promoters and friends of the Irish bill; he was offered, but he instantly and absolutely refused, a complimentary present of 500 guineas for his exertions. The passage of the bills had been peaceful, but a wave of Protestant agitation slowly gathered head in Scotland, and spreading south to London it broke in the agitation of the Protestant Association and the atrocities of the Gordon Riots during the June of 1780. Burke behaved nobly during the riots; he behaved nobly afterwards, both when he exerted himself with the government to secure merciful treatment for the rioters, and when he strenuously and successfully opposed any modification of the Catholic Relief Act of 1778 in obedience to Protestant agitation. But an invincible Protestant prejudice had been aroused; the Protestantism of every candidate was severely scrutinized in the General Election of 1780, as even Charles James Fox found at Westminster; and it is significant that Burke, in the great speech 'previous to the election' which he delivered at Bristol in September, by way of apology for his parliamentary career, found himself compelled to devote the greater part of his vindication to the issue of toleration. He knew that he spoke to a critical audience: the solid Protestantism of Bristol had trembled on the brink of a sympathetic riot against Popery only three months before, when London seemed to have lit a Protestant beacon-fire for the nation, and the Bristol Corporation had spent £85. 12s. 5d. in 'sundry expenses on account of a threatened and expected riot'. But he was not dismayed. He spoke warmly and generously, because he spoke from the full humanity of a deeply humane mind. He could never, he said, proscribe his fellow-citizens by denominations, and indeed persecution was so unnatural to all honest men that they gladly snatched the first opportunity of quitting it and returning home —home 'to our natural family mansion, to the grand social principle that unites all men, in all descriptions, under the shadow of an equal and impartial justice'. If he had laboured in the cause of toleration, it was of a piece, he pleaded, with his other labours; and here he mentioned, in illustration, those labours for the improvement of the law of debt which were one of the charges against his public conduct. Indeed, he urged, all he had done was of a piece; he could not suffer 'any kind of oppression or wrong, on any grounds whatsoever; not on political, as in the affairs of America; not on commercial, as in those of Ireland; not in civil, as in the laws of debt; not in religious, as in the statutes against Protestant or Catholic Dissenters'. This was Burke's swan-song at Bristol, save for the few words he uttered, three days later, in declining the poll and retiring from the contest, when he found that any chance of his election had utterly vanished. It is, upon any estimate, a very sufficient apology for his public conduct in Parliament upon all the main issues of the years of his membership. But it still leaves us with the inquiry, postponed for a while but now finally imminent, the critical and crucial inquiry into Burke's conception and practice of the duty, or right, of a parliamentary representative, not merely on particular issues, but in the humdrum of day-to-day contact with a lively and turbulent popular constituency.

We must first of all notice certain peculiar currents, and a sort of flurry of gusts and flaws in the atmosphere, which made navigation particularly difficult for a member of Parliament in this period. In 1769 the House of Commons, acting on its own discretion and proceeding by no fixed or known rule of law, had expelled and re-expelled John Wilkes, the popularly elected member for the county constituency of Middlesex, and it had finally crowned its action, at the third time of asking, by declaring that the candidate who stood second at the poll, and had received only 296 votes to the 1,143 of Wilkes, was the real choice of the electorate and the true Member for Middlesex. This was to enthrone Parliament over the electorate even in the elementary article of election itself; it was to make the House of Commons, and not the Middlesex electors, the electorate for Middlesex. Such extreme action naturally provoked a reaction to the other extreme. The extreme democratic doctrine of the sovereignty of the electorate—a reformed electorate, an electorate to be vastly increased in numbers and loftily elevated in consequence—began to lift its head. The year 1769, it has been said, is the birth-year of modern Radicalism. Democratic clubs sprang into existence; the democratic doctrines began to be preached that electorates should be larger, in order to exert their proper influence at the time of election, that Parliaments should be shorter, in order to feel that proper influence more frequently, and that, to make assurance doubly sure, the electorate should issue 'instructions' to Parliaments even during the course of their sitting. It was the doctrine of instructions or mandates, in particular, which was to produce immediate and turbulent consequences. Here the mercurial Wilkes, prolific of uncalculated and unexpected results, had set in motion a groundswell which was to agitate the course not only of Burke but also of many another Member of Parliament. Larger electorates and shorter Parliaments were both matters which required parliamentary statutes, and parliamentary statutes, never very easily brought to birth, would be more than usually slow when they had to be produced by a Parliament which, if it were not actually committing suicide by their production, was at any rate rigorously reducing its diet and its figure. Instructions, however, were on a different footing; it needed only a committee of electors and a little drafting, and there they were. Early in 1769 one of the members for the City of London was declaring that if he received instructions from his constituents contrary to his convictions, he 'would not oppose his judgment to that of 6,000 of his fellow-citizens'. Bristol was hardly behind London. At a dinner in honour of Wilkes, at the Cock Inn, in June, '45 gentlemen,' writes Latimer in his *Annals* 'sat down to a feast of 45 fowls, a 45 lb. ham, a 45 lb. rump of beef, 45 cabbages, 45 cucumbers, 45 loaves and 45 tarts, to which were added 45 gallons of ale, 45 glasses of brandy, and 45 papers of tobacco'—an ample celebration of No. 45 of the *North Briton*. A month later, at a meeting in the Guildhall, promoted by Champion and Harford, the very two citizens who five years later promoted the candidature of Burke, it was agreed that the electors should have 'their opinions represented, not guided, by members of their choice', and a petition in this sense, signed by 1,500 electors, was forwarded to Brickdale and Lord Clare, the sitting members, neither of whom, and least of all Clare, the Whig who was really a Tory, had ever set ear to the ground to detect their electors' opinions. Bristol had already shown its hand, and the more its citizens were affected, in their purses and their fortunes, by the growth of American and other troubles after 1769, the more ambitious they became to guide the action of their parliamentary representatives.

In 1770, in the *Thoughts on the Cause of the Present Discontents*, Burke had addressed himself to the current issue. He had admitted, he had even proclaimed, the distempers of Parliament. But even in 1770, when he might well have been tempted to use the democratic stick to beat the Court party which was the object of his attack, he had expressed himself with measured and circumspect caution. To the cry of larger electorates and shorter Parliaments he turned, as he always continued to turn, a deaf ear. Neither now nor at any time could he reconcile himself to disturbing the prescriptive structure and the balanced system of the English constitution by tinkering with its weathered brick and ancient mortar. On the issue of electoral guidance of parliamentary representatives he seems, at first sight, to go farther. He believes that until a confidence in government is re-established, the people should be excited to watch the conduct of their representatives more strictly. To this end, he would have meetings in counties and boroughs to settle the standards for judging the conduct of members; to this end, again, he would have frequent publication of parliamentary votes on all important issues. But this policy, we soon perceive, is not a policy of instructions. In the first place, it is a temporary policy, 'until a confidence in Government is re-established'; in the second place, it is a policy of watching conduct in the light of previously settled standards, and of remonstrating, after the event, whenever conduct fails to satisfy such standards; but it is not a policy of giving instructions in advance about the conduct actually to be followed. Even at this point—and it is perhaps the farthest point to which Burke went—he still leaves the member of Parliament a free if responsible agent. When he came down to Bristol in 1774 this idea of free if responsible agency—we may almost say, free *because* responsible, when we reflect how closely freedom and responsibility are intertwined by the very nature of moral action—had settled deeply in his mind. After all, he had acted as a free member for his quiet Borough of Wendover during the last eight years; after all, he had been associated for all that period with a Rockingham circle of grandees who, in any case, felt themselves free in virtue of their very position, but who also, over and above that, demanded for their associates the freedom from local ties and instructions which was the essential condition of a free and full entry into the bonds and connexions of party. Even in the desponding days of September, when his constituency of Wendover was slipping away, Westminster had proved a false hope, and Bristol seemed hopeless—even when he was wondering whether he 'ought not totally to abandon this public station'—he had written to Rockingham: 'Most assuredly I never will put my feet within the doors of St. Stephen's Chapel, without being as much my own master as hitherto I have been, and at liberty to pursue the same course.' What he said in the despondency of September he repeated in the election of November. Newly elected Member for Bristol, he might have been pardoned if he had followed the politician's way and hidden his convictions behind a fleecy cloud of vague and bland compliments. But with the fine general cast of his mind he had more of the thinker's obstinate loyalty to a settled conviction, grounded on general principles, than he had of the politician's suavity and *savoir faire*; and he preferred to be tactlessly and admirably truthful. He had been brought down to Bristol by Champion and Hartford, the promoters of the meeting and petition of 1769, and they were perhaps standing on the platform when he spoke his first words as Member for Bristol. He was following upon the speech of his colleague and senior member, and his colleague had just said: 'It has ever been my opinion that the electors have a right to instruct their members.' He might have said, with that studied vagueness which is the saviour of political reputation: 'On the whole, and in the main, and without forgetting the other side of the question, I say ditto to Mr. Cruger'—as, by the way, Mr. Cruger is apocryphally, most apocryphally, alleged on this very occasion to have said 'ditto to Mr. Burke'. Instead of this—perhaps with some working of the brow and a certain tight pressing of the lips, perhaps with some violent gesticulation and an undulating motion of the head—he said, at some little length (but every word was pregnant): 'I say the opposite.'

This was an early flash of lightning; and it was to be followed, on this side and on that, by many intermittent rumblings of thunder. It was a triple conflict which provoked the rumblings

—a conflict on the issue which we may designate by the name of 'living in'; a conflict on the issue of 'commissions'; a conflict on the issue of 'instructions'. Each deserves a brief examination.

By the issue of 'living in' I mean the question of the amount of local residence, personal presence, and social attendance which a constituency such as Bristol might fairly expect from its members. Under a statute of 1413 it had long been the rule of the constitution that members should be actually resident in the constituencies for which they sat. The rule had long been in abeyance, and it was formally abolished in 1774. But the very fact that the rule of law had just been abrogated made it all the more necessary to find some rule of manners, or convention of etiquette, to take its place. About this time the tendency in the great southern boroughs was setting in favour of the election of local merchants. If a member were elected who was not of that stamp, he might at any rate be expected to establish a local connexion and to cultivate local society. 'Will Mr. Burke be answerable to you? Will he reside among you?'—such had been the questions of an anonymous pamphleteer during the election of 1774. The answer was disappointing. A home-keeping man, who had no sooner reached England in 1750 than he wrote to an Irish friend to say that he found something pleasing in the good old expression, 'A family burying-ground', Burke never for a moment thought of exchanging his beloved Beaconsfield and its country church for Bristol or Bath. Boswell records how he once heard him say, 'very pleasantly' . . . 'Though I have the honour to represent Bristol, I should not like to live there: I should be obliged to be so much upon my good behaviour.' But even without living there, he might have resided there upon occasion; and he knew and confessed that something of the sort was needed. 'An annual complimentary visit', he wrote to Rockingham in 1775, 'is a mark of decent attention and respect, which they require from their members: at least, they require it from those who can show them no other.' Actually, he paid two visits, one in the September of 1775 and one in the August of 1776. For the next four years, until the General Election in the autumn of 1780, he seems to have been a steady absentee. This was inexcusable. We may admit in extenuation his home-keeping habits; we may recognize in mitigation 'the horrid expense of these expeditions'. But it was hard upon his supporters, who sent pressing and hospitable invitations, to be told in reply: 'I am really too ill,' or 'My affairs and the advanced and uncertain season of the year will not permit me', or 'I feel myself something weakened and extremely fatigued by the attendance in the most laborious session I remember since 1768'. After all, it only took sixteen hours, at the rate of threepence a mile, to get from London to Bristol, and Burke was under fifty years of age. We cannot absolve him from the charge of inattention to his constituents. But we may quote his own defence, which is not ignoble: 'My canvass of you was not on the 'Change, nor in the county-meetings, nor in the clubs of this city; it was in the House of Commons; it was at the custom-house; it was in the Council; it was at the Treasury; it was at the Admiralty. I canvassed you through your affairs, and not your persons.'

This brings us to the second issue—that of 'commissions', or, in other words, regular exertions on behalf of local interests, corporate or individual, at the instance of local solicitations. Strictly, this is another issue from that of 'instructions', which, in their proper and exact sense, are mandates on matters of national interest and public moment; but the two issues readily intertwined (a matter of public moment might affect local interests, or a matter of local interest raise questions of national importance), and their treatment can hardly be divided. In the politics of that age there were still some features of the sort which we are now apt to call American. There were borough 'bosses'; 'who does not know,' Burke asked in a speech on a bill for shortening the duration of Parliaments, 'that in all the corporations, all the open boroughs, . . . there is some leading man . . . some wealthy merchant or considerable manufacturer . . . who is followed by the whole flock?' There was an expectation of local 'log-rolling'; 'the candidate,' said Burke in the same speech, 'must bring . . . the power of serving and obliging the rulers of corporations, of winning over the popular leaders of political clubs, associations and neighbourhoods.' In Bristol these features were no worse, and perhaps no better, than they were elsewhere. Burke, whose election expenses (we have to remember) had been paid for him, had to reckon with the 'Union' and the 'Bell' Clubs among his own supporters. He had to reckon, in the general life of the City, with the Corporation, which was something in the nature of a clique of related oligarchical families;

with the Society of Merchant Venturers, which had a hall of its own, a master of its own, a policy of its own, and had somehow annexed the quays and the wharfage dues of the City; and with the African Company, which, as we have seen, was mainly a company of Bristol merchants. He had to reckon, in a more scattered and desultory way, with individual firms, affected (or feeling themselves affected) in their business interests by parliamentary policy or administrative action, and pressing accordingly for action in the House or intercession with the government on behalf of those interests. It was an age of influence, of patronage, of favours, of jobs; a word in season might mean a large entry on the cash side of the ledger; and Burke naturally received commissions, which might easily become instructions, to speak the word. It was a labour of love to solicit orders from his noble friends for Champion's china factory; but there were many other businesses which required an attention far costlier of time and patience. He might have to dun the Treasury in the matter of importation of fruit; at one time the soap-makers had a business for him, and at another time 'Mr. Cowles and some other gentlemen of the glass-trade' were calling at Beaconsfield to ask for assistance; on one occasion the fishing off Newfoundland would engage his attention, and on another a local fire-engine bill would be pressing. Burke sat tight to his duties: 'I do attend', he assured Champion in 1777, 'to the small tithes of my duty in Parliament . . . I shall endeavour to omit nothing to help the most trifling business or the most insignificant person in Bristol.' But he groaned under the obligation, which, he thought, was twice cursed in its effects on a member, not only distracting him from the weightier matters of the law, but also driving him towards dependence on a government which alone could grant the favours he was asked to secure. He could not repress a groan even in his speech to the electors on the eve of the General Election of 1780: 'I ran about wherever your affairs could call me, and in acting for you I often appeared rather as a ship-broker than as a Member of Parliament.'

What with private commissions which tended to become public instructions, and what with pure public instructions, whether to vote against free trade for Ireland or otherwise to deflect the direct and congenial course of his policy and ideas, Burke found himself hard pressed. He had something of the zeal of an apostle, and he felt himself enmeshed by clinging and impeding threads. The feeling broke out in the famous cry of his last great speech to his Bristol electors: 'Applaud us when we run; console us when we fall; cheer us when we recover; but let us pass on—for God's sake let us pass on.' This is a passionate impatience, certainly comprehensible, perhaps pardonable, and yet hardly conciliatory. But the question raised between Burke and his constituents was more than personal and psychological; it was, in its essence, as we have seen, a grave constitutional question, which went to the impersonal roots of politics. It was a question whether the representative should be a free and national representative, determining himself freely on national issues in association with a national party which he had freely entered and whose tenets he had voluntarily embraced, or whether he should be primarily the attentive member of a local constituency, regarding its wishes, discharging its commissions, and acknowledging a prior loyalty to its opinions and interests. It is a question which has long been settled with us; and the foundations of the settlement had been laid early in the eighteenth century, by Standing Orders of the House of Commons for Public Business, passed in the reign of Queen Anne, which prevented public money from being voted except on the motion of ministers of the Crown, and thus disabled the private member from procuring public grants for the advantage of local interests. But the question was by no means so definitely settled in 1780 as it is to-day. For one thing our modern parliamentary procedure for private bill legislation, which substracts private and local bills from the general House and remits them to a sort of judicial procedure in private bill committees, had not yet been developed, and a local member could still affect the fate of such bills by his speech and vote in the House. For another thing, the administrative procedure of the executive was still liable to be influenced in 1780 as it cannot be influenced to-day: a minister might buy a supporter by conceding a favour; and so long as such traffic was possible, the local member was always tempted to haggle for local favours. Under these conditions a great popular constituency, with all its local bills to be pressed and local favours to be sought, was apt to lie particularly heavy on its member. It became a question, as Burke said, whether we might not 'degrade our national representation into a confused and scuffling bustle of local agency'. It has been said by Dr. Lawrence Lowell, in a passage in which he deals with our system of private bill legislation, that the curse of most representative bodies at the present day is the tendency of the members to urge the interests of their localities or constituents. It is a curse which may still be found operative in France and the United States; it is a curse from which we have been saved by the Standing Orders of Queen Anne's reign, by our system of private bill legislation, by the growth of a firm tradition that the executive is not to be pressed by the private member, and (we may also add) by the stand which Burke made on the principle of the whole issue between 1774 and 1780. The Bristol idea—not the idea of the best minds in Bristol, but the idea of ordinary and average opinion—was in favour of a representative more or less of the nature of a French deputy, who discharges commissions in Paris ('down to the choice of a wet nurse', Lord Bryce has said, 'or the purchase of an umbrella'), and exerts his influence with the ministry to secure decorations, minor posts, and local advantages. Burke was willing to discharge many commissions; he was willing, as he said in the address he issued on the day of his election in 1774, to receive 'frequent advice and seasonable assistance'; but he stood by his conception of the national representative, and he would not stoop to 'the little silly canvass prattle of obeying instructions and having no opinions but yours'. There was so much, he felt, at stake. There was the dignity and position of the House of Commons. There was the whole future of party—whether it should be a national force under central direction, a band of brothers united for promoting by their joint endeavours the national interest upon some particular principle, or should sink into a local caucus immersed and lost in a confused and scuffling local bustle. Where so much was at stake, he was willing to stake himself. He staked, and he lost. But if he lost his constituency, he added a stone to the fabric of the English constitution. He was true himself, and he helped others after him to be true, to his own wish, which now stands carved on the base of the statue erected to his honour in Bristol: 'I wish to be a Member of Parliament, *to have my share of doing good and resisting evil.*'

It is easy, caught by the glow of Burke's own eloquence, to see only his side of the matter, and to see it wholly and entirely resplendent. But there is another side which must not be neglected or overlooked, however our eyes may be dazzled. To espouse without reserve the cause of Burke against Bristol would be, in effect, to deny the cause of democracy. Democracy is not 'living in', or 'commissions', or 'instructions', and so far as he protested against such things, Burke was not protesting against democracy. But democracy has some positive implications, to which he was perhaps a little blind. Foremost among those implications is the principle of the value of discussion. Discussion, we may almost say, is the life-breath of all communities which in reality, and not merely in name, are free and self-governing. In itself, and considered simply as a process, it is an intellectual gymnastic which elicits and enlists the energy of a people's mind; in its results, and considered in the light of its product rather than its process, it achieves a common purpose, an agreed object (or system of objects) of the common life, a general will which is the peace of the whole community. The area of a community's discussion must ideally be coterminous with the community; if it is narrower, if it is confined to a section or sections, it fails as an intellectual gymnastic, because it fails to elicit the whole energy of the community's mind, and it fails as the producer of a common purpose and a general will, because it produces only a sectional purpose and a partial will. Burke could write nobly on occasions, as he does in a passage in the *Reflections on the Revolution in France*, of mind conspiring with mind, and time producing that 'union of minds which alone can produce all the good we aim at'. But in his normal belief the union of minds was confined to a narrow circle, and the area of discussion was an area of the *élite*. He hardly regarded himself as engaged in discussion with the people of Bristol, or the people of Bristol as engaged in discussion with him; he rather regarded himself and his fellow members in the light of 'publick Counsellors', or as we may say, in the language of that book of Ecclesiasticus which he knew and quoted, 'leaders of the people by their counsels, and by their knowledge of learning meet for the people, wise and eloquent in their instructions'. He remained something of the scholar of Trinity College, 'damned absolute'; something of the professor, who even in the House of Commons was apt to speak *ex cathedra*; something of the associate of Rockinghams and Portlands, Richmonds and Cavendishes, who was perhaps a little prone to magnify the pearls of aristocratic wisdom.

It is interesting to cull the references to the people, the electorate, the multitude, from the letters Burke wrote and the speeches he delivered during the six years of his connexion with Bristol. The will of the people, he believes, must in the last resort always prevail, even when it is set towards parliamentary reform. It would be a dreadful thing, he writes, repeating himself almost in the very same words in two different letters of April 1780, if there were *any* power of strength enough to oppose with effect the general wishes of the people. But this, after all, is a negative attitude; and the same attitude recurs in a speech in Parliament of the same year. It is a great and glorious object, he says, to govern according to the sense of the people; this object can only be obtained through popular election; and (he suddenly and paradoxically concludes his syllogism) popular election is a great evil. We who are here may be elected—indeed we must be elected; but our office is to be faithful watchmen, and our duty to give the people information, not to receive it from them: 'we are not to go to school to them to learn the principles of law and government.' In the same strain, in a letter to a citizen of Bristol in 1780, he explained that the people of Bristol 'placed me in a situation which might enable me to discern what was fit to be done on a consideration of the relative circumstances of this country and all its neighbours; this was what you could not so well do yourselves'. To the assembled citizens of Bristol themselves, in his last great speech, he stated his belief that the opinions of even the greatest multitudes were not the standard of rectitude—a true enough proposition, but one which needs explanation, and is not in itself the whole of the truth. In his more familiar correspondence he was even more explicit. He wrote to Champion in 1780: 'The people only remain, and you know that I never expected much from the people.' He wrote to Harford, after the General Election of 1780, that the Bristol election had shown 'the madness of the common people's dream, that they could be anything without the aid of better fortunes and better heads than their own'.

Many, if not all, of these expressions of opinion belong to the year 1780. We must allow something for the tone of Burke's feelings in a year in which he might well say to himself that he was fighting with beasts at Ephesus—with anti-Irish prejudice, Protestant prejudice, anti-debtor prejudice, every manner of prejudice, all at the same time. We must also allow something for the pontifical and didactic manner of the period. We must not take Burke too seriously, for example, when he says, in a speech of this same year, 1780: 'The distemper of this age is a poverty of spirit and of genius: it is trifling, it is futile, worse than ignorant, superficially taught: with the politicks and morals of girls at a boarding-school rather than of men and statesmen.' But the expressions of Burke's views on the value of public opinion are not confined to the year 1780, or to solemn and pontifical passages. They are scattered through the six years of his connexion with Bristol, and they recur in different contexts. The people do not think, and they do not act; they must be guided and goaded; there must be party direction from the centre, and party agitation in each locality. Burke was not a wire-puller; but he was ready to pull the strings which would make the people speak in the sense he desired. No sooner was the election of 1774 over than he was urging Rockingham to mature public discontents by proper means, to give them direction, in a word, to organize, to agitate, to make the people felt by making the people feel. Along this line Burke was led to occupy his thoughts and his time with a solicitude of drafting petitions; of arranging meetings of counties and boroughs for their adoption; of promoting committees of correspondence which would keep the meetings in touch; of urging that petitions should be backed by what he called regular solicitation, and even pursued to the lengths of civil resistance and legal opposition. Under this aspect the people becomes a sort of managed multitude, which will provide the necessary political steam if only you stoke its fires and duly replenish its boilers. It would be absurd to suggest that Burke's view was confined to this aspect. He oscillated, as it is still easy to oscillate, between the idealist and philosophical view, which makes the people the *primum mobile* of the political universe, and the practical and psychological view which, upon a study of 'human nature in politics', issues in a technique of moving the *primum mobile*. Immersed as he was in practical politics, he was necessarily led, more than a pure theorist can ever be, into objurgations at the inertia of the thing to be moved and reflections on the skill of the moving agents; and with his frank nature and his habit of thinking aloud, not only in his correspondence but also before audiences, he stated freely his objurgations and his reflections. When he knew that he had the people with him, as, for instance, in his plans for the economical reform of an antiquated and corrupt establishment, he could bid the House, in a ringing peroration, to belong wholly to the people, to return to its proper home, 'to enter the friendly harbour that shoots far out into the main its moles and jetties to receive us'. 'War with the world, and peace with our constituents.' The steam was high in the boilers; Bristol itself, upon this issue, had petitioned in his favour; the people entered naturally (as it often does) to round a peroration. But in the same speech, in a passage delivered only ten minutes earlier, he had said: 'The people are the masters; they have only to express their wants at large and in gross; we are the expert artists, we are the skilful workmen, to shape their desires into perfect form. . . . They are the sufferers, to tell the symptoms of the complaint; but we know the exact seat of the disease, and how to apply the remedy.' The expert artist, the skilful workman, the cunning physician, must think ahead, over the heads of his constituents, beyond their immediate views. 'I am to look indeed to your opinions,' Burke said to Bristol in his final *apologia*, 'but to such opinions as you and I must have five years hence. I was not to look to the flash of a day.' The free prescience of the free member—this is the beginning and end of the matter. Even in advocating economical reform, for which he knew that he had popular support, he proclaimed his independence. 'I cannot indeed take upon me to say I have the honour to follow the sense of the people. The truth is, I met it on the way, while I was pursuing their interest according to my own ideas.' Burke had many Quaker friends. He cultivated their friendship, and they admired his genius. His love of toleration owes something to their quiet influence. But there was one Quaker idea which he never really learned. It is the idea of 'the sense of the meeting': the idea of a union of minds, in a common purpose, attained through a process of general thought to which we may all contribute, and by a mode of amicable discussion in which we may all participate. It is the idea which underlies any grounded belief in democracy.

Even a well-graced actor must leave the scene, and it is time to ring down the curtain and dismiss into the oblivion from which he has been conjured the figure of that Edmund Burke who represented Bristol between 1774 and 1780. There had always been a contrast, we may almost say an incompatibility, between the man and his constituency. Of the divergence between their views in matters of politics and economics enough has already been said. But there was also a personal divergence. He was an Irishman, rapid of speech, passionate of temper, a whirlwind of energy; his constituency lay beside the quiet county of Somerset. He was a scholar who understood 'everything but gaming and music'; his constituents, if they were not as illiterate as the backs of tombstones, belonged to the solid English middle class of their day. He was a poor man, associated with an aristocratic circle of which he carried the tinge and the flavour; his constituency, if it was one of the wealthiest in England, was also a popular constituency which naturally desired a popular and approachable member. He was a humanitarian, who could draft a Sketch of a Negro Code and protest against the cruelty of the English law of debt; his constituents were not inhumane, but they were satisfied with a slave trade which they thought permissible as well as lucrative, and with a law of debt which seemed to them justifiable as well as effective. He loved toleration, and they clung to a Protestant establishment; he was never happy except on the benches of St. Stephen's or in his Buckinghamshire home, and they thought that he should reconcile his happiness with attentive visits to Bristol.

As early as the middle of 1777 Burke had begun to wonder whether Bristol was not reserved for some more fortunate person at the next election. In 1780 he was still more dubious, and rumours began to circulate that he intended to retire. He had never visited the city for four years, and the odds were heavily against him. His stand for Irish free trade in 1778 had not been forgotten, even if North himself had capitulated on the issue at the end of 1779; and the Protestant passion aroused by the Gordon Riots of June 1780 was still an active force when the General Election began in the following September. But it was not in Burke to decline a contest. Parliament was suddenly dissolved on the 1st of September; on Wednesday, the 6th, he was in Bristol, and on that day he delivered the great speech in defence of his recent parliamentary action; on Friday, the 8th, he was nominated, along with Cruger, on behalf of the Whigs; and Brickdale and a Mr. Combe were nominated on behalf of the Tories. But it needed only a few days in Bristol to convince Burke that his chances were hopeless. He could not fight an election without an election fund; he could contribute nothing himself to such a fund; his wealthier supporters had been hard hit by the American War; the Cruger connexion was once more set on a policy of selfish isolation; the Tory candidates had a grant of £1,000 from the hands of the Secretary to the Treasury. There was no course open but to retire, and on Saturday, the 9th, he appeared at the Guildhall, on the opening of the second day of the poll, and declined the election. Mr. Combe had suddenly died on the previous day, at his house on College Green, immediately after his nomination, and the Tories had hastily substituted another candidate. Burke said a quiet and grave good-bye. 'From the bottom of my heart I thank you for what you have done for me. You have given me a long term, which is now expired. . . . I have served the public for fifteen years. I have served you in particular for six. What is passed is well stored. It is safe, and out of the power of fortune. What is to come is in wiser hands than ours.' And then, thinking of the death of Mr. Combe, and the littleness of human things in the face of death, who reads us all his lesson against being too much troubled, he added: 'Gentlemen . . . what shadows we are, and what shadows we pursue.'

With these words Burke passed from the stage of Bristol. The two Tory candidates were both elected: Brickdale was at the head of the poll, with more than double the number of the votes recorded for Cruger. On 28 October the Town Clerk of Bristol transmitted to Burke a copy of a vote of the Corporation passed on the motion of Mr. Harford, rendering him thanks for the faithful discharge of his duty in Parliament, assuring him that 'though he ceases to be the representative of this city in Parliament, yet this Corporation will always retain for him the strongest sentiments of friendship and regard', and expressing 'the respectful and grateful sense this Corporation entertains of his merits and services, as a senator and as a man'. In April 1782 the Corporation sent him a further vote of thanks, by the hands of a deputation of five gentlemen, for his great scheme of economical reform. In 1783 his brother, Richard Burke, a barrister and a wit, who had more than once acted in his interests at Bristol, was appointed Recorder of the city by the Common Council, and held the office until he died in 1794. A hundred years after Richard Burke died, and the name of Burke seemed finally to have departed from Bristol, a statue was erected to the memory of Edmund in Colston Avenue.

Brickdale, the victor in 1780, lived to a good old age, and died in 1831. Reduced to poverty, he spent his last days with a son and daughter who held offices in the Custom House, 'sitting in a chair which had been assigned to him in the Long Room ... and generally ... in a drowsy condition'. Cruger became Mayor, and also Master of the Society of Merchant Venturers, in 1781; he was elected Member for Bristol, along with Brickdale, in 1784, and Bristol thus returned to its usual policy of 'a blessing upon both your houses'; but he retired to New York, his native city, about 1790, and he died there in 1827. Champion, after serving as Deputy Paymaster-General during his friend's brief tenure of that office, emigrated to South Carolina, where he died in 1791. Harford, promoter with Champion of Burke's election in 1774, and mover of the thanks of the Corporation in 1780, followed Burke's lead by becoming chairman, in 1788, of the first local committee formed for the abolition of the slave trade; and he followed him further a few years later when he left the Whig party and the Society of Friends to throw himself ardently into the war against France. Burke died in 1797, at the age of sixty-eight. He lies in the same grave with his brother and his only son, who had both preceded him in 1794, and with his wife Jane, who followed him fifteen years later in 1812. He had come to rest, after nearly half a century of splendid turbulence, in the 'family burying-ground' of which he had dreamed when he came to England in 1750. He slept, as he had wished, in a little country churchyard; and there, as he had also wished, his dust mingled with kindred dust.

Essay Seven

BURKE ON THE FRENCH REVOLUTION

I

THREE events, in three great countries, marked the year 1789. Let us look at them in their chronological order. On the morning of 30 April in that year George Washington, the first President of the United States of America (which had recently framed its new federal constitution in 1787), appeared on a balcony overlooking Wall Street, in New York, and took the oath to preserve, protect, and defend the constitution. On the morning of 5 May, in the Salle des Menus Plaisirs at Versailles, Louis XVI opened the session of the States General: on the following morning, in the same room, the deputies of the Third Estate held their first separate meeting; and the French Revolution had begun its course. On 4 November, the various local Revolution Societies in England (which had been revivified in the previous year by the celebration of the centenary of the Revolution of 1688) met as usual to dine and to toast the memory of 'the deliverer', King William III, who had landed in England on a November day to aid its people in rescuing themselves from the tyranny of James II and establishing a new 'Revolution Settlement' of their liberties. But a new thing, different from the ordinary ritual, happened in 1789 at the meeting of the Revolution Society in London, which was attended by the Lord Mayor and several members of Parliament. An address of congratulation to the National Assembly of France, 'on the Revolution in that country and on the prospect it gives to the two first Kingdoms in the World of a common participation in the blessings of Civil and Religious Liberty', was moved and sent. It was received by the National Assembly with 'a lively and deep sensibility'; and it thus seemed as if the English Revolution of 1688 was saluting in amity the French Revolution of 1789, as that had saluted or copied the American of 1776, and as if the three countries of the West were beginning to move in step.

But here there arose a deep and fundamental question. The Revolution Society of London was only a small and narrow body. What would be the general sentiment of England towards the French Revolution? Would Englishmen at large believe that their own revolution, now a century old, was congruous with the revolution in France, and that the two countries should therefore march shoulder to shoulder? Or would they see a gulf of division between their own historical and legal revolution and the new and metaphysical revolution of France? This was a question which was destined to be answered, as much as it could be answered by any one man, by the writings and speeches of Edmund Burke.

The two great political parties of England, the Whig and the Tory, were confronted by a new situation and a certain *bouleversement des croyances* in 1789. Hitherto the Tory or Conservative party had been the party friendly to France, as indeed was natural so long as France was still the France of the *ancien régime*. The Whig or Progressive party (not that it was ever very remarkably progressive) had been generally opposed to France—partly on commercial and colonial grounds, but mainly on the political ground that France had originally been the enemy, and had never become the friend, of the Revolution Settlement established by the Whig party in 1688. When France herself began, in 1789, to establish a revolution settlement, the natural result was to alienate the Tories, and at the same time to conciliate—but in a very much smaller measure—the sympathies of the Whigs. It was here—that is to say, in the attitude of the Whigs—that the *bouleversement des croyances* failed to establish itself effectually. The Tories indeed swung round, and adopted an attitude of hostility to revolutionary France; but the bulk of the Whigs stood where they were, in opposition to France, even though France herself was changing direction and moving along the path of constitutionalism. It was only a minority of the Whigs—the minority which cherished a tradition of popular sympathies—which eventually espoused the cause of the French Revolution. The majority—aristocratic like the Tories, if not more aristocratic, and no less conservatively inclined, even if they could plead that they only sought to conserve the liberties of 1688—remained in their old position of general opposition to France. On this issue too, by his influence on the attitude and action of parties, and more particularly on the attitude and action of the Whig party, Burke, himself a Whig of the Whigs, played a decisive part.

The traditional political parties were not the only political forces which swayed the public opinion of England in 1789 and afterwards. There were two other forces, or bodies of opinion, which also counted. The first of these may be called by the general name of Radicalism. It was not a party: it was rather a general progressive sentiment which existed outside the political parties, among the ranks of the people and in the unenfranchised masses. The forms or organizations in which Radicalism expressed itself were various; but they were generally favourable to the French Revolution—at any rate until the beginning of 1793, when France and England became engaged in hostilities. There were, first of all, the sporadic Revolution Societies already mentioned, in London and in other towns, founded to commemorate the English Revolution of 1688, but passing over into allegiance to the French Revolution of 1789; there was, next, the Society for Promoting Constitutional Information, which had been founded in 1780 on a moderate basis of parliamentary reform, but by 1792 had adopted the cause of Radicalism and the French Revolution: there was, finally, the London Corresponding Society, which was founded only in the beginning of 1792, but rapidly became the most vigorous of the radical organizations. It drew its members from the working classes: it had branches, with which it corresponded, in the Midland, Northern, and Scottish towns: its members called themselves 'citizens', and followed the teaching of Tom Paine and his pamphlet on *The Rights of Man*.

The other force, more serious and more solid, was English Dissent or Nonconformity—the body of Congregationalists, Baptists, and Wesleyans who dissented from the established Church of England and, in virtue of that dissent, were legally excluded from membership of municipal corporations and from holding office under the Crown. Excluded, under the constitution as it stood, from the benefits of active citizenship, the Dissenters naturally sympathized with the cause of Radicalism and constitutional reform. Their leaders, such as Priestley and Price, wedded religious Nonconformity to political Radicalism—necessarily, in their own view, because they were compelled to alter the general constitution if they were ever to remove their own religious disabilities. The rank and file had already been excited by parliamentary movements for the relief of their disabilities in 1787 and 1789: they were still more excited by the course of the Revolution in France, as it moved to the reform and the recasting of an old established Church. The result of this excitement was the paradox of a tacit alliance between the convinced religious fervour of English middle-class Nonconformity and the convinced anti-clericalism, mixed with agnosticism, of the prevalent opinion of France. This was the paradox which Burke sought to explain and expose in his 'Reflections on the Revolution in France and on the proceedings of certain societies in London relative to that event'. It was indeed a paradox which in its nature could not last. The English Revolution of 1688 had been a 'Protestant' Revolution, founded upon a religious basis. It could not hail the Revolution of 1789 as a brother. The Dissenters, just because they were wedded to 1688, could not embrace 1789. Far from helping to promote a revolution in England, parallel to that in France, they were one of the forces which, in the issue, made a revolution in England improbable, and indeed impossible. The zest which in France went into revolution went in England into Dissent; and English Dissent became, in the issue, a safety-valve for the passions and feelings which were destined to act, across the Channel, as an explosive force. The Dissenters, in spite of their disabilities, could find a satisfaction in their congregations which made the world tolerable for them; and they soon drew away from the tumult and shouting of revolution into the quiet inner life of their own communities.

II

THIS was the general English background of the thinking and writing of Burke. Already in 1773, on his first and only visit to France, he had been alarmed by the radical rationalism which he detected; and already in that year he had spoken of the atheism, and 'the confederacy of the powers of darkness', which undermined 'the props of good government'.[1] This was the

---

[1] Speech of 1773 in Burke's *Works*, the Rivington edition, vol. x, p. 39, on a Bill for the relief of Protestant Dissenters. Burke was arguing in favour of the bill, on the ground that all Christian confessions, whatever their differences, must be united in opposition to atheism; see above, p. 188.

harbinger of the temper of 1790, which culminated in the publication of the *Reflections* in the November of that year. A number of causes combined to impel Burke towards that temper. Prominent among them was a strong churchmanship of the type of Hooker, which led him to believe that Church and State were simply two aspects of a single society; that this single society was maimed and secularized if it were deprived of its religious aspect by the ending of establishment, which was the public recognition of that aspect; that this maiming and secularizing had happened in France; and that it would happen in England if the combined effects of Radicalism and militant Nonconformity led to imitation of the pattern of France.[1]

Another cause, less lofty and more secular, which impelled him to challenge the revolutionary development of France was his own aristocratic bias. This bias, natural in one who was closely connected with an aristocratic group of the Whigs (the Rockingham connexion), led him at once to glorify, in an ideal light, the chivalry of the nobility of France, and to decry, with a sombre alarm, the growth of an unchecked and *sansculotte* democracy. His contact with French *émigrés* in London, during the latter part of 1789, heightened his feelings; and his old Whig doctrine of the balance of the constitution—a balance which could only be preserved if aristocracy continued to stand as an independent factor between monarchy and democracy—gave a rational ground to his fears.

Deeper still, among the causes of his antagonism to France, was the whole cast of his thought. An Irishman, he had something of a Celtic feeling for the sanctities of the past; a newcomer in English historic life, he was fascinated (as may well happen to a new-comer of genius and insight) by the continuity of its tradition. His mind, deeply historical in its tinge, and all the more devoted to history because his religious feeling tended always to consecrate historical experience as 'the known march of the ordinary providence of God', divorced him utterly from

---

[1] Burke's feelings in this respect were expressed with a particular logic in a speech of 1792 (*Works*, the Rivington edition, vol. x, pp. 41–62), on a petition of one of the dissenting bodies, the Unitarians, for relief from their special disabilities. He now opposed the granting of any relief to Unitarians, who unlike other Nonconformists refused to recognize the divinity of Christ, on the ground that the toleration of such a confession by the State would imply that it was ceasing to recognize and support the Christian Church.

what, in his view, was the French passion for the *tabula rasa*, the French combination of *a priori* metaphysics with geometrical areas of local government and an arithmetical electorate, the general French rejection of the God of History. It may seem inconsistent that Burke should have welcomed, and even advocated, the beginnings of the American Revolution, down to 1776, and then disliked and even attacked the beginnings of the French Revolution. But his point of view was fundamentally the same in regard to both; and in either case he took the same historic ground. He championed the American colonists because he believed that they were standing for historic rights, and were being attacked in the enjoyment of those rights by metaphysical notions of the sovereignty of the British Parliament. He equally championed the monarchy, the nobility, and the Church of France because he believed that they had historic rights, and were being attacked in the enjoyment of those rights by metaphysical notions of liberty and 'national sovereignty'.[1]

Religious feeling, aristocratic bias, and an historic cast of thought combined to produce in Burke's mind a fourth and more general cause of antagonism to the French Revolution. He was led to feel, not altogether unjustly, that the Revolution meant not the rise of a new form of state within old territorial limits, but the rise of a new movement—at once irreligious and religious; at once hostile to established religion and resolved to be a religion itself—which, as such, could stop at no limits. He adopted the same attitude towards the French revolutionaries which has been adopted by many, in more recent times, towards the Bolsheviks and the Comintern; and he cherished the same idea that what was being attempted was not the reconstruction of a territorial state, but the dissemination of a gospel or mode of belief which sought to be non-territorial and of universal validity. It was 'a strange nameless wild enthusiastic thing'[2] that he saw emerging from France, and threatening to cover the world. He detected 'a general apostolic mission': he saw 'a spirit of proselytism'. These are phrases from his *Reflections* of November 1790. In a letter to a member of the National Assembly, written

---

[1] He states this argument himself in his *Appeal from the New to the Old Whigs*, in 1791.
[2] Letter of January 1791 (written two months after the appearance of the *Reflections*) in Burke's *Correspondence*, vol. iii, p. 185.

shortly afterwards, he goes to the length of speaking of 'a college of armed fanatics', and of citing the example of Mahomet; and in the same sense he says, in his *Appeal from the New to the Old Whigs* (of the year 1791), that 'a theory concerning government may become as much a cause of fanaticism as a dogma in religion'. He already foresees, nearly two years in advance, the fraternity decrees of November 1792: he already believes that all metaphysical positions must tend to claim universal validity, and to threaten in every country the existing system of historical order. His desire becomes a burning desire to fold in his arms, for its preservation, the insular historic life of the English nation, and to annihilate English sympathies with the invading flood.

III

By the autumn of 1789 Burke was already beginning to entertain grave doubts about the course of the Revolution. In a letter written in the month of October to a French correspondent, M. Dupont (the same correspondent to whom the *Reflections*, which were couched in the form of a letter, were nominally addressed), he confesses that, though he is very imperfectly acquainted with the political map of France, he is sceptical about the progress made during the six months since the meeting of the States General in May. It is a profound letter, which already contains in the germ many of the ideas expressed a year later in the *Reflections*. 'You may have made a revolution', he tells his correspondent, 'but not a reformation. You have theories enough concerning the rights of men; . . . it is with man in the concrete . . . you are to be concerned. . . . You ought not to be so fond of any political object, as not to think the means of compassing it a profound consideration.'[1] The train of thoughts here expressed, in October 1789, continued to march and to deploy its sequence in his mind. In a speech on the army estimates, delivered on 9 February 1790, he showed that he was already parting company with Fox and those of the Whigs who sympathized with the Revolution, and that he already detected in the political life of France a danger from anarchism, and in her religious life an equal danger from atheism. The *Reflections* were being composed at the time when he made this speech; we know from a letter of Philip Francis, dated 19 February 1790, that he had already

[1] Ibid., pp. 102-21.

read some of Burke's proof-sheets, that he was critical of his argument, and that he thought his praise of Marie Antoinette 'pure foppery'. But the composition of the *Reflections* proceeded slowly: indeed it seems to have been undertaken at two different times and in two different sections, with the result of some repetition and a double covering of the same ground; and it did not finally appear until the month of November.

New vials had meanwhile been added to Burke's simmering indignation by his sense of the growing radical and Nonconformist sentiment in England (as he thought, an unreflective and miscalculated sentiment) in favour of the French Revolution. Since the sending of the address of congratulation to the National Assembly, in November 1789, there had been a fermentation of radical clubs and societies, often affiliated to democratic clubs in France; and on the anniversary of the capture of the Bastille, in July 1790, a celebration was held by the Revolution Society of London, and a speech of eulogy was made by Price, the main leader (along with Priestley) of dissenting opinion. This was the state of feeling, at any rate on the surface (for the solid opinion of the country at large had hardly yet been formed), when the *Reflections* appeared at the end of 1790. The immediate effect was a storm of controversy. Some forty answers to the *Reflections* were published. One of the first was Tom Paine's *Rights of Man*, 'being an answer to Mr. Burke's attack on the French Revolution', which was hastily written at an inn in Islington, printed in time for the meeting of Parliament in February 1791, and finally published in March of that year.[1] Paine was a famous publicist and pamphleteer who had played a part in the American Revolution from 1776 onwards; he had established, from 1787 onwards, connexions with the leading Liberal politicians both in England and France; and after the publication of his pamphlet in reply to Burke he was made a French citizen by the Legislative Assembly (along with Priestley, Bentham, and others) in August 1792, and afterwards elected, in September of that year, as one of the representatives of Calais in the Convention. The battle engaged in English thought in the course of 1791 was pre-eminently a battle between Burke

---

[1] In strict accuracy, this was only the first part of Paine's pamphlet. A second part, of equal length, appeared a year later, early in 1792; and the full text of *The Rights of Man* includes both parts.

and Paine; and Burke himself cites Paine (though without mentioning his name, and under the anonymous style of 'they') as the great exponent of the Revolutionary cause, in the pamphlet defending his *Reflections*, and entitled *An Appeal from the New to the Old Whigs*, which he published in the latter part of 1791.

Among the other answers to Burke there are two which deserve some notice. One, entitled *A Vindication of the Rights of Man*, which was the first to appear, was written by a woman, Mary Wollstonecraft, the first wife of the philosopher Godwin, and the mother of the second wife of the poet Shelley. Another reply, which came not from the Radicals, but from the Left wing of the Whig party, and which was one of the most temperate and cogent of all the replies, was the *Vindiciae Gallicae* of James Mackintosh, published about the end of April 1791. Mackintosh's *Vindiciae* and Paine's *Rights of Man* were the most successful of all the replies. The former ran into a fourth edition in the course of 1791: of the first Part of the latter, if Paine himself may be trusted, between forty and fifty thousand copies were sold in the course of the same year. But in spite of the vogue of the answers to the *Reflections* the tide ran steadily in favour of Burke. On 6 May 1791, in one of the famous scenes in our parliamentary history, he broke with his own party, which he had loved so dearly, and with its leader, Fox. He seemed to go into isolation, leaving the general body of the Whig party adhering to the cause of the French Revolution; but within a year the party was utterly divided, and in the course of three years the bulk of the party had rallied to the side of Burke, leaving Fox and the rest of its own Left wing in a small minority. His influence had triumphed; and at his call the Whig party had decided that by the very virtue of its own Revolution of 1688 it was a non-revolutionary party—a party of monarchy (limited, but still monarchy); a party of property, of aristocracy, and even (in spite of its Nonconformist connexions) of the established Church. Meanwhile the country at large began to show signs of a tenacious conservative sentiment, opposed to the agitation of the Radical societies and pamphleteers which had alarmed Burke's mind and inspired his pen. It was a significant sign that when the Revolution Society in Birmingham (by no means a conservative city) announced its intention of celebrating the second anniversary of the capture of the Bastille on 14 July 1791, there was an immediate riot, which lasted for some days. Nonconformist meeting-houses were destroyed: Priestley, who lived in the city, lost his house, his library, and his manuscripts. This was mere mob violence; but Burke could justly claim, as he did in the beginning of his *Appeal from the New to the Old Whigs*, that he was a faithful representative of the general sentiments of the people of England. Price died in the course of 1791: Priestley, after moving to London, ultimately emigrated to America; Paine finally left England for France in September 1791. Sympathy for the French Revolution still lingered among the various radical societies and the members of the working classes who belonged to these societies. But the repressive hand of the government began to fall upon the societies and their adherents: and a sad chapter in the history of English liberty, which began with the proclamation of 21 May 1792 against seditious meetings and publications, was finally closed by an Act of 1799, 'for the more effectual suppression of societies established for seditious and treasonable purposes', which ended, along with others, the London Corresponding Society.

IV

WE may now turn to estimate the argument and the importance of Burke's *Reflections*. It is many things in one, all welded together by the fire of genius—a great apology for romanticism; a great and glowing proclamation of the place of religion in the life of the state; a great defence of historicism and of historical experience; a great vindication of political empiricism and the wisdom of political compromise. It is one of the profoundest treatises on politics that ever was written, as it is also one of the most stimulating; nor was it idly, or altogether ironically, that at a dinner of the friends of liberty, held in London on 14 July 1791, Burke was toasted by his enemies 'in gratitude for his having provoked the great discussion which occupies every thinking person'. He saw the French Revolution with a wide and magnificent, if also with a prejudiced and passionate, vision. (But the prejudice grew more bitter, and the passion more intense and disordered, after the attacks on the *Reflections*, and especially after his breach with Fox in May 1791; and the view which he took of the Revolution at the end of 1790, even if it is already partisan, is far more philosophic, and far more profound, than his later view.) He felt the greatness of the Revolution, 'the most astonishing that has hitherto happened in the world'. He could foresee some of its ultimate tendencies: he feared already the coming of the revolutionary tribunal and of the guillotine ('there must be blood: the want of common judgement manifested . . . in all their kinds of civil and judicial authorities will make it flow'): he feared the coming of Caesarism and of a military autocracy. 'Some popular general', he wrote, 'who understands the art of conciliating the soldiery, . . . shall draw the eyes of all men upon himself. The moment in which that event shall happen, the person who really commands the army is your master . . . the master of your whole Republic.'

On the other hand, there was also much which he failed, partly through ignorance and partly through wilfulness, to understand. He was far too tender to the *ancien régime*. In a passage which excited the animadversions of Philip Francis,[1] as it continued afterwards to excite general criticism, he spoke of the French as having had before 1789 'the elements of a constitution very nearly as good as could be wished'; and though in a later passage he spoke of the pre-revolutionary government in France as 'full of abuses', he seemed to condone the abuses of which he spoke. The passage on Marie Antoinette and the age of chivalry, which Francis described as 'pure foppery' and which led Paine to make the fine and caustic remark, 'He pities the plumage but forgets the dying bird', was of a piece with his general idealization of the old French court, the old French aristocracy, and the old French Church. He made the error—natural in 1790, but still an error—of thinking that France was degenerating into a congeries of little democracies, and therefore into military impotence. He made the graver error—again perhaps natural in 1790, but hardly excusable even then—of thinking that the Revolution was undermining property, when the fact was that property was being consolidated more firmly than ever, and on a far more equal basis, in the tenacious grip of the middle class and the peasantry. He was blind to the ideals of the Revolution —its passion for liberty, and its still deeper passion for equality: he was no less blind to some of the profoundest and the most permanent of its actual tendencies and achievements.

[1] Burke's *Correspondence*, vol. iii, pp. 167–8.

V

THE first effort of Burke's thought, in the beginning of the *Reflections*, is directed to comparing, contrasting, and dissociating the English Revolution of 1688 and the French Revolution of 1789. He was anxious to prove to the Whigs that they need not sympathize with one revolution because they themselves, a century ago, had conducted another: he was anxious to prove to the English people at large that they need not applaud the resistance of the French people to the *ancien régime* because they themselves had once resisted the régime of James II. There is justice in Burke's dissociation of 1688 and 1789. The English Revolution of 1688 had been achieved by the aristocracy, not unaided by the Church, and it had been achieved within the four corners of the historic tradition and the legal inheritance of the nation: the French Revolution of 1789 sprang from the people, rejected the Church and the aristocracy, and appealed for its sanction to natural law and first principles. But there were similarities as well as dissimilarities; and the subtlety of Burke's thought glossed and dissimulated the similarities. If there was no social revolution in England in 1688 and afterwards, as there was in France in 1789 and afterwards (that is the fundamental and indisputable difference between the two revolutions), there was none the less a genuine political revolution in England in 1688, different indeed, but not fundamentally different, from the political side of the revolution begun by France in 1789. Sovereignty was definitely transferred by the Revolution of 1688 to the people as represented in Parliament; this was the theory of Locke, and it was also the actual logic of fact. France simply attempted a similar transference by her Revolution of 1789. But a just comparison of England and France must go still farther back. We have to remember (what Burke never pauses to remember) that the English Revolution really began before 1688. It had begun as early as 1641: it had entailed civil war and the execution of King Charles I. The year 1688 cannot be isolated. When we take the English Revolution in its length and its breadth, from 1641 onwards, we attain a juster comparison with France. And on that comparison, while difference still remains, a fundamental similarity emerges. England and France, in their different ways, were facing the same political problem.

They were attempting to discover the secret of parliamentary democracy.

Burke, entrenching himself resolutely in the limited area of 1688, and only able to see, with the inevitably limited scope of contemporary vision, the first desperate struggles of a France which had none of the treasures of historic precedent or of an historic Parliament possessed by the English revolutionaries of the seventeenth century, saw only difference—pure sheer difference—between the revolutions. He smoothes and planes the English Revolution, in order to accentuate its difference from the French, until it becomes the politest and the least revolutionary of all conceivable revolutions. Writing in the very spirit of Loyseau, who had argued, in his *Traité des Offices*, that 'by the prescription of long possession kings had become the owners of sovereign power', Burke connects the rights of monarchs with the general system of rights of property; and he contends that the Revolution of 1688 had scrupulously respected the existence, if it had somewhat altered the extent, of the vested and hereditary rights of monarchy. There was nothing, he argues, in the Revolution to prove that people had the right to form a government for themselves *de novo* or *in vacuo*. On the contrary, the Revolution had been entirely conducted for the purpose of restoring a system of government already existing, and already historically consecrated by the fact of long inheritance—the system of a mixed constitution, in which King, Lords, and Commons all played their historical parts, and enjoyed their hereditary rights, under the sanction of an inviolable pact or engagement which had always tied them to one another. The Revolution might be called, at the most, no more than a reformation; but even as a reformation it was both limited and conservative—limited to the one purpose of removing the innovations upon the constitution which had been introduced by James II when he exaggerated the rights of the monarchy; conservative in the sense that it was based upon the previous constitution, which it simply sought to restore in its proper and traditional balance. In a word, the Revolution was like Magna Carta itself: it was simply a restoration of the *mos majorum*.

It is to the *mos majorum* that Burke makes his final appeal. All English liberties, in his view—including the liberties vindicated in 1688—are based not on rights of men, which are uncertain and susceptible of as many interpretations as there are interpreters, but on the rights of Englishmen, which are certain and known because they constitute 'an entailed inheritance ... an estate specially belonging to the people of this Kingdom'. History and the principle of inheritance unite an inheritable crown, an inheritable peerage, and the inheritable rights of the House of Commons and the people. It almost seems as if Burke were applying to politics the analogy of the contemporary English land-laws, and as if he were making the English state a sort of family concern, where public rights were tied up in the members, and entailed upon the members, in the same sort of way as private rights to the ownership of land were entailed upon, and tied up in, an aristocratic family by the system of the 'family settlement'. But Burke soon rises above his analogy to greater heights and a broader sweep. He attains the idea of what may be called (if we may borrow a term from Nicholas of Cusa) 'the divine concordance of the universe', in the scheme of which inheritable land and an inheritable constitution are linked, by the disposition of a stupendous wisdom, with the great and general principle of the continuous inheritance of life in the whole of the realm of nature.[1] Here, though his immediate debt is a debt to the Middle Ages, we may say that Burke is already reaching forward into the nineteenth century. He has a feeling for biology and biological analogy; he is averse from mechanics and the engineering analogies which were so dear to the eighteenth century, and especially to Paine.

But the argument of inheritance, of which we have just been speaking, in not only connected with the idea of 'the divine concordance', and with a feeling for biology: it has also its affinities

[1] The idea of the divine concordance of the Universe, which includes the State in its scheme, haunted the mind of Burke. Not only does it occur in the *Reflections* of 1790 (Burke's *Works*, the Bohn edition, vol. ii, p. 307; cf. also pp. 368–9, where he speaks of the 'eternal society ... connecting the visible and invisible world, according to a fixed compact sanctioned by the inviolable oath which holds all physical and all moral natures, each in their appointed place') : it already appears in his speech of 1783 on the East India Bill (ibid., p. 220). It is also, and finely, expressed in his *Appeal from the New to the Old Whigs* in 1791 (vol. iii, p. 79), where he speaks of the predisposed order of things in which, by a divine tactic, we are all disposed and marshalled to act the part which belongs to the place assigned us. The underlying philosophy, as we shall have reason to notice later, is fundamentally Catholic or Thomistic (though Burke himself was a loyal member of the Church of England); or again it may be said to find its analogies, though not its sources, in the philosophy of Suarez and the other theologians of the Counter Reformation.

with literary romanticism and its historical passion. This clearly appears in one of the passages of the argument, where he passes from the mention of inherited liberties to speak of 'canonized forefathers', of 'a pedigree and illustrating ancestors', of 'bearings ... ensigns armorial ... gallery of portraits ... monumental inscriptions'. Burke has a large vein of what Sir Walter Scott called 'Gothic sentiment'. He bows before the pageant of history and worships its sanctities.

VI

IN this frame of mind he opposes history to metaphysics, and the historical tradition of England to the first principles of France. He rejects the dry anatomy of natural rights for the living physiology of historical experience. The denunciation of metaphysics is as frequent in the *Reflections* as it had been, some fifteen years before, in the speeches on the American Revolution—with the one difference that then he had denounced the metaphysics of sovereignty professed by the English Parliament in opposition to the Americans, and now he denounces the metaphysics of liberty professed by the National Assembly in opposition to the *ancien régime*. Along with metaphysics he also repudiates, in the *Reflections*, what he calls arithmetic and geometry—in other words, the arithmetical treatment of men, for electoral purposes, as mere mathematical integers, and the geometrical treatment of the country, for purposes of local government, as mere Euclidean space. To the nakedness and solitude of metaphysical abstractions, clothed (and yet not clothed) by arithmetic and geometry, Burke opposes the three living articles of his belief. He opposes circumstances: he opposes moral policy (which may also be called, in a high sense of that word, expediency): he opposes the collected wisdom and the general treasure of history.

Circumstances, as he understands them, are the factors which give a distinguishing colour and a discriminating effect to all political principles when they come to be actually applied. You must not, he feels, make your principles iron: you must bend them (as Aristotle said that the leaden rod of Lesbian architecture bent) to suit the material of the environment and the circumstances of the situation. There is something Aristotelian in this contention (Burke was always an Aristotelian, perhaps because he was also, even if unconsciously, a Thomist); and in what he proceeds to say about moral policy there is a still more Aristotelian strain.

Adopting, initially, the term 'political reason', he argues that such reason is indeed a 'computing principle', but the units which it computes are true 'moral denominations', and the method which it uses is moral and not metaphysical. In other words, the units of political computation are not the uniform integers of individual citizens, or bare geometrical spaces, but the various social factors (which may also be called 'moral denominations') such as property, the Church, the Estates, or the historic provinces of a country; and the method of computation is not that of mathematical calculation, but that of moral policy or prudence (or what Aristotle called 'phronesis'), which appreciates the factors of computation by virtue of moral insight. In dealing therefore with a factor such as monasticism and its congregations, one must compute and appreciate the moral value of security, which would be disturbed by expropriation; one must compute and appreciate the moral interdependence of institutions, which unites the cause of religious congregations to that of other 'social faculties'; and, finally, one must also compute and appreciate the 'purchase' or opportunity which is offered to the statesman by any social factor, even if it is growing wild—a purchase which he will be wise to use by reforming and training the factor for the general social advantage.[1] This, in a word, is a plea for expediency at its best.

From circumstances and moral expediency Burke turns to history, the root of his belief and the ground of his counter-metaphysic. There were two reasons which moved his mind towards a belief in history. The first and lower reason was a reason on the plane of humanism. He felt that, even if you were content to follow the mind of man as your highest guide, there was a better thing than the individual mind of the individual metaphysician; and that was the collective mind of mankind working in history.

[1] *Reflections*, in Burke's *Works*, vol. ii, pp. 428–9. The same argument is repeated, in a letter of 1 June 1791 (*Correspondence*, vol. iii, pp. 206–15), with regard to the Emperor Joseph II's 'enlightened' policy for dealing with monastic corporations in the Netherlands. It had already been anticipated in a passage of a speech delivered in 1780. 'The excellence of mathematics and metaphysics is to have but one thing before you; but he forms the best judgement in all moral disquisitions, who has the greatest number and variety of considerations in one view before him, and can take them in with the best possible consideration of the middle results of all' (*Works*, Rivington edition, vol. x, p. 74).

Better than 'the private stock of reason' was the general bank and capital of nations and of ages'; better than the explosion of general prejudices was the discovery of the latent wisdom which prevailed in prejudice itself. This is a profound element in Burke's thoughts, to which we shall have to return. But he had a second and higher reason for his belief in history; and this was a reason on the plane of a devout and convinced theism. God worked in history: God willed the state; and the rules of prudence in political affairs were therefore 'formed upon the known march of the ordinary providence of God'[1] proceeding through history. By history therefore you may know both the collected treasures of the mind of man and the working of the providence of God.

VII

IN the temper of this conviction Burke rings the changes on four bells, which we may call by the names of Experience, History (in the more specific sense of the written record of the past), Prescription, and Prejudice. Let us first hear the bell which is called Experience. Experience should not be despised as the wisdom of unlettered men. It has done a great work for general humanity. 'No discoveries are to be made in morality; nor many in the great principles of government, nor in the ideas of liberty, which were understood long before we were born.'[2] In a far profounder phrase, which goes far more to the root of the matter, he proclaims, 'Mind must conspire with mind: time is required to produce that union of minds which alone can produce all the good we aim at.'[3] The co-operation of mind with mind, 'enjoying the benefit of time' and enjoyed by virtue of that benefit—

[1] Letter II on a Regicide Peace, of the year 1796, in Burke's *Works*, the Bohn edition, vol. v, p. 236.

[2] *Reflections*, in Burke's *Works*, ibid., vol. ii, p. 94. The thought has its parallel in Aristotle, criticizing Plato (Aristotle on Plato has his analogies with Burke on the French Revolution): 'We are bound to pay some regard to the long past and the passage of the years, in which these things (the things advocated by Plato as new discoveries) would not have gone unnoticed if they had been really good. Almost everything has been discovered already; though some of the things discovered have not been co-ordinated, and some, though known, are not put into practice' (*Politics*, ii. 5. 16). But the difficulty of an argument which can be applied equally in 330 B.C. and in A.D. 1790 is that it cannot have been equally true at both times. After all, something had happened, and some new things had been discovered, in those 2,000 years and more.

[3] *Reflections*, in Burke's *Works*, the Bohn edition, vol. ii, p. 439.

this was what filled the rich cup of experience from which Burke wished men to drink. In a sense this is pure conservativism; and Lord Acton has accordingly spoken, in his lectures on the French Revolution, of 'the great conservative maxim that success generally depends on knowing the time it will take'. But there is far more than conservatism in Burke's deep sense of experience. There is a passage in one of his speeches, delivered in May 1782, on the theme of parliamentary reform, which contains the very quintessence of his thought. (It is eight years, and more, prior to the *Reflections*; and it proves abundantly, if that needed to be proved, that the Burke of the *Reflections* was not a new Burke, but the same that he had always been.) It is a passage which deserves to be quoted, and studied, and remembered.

'A Nation is not an idea only of local extent, and individual momentary aggregation, but it is an idea of continuity, which extends in time as well as in numbers and in space. And this is a choice not of one day, or one set of people, not a tumultuary and giddy choice; it is a deliberate election of ages and of generations; it is a Constitution made by what is ten thousand times better than choice; it is made by the peculiar circumstances, occasions, tempers, dispositions, and moral, civil and social habitudes of the people, which disclose themselves only in a long space of time. It is a vestment which accommodates itself to the body. Nor is prescription of government founded on blind unmeaning prejudices—for man is a most unwise and a most wise being. The individual is foolish. The multitude, for the moment, is foolish, when they act without deliberation; but the species is wise, and when time is given to it, as a species, it almost always acts right.'[1]

Profound words, on which one can build a whole philosophy—a philosophy which would seek to explain how in every society the collective mind of man (not a single 'group-mind', but the interpenetration and co-operation of many individual minds) has been active through the generations in building a fabric of social and political experience and a system of social and political values—justice, liberty, equality, fraternity—which are made of mental stuff, and indeed *are* a mental stuff, and therefore deserve, and demand, to be appreciated and justified by the reflective power and the mental insight of the philosopher. But this fabric

[1] Speech on Representation of the Commons in Parliament, *Works* (Rivington's edition), vol. x, p. 97.

of past experience, this system of inherited values, also needs to be criticized, in each generation, for each generation, by each generation, if it is ever to be carried to a higher stage; and this is a necessity which Burke tended to minimize and even to ignore. Paine saw the necessity only too clearly, arguing that each generation is and must be competent for its own purposes; but he was blind to the claims of the past, and he exaggerated the rights of the present. Burke was prior to Hegel, but he had an Hegel within him; and he well knew—indeed he knew only too well—the working of 'objective mind', as it operates in time and moves on its course through the ages.

It is time to turn from the bell of Experience, to which we have been listening too long, to the bell of History, and to note the changes which Burke rings on that word when he is using it specifically and distinctively, in its more particular sense, to denote the written record of the past. 'In history', Burke writes, 'a great volume is unrolled for our instruction.' But there is an abuse, as well as a use, which can be made of that volume. It is abused if it is employed to kindle and to fan brooding memories of past wrong. It is equally abused if it be employed without respect to circumstances, and without the use of moral prudence, in which case 'you will be wise historically, a fool in practice'. This argument suggests, and suggests inevitably, that history needs selective interpretation; and that in turn suggests that there is a weakness in the appeal to history, since history has itself to be weighed before it can weigh in the balance.

But we have to remember that history is something more than a collection of justificatory pieces, which may be used in this way or that according to the selector's choice. We have also to consider the historic process behind any system of institutions, which forms their connecting cement. This we may call by the name of Prescription. We have equally to consider the historic feeling which forms the support of institutions, and constitutes a vitalizing sentiment active on their behalf. This we may call by the name, if we understand it in its highest and best sense, of Prejudice.

We have already seen, in speaking of Burke's view of the Revolution of 1688, the nature of the changes which he could ring on the idea of Prescription and the *Mos majorum*. We have seen how, in his view, the prescription of inheritance unites with one another the several rights of all subjects, and then unites the whole of their rights with the similarly inheritable and similarly prescriptive rights of monarchy. 'Prescriptive right' may be called his keyword, as 'natural and imprescriptible rights' may equally be called the keyword of Paine and of all the sympathizers with the Revolution.

Prejudice is another term of art in Burke's philosophy. Prejudice, as it has a latent wisdom, serves also as a vitalizing sentiment. 'Prejudice, with its reason, has a motive to give action to that reason, and an affection which will give it permanence.... It previously engages the mind in a steady course of wisdom... and renders a man's virtue his habit.'[1] This theory of the sentiment of Prejudice, which thus provides a motive, and conciliates a sentiment of affection, for the discharge of civic duties, may be connected with Burke's somewhat similar theory of what may be called the politico-aesthetic sentiments, which appears in the 'Age of Chivalry' passage.[2] His first work had been an aesthetic essay on *The Sublime and Beautiful*; and it is not surprising that in his later years he should seek to trace the connexion between politics and aesthetics. Authority, he felt, must wear an aesthetic guise and possess an aesthetic quality, in order that it might be supported by the aesthetic sentiment: otherwise it would possess only the quality of power, and be supported only by the sentiment of fear. Manners and faith—'the spirit of a gentleman, and the spirit of religion'—must cover the bare bones of politics with a vesture of beauty, which would conciliate man's sense of beauty both to itself and to what it covered. 'To make us love our country, our country must be lovely.' Historical romanticism, such as Burke preached (not that it was the only or the deepest thing which he preached), has a natural alliance with aesthetics.

VIII

But the 'spirit of religion' meant far more for Burke than a vesture or decoration. It was the inmost essence of his theory of politics. Already in his *Thoughts on the Cause of the Present Discontents*, which goes back to the year 1770, he is professing a theory of government which had already been enunciated by St. Thomas Aquinas. St. Thomas, who has been called by Lord

---

[1] *Reflections*, in Burke's *Works*, the Bohn edition, vol. ii, p. 359.
[2] Ibid., pp. 348–51.

Acton 'the first Whig', developed a theory of government (or *potestas*) according to which the *principium*, or essence, of power was an emanation or delegation proceeding from God, and accordingly based on divine right, but the *modus* or constitutional form of power was determined, and the *exercitium* or actual enjoyment of power was conferred, by the people. This was a combination of a doctrine of the divine right of authority with a doctrine of its popular origin. Burke made the same combination, in practically identical terms. 'Government certainly is an institution of Divine authority, yet its forms, and the persons who administer it, all originate from the people.'[1] Here the emphasis in the combination seems to rest particularly on the element of popular origin, though the element of divine right is definitely acknowledged. The emphasis shifted as he grew older. It was less that he grew more conservative: it was rather that he grew more deeply convinced of the great and fundamental claims of religion. It is this deep conviction which inspires the greatest passage in the *Reflections*.[2]

'Religion is the basis of civil society,' so the passage begins, 'and man is by his constitution a religious animal.'[3] God has willed the state, and he has given divine authority to its government. The constitution of the state, under the inviolable pact or engagement which ties its parts together, includes an established Church as well as an established monarchy, an established aristocracy, and an established democracy, and it includes each in its degree. (This, it is true, is intended as a philosophy of England, but it is a philosophy which readily assumes in Burke's

[1] *Thoughts*, in Burke's *Works*, the Bohn edition, vol. i, p. 348. How Burke came to know and to use the theory of St. Thomas is a problem which deserves investigation. In the *Reflections* he also uses the same Thomistic terminology, when he speaks of the Bill of Rights of 1689 as 'not changing the *substance*, but regulating the *mode* and describing the *persons*' [vested with the exercise of power]; *Works*, vol. ii, p. 295.

[2] The passage comes in Burke's *Works*, the Bohn edition, vol. ii, pp. 362–72. It should be compared with the speech on the petition of the Unitarians, delivered on 11 May 1792 (*Works*, the Rivington edition, vol. x, pp. 41–62, and especially pp. 41–5). It may also be compared with the speech on a bill for the relief of Protestant Dissenters, delivered in 1773 (ibid., pp. 22–40, and especially pp. 35–40). This last speech, with its fear of atheism, seems to have been composed under the influence of his recent visit to France in the year 1773: see above, p. 208.

[3] Burke is consciously altering Aristotle's definition of man as 'naturally a political animal'. He had used an analogous phrase in his speech of 1773 just mentioned —'the glorious and distinguishing prerogative of humanity, that of being a religious creature'.

view a universal validity; for he, too, though he condemns the universalism of French metaphysics, has a universalism of his own.) But an established Church is not only a part of the constitution, sympathetic with other established parts; it is 'the foundation of the whole constitution'. Here we have to remember Burke's idea, borrowed from Hooker's *Ecclesiastical Polity*, that a people or nation is a single and indivisible society, of which Church and State are simply two aspects, mutually implying one another. Hooker had said that 'in a free Christian State or Kingdom . . . one and the self-same people are the Church and the Commonwealth'.[1] Burke himself, in a speech of 1792, argued that 'in a Christian Commonwealth the Church and the State are one and the same thing, being different integral parts of the same whole'.[2] The same idea inspired the *Reflections*. 'Church and State are ideas inseparable in our minds.'

On this basis he goes on to argue that the mind of a people, acting historically under the inspiration of the God who willed the State, has been taught, or has taught itself, not only to build a political structure, but also to consecrate the structure which it has built. It has achieved this consecration by making the State also a Church, and by establishing the organization of that Church as a part, or rather as the foundation, of the constitution of the State. Two great ends are achieved by means of this consecration.[3] In the first place the persons of the government, by their connexion with the Church, are led to realize clearly that they hold and exercise powers of divine institution, and that the 'principle' of their authority comes from God. This is an idea which, as we have seen, Burke had already used, twenty years earlier, in his *Thoughts*. In the second place, and even more, the people themselves, who in order to be free must enjoy some

---

[1] *Ecclesiastical Polity*, VIII. iii. 6.
[2] *Works*, the Rivington edition, vol. x, p. 44.
[3] If we examine Burke's conception of the ends of government, we cannot but be struck by a passage in his speech of 1792 in which he argues that religion is not only the care of the Christian magistrate, but 'the principal thing in his care, because . . . its object is the supreme good, the ultimate end and object of man'. In the same way St. Thomas, in stating the hierarchy of the ends pursued, or the duties discharged, by government, had concluded with its supreme duty of helping men to attain the heavenly sovereign good. In the *Reflections*, however, Burke is concerned only with the ends achieved by a system of Church establishment in the way of moderating and sobering the action of government (and also of the people) *whatever may be the purposes to which its action is directed.*

determinate portion of power and thus form a part of the total scheme of government,[1] are equally led, by the establishment of a national Church, to realize that they too are responsible to God for the use of the power which they also hold as a trust derived from Him. Burke lays an especial emphasis on the effect of establishment on the people. The danger which threatens the people is the danger of irresponsible use of a power imagined as absolute: it is the danger of the enthronement of popular will as the final standard of right. Unchecked, democracy is 'the most shameless thing in the world': the people need to realize, more than any other bearer of power, that the share of power which they exercise, if it is 'to be legitimate, must be . . . according to . . . eternal, immutable law'.

Burke sees another and a third end which is also achieved through the consecration of the State by an establishment of the Church. Such an establishment secures the idea and the fact of the continuing and immortal life of the State, which is thus recognized as an integral part of the continuing and immortal society of the universe ordained and moved by God: it ensures thereby a sense of responsibility to the past and future of the State, and to the past and future of the whole eternal society to which it belongs. Otherwise the commonwealth falls 'into the dust and powder of individuality'; it becomes the '*moleculae* of a disbanded people'.

Such is Burke's conception of the Christian State. Nerved by that conception, he could not but attack the Revolution in France, which, in his view, had departed so widely from it. In France he saw a combination—hostile to the established Church, and therefore hostile to the Christian State—between a new monied interest, anxious to enrich itself by ecclesiastical property, and the literary cabal of the *Encyclopédistes*, anxious to proselytize recruits for their own atheistical tenets. He foresaw the triumph of a view that 'a State can subsist without any religion rather than with one'—a view which would enthrone, in place of religion, a calculated species of utilitarianism under the name of civic education.[2]

[1] It may be noticed that Burke here assumes that the people must necessarily, in its nature, possess political power in order to be free—whether or no it possesses political capacity. We shall see later that, in another passage of the *Reflections*, he modifies this view.
[2] *Reflections*, in Burke's *Works*, the Bohn edition, vol. ii, p. 419.

IX

But the conception of the Christian State which he had finally developed in the *Reflections* not only made Burke critical of the Revolution: it also affected and modified his conception of the part played by the people in the constitution of the State. We have spoken of his combination of the doctrine of the divine right of authority with a doctrine of its popular origin; we have noticed that, in 1770, his emphasis seemed to lie on the doctrine of popular origin. In 1790 the emphasis has shifted. This appears particularly in the theory which he now enunciates of the nature of rights. There are no such things as natural rights. All rights are socially created: they belong to 'the civil social man, and no other'. Convention creates a civil society. That society, thus created, in turn creates rights; in other words, it produces, by the fact of its existence, advantages which become the rights of its members in virtue of their being the makers of the convention, and thereby of society, and thereby, again, of all the advantages produced by society. But the convention which creates society, and thereby social rights or advantages, must be free to limit and modify the rights which it creates—the right to property; the right to 'instruction in life and consolation in death' (or, in other words, the right to enjoy the benefits of education and religion); the right to enjoy a government which is 'a contrivance of human wisdom to provide for human wants'. All these rights are subject to (since they are produced by) the convention of society: all these rights are determined, limited, modified, and specified by that convention.[1]

On what basis, then, will the convention of society determine and specify rights? In respect of things other than political—or, in other words, in the domain of civil rights, such as the right of property—the convention will treat all equally: it will recognize that all men have equal rights. But in respect of political things, and in regard to the right of active participation in government

---

[1] Burke had used the same argument in a speech of 1772 (*Works*, the Rivington edition, vol. x, p. 16): 'to annex any condition you please to benefits, artificially created, is the most just, natural and proper thing in the world. When *e novo* you form an arbitrary benefit, an advantage ... not by nature but institution, you order and modify it with all the power of a creator over the creature.' The new thing in the *Reflections* of 1790 is that Burke applies this argument even to the rights of the people, as he had not hitherto done.

(as distinct from the right of passive enjoyment of the advantages of government), the convention will proceed on a different line. It will not necessarily give active political rights to more than a small minority. All men have indeed a right to enjoy government in the sense of being governed; but all have not a right to enjoy government in the sense of participating in government. To govern is not a right or advantage, which as such may be claimed by all: it is a convenience calculated to produce rights or advantages; and it must be settled in the way which is most convenient, or, in other words, in the way best calculated to produce the most advantages. This means, in effect, that government must be vested in those who, by reason of virtue and prudence (that is to say, on moral and intellectual grounds), are most likely to be most efficient. Burke accordingly proceeds to argue that any right of the people to share actively in government is not a power, or a thing based upon power: it is rather a capacity for producing advantages, or a thing based on such capacity; and it must therefore depend on the virtue and prudence of the people, and will exist in so far (but only in so far) as those qualities exist.[1] But this is a modification, and indeed a vital modification, of the theory which he had previously held, and had stated in the *Thoughts* of 1770—the theory that the people, by the nature of its being, has the right to determine the 'mode' and to confer the 'exercise' of power. In the new theory of the *Reflections* the people has no certain or inherent political rights. It may have such rights if it is virtuous and prudent: otherwise it will have none. By 1790 Burke has come to regard the people as passive rather than active[2]—'a protected, satisfied, laborious, and obedient people'. Passive rather than active in the political sphere, the people may also be said to be inferior rather than equal even in the civil sphere. 'All men have equal rights: *but not to equal things.*' The qualification enables

[1] Here Burke unconsciously modifies, or abandons, a view which, as we have seen, he had himself expressed in another passage of the *Reflections*.
[2] There is a notable passage early in the *Reflections* (the Bohn edition, vol. ii, p. 322), in which Burke explains the idea of such a society, and refers for support to the Book of Ecclesiasticus (xxxviii. 24–xxxix. 5). 'The occupation of a hairdresser, or of a working tallow-chandler, cannot be a matter of honour to any person—to say nothing of a number of other more servile employments. Such descriptions of men ought not to suffer oppression from the State; but the State suffers oppression if such as they, either individually or collectively, are permitted to rule. In this you think you are combating prejudice, but you are at war with nature.'

Burke to move back to the idea of a graded and hierarchical society.

There is thus, after all, some recoil in Burke's thought (as it fixed itself in 1790 and the years that followed) from his earlier ideas and convictions. He was not so consistent as he believed—and as he argued in his *Appeal from the New to the Old Whigs*—with his own previous attitude. But the French Revolution was the explosion of a tremendous force, and its impact might well shake the stability and the consistency of even the most established of thinkers. Burke, with his Catholic cast of thought, had never been a believer in the sovereignty of human will, and least of all a believer in the sovereignty of the popular will of the moment. Behind human will he believed that there was always a final Sovereign Will, moving in its own mysterious way; and as early as 1782 he had said, of 'the multitude for the moment', that it was foolish when it acted without deliberation. He saw in the French Revolution an explosion of 'the multitude for the moment'; he saw in it a titanic insurrection of mere human will. It is impossible not to be moved by the profundity of Burke's feeling about the insurrection of human will. It is already expressed in October 1789, in the letter to M. Dupont which has already been mentioned. 'The moment *will* is set above reason and justice, in any community, a great question may arise in sober minds, in what part or portion of the community that dangerous domination of *will* may be the least mischievously placed.'[1] The same feeling reappears in the *Reflections*. 'It is . . . of infinite importance that they (the people at large) should not be suffered to imagine that their will . . . is the standard of right and wrong. . . . When the people have emptied themselves of all the lust of selfish will, . . . and exercise . . . the power which to be legitimate must be according to that eternal, immutable law in which will and reason are the same, they will be more careful how they place power.'[2] Finally, the same feeling is expressed, once more, in the *Appeal from the New to the Old Whigs*. 'Neither the few nor the many have a right to act merely by their will, in any matter connected with duty, trust, engagement or obligation. . . . The votes of a majority of the people . . . cannot alter the moral any more than they can alter the

---

[1] Burke's *Correspondence*, vol. iii, p. 107.
[2] Burke's *Works*, the Bohn edition, vol. ii, pp. 365–6.

physical essence of things.' To think otherwise is 'to subject the sovereign reason of the world to the caprices of weak and giddy men'.[1]

X

'The sovereign reason of the world.' It is a phrase which brings us back, in the conclusion of the argument, to the ultimate foundation of Burke's philosophy. Eternal reason, revealing itself objectively in that 'general bank and capital of nations and of ages' which the mind of man accumulates by its long and collective reasoning, guides the process of history and the life of States. Immortal and continuous itself, it expresses itself in the immortal and continuous life of the State, which is part of the continuous and immortal life of the universe. But this eternal and sovereign reason, though it pervades everything by its 'divine tactic', and though it summons the States of men to partake in its own immortality, imposes no inevitable fatalism on human thought and action. On the contrary, it summons men to collaborate, and to collaborate by that same process of the gradual unfolding of thought, and the gradual making of order, by which it is always acting itself. God operates, and man, under His guidance, co-operates. Holding this view, Burke can believe, at one and the same time, in the immortality of the State and the experimentalism of politics. He can hold, at one and the same time, that we cannot escape from the past, and that we can and must escape from the dead hand of metaphysical theories of politics which would cast life unalterably and irrevocably in one hard iron mould. The immortal State, and the experimentalism of the politics by which the State is guided and governed—this is the paradox, the seeming paradox, with which Burke seeks to confront the votaries of the Revolution. On the one hand, the State is immortal—doubly and trebly immortal; immortal because it is a system of inherited rights and obligations for ever marked by a biological continuity of transmission; immortal because it is a Church as well as a State, and because it is consecrated for immortality by its consecration in the character of a Church; immortal, because it is a necessary and linked part of an

---

[1] Ibid., vol. iii, pp. 76–7. The whole passage which follows, down to p. 87, is cardinal to the understanding of Burke's thought.

immortal universe proceeding according to a divine concordance which holds all physical and all moral natures eternally together. The immortal State must keep its faith in the appointed scheme —respecting its own past; respecting, in the present, the balance and engagement between its own parts or elements; respecting the whole 'bank and capital' of collective historical thought on which, under God, it is based. 'But this', a critic will naturally say (as Tom Paine actually said), 'is just the dead hand of the past, restricting a present which is, and must be, competent for its own purposes.' Burke has his own reply to the critic. The past is not a dead hand, but a moving finger of guidance. If we respect the past, and the present in which the past lives, we are essentially and fundamentally free. We are engaged in that tentative and experimental progress through time which is the essential liberty of man. The real tyranny, the real dead hand, which is to be feared, is the tyranny and the rigidity of fixed metaphysical principles. Politics is not, and can never be, metaphysics or geometry. It is a moving art of moral prudence. It is an experimental science, and, 'like every other experimental science, not to be taught *a priori*'. Here Burke was true to the country in which he lived and wrote—a country which has always preferred experiment to doctrine. But was not France herself, after all, engaged in experiment? Was Burke really true to his own faith, or to the lessons of his own country's history, when he frowned so sternly on the great experiment of France? Was he loyal to his own idea of the moving finger of historic guidance? Was he not so gravely alarmed by the dead hand of metaphysics —which, on another valuation, may be rather accounted a lively brain—that he fell himself into a worship of the dead hand of history?

It was a serious choice by which men were confronted in those profound and stirring years at the end of the eighteenth century. An observer living in France had written, even before 1789, 'There is scarcely a young man who on leaving College does not form a project of establishing a new system of philosophy and of government.' In and after 1789 the systems scintillated, and their lightning was destructive. Burke retreated into the shelter of the historic state, and did homage to its dignity.

> We do it wrong, being so majestical,
> To offer it the show of violence.

This was conservatism. But it was also magnificent; and its magnificence, mixed though it was with extravagance, has established Burke's *Reflections* as one of the permanent possessions of man's mind in its voyage through the seas of thought.

PART III
ESSAYS ON THE RELATION OF THE CHURCH TO SOCIETY AND THE STATE

Essay Eight

ST. AUGUSTINE'S THEORY OF SOCIETY

I

ST. AUGUSTINE was born (A.D. 354), and spent his life, in the eastern part of what is now the French province of Algeria; and for the last thirty-five years of his life he was bishop of what is now the French port of Bona. In his lifetime, and to the very year of his death (A.D. 430), when the Vandal Gaiseric began a Teutonic conquest, the land was part of the Roman province of Africa. St. Augustine was thus an 'African'; and he shows in *The City of God* some traces of that nationalism which, in Africa as well as elsewhere, but perhaps more than elsewhere, emerged from the decline and fall of Rome. The Roman province of Africa, many centuries ago, had been governed by ancient Carthage; the language of ancient Carthage, Punic, still lingered in the province, and formed a vernacular basis of African nationalism. St. Augustine drew illustrations from the old speech: he urged on the Christian clergy of the province the need for acquainting themselves with it; and when he speaks, in *The City of God*, of the Punic Wars, he betrays a sympathy with the *victa causa* of Carthage.

The archaeological research of our own day proves more and more abundantly the culture of Roman Africa. Born among this culture, St. Augustine began to imbibe it at an early age. By the year A.D. 370, at the age of 16, he was engaged in study at Carthage. He mastered the Latin classics—particularly Cicero, Virgil, and the encyclopaedic Varro, whose *Antiquitatum Libri* (in forty-one books, now lost) is quoted again and again in *The*

City of God. He also read (in translations) the *Categories* of Aristotle and many of the dialogues of Plato. He was particularly influenced by Plato; and one of the chapters of *The City of God* is headed: 'Of the means by which Plato was able to gain such intelligence that he came near to the knowledge of Christ.' He became a teacher of classical culture: he professed 'rhetoric' at Carthage as early as 377, and was professing the same subject at Milan in 384. . . . And then, by the ways which he has himself described in his *Confessions*, he was led to the Christian cause. Henceforth there are, in a sense, two men in St. Augustine—the antique man of the old classical culture, and the Christian man of the new Gospel. It is the great fascination of *The City of God* (and particularly perhaps of the nineteenth book) that we see the two men at grips with one another. This is what makes the work one of the great turning-points in the history of human destiny: it stands on the confines of two worlds, the classical and the Christian, and it points the way into the Christian. For there is never a doubt, in all the argument, from the first words of the first chapter of the first book, of the victory of that 'most glorious city of God' proclaimed, as with the voice of a trumpet, in the very beginning and prelude.

St. Augustine was baptized in 387 at the age of thirty-three. After an absence of five years in Italy, he returned to Africa in 388. Three years later, in 391, he was directly ordained a presbyter, omitting all minor orders; and he was set by his bishop (the Bishop of Hippo, which is the modern Bona) to expound the Gospel and to preach in his presence. He was thus directed, early in his career, to the task of Christian exegesis; and having a ready pen as well as an eloquent voice—burning, in every way, with a great gift and a fine passion of communication—he set to work on his lifelong task of justification and interpretation of the Christian faith. He was consecrated bishop in 395. His episcopal duties were far from light. For one thing, he had a heavy burden of judicial duties: the episcopal court, in the custom of the age, was a court of general resort, even for civil cases.[1] For another thing, he was organizing around him (as he had already begun to do when he was first made presbyter) a community of clergy,

---

[1] When St. Augustine (e.g. in Book xix. 6) speaks of the difficulties of the judge and 'the error of human judgements when the truth is hidden', he is speaking from a full experience.

or canons, living a common life under a rule; and he was thus occupied in the foundation of what, in the language of a later day, would have been called a religious order—a task which a St. Benedict or a St. Francis found engrossing enough in itself. But whatever the burden of his judicial work, and whatever his obligation to the clerical community gathered round him, he never ceased to write till the very year of his death. He began in 397 a work *De Doctrina Christiana*: it was not finished until 426. He began in 413 *The City of God*; and that too was not finished until 426. (We have to remember, in reading it, that it appeared, part by part, over a period of thirteen years; and then we can understand its length, its repetitions, its diffuseness, its lack of a single controlling scheme of arrangement. The bishop was giving to his flock and to the world—part by part, and section by section—the thoughts that had poured into a fermenting brain, the experiences which had filled a rich life, in the intervals between the publication of one section and the appearance of the next; and his flock, and the world of his readers, had come to expect their recurrent food in its season.) But the treatise on *Christian Doctrine* and that on *The City of God* are only two among a multitude of others. There are the *Confessions*, for instance, which were finished before 400; there are commentaries on Genesis, the Psalms, and the Gospel of St. John; there are homilies, *De Bono Conjugali* and *De Nuptiis*; there are treatises on Free Will and Predestination, the Trinity and the Grace of Christ; there are, at the end of his life, the *Retractationum Libri*. It was an indefatigable pen which finally ceased its work in the last days of August 430 in that city of Hippo in which he had spent more than half of the seventy-four years of his life. The city was being besieged by the Vandals as he died; and within five years of his death they had settled in a large tract of the Roman province, with their capital at Hippo. For his own city, at any rate, St. Augustine had been the 'last of the Romans'.

He was a man of vital personality, with an abounding gift of self-expression. One of his phrases, as Mr. Bevan has remarked in an essay on the 'Prophet of Personality',[1] is the solemn and profound phrase, 'abyssus humanae conscientiae', 'the abysmal depths of personality'. He knew the depths of the soul, and he could express its secrets, in a way which was new among the

[1] Essay VII in *Hellenism and Christianity*.

ST. AUGUSTINE'S THEORY OF SOCIETY 237

writers of the ancient world. He had at his command a remarkable style and a Latinity which was at once nervous, subtle, and sinuous. 'We should perhaps never have dared to forecast,' Mr. Bevan writes of his Latin, 'how this speech of massive construction, made for rock-graven epigram or magisterial formula, could be used to convey the outpourings of mystical devotion, to catch the elusive quality of shadowy moods, to enter into the subtleties of psychological analysis.' The glory of his Latinity, and of the vision which it expressed, was destined to work permanently on the imagination of all the Middle Ages. When Abelard sings his great hymn—

> O quanta qualia sunt illa sabbata,
> Quae semper celebrat superna curia,

he is borrowing the very words of St. Augustine, and particularly of that last chapter of the last book of *The City of God* which is entitled, 'of the eternal felicity of the city of God and its perpetual Sabbath'. And when Dante climbs into Paradise, he is following St. Augustine's footsteps.

It is tempting to quote some of the great sayings of St. Augustine.[1] 'Thou has made us for Thyself, and our heart is restless until it find rest in Thee.' 'This is the sum of religion, to imitate whom thou dost worship.' 'A man shall say unto me, *Intelligam ut credam*; and I will reply to him, *Immo crede ut intelligas*.' 'There is one commonwealth of all Christian men.' 'That heavenly city which has Truth for its King, Love for its Law, and Eternity for its Measure.' 'Whosoever reads these words, let him go with me, when he is equally certain; let him seek with me, when he is equally in doubt; let him return to me, when he knows his own error; let him call me back, when he knows mine.' All these sayings show the man. Many of them became the great commonplaces of future ages. To remember them is to remember the essence of the writer's thought. Who can forget the deep meaning of his cry to God, 'Da quod jubes—et jube quod vis'?

II

The occasion of the writing of *The City of God* was the sack of Rome by Alaric and his Goths in 410. The sack was not in itself

[1] They are collected in Bishop Welldon's edition of the *De Civitate Dei*, vol. ii, pp. 656–8.

the most terrible of visitations. Gaiseric and his Vandals sacked it again in 455, plundering at leisure for a fortnight. The Normans under Guiscard sacked it once more in 1084, and their ravages exceeded the ravages of Goths and Vandals. But the sack of A.D. 410 impressed the imagination of the age profoundly. Rome herself, intact from a foreign invader for nearly a thousand years—Rome, the founder, the mistress and the capital of the Empire—had fallen. She had fallen in the hour of the victory of Christianity; she had fallen (murmured those who clung to the ancient ways) in consequence of that victory. News of the fall of Rome had come flying over the seas to Carthage; and fugitives from Rome had come flying in the wake of the news. Here was a great question for Christian apologetics. Were the barbaric invasions and the decline of the Empire, which had just culminated in the resounding crash of the 'Eternal City', the result of abandoning the old civic gods and the old civic faith? If they were not, what was their meaning, and what 'philosophy of history' could Christians produce to explain and justify the march of events? These were the questions to which Augustine turned, and which formed the original inspiration of *The City of God*.

But a work which, as we have already had occasion to notice, took thirteen years in composition, and eventually ran to twenty-two books, was bound to transcend its original design. St. Augustine indeed deals with history in *The City of God*; but he left a good deal of the historical theme to Orosius, a Spanish monk who had come to Hippo in 414 (the year after *The City of God* had been begun) and was entrusted with the writing of an *Historia adversus Paganos* by way of an appendix or corollary—not of a very high order—to his master's work.[1] St. Augustine himself took a higher flight. He had been drawn into a connexion with Volusianus, the proconsul of Africa, a philosophical pagan engaged in the study of Christian evidences. The connexion gave a new theme and fresh motive to the development of his treatise on *The City of God*. He was no longer only concerned to provide a philosophy of history in answer to pagan

---

[1] 'Orosius's cue was this: the world, far from being more miserable than before the advent of Christianity, was really more prosperous and happy. Etna was less active than of old, the locusts consumed less, the barbarian invasions were no more than merciful warnings.' Dr. F. F. Stewart, in the *Cambridge Ancient History*, vol. i. pp. 576-7.

murmurings; he was also concerned to provide a justification of the whole *philosophia Christi* in answer to the human philosophy of the ancient world. It was this double purpose which determined the trend and the argument of *The City of God* as the work developed down to 426.

St. Augustine himself has given his own account of the scope of his work in a passage of the *Retractationum Libri*. The twenty-two books, he explains, fall into two parts—which, as we shall see, correspond to the two purposes of which we have spoken. The first part, embracing the first ten books, falls itself in turn into two divisions. The first division (Books i–v) is directed against the belief that human prosperity depends upon the maintenance of a civic worship of the many gods of the pagan pantheon; and in particular it is intended to disprove the opinion that the prohibition of such worship, which had been recently enacted by Gratian and Theodosius (*c.* A.D. 380), was responsible for the late calamities—the barbarian invasions, the decline of the Empire, and the sack of Rome. The second division (Books vi–x) is directed against a more moderate trend of pagan belief and opinion: it is intended to refute the thinkers who, admitting that calamities were the inseparable and perpetual companions of humanity—admitting, therefore, that the late calamities needed no special explanation of ancient gods irate at the special oppression of their worship—nevertheless believed that for the course of the life to come (if not for the course of this life) the worship of the ancient gods had its own advantages. The argument of both the divisions of the first part is thus critical and destructive: it is an *argumentum adversus paganos*. But criticism was not enough: St. Augustine desired to be constructive as well as destructive; he desired not only to put to flight pagan murmurings about the sack of Rome, but also to draw over to the Christian side the thoughtful pagan (such as Volusianus) who was pondering the truth of Christian evidences. 'As I did not wish', he says, 'to be accused of having merely controverted the doctrines of others, without stating my own, this (that is to say, the statement of his own doctrines) is the theme of the second part of this work, which is contained in twelve books.' This second part is divided by St. Augustine into three divisions. The first (Books xi–xiv) 'contains the *origin* of the two cities, the City of God and the city of this world'; the second (Books xv–xviii) 'contains their *process or progress*'; the third (Books xix-xxii) deals with 'their appointed *ends*'—in other words, with the goal towards which they move and the consummation in which the logic of their process necessarily culminates.

III

ST. AUGUSTINE, taking over the idea from the philosophers of antiquity, distinguishes four grades (or, we may say, concentric rings) of human society. The first is the *Domus* or Household. Above that, and wider than that, is the *Civitas*—which had originally meant the City, and the City-State founded upon and co-extensive with it, but had been extended (as Rome, for example, grew, and from a city became an empire) to mean the great State of many cities, and many tribes and kingdoms, united in a common allegiance to the person of a common ruler. Above the *Civitas*, and wider than it, comes the *Orbis terrae*—the whole Earth and the whole human society which inhabits the Earth. Finally, and widest of all societies, there is the Universe, *Mundus*, which embraces the heavens and their constellations as well as the earth, and includes God and His angels and the souls of the departed as well as the human society now sojourning upon the earth. In the light of this classification we may make some preliminary observations on St. Augustine's conception of the City of God.

Strictly, the City of God transcends the grade (or the concentric ring) of the *Civitas*. It belongs to the great society of the Universe; it is coextensive with the *Mundus*. But for centuries past, by a natural metaphor, the conception of *Civitas* (or πόλις) had been applied to the universal society; and such society had been regarded, and described, as a city. Men naturally sought to import the warmth and the intimacy of the close and familiar civic community into the Universe, as soon as they began to regard it as a unity or society; they felt that they had made themselves at home in the Universe when they had called it a 'city', in which the Divine and the human dwelt together in a common 'citizenship'. The Stoics, about 300 B.C., had already begun to go this way; and indeed the Cynics had already trodden the way before them. They had spoken of the κοσμόπολις, the City which is as wide as the whole κόσμος (the Greek word for Universe which was translated by the Latin *Mundus*); and in the process of time, as we find in the *Meditations* of Marcus Aurelius (iv. 23), the very term 'City of God' began to be applied to the Cosmos. Turning to it, the Emperor cries, 'All fits together for me which is well-fitted for thee, O thou Universe; from thee are all things, in thee are all things, to thee come all things; the poet saith, "Dear City of Athens", but wilt thou not say, "Dear City of Zeus"?' (ὦ πόλι φίλη Διός.) St. Augustine had thus the great phrase ready to his hand; but he had even more than the phrase. He had a picture, inherited from the past, of the lineaments of the City of God.

The picture was a double picture, and it had been painted by two men, both of whom came from the same corner of the Eastern Mediterranean.[1] One of them was Posidonius of Apamea, an eclectic philosopher who blended Stoicism with Platonism, and gave to the world of the first century B.C. (the world into which Christianity was born) its prevalent body of philosophic ideas. Mr. Bevan has described, in his book on *Stoics and Sceptics*, the picture which Posidonius drew of the Universe. The outer spheres of the Universe (the spheres of the fixed stars and the planets and the sun) were composed of pure ether; and this pure ether was the place of God, and indeed it was God. As you came inward, towards the earth, purity diminished with the admixture of baser substance; and from the sphere of the moon to the central earth there was an increasing degree of impurity. What happened within this Universe was simple. At death the soul of man (now a *daimon*) tried to fly away to the pure ether and to be with God. It got as far as its life on earth warranted; and so the inner Universe, between the earth and the outer spheres, was peopled with *daimones*. 'You will see,' Mr. Bevan writes, 'that when the Stoic books talked about the world as one great city, of which gods and men were citizens, it was really a much more compact and knowable whole which was presented to their imagination than is suggested by the Universe to ours. Even to

[1] It is one of the curiosities of history that three great thinkers came from the neighbourhood of the Gulf of Cilicia, and all went to Athens to learn or to teach. The first was Zeno, from Citium in Cyprus, who came to Athens about 300 B.C. and founded Stoicism. The second was Posidonius of Apamea, who was in Athens about 100 B.C. The third was St. Paul of Tarsus, who was preaching in Athens about A.D. 50. An Englishman can hardly refrain from adding the name of Theodore of Tarsus, who became Archbishop of Canterbury in A.D. 668, and organized the English Church. He, too, had studied in Athens, and was called 'the philosopher'.

Posidonius, indeed, the spaces of the heavens were vast, as compared with the globe of earth; yet he could see the fiery orbs which marked the outer boundary of the Universe, *flammantia moenia mundi*, and there was nothing beyond it. . . . The whole of reality was contained for him within the envelope of fiery ether, one world, knit together by a natural sympathy between all the parts.'

The other man who painted a picture of the City of God was St. Paul. A number of inspirations combined to produce his picture. In the first place he was a Jew, and he knew the City of Jerusalem; he knew, too, the old Hebrew dreams of the Holy City of Zion, to which all the nations should resort, and which should gather the world into its glory. Again he was versed (like St. Augustine himself in his day) in the teachings of the Greek philosophers; and a knowledge of Stoic philosophy peeps again and again through his Epistles. Above all he was an Apostle, and he knew the teaching of our Lord: he had received the gospel of the 'Kingdom of Heaven', into which all men might enter by regeneration, if they believed in God and His Son and their belief were counted to them for 'Righteousness'. Under these various inspirations, but especially and particularly under the last, St. Paul spoke of a commonwealth (a πολίτευμα, or organized civic body) as 'existing in the heavens',[1] and yet as including Christian believers here on earth who had attained (or, more exactly, had been given by the grace of God) the gift of 'Righteousness'. It is to that Divine commonwealth, or City of God, that all Christians really belong; and St. Paul thus speaks of them as fellow-citizens (συμπολῖται) of the Saints.[2] But meanwhile Christians are also sojourning below in another polity; and in that other, or earthly, polity they may be called 'strangers and pilgrims'[3]—or, as a Greek would have said, 'resident aliens' (ξένοι μέτοικοι), who, belonging as citizens to another city, are temporarily resident as strangers in a foreign body of citizens. It is here, and in this picture (sketched with a few bold strokes) of the commonwealth in the heavens and the pilgrimage on earth, that we find, as it were, the original drawing from which St. Augustine painted the great canvas of *The City of God*.

---

[1] Phil. iii. 20. [2] Eph. ii. 19.
[3] The words are those, not of St. Paul, but of St. Peter (1 Pet. ii. 11). I would add that I owe these references to Bishop Welldon's edition of the *De Civitate Dei*.

We must pause, at this point, to notice some fundamental differences between the picture of St. Paul and the picture of Posidonius and the Stoics. For the latter there is really but a single city, reaching from earth to heaven—a city in which the baser sort (the *Stulti*, as the Stoics called them) will indeed occupy a far lowlier position, never attaining near to the outer ether, but which, none the less, includes the Divine and the *daimones* and all humanity in its wide embrace. St. Paul implies two sorts of cities—the Divine commonwealth in the heavens, and the human commonwealth on earth. (Just in the same way St. Augustine distinguishes the *Civitas Dei* and the *terrena civitas*.) And the reason for this distinction of the two sorts of cities is, in one word, 'Righteousness'. For the Divine city is the city only of the righteous; and no unclean thing may enter into it. Here, in this one word Righteousness, which in Latin is *Justitia*, we touch one of the great key-words of human thought—a key-word to the thought of St. Augustine, a key-word to the thought of the Middle Ages. It is a word which we must study; and we shall find that its study takes us back to Plato.

Language plays great tricks with the human mind. Words of a mixed and wavering content are the greatest of all tricksters. Among these words is the Latin word *Justitia*. When the thought of the Greeks—the thought of Plato and of St. Paul—came to the Latin West, there came with it the word Δικαιοσύνη, which (so far as it has an equivalent in our language) may be translated 'Righteousness'. The translation which it received in the Latin language was *Justitia*; and that translation had large (and sometimes disastrous) consequences in the field of theology and of moral philosophy. It legalized a term which in the original Greek was something more than legal; and a legal tone (a tone of wrongs, penalties, sanctions, and 'justification') thus came to affect the thought of Latin Christendom. This had not been the tone of Greek writers. Plato, for example, had written a dialogue called *The Republic, or Concerning Righteousness* (πολιτεία ἢ περὶ δικαιοσύνης); but the Right (τὸ δίκαιον) had meant for him the ideal good of a society in the whole range of its collective life (and not merely in the field of legal relations), and Righteousness had meant accordingly the ideal goodness of a whole society in all its breadth. The idea of Righteousness in Plato was a moral idea (which at its highest seemed to pass into a religious idea) rather than an idea of law; and what is true of Plato is also true, and even more true, of St. Paul and his use of the idea of Righteousness. It is also true, as we must now proceed to show, of St. Augustine.

St. Augustine, as we have already had occasion to mention, was particularly influenced by Plato. He had read his dialogues in a Latin translation; he had read the Neoplatonists' interpretations of their master; and he cites Plato again and again in the course of *The City of God*. We are here concerned only with the influence of the Platonic conception of Righteousness, and that only as it bears on the social and political theory of St. Augustine; but the influence of Plato upon St. Augustine goes farther than that. St. Augustine carried the *general* thought of Plato into his own *general* thought; and through him, as we shall later have reason to notice, Plato influenced the subsequent course of Western theology throughout the Middle Ages and down to the Reformation, which was indeed itself, in some of its aspects, a return to Plato and St. Augustine. 'The appeal away from the illusion of things seen to the reality that belongs to God alone, the slight store set by him on institutions of time and place, in a word, the philosophic idealism that underlies and colours all Augustine's utterances on doctrinal and even practical questions and forms the real basis of his thought, is Platonic.'[1]

In *The Republic* Plato had constructed an ideal city, based upon Right and instinct with Righteousness, which might almost be described as a City of God, and is actually described by Plato as 'laid up somewhere in heaven'. This ideal city was to be a model; and looking upon it, and trying to copy it, men might blot out some features from their cities, and paint in others, until 'they had made the ways of men, as far as possible, agreeable to the ways of God'.[2] Over against the ideal city Plato had set, in the later books of *The Republic*, a description of the actual and earthly cities of men, tracing the progressive corruption of the ideal in their successive forms. The ground of the distinction and contrast was simple. In the ideal city there was Righteousness. Each of its citizens took his particular station; each of them performed—performed only, but performed to the best of his power—the appointed function of that station; and since Righteous-

---

[1] Dr. Stewart in the *Cambridge Modern History*, vol. i, p. 579.
[2] *The Republic*, 501 B–C.

ness consisted in 'performing the function of station' (τὸ αὐτοῦ πράττειν), a city on such a foundation was Righteous. In the actual and earthly cities, on the other hand, Unrighteousness reigned; men departed more and more from their station, and encroached more and more on the stations of others; there was no order; there was no system of stations; there was no system of right relations duly based on a system of stations.

We may almost say that St. Augustine takes the Platonic distinction, and Christianizes it. Righteousness is lifted to a higher plane: it ceases to be a system of right relations between men, based on the idea of social stations, and it becomes a system of right relations between man and God (but also, and consequently, between man and man), based on the idea, first of man's faith in God's will for a system of right relations, and secondly of God's grace as rewarding such faith by creating (or rather restoring), through the 'election' of the faithful, the system of right relations interrupted by sin but renewed by faith and election. *Ordo* is a great word in St. Augustine; and *ordo* is closely allied to what I have called a 'system of right relations',[1] as that in turn is closely allied to, and indeed identical with, the idea of Righteousness. We can now understand St. Augustine's transfiguration of the old Platonic conception; we can understand his distinction of the City of God and the terrene city; we can understand his saying (iv. 4), 'Remove righteousness, and what are kingdoms but great bands of brigands'? The City of God is the the city of the righteous, a city pervaded by a system of right relations (*ordo creaturarum*) which unites God and His Angels and the Saints in Heaven with the righteous on earth. It is a city of the Universe (*Mundus*); and yet it does not embrace the whole Universe, for it excludes the fallen angels, the souls of the unrighteous, and the unrighteous who are living on earth. It is an invisible society: it cannot be identified with any visible society; it cannot, in strictness, be identified with the Church, because the Church on earth contains baptized members who belong to *its* society, and yet are not righteous, and cannot therefore belong to the society of the City of God. Look at the City of God in its earthly membership (remembering that this is only one part of the whole), and you will see that, so far as religious society on earth is con-

[1] 'Ordo est parium dispariumque rerum sua cuique loca tribuens dispositio' (xix. 12).

cerned, the City contains most, but not all, of the members of the Church: you will see again that, so far as secular societies are concerned, the City 'summoneth its citizens from all tribes, and collecteth its pilgrim fellowship among all languages, taking no heed of what is diverse in manners or laws or institutions' (xix. 18). Compare it then with its opposite, and you will readily see the nature of the earthly city. That again, in strictness, is no formal, visible, enumerable society. It is simply all the unrighteous, wherever they be in the Universe—the fallen angels, the souls of the unrighteous, the unrighteous who are living on earth. You cannot identify it with any actual organized society: you cannot, for instance, identify it with the Roman Empire. It is something more—it includes fallen angels as well as men; it is something less —it does not include the righteous, who are to be found in any actual State.

We can now see, as it were face to face, the lineaments of the City of God, 'Two loves have created two cities: love of self, to the contempt of God, the earthly city; love of God, to the contempt of self, the heavenly' (xiv. 28). Of the heavenly city St. Augustine writes further in one of his letters (cxxxvii) saying, 'The only basis and bond of a true city is that of faith and strong concord, when the object of love is the universal good, which is, in its highest and truest character, God Himself, and men love one another, with full sincerity, in Him, and the ground of their love for one another is the love of Him from whose eyes they cannot conceal the Spirit of their love'.... And these two cities, and these two loves, shall live together, side by side, and even intermixed, until the last winnowing and the final separation shall come upon the earth in the Day of Judgement.

Two things remain to be said—one concerning the State and its institutions in their relation to this distinction of the heavenly and the earthly cities; the other concerning the Church and its relation to the same distinction.

We might think, at first sight, that the State corresponded to, or was somehow identical with, the earthly city or some form of that city. But, as we have just seen, it would be as great a mistake (or an even greater mistake) to identify the earthly city with the Roman Empire, or any form of actual State, as to identify the heavenly city with the Catholic Church. The earthly city, like the heavenly city, is an ideal conception; or rather, and to speak more exactly, it may be called the ideal negation, or antithesis, of the ideal. It is a city of Unrighteousness. The actual State, as it really exists, is something different. It is not absolutely unrighteous. On the contrary, it has a sort of *Justitia* of its own; and not only so, but the citizens of the heavenly city avail themselves of the aid of this *Justitia* in the course of their pilgrimage, so that the State is thus, in its way, a coadjutor of the City of God.

In order to understand this view of the State we must make a distinction between absolute and relative righteousness. Absolute righteousness is a system of right relations to God—relations which are at once religious, moral, and, if you will, legal: relations which are, in a word, *total*. This system, or *ordo*, has not to reckon with, or to be adjusted to, any defects; it has not to reckon with, or to adjust itself to, the defect of sin, for sin has been swallowed up in faith and grace. Relative righteousness is a system of right relations mainly in the legal sphere, and it is a system of right relations reckoning with, and adjusted to, the sinfulness of human nature. It is the best possible, *granted the defect of sin*; but again, and just because that defect has to be assumed, it is only a second best. This is the basis of St. Augustine's conception of the State and all the institutions of the State—government, property, slavery. All of these institutions are forms of *dominium*—the *dominium* of government over subjects, the *dominium* of owners over property, the *dominium* of masters over slaves. All *dominium* is a form of *ordo*, and to that extent good; but the order is an order conditioned by, and relative to, the sinfulness which it has to correct, and it is therefore only relatively good. The argument may be illustrated from the example of property. Ideally, for the righteous, all things are in common, and we read of the early Christians that 'they had all things common'. But sinfulness continues and abounds; and a form of sinfulness is greed. Partly to provide a punishment for greed, and partly to provide a remedy, private property becomes a necessity and an institution of the organized State. It is not *quod postulat ordo creaturarum*; but at any rate it is *quod exigit meritum peccatorum* (xix. 15). We may say, therefore, that property is an institution, not indeed of absolute, but at any rate of relative righteousness. We may even say that it is willed by God, who wills a relative righteousness where sin makes absolute righteousness unobtainable. What is true of the institution of property is true of the whole State. 'God willed the State,' in the view of St. Augustine (as afterwards in that of Burke); but he willed it *propter remedium peccatorum*.

The State, therefore, if it falls far below the heavenly city, may be said to rise above the earthly city of the unrighteous. It stands somewhere between the two, though it must be admitted that the language of *The City of God* often seems to suggest that the State and the earthly city touch and blend. From this point of view we can understand how St. Augustine can speak of the heavenly city as using the aid of the State. The State has its *ordo*, though it is not the order of creation: the State has its *pax*, though it is not the true and eternal peace. 'Therefore the heavenly city rescinds and destroys none of those things by which earthly peace is attained or maintained: rather it preserves and pursues that which, different though it be in different nations, is yet directed to the one and selfsame end of earthly peace—provided it hinder not religion, whereby we are taught that the one highest and true God must be worshipped. Therefore, again, the heavenly city uses earthly peace in this its pilgrimage: it preserves and seeks the agreement of human wills in matters pertaining to the mortal nature of men, so far as, with due regard to piety and religion, it can; and it relates that earthly peace to the heavenly peace, which truly is such peace that it should be accounted and named the only peace of the rational creature, being as it is a most ordered and most concordant companionship in the enjoyment of God, and, again, in the enjoyment of one another in God' (xix. 17).

Here, it might seem, we touch St. Augustine's theory of the relation of Church and State. In a sense that is true, though we have to remember that, so far as our argument has hitherto gone, the Church and the heavenly city are not the same, and it is of the heavenly city that St. Augustine is speaking in the passage which has just been quoted. This much, at any rate, we may believe about the State, that it is not an unblessed or Satanic institution. It has its own 'order': it has its own relative 'righteousness'. It is not a *magnum latrocinium*; for you *cannot* remove righteousness from it, and St. Augustine only said that kingdoms were great bands of brigands *if you remove righteousness*. Nor again was it founded by Satan (even though Gregory VII, at a far later date, might say in a hot moment that kings took their beginnings from those who were instigated by the prince of this world to desire dominion over their fellows); on the contrary, it is willed and intended by God. It can stand up, on its own basis, with its own justification, to aid the heavenly city. The State has thus assumed a clear character; but we are still left with the question of the position of the Church, of its relation to the distinction of the heavenly and the earthly cities, and, again, of its relation to the State.

We may begin by noticing that, at the time at which St. Augustine was writing, a distinction had already established itself between the Church in the East and the Church in the West. The Eastern Church had become something of the nature of a State-Church, with a reverential awe for its Emperor at Constantinople and a veneration for the memory of Constantine as 'equal to the apostles'. The Church of the West was far more independent. St. Ambrose had but lately rebuked and controlled the great Emperor Theodosius; the Pope at Rome, all the more as the Emperor had recently withdrawn to Ravenna, stood ready to assume the purple. Did *The City of God* prepare the way for the pretensions and the power of the medieval papacy? A great ecclesiastical scholar has written the words, 'St. Augustine's theory of the *Civitas Dei* was, in the germ, that of the medieval papacy, without the name of Rome. In Rome itself it was easy to supply the insertion, and to conceive of a dominion, still wielded from the ancient seat of government, as world-wide and almost as authoritative as that of the Empire.'[1] In what sense, if any, may it be said that *The City of God* was the germ of the medieval papacy?

What St. Augustine might be interpreted into meaning, or used to suggest, is a different thing from St. Augustine's own teaching. We may admit, and admit readily, that the whole picture of the *gloriosissima civitas Dei* might easily be transferred to the medieval Church and the papacy. After all, that Church was based on the 'righteousness' of the *lex evangelica* (*Justitia* was the cry of Hildebrand, and his dying words were *Dilexi justitiam*); after all, it sought to spread the reign of 'righteousness' by the action of its papal Head in every State and upon every Estate or condition of men: why should it not be counted the heir of *The City of God*? But we are here concerned with St. Augustine himself, living and writing in nationalist Africa (and no little of a nationalist himself, as witness his references to ancient Carth-

[1] The late Mr. C. H. Turner in the *Cambridge Mediaeval History*, vol. i, p. 173.

age) between the years 413 and 426. What was his actual conception of the Church, in his own day and for his own generation?[1]

We must turn to some of his other writings to get the outlines of his conception clear. He believed in a universal Church comparable to the moon; he believed in particular Churches (*particulatim per loca singula Ecclesiae*) comparable to the stars. He held that an especial authority resided in the particular Churches founded by the Apostles; and among these he recognized a primary or still more especial authority in the Roman Church. The Roman Church might therefore be particularly consulted for an authoritative pronouncement on disputed questions, though at the same time St. Augustine speaks of an appeal to 'a plenary Council of the Church Universal'. Roughly, we may say that he believes in a universal Church as a single unit of faith and Christian society: he believes in particular or local Churches as units of organization; he allows a special authority to some, and a still more especial authority to one, of these; but he has no single Church which is at one and the same time a unit of faith, of organization, and of authority.

We may now inquire into the relation of the universal Church, as a unit of faith, to the City of God. We can only say that the thought of St. Augustine about this relation varies, according as his thought glows into a fervour of incandescence, or restricts itself within the bonds of his theological logic. Logically, there is a difference between the Church and the City of God. Not all who formally belong to the Church as a unit of faith—not all who have been baptized and confirmed—are righteous; and the Church may thus contain members who are not also members of the City of God. But the fervour of faith may sweep away the difference; and there are passages in which the Church is made the same as the City of God. 'The ark is a figure of the City of God on its pilgrimage in this world, *that is to say of the Church*, which is saved by the wood on which hung the mediator of God and men, the man Christ Jesus' (xv. 26). 'Therefore even now the Church is the Kingdom of Christ and the Kingdom of the Heavens' (xx. 9). A number of other passages might readily be collected to the same effect. We can only say that the Church, as a unit of faith,

---

[1] In seeking to answer this question, I have drawn on Appendix H of Bishop Welldon's edition.

sometimes glows with the greatness of the City of God, and sometimes falls short of that measure.

What, then, shall we say of the relation of Church and State? It is a question that hardly enters into St. Augustine's thought, in the form in which it presented itself to the Middle Ages, or presents itself to us to-day. There is no question, in *The City of God*, of any system of 'concordat' between Church and State, or of any State 'Establishment' of the Church, or of the superiority of the *sacerdotium* over the *regnum*, or of the power of the keys, or of the Donation of Constantine,[1] or of anything of the sort. The Church is a pilgrim society, living by faith and looking to the Hereafter. It lives on earth by the side of the State; it uses the *terrena pax* of the State; it acknowledges the divine institution and the relative righteousness of the State. But it simply moves as a pilgrim past the grandeurs and dignities of this world, 'nihil eorum rescindens vel destruens, immo etiam servans et sequens', but always looking beyond, and always with eyes fixed elsewhere. What has a pilgrim to do with a king, except to acknowledge that he is king, to render to him due obedience in matters of worldly peace, and to pass on?

Yet there is a sense in which the doctrine of *The City of God* is inimical to the State, and even subversive of its existence. St. Augustine shifts the centre of gravity. The men of the ancient world had thought in terms of the *Civitas Romana* as the one and only society; they had deified the Roman Emperor as its living incarnation, and they had thereby given a religious sanction to its claims: they had pent all life—religion, politics, everything—in a single secular framework. Writing at a time when the framework seemed to be cracking and breaking, St. Augustine says, in effect: 'This is not all; nor indeed is it the half of the matter. There is another and a greater society; and it is towards that society that the whole of creation moves.' The ultimate effect of *The City of God* is the elimination of the State: it is the enthronement of the Church (or at any rate of the heavenly city which again and again is identified with the Church) as the one and only *final* society. Rome has fallen: Christ has risen. The process of history is a process making for His Kingdom. When we remember that St. Augustine himself, as a consecrated officer of the Church, was already doing justice from his own episcopal tribunal in all sorts of cases, and thus taking the place of the State in the great sphere

[1] The idea of the Donation first emerges in the eighth century.

of jurisdiction, we can see that the way was prepared, alike in his thought and his life, for the enthronement of the Church upon earth.

IV

THE student who seeks to acquaint himself with the thought of St. Augustine may well be dismayed by the 1,200 pages of a Latin edition of the *De Civitate Dei*, such as that which was published by Bishop Welldon in 1924. He may even be alarmed by the 800 pages of the English translation printed recently (1945) in Everyman's Library.[1] Perhaps he may be wise to steep himself in some single book of the twenty-two. The argument of *The City of God* is not a sustained argument in distinct and successive logical steps. Writing as he did in separately published parts, and repeating and reinforcing his cardinal views, St. Augustine may be studied, as it were, in a 'sample'. The sample will not give the whole of his thought; but it may indicate its general drift and tendency. Such a sample may be found in Book xix.[2]

The City of God, it was said above, 'stands on the confines of two worlds, the classical and the Christian, and points the way forward into the Christian'. The nineteenth book particularly illustrates this sentinel attitude. On the one hand, St. Augustine looks back upon the theories of classical philosophy in regard to the nature of the Supreme Good, and reviews the attempts of antiquity to construct a gospel of human happiness within the confines of our mortal existence; on the other hand, he looks forward to the peace and happiness of the heavenly city of God, alike in the time of its earthly pilgrimage and in the eternity of its perpetual Sabbath.

In the early chapters (1-3) St. Augustine, using, as he so often does, the compilation of Varro, begins by stating the best features of the theories of classical antiquity in regard to the nature of the Supreme Good. He finds these features represented in the opinions and doctrines of the Old Academy—that is to say, in the Platonic

---

[1] The translation printed in Everyman's Library is the Jacobean translation of John Healey, published in 1610. The editor of the text, the Rev. R. V. E. Tasker, has incorporated most of the corrections made in the later edition of 1620, and has added some further corrections and emendations.

[2] Mr. R. H. Barrow, in his 'St. Augustine, *The City of God*' (1950), prints the Latin text of Book xix (with some few omissions), and an English translation facing the text, on pp. 62-133. He adds an analysis, and a full commentary, on pp. 177-263.

tradition. We may summarize these opinions and doctrines in two propositions. (1) The Supreme Good, in which lies happiness, is composed of the goods both of the body and of the mind; but since virtue, the highest quality of the mind, is incomparably the greatest of all goods, the life of man is most happy (and the Supreme Good is most perfectly attained) when he enjoys the possession of virtue, with the other goods of mind and body without which virtue is impossible. (The Christian answer to this theory is stated by St. Augustine in the fourth chapter.) (2) The happy life is social, and the Supreme Good can only be attained in society. Men desire the good of their friends: they desire that good for its own sake; they wish for their friends, for their friends' own sake, the good which they wish for themselves. Society thus arises, and appears in four grades—the grades we have already mentioned—the *domus*, the *civitas*, the *orbis*, the *mundus*; and society is essential to happiness. (To this line of thought St. Augustine cannot but give, as he says, a 'far ampler approval'; and therefore, partly in agreement with it, and partly in correction of it, he devotes twelve chapters (5–17) to a consideration of society and its relation to the Supreme Good and the happiness of man. It is these twelve chapters which give to the nineteenth book its particular interest for students of the social and political thought of St. Augustine.)

In stating these two propositions, we have incidentally indicated the gist of the first seventeen chapters, which form more than two-thirds of the nineteenth book. But there is another and final section of the book which also bears particularly on St. Augustine's political theory. After three intervening chapters (18–20), which are partly occupied with some details of the opinions of the Academy, and partly with an insistence on the idea that Christian happiness is an anticipatory happiness (*spe*, as he says, rather than *re*), he starts, in chapter twenty-one, to discuss Cicero's definition of *populus*. It was natural that, after discussing *societas* in general, he should turn to a discussion of *populus* and *respublica*; and thus a final and peculiarly political section is added to the book (21–27). But there is a long theological digression early in the section (22–23, but particularly 23); and the conclusion of the section, rising to higher than political themes, first treats of the relations between religion and morality, and then ends with the end of the wicked.

There are three themes which emerge from this brief analysis of the nineteenth book. The first is St. Augustine's criticism of the moral theory of the ancient philosophers. The second is his own theory of *Societas*. The third is his definition of *Populus* and *Respublica*.

(1) His criticism of the moral theory of the ancient world begins in and ends with the affirmation of the opposing tenets of the Christian faith. 'The City of God will make answer that eternal life is the Supreme Good, eternal death is the Supreme Evil; and it is therefore for the sake of gaining the one, and shunning the other, that we must live rightly.' There can be no Supreme Good or Happiness in this life only—and it is to this life only that pagan philosophy has its regard. Sickness assaults the body: afflictions threaten the senses; insanity menaces reason itself; and even virtue, the highest reach of mere mortal faculty, is always a struggle against the lusts of the flesh—a battle, and not a felicity. One by one St. Augustine examines the four cardinal virtues of ancient theory—Temperance, Prudence, Justice, and Fortitude —and of each in turn he proves that, so long as it is a merely mortal virtue, without the comfort of faith in God and the corroboration of the hope of eternal life, it must necessarily absent itself from felicity. Consider, he urges, Fortitude; consider its culmination in Stoic theory, which was a theory of Fortitude; and what do you find at its peak but Suicide, glorified as the last and greatest fling of the brave heart? And how can a theory which ends in *that* be a theory of the Supreme Good or of Happiness? This is a shrewd and vital criticism of the moral theory of the ancient world: the gaunt figure of Suicide standing on its summit is the index of its inherent inconsistency. 'O vitam beatam, quae ut finiatur mortis quaerit auxilium'—'O strange Happiness, that seeketh the alliance of Death to win its crown.' From the gospel of Death St. Augustine turns to point to the gospel of Life, the Life of Eternity. Seek the righteousness which comes from faith in God, and you shall have the hope of immortality; and in that hope you shall have both *salus* and *beatitudo*—the Salvation and the Happiness which philosophy seeks in vain. 'Talis salus, quae in futuro erit saeculo, ipsa erit etiam finalis beatitudo.' The supreme Good and Happiness are not in the Here and Now: they are in the Yonder and the Hereafter; it is in terms of eternal life alone that the 'Good' of man can be understood, and won.

(2) The philosophers have said that the moral life is *vita socialis*. Therein they spoke wisely, and we may agree with their saying; for how could the City of God, itself a society, have its beginning, or its course, or its consummation, *nisi socialis esset vita sanctorum*? But if happiness be social, society (in itself) is not happiness; and St. Augustine (looking always to Eternity) proceeds to show the troubles and the misfortunes to which society is prone. He takes each of the four ranges of society. The domus, *commune perfugium*, has none the less its losses and griefs, its disputes and its angers. The society of the *Civitas* suffers from the problems of litigation and the perils of civil war. (On the problems of litigation St. Augustine, himself a judge, writes a pregnant chapter (6). How difficult it is for the judge to find the truth, and yet how necessary is his office; how gladly would he leave his bench, but how strictly is he constrained to his duty by human society, 'which he thinks it a crime for him to desert'; how fervently can he repeat the Psalmist's cry to God, '*De necessitatibus meis erue me*'.) On the city follows the *orbis terrae*, the third range of human society (7); and lo! the earth is full of misfortunes and troubles. The difference of languages has kept the human race sundered; and if the *imperiosa civitas* of Rome has imposed her own language on conquered nations through the peace of the great society she has achieved, the price of her achievement in the past has been war, as the price of its maintenance to-day is still war—war without, or war on the frontier: war within, or civil war, which the very extent of the Empire inevitably breeds. And if it be said that there is such a thing as 'just war' (the Christian canonists were later to elaborate a theory of *justum bellum*), it may also be said that even the just war is a 'cruel necessity', unavoidable, indeed, if the unjust aggressor is to meet his due, but none the less, in itself, a trouble and a misfortune.

At this point St. Augustine turns aside to speak of friendship (8). It is a consolation and a delight; but when we give our heart to our friends, we give it over to perils. Our friends may suffer—and then we suffer; they may be corrupted—and then we suffer even more. The society of friends is precious, but it is as perilous as it is precious; and in it, as in all the three ranges of society through which the argument has run, there is no exemption from misfortune and trouble. Nor is there any exemption in the fourth and highest range of society, the *Mundus*, which brings us into the society of spirits (9). We cannot see the angels familiarly; and Satan sends false angels for our deception. It is these false angels, masquerading as gods, who have produced pagan polytheism. Even the true Christian, who has not yielded, like the pagan, to such guile, is never secure from the assaults of deception (10).... But the trouble from which he suffers serves only to whet the fervour of his longing for that final security in which peace—peace as complete as it is certain—is at the last to be found.

Peace now becomes the note of St. Augustine's argument (11). Society is a good thing; but we want a society free from trouble and misfortune; we want a society which is at peace. We may say therefore that the Supreme Good, which was defined before as eternal life, is also, and at the same time, peace (11). It is not idly, continues St. Augustine, that Jerusalem, which is the mystical name of the Heavenly City, should also signify peace; for the Hebrew *Salem* is the Latin *Pax*. And yet peace is not enough in itself to denote the Supreme Good (for peace may also exist in a lower sense); nor again is eternal life enough in itself (for we read of the eternal life of the wicked, which is the Supreme Evil); and we must therefore put both together, and define the Supreme Good as 'Peace in Eternity' or 'Eternity in Peace'.

Having thus vindicated eternal peace as the Supreme Good, St. Augustine proceeds to show that the highest peace is but the finest music of a chord which runs through all creation (12). Peace is the diapason[1] of the Universe. Peace is the object of war: the breaker of peace desires peace—only a peace more after his own mind; conspirators and robbers need peace—if it be only peace with one another. The very animals seek peace and ensue it; and it is by the gate of their instinct for peace that they pass into the life of the herd or society, of which that instinct is the condition and (we may almost say) the origin. Man is especially moved by the laws of his nature to enter upon society and to seek peace with all men. It is only a perversion of a genuine instinct when a man seeks, by conquering and dominating others, to make his will their peace. Properly, naturally—by the law of his nature, which is part of the universal law of all nature—man should seek to live in equality with others under the peace of God: improperly, unnaturally, violating that law, he seeks to make others live in

---

[1] Diapason, if we go back to the Greek, is ἡ διὰ πασῶν τῶν χορδῶν συμφωνία.

inequality and subjection under a peace of his own imposition. But even in violating nature (that is to say, in instituting *dominium* over others to the end of securing an imposed peace), man does homage involuntarily to nature; and he does so because he seeks and ensues, in his own way, the peace which is nature's purpose and chord and law. 'No man's vice is so much against nature that it destroys even the last traces of nature.' This great phrase is like that of Shakespeare:

> There is some soul of goodness in things evil
> Would men observingly distil it out.

The free will of man cannot entirely defeat the purpose of nature; and all nature, as the creation of God, is intrinsically good. 'Even what is perverse must be peaceably set in, or in dependence on, or in connexion with, some part of the order of things.'

St. Augustine's idea of universal peace is thus closely connected with the idea of a universal order or law, proceeding from God and pervading creation. *Pax* and *ordo* go together; they are like obverse and reverse of the same coin. From the connexion of *pax* and *ordo* St. Augustine rises to one of the finest and most philosophical of his arguments (12, end). Imagine a living human body suspended upside down. It is a thing contrary to the order, the natural law, the peace of that body. Imagine the body left alone, day upon day, day upon day. Order, natural law, peace, all return. The body dies, dissolves, is resolved into the earth and air: it returns to its order, its nature, its peace. 'It is assimilated into the elements of the Universe; moment by moment, particle by particle, it passes into their peace; but nothing is in any wise derogated thereby from the laws of that Highest and Ordaining Creator by whom the peace of the World is administered.' The words (with their suggestion of the sovereignty of nature's great laws and the conservation of all nature's energy) have the ring of modern science[1]; but they have at the same time the solemn overtone of Christian faith.

We now see that many things work together, and are fused, in St. Augustine's thought. We spoke of righteousness as a system of right relations, an order; and St. Augustine himself (4) speaks of righteousness as a *justus ordo naturae*. Peace, too, is an order—the

---

[1] See Dr. Cunningham, *St. Austin*, Appendix A (St. Austin and the Observation of Nature).

order of an 'ordaining' God who pervades an 'ordinate' creation, and always and in everything acts by law, in Heaven above and on the earth beneath. This order of peace is an order which everywhere, and in all creation, composes part to part (both among things animate and among things inanimate) according to law; it is an order, therefore, issuing in society—the society of the whole articulated Universe as well as, and in the same way as, the societies of men. *Pax, ordo, lex, societas*—the words are like four bells ringing a peal in all the Universe. Burke, who knew the writings of the Fathers, has a noble passage in the *Reflections on the Revolution in France*, which is a modern counterpart of St. Augustine. *Pactum*, or contract, is his key-note rather than *pax*; but he makes *pactum* pervade the Universe just as St. Augustine made *pax*. 'Each contract of each particular State is but a clause in the great primeval contract of eternal society, linking the lower with the higher natures, connecting the visible and invisible worlds, according to a fixed compact sanctioned by the invisible oath which holds all physical and all moral natures each in their appointed place.'[1]

In the following chapter (13) St. Augustine proceeds to enumerate the phases and manifestations of peace. There is a peace of the body; a peace of the irrational soul; a peace of the rational soul; a peace of both body and soul in their union with one another. There is a peace between man and God, which is 'ordered obedience in faith under eternal law'; there is a peace between man and man, which is 'ordered concord'; and, as species of this latter, there are the peace of the household ('ordered concord of its members in rule and obedience') and the peace of the *Civitas* or State ('ordered concord of citizens in rule and obedience'). Finally, there is the peace of the City of God, 'a most ordered and concordant companionship in enjoying God and one another in God'; and there is the universal peace of all things, which is 'the tranquillity of order'. This peace of order, in all the range of its phases and manifestations, is a system of righteousness; but it embraces even the unrighteous. They have, in one sense, gone out of the order; they are, in another sense, caught fast in the order. So far as they are miserable, and justly miserable, their misery is only the 'return' upon them of the order which they have violated; so far as they are free from disturbance, it is because they are

[1] Burke's *Works*, vol. ii, p. 368 (Bohn edition): see above, p. 218, n. 1.

adjusted, by a sort of harmony, to the conditions in which they are placed; and in this way they possess a sort of tranquillity of order, and therefore a sort of peace. We may gloss this argument by saying that the institutions adjusted to unrighteousness (the State and its government, slavery, property) are institutions fundamentally righteous, because they represent the return—the inevitable return—of interrupted right and order and peace. Nothing can exist outside order. Nothing can be in its nature utterly bad.[1] God made creation, and made it good. If His creatures, by their will, introduce evil, the overruling order of His will returns, and instils good into that evil. The State is the return of the order of God upon the evil introduced by man's sin.

In the fourteenth chapter the argument begins to trend more definitely in a political direction, and the fifteenth and sixteenth chapters (more especially the former) contain some of the most essential elements in the political thought of St. Augustine. He goes back to one of the phases or manifestations of peace which he has mentioned in the previous chapter. The highest peace of man (considered, for the moment, simply as man) is the peace of his highest faculty. This is his rational soul; and its peace may be defined as an 'ordered harmony of knowing and doing'. Knowing precedes doing; but for any true knowledge man needs a Divine Master whom he can follow in certainty, and a Divine Helper whom he can obey in liberty. The Master and Helper has given us two commandments—that we should love God, and that we should love our neighbours as ourselves. It follows that we should serve and aid our neighbours to love God, since that is the greatest love and the highest service we can give them. If we do that, we shall be living in peace—which is 'ordered concord', which again is 'society'—with our neighbours. The rules of this society will be, first and negatively, to injure no man, and secondly or positively, to aid all men whom we can. The first circle of such society will be the family; and in the family there will be authority and subjection. But since the rule of the society is love, and love means service, any authority will only be a mode of service, and it will be exerted in the spirit of service. 'They who exercise authority

---

[1] 'There cannot be a nature in which there is no good. Not even the nature of the Devil, in so far as it is nature [and therefore the creation of God], is evil; but perversity maketh it evil.... He abode not in the tranquillity of order; but he hath not therefore escaped from the power of the Ordainer.'

are in the service of those over whom they appear to exercise authority; and they exercise their authority, not from a desire for domination, but by virtue of a duty to give counsel and aid.'

St. Augustine here started a line of thought which was long to endure. More than a thousand years afterwards, in 1579, the author of the *Vindiciae contra Tyrannos* echoed his words when he wrote, 'Imperare ergo nihil aliud est quam consulere'; and a writer of our days has similarly said of the State, 'It commands only because it serves'. But St. Augustine has no sooner started this line of thought than he sees, and faces, a difficulty. He has been speaking of the circle of the family; and the family, in his day and generation, included slaves. Can the position of the slave be reconciled with the idea that authority is only a form of service? St. Augustine attempts an answer in the fifteenth chapter. The free society, in which *imperare est consulere*, is argued to be both the prescription of natural order and the rule imposed at the moment of creation. God gave the first man dominion only over the animal world. 'He would not have reasonable man, made in His own image, to exercise dominion save over unreasoning beings: He set man not over man but over the beasts of the field. Therefore the righteous of the first days were rather made shepherds of flocks than kings of men, in order that God might, even after this manner, suggest what it is which is required by the order of created beings, and what it is which is demanded by the desert of sin.' For there is a great gulf between these two things; and slavery is explained, and justified, by that gulf.

Slavery is the result of sin; and it is a condition rightly imposed on the sinner. It comes to pass by the judgement of God; it is justified by His judgement. There is even a sense in which it is the result, or rather the 'return', of natural order. 'No man, indeed, is a slave to man, or to sin, by the nature in which God first created man. But penal slavery is ordained by that law, which commands the preservation and forbids the violation of natural order.' Thus even the unrighteous, as we have already had reason to notice, are caught fast in the system of righteousness; and even what seems the unnatural institution of slavery is but the 'return' (in the form of retribution for 'the desert of sin') of the order of nature. The question one naturally asks to-day (though St. Augustine did not pause to put it) is whether an actual slave has ever really committed any unrighteousness other than, or beyond, that committed by the rest of mankind? And if the answer to that question be 'No', it is difficult to explain why he should be placed none the less in a totally different condition from other men.

But if slavery be a result, or a 'return', of natural order, the true master of slaves must nevertheless look to their eternal happiness (16). He must serve and aid them (for they, too, are his neighbours) to love God; and meanwhile he may hope to be released from the burden of his mastership in the Hereafter. For it *is* a burden, in the same way and the same sense as St. Augustine has argued before that the office of judge is a burden: it involves, in the same way, the duty of discipline and the office of correction. The master, like the judge, may cry for deliverance (*De necessitatibus meis erue me*), 'longing and praying to reach that heavenly home, in which the duty of ruling men is no longer necessary'. (How often must any 'administrator' echo that cry!)

We might expect, after this discussion of the household, to be carried into a discussion of the *Civitas* or State. But St. Augustine, omitting to speak of the *Civitas* at large in general terms, flies away at once, in a chapter (17) which concludes his long discourse on society, to a consideration of the heavenly city. His theme is its relations—its relations both of agreement and of disagreement—with the earthly city. It is, in a way, the theme of the relations of Church and State. In some things, says St. Augustine, 'the things which are necessary to this mortal life' (roughly, we may say, the preservation of law and order), both cities can readily share together. The heavenly city (or, more exactly, the part of it which is now making its earthly pilgrimage) accordingly uses the earthly peace of the earthly city; its members enter into the agreement of wills concerning the things pertaining to mortal life; they obey the laws regulating these things, 'that as mortality is common to both cities, so concord may be preserved between both in matters pertaining thereto'. But there is a sphere of things, 'the things pertaining to immortality', in which no concord is possible. Polytheistic thinkers have introduced supposed gods as civic deities into the affairs of the earthly city; and the heavenly city, devoted to the one true God, cannot therefore have any laws of religion in common with the earthly city. It has therefore followed the way of Dissent; it has trodden the hard road of Persecution—'until the days [they had already come in St. Augustine's time] when at length it may make the spirits of its adversaries recoil before the terror of its multitude'.

(3) The final theme of the nineteenth book is the nature of a *Populus* and of the *Respublica* in which a *Populus* is organized. The theme, as we have already had occasion to notice, would naturally follow on the discussion of *Societas*; but in fact it is treated separately, and the chapters concerned with the theme are in the nature of an appendix. St. Augustine had promised, in an earlier book (ii. 21), to prove that, on Cicero's definition of the term, there had never existed a *Respublica* at Rome. What he has said in the nineteenth book about the heavenly city, as the only home of true Righteousness, reminds him of his promise, and he sets about its performance.

A *Respublica* is *res Populi*: what then is a *Populus*? In Cicero's definition it is 'the union of a number of men associated by the two bonds of common acknowledgement of Right (*jus*) and common pursuit of interest' (21). It is the word Right, or *Jus*, which offends St. Augustine. In the Latin usage *Jus* is a legal term; and it signifies simply the body of legal rules which is recognized, and can be enforced, by a human authority. On the basis of this significance of *Jus* there is little in Cicero's definition with which we need quarrel. It might, perhaps, go farther; but it is correct enough so far as it goes. But St. Augustine had his own preconceptions; and they made him resolved to quarrel with Cicero's definition. With his mind full of the idea of Righteousness (the Greek Δικαιοσύνη, as it appears in Plato and in St. Paul), he twists the sense of *jus*. He identifies *jus* with *justitia*; he identifies *Justitia* with *vera justitia*; and he argues accordingly that 'where there is no true righteousness, there cannot be a union of men associated by a common acknowledgement of Right'. Here he has already departed far from Cicero's sense; but he proceeds to depart still farther. *Justitia*, he argues, is the virtue which gives to each his due. It must therefore include, and include particularly, the giving of His due to God. In other words, it must include true religion; for it is only true religion which gives to God His due. But if *Justitia* thus involves true religion, and if *Justitia*, as has already been assumed, is necessary to the existence of a *Populus*, it follows that true religion is necessary to the existence of a *Populus*. The worship which gives to God His due is the *sine qua non* of the existence of a

Populus, and therefore of a *Respublica*. It is therefore proven that, on Cicero's *definition*, there never existed a *Populus* at Rome; for the *populus Romanus* never gave God His due.

We may rejoin that this has only been proven on the basis of assumptions about the significance of *Jus* which Cicero would never have admitted. But if we make that rejoinder, we must also make an admission. We must admit that century upon century was destined to hold, and to hold tenaciously, the view which St. Augustine implies—the view that a people, in order to be a true people, must not only be a legal society, but also, and in the same breath, a religious society worshipping God in union and uniformity. This is the Elizabethan view, implied in the Act of Uniformity and expressed in the philosophy of Hooker: the commonwealth of the people of England must be a Church as well as a State in order to be a true commonwealth, and its members must be Churchmen as well as citizens in order to be truly members. Indeed, so long as a form of Establishment lasts, there still remains a relic of the idea that religion is necessary to the existence of a *Respublica*.

And yet St. Augustine is willing, after all, to allow that there may be a people without any confession of true religion. He had only set out to prove, and he was content with having (as he thought) proved, that *on Cicero's definition of the term* there could not be a people without a confession of true religion. *If* (he had argued) you say that there must be 'common acknowledgement of Right', *then* there must be common acknowledgement of God, for *that* is involved in common acknowledgement of Right. But you need not say that there must be common acknowledgement of Right. You may pitch the key lower, and simply say that a people is 'the union of a reasoning multitude associated by an agreement to pursue in common the objects which it desires' (24). On this definition the end and criterion of a people is not *Jus*; it is simply—whatever it is. On this definition, again, the objects desired may be higher or lower; and a people will be better or worse accordingly. On this definition, finally, the Roman people was a people, and the *Respublica Romana* a *Respublica*; but history shows the quality of the objects it desired, and history testifies how it broke again and again, by its civil wars, the agreement on which the salvation of any people depends. This is equally true of Athens and other States of antiquity. We may allow that they were 'peoples': we must also allow that they were 'cities of the ungodly, devoid of the truth of Righteousness'. And therefore the conclusion of the matter is that, though a people may be a people without confessing the true God, no people can be a good people without that confession.

And so St. Augustine argues, in the last chapters of the book (25–27), that true virtue cannot exist apart from true religion. Indeed, virtue which does not come from the knowledge and love of God is a vice rather than a virtue; it is a matter of peacock pride and idle vainglorying. 'Not from man, but from above man, proceedeth that which maketh a man live happily.' And yet (the argument proceeds, as St. Augustine turns to the other side of the matter), even a people alienated from God, destitute as it is of virtue, has 'a certain peace of its own, not to be lightly esteemed' (26). It is indeed to the interest of the Christian that it should have this peace; 'for so long as the two cities are mixed, we too use the peace of Babylon'. Here St. Augustine returns to the old problem of the relations of the heavenly and the earthly cities (*supra*, p. 248); but he adds a fresh tribute to the service and the claims of the earthly city when he cites the Apostle's exhortation to the Church to 'pray for kings and those in authority'. The peace of this world, after all, deserves its acknowledgement. Not but what the Christian, even in his world, has a peace of his own which is higher than the peace of this world—the peculiar peace of his faith (27). And yet even that higher and peculiar peace has its miseries, so long as it is enjoyed, precariously enjoyed, in this mortal life. Sin besets us always: even upon the brave fighter 'subrepit aliquid . . . unde, si non facili operatione, certe labili locutione, aut volatili cogitatione, peccatur'. (The words have a beauty and a subtlety beyond translation.) Only at the last 'will there be such felicity of living and reigning as there shall also be serenity and facility of obeying; and this shall there, in all and in each, be eternal, and its eternity shall be sure; and therefore the peace of this beatitude, or the beatitude of this peace, shall be the Supreme Good'.

V

We have seen the philosophy of sunrise seeking to dispel the philosophy of night. It only remains to say some words on the future influence of *The City of God*. It was studied by Gregory the Great: it was read and loved by Charlemagne, who believed that he had inaugurated the *Civitas Dei* upon earth. Abelard wrote hymns in the strains, and even the words, of the great prose of St. Augustine; and Dante, though he only refers to him twice in the *Divina Commedia*, uses his teaching in his *De Monarchia*.[1] But the deeper influence of St. Augustine is not to be traced in particular writers. It is to be traced in the general theory of the canonists and the general theological tradition of the Middle Ages.

One element in the theory of St. Augustine which particularly influenced the canonists was his teaching with regard to property—that by the natural order all things are enjoyed by the righteous in common: that private property is the result of sin; but that none the less it is justified (on that doctrine of the 'return' or recoil of natural order of which we have spoken), because it is, after all, a remedy for sin, and because it canalizes, as it were, and reduces to order the greed of possession which came with sin. This teaching passed to Gratian and the canonists; and it gave them, as Dr. Carlyle has shown (*Medieval Political Theory in the West*, II. ii. 6), their technical doctrine in regard to property—that it is not a primitive or natural institution; that its origin must be sought in sinful appetite; that its title rests on the sanction of custom and civil law. It is tempting, but it is impossible in this place, to investigate the debt of Wyclif's theory of *Dominium* to the teaching of St. Augustine. It can only be said that Wyclif, in this as in other points of this theory, was steeped in St. Augustine, even if he carried the premises of his teacher to conclusions at which the teacher himself might have stood aghast.

If the teaching of St. Augustine certainly influenced the canonists' theory of property, it is a much more difficult thing to say how far his teaching influenced their theory of the relations of *regnum* and *sacerdotium*. Of this theme we have already spoken; and there is but little to be added here. It is sufficient

[1] On Dante and St. Augustine, see Moore, *Studies in Dante*, I. One might have dreamed that Virgil would have been succeeded by St. Augustine (who, by the way, loved Virgil) when the end of the *Purgatorio* was being reached. But Beatrice appears instead to guide Dante upward to the Heavenly City. In the *Paradiso* Dante simply mentions St. Augustine as the founder of canons, by the side of St. Benedict the father of monks and St. Francis the founder of friars.

to say that, between the time when St. Augustine finished *The City of God*, in 426, and the outbreak of the War of Investitures, in 1075, a whole stock of new weapons had been added to the armoury of polemics. There is the Gelasian theory of the parity or 'diarchy' of the two powers (*c.* 500); there is the weapon of the 'Donation of Constantine', fabricated about 760; there is the argument from the 'Translation of the Empire', deduced from Charlemagne's coronation in 800; there are the theories drawn by later controversialists from the 'Keys' and the 'Two Swords' and the analogy of 'Sun and Moon'; there is the application of feudal theory to the relations of Church and State. It was from materials such as these that the Middle Ages proper constructed a theory of the relations between *regnum* and *sacerdotium*; and the teaching of St. Augustine could only be one ingredient in a large and varied amalgam. It is tempting to trace a connexion between the saying of St. Augustine, 'Remove righteousness, and what are kingdoms but great bands of brigands?', and the outburst of Gregory VII in his letter to Hermann of Metz, 'Who can be ignorant that kings took their beginnings from those who by way of rapine, at the instigation of the prince of this world, desired to have dominion over their fellows?' But before we attempt to trace the connexion, or to conclude that St. Augustine taught Gregory VII that States were organizations of brigands, we must remember two things. The first is that, as we have already seen, St. Augustine taught nothing of the sort. The second is that the outburst of Gregory VII stands in isolation, and is contradicted by his other statements. Little can be made of the influence of St. Augustine in this particular connexion; and it must remain doubtful how much can be made of it in other respects. Scholars have differed upon the issue whether the teaching of St. Augustine tended, or did not tend, to depress the State and to promote the rise of a theocracy. Harnack has said, 'He roused the conviction that the empirical Catholic Church *sans phrase* was the kingdom of God, and the independent State that of the Devil'.[1] (This is a saying which cannot be justified.) Gierke has said, 'The theory of *The City of God* left the worldly State practically destitute of importance, except in so far as it ranged itself, as a subordinate member, within and

---

[1] I have borrowed these quotations mainly from Bishop Welldon's edition, vol. i, pp. 51-2. The reference to Troeltsch is my own.

below the Divine State which was realized in the Church'. (This is a saying, again, which the reader of St. Augustine's actual text can hardly accept.) Dubief has said (as it seems to me with more justice), 'It is impossible to find in St. Augustine's words those comparisons between the spiritual power and the temporal power which are intended to establish the pre-eminence of the former above the latter, and denote the intention of subordinating the State to the clergy'. Perhaps Ernst Troeltsch, in his massive way, gives the best and soundest view of the matter[1]: 'St. Augustine admitted that view of the State and its laws which brings them both into connexion with natural law, but he confined that view within narrower limits than the other fathers: he wanted room for the possibility of irreligious Emperors (regarded as a visitation of God and a punishment of sin), and for the moral rejection of the powers that be in so far as they did not allow themselves to be guided by Divine Righteousness.' There were, Troeltsch argues, two elements in the thought of the contemporary world. One was a belief in the *Naturrecht* of the State (in other words, a belief that it was based on what St. Augustine calls *naturalis ordo*); the other was the theocratic belief of a newly victorious religious society that its principles were the sovereign principles, and must therefore prevail even in the area of political organization. 'The latter, as is well known, was particularly expounded by St. Augustine in his great work. But what is less noticed is that in it he also enunciated and maintained the former. In the irreconcilable struggle of the two points of view lies the double nature of the work of this great thinker—a work which, for this very reason, transmitted also to the future a double tendency. Theocracy and *naturalis ordo* are both made to consecrate the State: what the one cannot do the other will; and in any case the Emperor is primarily determined by his quality of existing *Dei gratia* and by his theocratic connexions. Yet the State itself remains, for all that, the incarnation of "the world".' After this account of St. Augustine's own position, Troeltsch turns to his influence on the Middle Ages. 'Chrysostom, Leo I, Gelasius I, St. Augustine might indeed demand the theocratic subjection of the Emperor under the clergy, on the analogy of the Old Testament, and they might sketch the "Programme of

---

[1] I have translated or summarized four passages in his *Soziallehren der christlichen Kirchen*, pp. 168, 170, 191, 215.

the Middle Ages". But the programme was never realized at all in the East, and it was only realized in the West after five centuries had passed.' When these five centuries had passed, and the realization of the programme was attempted, St. Augustine's treasures of thought were used. But (and this is the important point), if 'the harsh sayings of St. Augustine about the State were again brought into play, they underwent a radical intensification in the process; and an exorbitant exaggeration of emphasis was laid on the sinfulness of the State, on which St. Augustine had indeed laid stress, but behind which he had always recognized the existence of a basis of natural law'.

The influence of St. Augustine on the theological tradition (as distinct from the social and political doctrines) of the Middle Ages is a vast theme, upon which we cannot embark, but which it would be almost a treason not to mention. St. Augustine enters into the *Summa* of St. Thomas; he influenced Wyclif profoundly; he influenced Luther no less profoundly. 'The history of Church doctrine in the West,' Harnack has said, 'is a much disguised struggle against Augustinianism.' This is a deep saying, and we must attempt to gloss it. St. Augustine, we may say, imbued as he was with Platonic philosophy, always believed in the unchanging perfection of a God who always and everywhere acted by law. In his theory, God is always determined (or to speak more exactly He always determines Himself) by *rationes exemplares*[1] (or, as Plato would have said, 'ideas'); His relations to His creatures are always relations in the sphere of immutable order; any apparent change is a change not in God, but in the creature, and God must adjust Himself to the changing creature in order to remain unchanged in His own unchanging essence. Against this clear and pure rigour of an unswering general order (the rigour which Wordsworth celebrates in his *Ode to Duty*), it was natural that those should revolt who wanted a mysterious and emotional world, rich in insoluble riddles, and needing a mediatory and miraculous Church to give a mystical clue. Such a revolt was that of the Nominalists of the later Middle Ages; and here we find one of those 'much disguised struggles against Augustinianism' of which Harnack speaks. *Latet dolus in generalibus*, said the Nominalists; and they accordingly laid their emphasis on the Particular in its unique and concrete 'reality'.

---

[1] I have borrowed the phrase from Wyclif.

Their emphasis on the Particular led them to lay stress on individuality and personality, alike in man and in God; and their study of human individuality helped them to make some of the first modern researches in psychology. But the trend of their thought turned them also towards obscurantism. The individual became an ultimate mystery: God Himself became an inscrutably omnipotent individual, acting indeterminately by His individual will. The Nominalists thus came to magnify the authority of the Church as the only escape from 'the burden of the mystery'; they believed in *fides implicita*; and in them may be traced the tendency of the over-subtle intellect to pass through obscurantism to the acceptance of mere authority. It was against the Nominalists that Wyclif and Luther were both in revolt; and they both went back to St. Augustine for comfort and countenance. It would be too bold to say that St. Augustine inspired the Reformation. But it would perhaps be true to say that he took the sixteenth century back to the idea of a Divine general order of the Universe, and back to a conception of Righteousness based upon that idea.

Essay Nine

THE COMMUNITY AND THE CHURCH

I. *Community*

WE use a number of words in English—people, nation, society, and community—which have all different shades of meaning, but which are all so closely related that they possess, or at any rate seem to possess, a fundamental unity. We also use a word which is common to most European languages—the word 'state'. It is a word related to the first set of words; but it is not so much related but that it may, and must, be distinguished. To state its differentia, and to express its particular connotation, may be the best way of arriving at an understanding of the first set of words.

A State is a legal association, or, as some say, a juridical organization. Membership of the State is a legal fact, depending on some sort of legal act, such as registration or naturalization. The State itself is constituted by a legal act, or a series of successive legal acts, called a constitution; it is 'constituted' in the sense that the mode of its activity is determined by such act or series of acts. That activity always assumes a legal form. It consists in the declaration and enforcement of general rules of law, within the terms and subject to the prescriptions of the constitution. The State exists by the grace of law, and for the purpose of law. We may almost say that it *is* law.

To say that the State is constituted—which means, in effect, created—by a legal act is not to say that it is created by the putting together of individuals hitherto separate, or, in other words, by an act of contract between such individuals. What actually happens is something at once more simple and more subtle. It is possible to conceive a legal association or juridical organization as being 'constituted', not by the drawing together of parts which were hitherto separate into a whole which is utterly new, but by the turning of some whole which already existed, but existed in another form, into the new form of such an association or organization. What is new, in such a case, is not the whole itself, but the new form of the whole and the new mode of its activity. The whole which existed before still continues to exist, in its old form and with its old mode, or modes, of activity; but henceforth it assumes, or rather adds, a new form and a new mode of activity. This is a line of thought, and a method of interpretation, which we may properly apply to the state. It is a legal association, or juridical organization, which has been constituted from a previously existing whole. That whole is a people, nation, society, or community. When it becomes a State, or comes to be regarded as a State, this whole does not cease to be what it was. It does not lose its previous form or its previous modes of activity. It simply adds a different form and a new and separate mode or modes.

It is difficult to avoid the language of time, or to speak otherwise than in terms of an 'old' or 'previously existing' whole and a 'new' or 'added' form of that whole. There is this justification for such language that we sometimes find an existing group, which describes itself as a 'people' or 'nation', constituting itself as a State at a definite point of time. This is what happened, for example, in Czechoslovakia in 1920; 'we, the Czechoslovak nation, desiring to consolidate the perfect unity of our people ... to guarantee the peaceful development of our native Czechoslovak land ... have adopted in our national assembly the following Constitution for the Czechoslovak Republic.'[1] But the separation, or distinction, between a people or nation and a State is not really a matter of time. It is a matter of idea. There are constitutions, such as the English, which can hardly be dated in time. There are countries or areas where the conception of the people, nation, society, or community and the conception of the state seem coeval. But the two conceptions none the less remain distinct. There is the conception of the State—the legal association, constituted by the constitution and acting in the mode of legal activity. There is the conception of the people, nation, society, or community, which we have still to examine. The two may be one, so far as concerns the body of persons which they embrace. In a perfect 'national state' the State is the nation, and the nation the State. But the two are two, and remain two, so far as concerns their form and their

[1] Preamble to the preliminary law and constitutional charter of 29 Feb. 1920.

modes of activity. 'By the State', says Bosanquet, 'we mean society as a unit recognized as rightly [legally?] exercising control over its members through absolute physical power [an adequate power of enforcing legal sanctions?].'[1] That still leaves open the question what we mean by society, or community, or people, or nation, as something other than such a unit.

2. Before we seek to answer that question—but also in order to prepare the way for an answer—it is well to choose one of the four alternative terms thus presented to us by the ordinary use of language. We want a single word related to the word 'state', but not so closely related that it may lead to confusion between the conception of the State and the other conception which we are seeking to express and to define. The word 'people', in our usage, has a definite political connotation, and is closely related to the conception of the State. It is connected with the idea of democracy: when we talk, for example, of 'the will of the people', we are apt to think of the electorate; and the adjective 'popular', which is totally different from the German *völkisch*, suggests the idea of democratic government. The word 'nation' has in some ways a broader sense; but it also suffers from some defects. It too is closely connected, if in a different way, with the conception of the State; indeed when we speak of the United Nations we are using the two words as if they were simply convertible, and when we speak of a 'national' we are apt to mean a member of a State. The word 'nation' is too much of an *étatiste* for our purposes; and it has besides the suggestion of a blood-group, or body of kinsmen, which narrows its meaning and restricts its range. We are thus left with a choice between the words 'society' and 'community'. Either will serve our purpose.[2] Our English thinkers generally use the word 'society'. There is a danger in that word—not for ourselves, but for continental thinkers, who may read into the word suggestions which it does not carry for us. They may think that it suggests ideas of the *societas* of Roman Law and the *société* of French Law, and that it therefore conveys notions of a business partnership or commercial company. No

[1] B. Bosanquet, *Philosophical Theory of the State*, p. 185.
[2] This essay was written before the appearance of the late Professor Collingwood's *The New Leviathan* (1942). The discussion of society in Part II of that book is of the first order of importance; and the distinction there suggested between society and community is one to which the author of this essay, who has treated the two terms as generally synonymous, desires to refer all his readers.

such idea or notion enters into our own usage; if there is any danger in the term, among ourselves, it is rather that it suggests, in common speech and ordinary parlance, the notion of 'good society' or *le grand monde*. 'Community' has no dangers: the only objection to it is that it escapes from any particular colour so successful that it is almost colourless. But it is coming into more general use and acquiring a more definite connotation. We speak, for example, of the Dominions as 'autonomous communities', freely united in a broader community (or 'commonwealth') which is something more than a legal association, though it has some of the characteristics of such an association. We speak again of 'community associations'—the voluntary bodies which have freely formed themselves for social and cultural purposes on our new municipal housing estates—and we speak of the 'community centres' in which they freely meet and act. These usages indicate a sense of community as something which—whatever the area of its operation, large or small—is essentially free and essentially voluntary.

3. It is important to notice at this point that 'the community' is for us a multi-coloured sort of thing. It has many areas of operation. The German word *Volk* is a unitary word. There is one *Volk*, though it may have two different manifestations according as we are thinking of the *Volk* already included in the boundaries of the German State or of the broader *Volk* which transcends those boundaries. Our word 'community' is essentially multiform. There is first the community of the British Commonwealth. It is real; but it is not readily definable by any objective criteria of blood or speech or creed or culture. Then there is the community of Great Britain. It is real; indeed, it is even more profoundly apprehended than the community of the Commonwealth, and its unity may be described by more definite marks or attributes. But it is not unitary or exclusive; and just as it coexists with the broader community of the Commonwealth, so it also coexists with the narrower communities, contained in itself, of England, Scotland, and Wales. None of us can use the word community with the simple intensity with which the German uses the word *Volk*. When we think of community, we see successive circles, which are far from fitting neatly into one another with geometrical precision. When we think of the relations of Church and Community, we are thus thinking of

something different from the relation of *Kirche* and *Volk*. We are thinking of the relations of a Church, which itself (as we shall see later) takes a number of different forms, to a community which is also multiform. The problem, for us, is far from simple. Perhaps for that reason it is not an acute or dangerous problem. When *Kirche* confronts *Volk*, there may emerge either a plain dualism of the two, or a blunt demand for their assimilation. When Church confronts Community, there is time to stop and think.

It is tempting to classify our different spheres or areas of community in different categories. We might, for example, regard the community of the British Commonwealth as a general 'culture-circle': we might regard the community of Great Britain as largely, or even mainly, a 'political community'—though also something more: we might regard the community of Scotland or that of Wales as a 'national minority', which as such has claims or rights to equal treatment with the national majority and to equal respect for its speech and customs. The use of such categories would not help us: on the contrary, it would confuse understanding by suggesting differences which do not exist. The community of the British Commonwealth is a political community as well as a 'culture-circle': the communities of Scotland and Wales are more than 'national minorities'. There is a general notion of community which is common to its different circles or separate manifestations; and though this general notion may be qualified, or rather specified, in some particular way in each particular circle or manifestation, the general notion still persists.

4. What is this general notion? It may be wise, before attempting to answer that question, to begin by saying what it is not. When we use the words community or society, there is no suggestion, such as tends to be conveyed by words like *Volk* or *Nazione* or *Nation*, of a particular colour due to particular characteristics, or of a consequent partiality. In itself, and in its intrinsic connotation, the idea of community is not coloured by any peculiar reference to particular characteristics of race or soil or language.

It is true that a territorial community, because it consists of physical human bodies in a common physical environment, will tend to have common physical characteristics which may be roughly designated as racial. But the face of the earth is old; it has been swept over, again and again, by successions of different men, who have all left their traces and their blood; and if a community actually shows common physical characteristics, they will be the characteristics not of a race but of an amalgam of races. Moreover, common physical characteristics, however common they may be, and however generally diffused, have no great bearing on the character and nature of a community, unless they are accompanied by common mental and moral qualities; and there is no proof that common physical characteristics —in themselves, and apart from other causes—produce common mental and moral qualities. Nor can it even be admitted that every human community has common physical characteristics. The British Commonwealth is a community, and India is a community within that community; but both the one and the other are diversified by differences of physical characteristics; and the differences within the former grow steadily greater as new physical types (for instance the Australian) develop themselves under the influence of a new climate and a new soil.

A common soil is no doubt necessary to any community; and the character of its common soil will no doubt affect, as indeed has just been suggested, the community which lives on the soil. But when we speak of a common soil, we may easily fall into errors and exaggerations. Different parts of the soil may well be very different; and in that case what is common in the common soil is not the soil itself, but our feeling about the soil. In any case there is no predestined harmony between soil and community. The soil is the environment of the community: that environment acts upon the community, and the community, in turn, reacts upon the environment: some *modus vivendi*, and some measure of harmony, is attained by the action and reaction; but this *modus vivendi* has to be attained, and can be attained, by *any* community in *any* environment.

Even a common language, though it is valuable, and indeed particularly valuable, is not an indispensable necessity of the life of a community. Not to speak of the Swiss community, there are communities in the British Commonwealth, such as the Dominion of Canada and the Union of South Africa, which are none the less communities although they are divided in language. Linguistic differences may possibly create additional difficulties;

they certainly make additional demands on the spirit of mutual understanding and mutual comprehension; but far from making that spirit impossible, they may even encourage its exercise.

We must recognize that community has roots in the physical or quasi-physical—in some peculiar amalgam of 'racial' ingredients: in a common soil, which may none the less be various and diversified: in a common mode of utterance, which may yet be consistent with varieties—but when we have recognized that fact, we have to disengage community itself from its physical or quasi-physical bases. These things, or some of them (they are not all always present), may be, in the language of Aristotle, 'necessary preliminary conditions' ($\hat{\omega}\nu$ ο$\dot{\upsilon}$κ ἄνευ), but they are not 'integral parts' ($\mu\acute{o}\rho\iota\alpha$). Just as we have to distinguish community from the legal association of the State which is erected upon it, so we have to distinguish it again from the natural basis of stock and soil and language on which it is itself erected. The old idea of the Social Contract has gone out of fashion before the advance of historical and scientific studies. It was indeed an imperfect and confused idea. It supposed natural men to be furnished with the legal wisdom and the professional caution of solicitors, and it made them con and perpend a contract of partnership 'in the woods'. It confused community or society with the state, and it made them both spring into existence together by a single act of immediate creation. But behind its confusions there lay a kernel of truth. Those who held the idea were aware of the fact that a community of men is somehow, and in some sense, a human creation, superimposed on the natural or physical grounds of human existence.

5. A community involves *communication* or sharing. Sharing, in turn, involves two ideas—the idea of a something *in* which you share, and the idea of a number or body of persons *with* whom you share. Of these two ideas the more important and the more fundamental is the idea of the something in which you share. That is the prior idea, in the sense that it tends to determine the number of persons who share. The number who can share with you in something must obviously depend in the main on the nature of that in which they are invited to share. But this is not the only factor. The area of a community, or the number of its members, will also depend on the possibilities of human intercourse. It will depend, in other words, on the range of physical

and mental communications—on the ease or difficulty of physical transport and actual personal intercourse; on the ease or difficulty of what may be called mental transport, which enables us to communicate with one another, without actual personal intercourse, through written or printed or photographed material presented to our eyes, or broadcast matter presented to our ears. One of the difficulties of our times is that communities formed in one stage of physical and mental communications persist in a different stage. No doubt they will continue to persist. They have had a long existence in their own appropriate stage, and they have developed, in the course of that long existence, a general tradition and individuality. If the past did not exist, and we were free to make our own community today, in the light of our present methods of communication, we might make a world-community. If steamships and wireless communication had existed at the time of the War of American Independence, probably the North American colonies would never have seceded from their mother-country. But they *did* secede: the past *does* exist; and it cannot be liquidated. Our actual communities are a legacy of the past, bequeathed to a different present, but inevitable in the present to which they have been bequeathed. We must accept the legacies of history. . . . But we need not deify them.

What is the something which has led men, in order that they might share in it, to live together in a community—a community with an area of membership determined partly by the nature of the thing to be shared, and partly by the range of men's power of communicating with one another? To ask this question is not to inquire into the purpose or end of the State (that is another matter): it is only to inquire into the common substance—the shared and common treasure—of community or society. We can only say, if we make this inquiry, that there is no limit set to this common substance. Community, or society, does not mean a sharing with others in some one particular substance, some one particular good or commodity or benefit. Men may share in blood, and be a race, without being a community. They may share in language, and be a linguistic group, without being a community. They may even share in a common system of law and government, and be a State, without being a community. The old Austro-Hungarian Empire was a State, but it was not a community. In order that there may be a community, there must be conscious and purposive sharing (it is in this sense that a community of men is necessarily a human creation); and the sharing must be a sharing in the *general* business of life and in its *general* conduct.

6. Two things are here predicated of community. The first is that it involves a conscious and purposive sharing. This is what Burke meant when he wrote that 'society is indeed a contract', or, in other words, a partnership. However it may need, and however it may be connected with, 'necessary preliminary conditions' of a natural or physical order—a natural sense of kinship, or a natural contiguity in space, or a natural bond of speech—it yet transcends these conditions, and is superimposed upon them by a purpose of further and higher communication. The second thing predicated is that community involves a sharing in a general way of life. This, again, is what Burke meant when he said that 'it is not a partnership in things subservient only to the gross animal existence of a temporary and perishable nature; it is a partnership in all science; a partnership in every virtue and in all perfection'.[1] Whatever the mind of men can reach—in the way of common and mutual fulfilment of moral obligation; in the common practice of religion; in the common furtherance of science and art in their widest sense; in the common advancement of economic prosperity and the common upholding of economic standards—this is the affair of community, so long as this is done by voluntary and spontaneous effort in the spirit of free partnership. Whoever can join in this, whatever his blood or speech, is a member of society and a partner in community.

In the great passage from Burke which has just been quoted community, or society, is still identified with the State. He begins by speaking of 'society': he glides, in the very next sentence, into speech of the 'state', as if the two terms were synonymous.[2] A passage from a contemporary writer, Professor George Unwin, may illustrate the difference of the two terms, as we interpret them in England today.

[1] Burke, *Reflections on the Revolution in France*, vol. ii, p. 368 of the Bohn edition of Burke's *Works*.
[2] '*Society* is indeed a contract. Subordinate contracts for objects of mere occasional interest may be dissolved at pleasure—but the *state* ought not to be considered as nothing better than a partnership agreement' (ibid.).

'I mean by the state that one of our social cohesions which has drawn to itself the exercise of final authority, and which can support that authority, if need be, by the exercise of physical force. And I mean by society all the rest of our social cohesions—family, trade union, church, and the rest. . . . Primitive man was restricted to a single social cohesion, which controlled him with supreme authority. Life was impossible outside his tribe. Freedom was impossible within it. The great array of differentiated social cohesions, which represent in their totality the free society of modern civilization, and from which the authority and force embodied in the state have withdrawn themselves, furnish the individual with that great variety of choice which constitutes real freedom.'[1]

The conception of community which is here implied has had a long history in our country. It may not have been explicit even in the days of Burke. But it had been implicit long before. If we go back to the Middle Ages, we find that our English law—the very law which seems the special and peculiar province of the state—was being built, in no small measure, by independent communities of lawyers, the Inns of Court, from which the judges were drawn, and which stood behind the judges. The Tudor age of the sixteenth century was in some ways a set-back (as ages of 'unification' are, whatever benefit they may bring): it was an age of one commonwealth, one State, one Church, and everything unified. But the seventeenth century marks a new advance of free community-action. The debt which we owe to our 'Free Churches' (and to the general movement of Nonconformity) from the seventeenth century onwards is incalculable. They were the beginning of a new advance; but that advance also showed itself, and showed itself increasingly, in a number of other ways. The movement of English colonization was a movement of the community. 'The expansion of England in the seventeenth century was an expansion of society and not of the state.'[2] When England awoke to new life, in the latter half of the eighteenth century, the new life expressed itself in the form, not of political revolution, but of religious and philan-

[1] G. Unwin, *Studies in Economic History*, p. 459. In another passage he distinguishes (p. 28) between society as the set of forces from below, the forces of spontaneity, of germination, and the State as the set of forces from above, the forces of authority, of formulation. He adds that, in his view, 'the main feature of British history has been the remoulding of a State by a powerful society; the main feature of German history in the same period has been the remoulding of a society by a powerful State'.
[2] Ibid., p. 341.

thropic movements in the general community. When at last Parliament was reformed and the reformed Parliament began to stir itself, in the course of the nineteenth century, it did not seek to oust the action of the community in order to install the action of the State. Our nineteenth-century method (and it is still our method in the twentieth) was that of co-operation between a democratic State and a free community. 'It is a feature of the typical nineteenth-century development', Mr. Sidney Webb wrote in 1910, 'that voluntary association and government action have always gone on side by side, the one apparently always inspiring, facilitating, and procuring successive developments of the other.'[1]

7. We may now draw together some of the conclusions which are implied in the course of the argument.

(a) A community or society, taken as a whole, is a body of persons sharing with one another in the common substance of a general civilization, which is not limited to any particular activity. Viewed in regard to the substance in which it shares, a community is inclusive, total, we may even say totalitarian. But that word 'totalitarian' may give us pause, and we must remember the qualifications to which its use is subject. In the first place it is the community, and not the State, which is total. The State is limited by its legal character, and confined to the one common substance of declared and enforced law. In the second place, the community itself is not totalitarian in the sense that it acts as a *single whole* when it seeks to cover the whole of life. A community is itself a sum of interacting and complementary communities. It acts in and through the communities which it contains; and it is only total in so far as it contains sufficient riches of community-organization to correspond to all the different aspects of human life and to enable men to share in all the different ways in which sharing is possible. A community without any Church could not be a total community. A community in which family life was abrogated or truncated could not be a total community. A community in which there was no room and no place for trade unions would not be a total community.

(b) It follows that a community is federal in character. It is not a federation, since it is not a union of states; but we may understand its nature by the analogy of a federation. It is 'a

[1] *Cambridge Modern History*, vol. xii, p. 747.

great array of differentiated social cohesions'—religious, economic, social, charitable, educational, artistic, and scientific—which unite and co-operate to form the total social cohesion. Not that the units which form a community ever club together, by any sort of federal act, to bring it into being. Such an idea would be absurd, though there are some forms of theory (of the 'pluralist' or 'functionalist' or 'syndicalistic' order) which seem to look in that direction. On the contrary, the community is prior to its contained communities; and they develop or differentiate themselves within it as it seeks to attain a greater fullness. Yet there is also a sense in which we may say that the reverse process also happens—that the germination of new forms of social cohesion helps to shape a community, or at any rate so broadens and enriches it that it becomes more conscious of what it is and more aware of the common substance in which it shares. It has often been pointed out, for example, that the conversion of Anglo-Saxon England to Christianity, and the formation of a Christian community in England, helped to create a general or national community.

There is no single formula in which we can comprehend the relation of the growing contained communities to the growth of the whole community, or the relation of the general grown community to its various contained communities. Sometimes the contained communities may even seem not to be contained at all. A branch of the Roman Catholic Church contained within any given general community is also contained within that Church at large; and it may be drawn so much to the one that it almost escapes the other. Yet it may perhaps be asserted that generally, and upon the whole, each community contains, or at any rate colours, all the different social cohesions in its area—whether they have germinated within it, or been introduced into it; whether they exist solely within it, or ramify outside it. On the one hand, they build it up, like a branching coral-reef; on the other hand, it draws them together, without any violence and without any force, in the terms of a common life. There is a sense in which the English family, the English trade unions, and the English Churches, all correspond, and all answer to one another.

(*c*) The general community, with all its contained communities, employs no force. That is not to say that it does not exert influence, or even employ a discipline, upon its members. But at its utmost range it is pedagogic rather than legal; it is a school rather than a State. It is a free partnership of minds, for the exploration of all the fields of the mind; and it always retains the note of freedom, initiative, experimentation. We may alter the metaphor of the school, or rather we may carry it farther; we may speak of the laboratory. This is a metaphor which has been employed even by an apostle of the State—Professor Bosanquet. He admits—indeed he contends—that

'the content of legislation and administration with a view to the public good—the inventive, experimental, creative element—is almost entirely supplied by one or other of the forms of social action which are not due to the initiative of the state.... True social work, independent of the public power, is the laboratory of social invention. ... The work of the state is *de facto* for the most part "endorsement" or "taking over"—setting its *imprimatur*, the seal of its force, on what more flexible activities or the mere progress of life have wrought out in long years of adventurous experiment or silent growth.'[1]

The community is thus a laboratory for the State. But that is not all. The community is also a laboratory for itself. It may hand over some of its inventions to be 'endorsed'. But there is much that need not be endorsed, and cannot be endorsed. There are things we can discover for ourselves, and do for ourselves, in the field of community-life, which had better remain in that field, and indeed *must* remain in that field. The partnership in science and art, 'all virtue and every perfection', must again and again run into the form of law; but it must equally, and even more, remain at point after point in its own fluid form—for otherwise science and art and virtue and perfection will be petrified in the form of compulsion.

There is also another sense in which the community, if it be regarded as a community of communities, is the home of freedom and experimentation and choice. The free community permits us all to make our choice among its riches. We can choose, enter, and relinquish the societies which it contains. No doubt they, too, like the whole community itself, exert an influence, and even employ a discipline, upon us, *so long as we are members*. But even so, as Professor Unwin has argued, 'they are not a

[1] Bosanquet, *Philosophical Theory of the State*, Introduction to the second edition, pp. xxxii–xxxiii.

mere instrument of social pressure' on the individual. 'He can react through them upon society, and this reaction of a strong and clear will upon society is freedom. But this is only possible on condition that he freely selects his social cohesions.'[1] A community in which each man has this capacity of free selection—among parties, churches, professional and occupational societies, and all forms of voluntary grouping—is a laboratory not only for general social experiment, but also for the testing and trying out of individual character and personality.

(*d*) It follows that the community is in no sense a transcendent being which stands above the individual and determines his being and his duties in terms of its own higher nature. It is true enough that the long course of social experiment has resulted in a tradition of social experience; that this tradition of social experience elevates every individual, in a greater or less degree, according to his capacity for entering into its inheritance; that a great part of the content of every individual mind is a social content; and that membership of any community involves a long process of education in the tradition of the community. But we cannot leap from this simple truth to the very different assumption that there is some higher being in the music of which all individuals are merely so many stops—'an organism with ends, a being, and means of action superior, in power and duration, to those of the individuals, separate or grouped, who compose it'.[2] A common content of many minds does not involve a common mind—at any rate when we are thinking *sub specie humanitatis* and dealing with the sphere of our transitory human groups. (The conception of a Church in which there is an indwelling Spirit of God belongs to a different plane of thought. But we only confuse thought, with sad and tragic results, when we take what belongs to one plane and transfer it to another and different plane. 'I only am holy, saith the Lord.') A human community is its own members, and no more than its own members (though it is more than its present members, since its past members, who are now gone, still live on in any element of its tradition which they have bequeathed, and its future members, who have still to come, already belong to it, in the sense that it owes

[1] G. Unwin, *Studies in Economic History*, p. 459.
[2] Article I of the Carta del Lavoro, approved and promulgated by the Fascist Grand Council of Italy, 21 April 1927.

a duty to them and to their well-being); it simply consists in the intercourse of those members, their relations to one another, their sharing *with* one another, and the common ideas and ideals which they have constructed and *in* which they share. This is its essence. And if it has some natural or physical basis—some 'touch of nature' and consciousness of kin; some clinging to mother-earth and some sense of the common soil—this is not of that essence, though it may be a primitive stuff which enabled the essence to emerge and grow. A community is something different from its own basis, and something above its necessary preliminary conditions. But it is also something less than a transcendent and superior Being or Mind, which stands above its members. It is just itself—a free partnership of individual minds, with its roots embedded in nature, but with its branches spread in the common air and the common light of the human spirit.

II. *Church*

8. IN what has been already said the relation of Church to community has already been, at any rate by implication, suggested or foreshadowed. A Church (or a number of Churches) is part of the federal nature of community. In many respects it is parallel with, and analogous to, other parts. Some of its objects may be similar to the objects of other parts, and they may even overlap with them: the educational objects of a Church, for example, are similar to those of a specifically educational society, and they have some affinity even with those of a trade union which makes the advancement of education among its members one of its aims. In formal organization, again, a Church may be closely analogous to other societies within the community; it may adopt a similar type of internal government; it may stand in a similar relation to the government of the State, and may occupy a similar position in the eye of the law. In England, for example, the 'Free Churches' and the trade unions alike vest their property in trustees, under a trust deed which binds the trustees to use the property for the objects and in the ways which are specified in their rules. But it would be dangerous, and very erroneous, to press these analogies too far. A Church, partly in virtue of the past history of its life, but above all in virtue of its own permanent and peculiar nature, stands in a special relation to the community. It has also stood, and in some countries still stands, in

a peculiar relation to the State. These are two different matters; but they cannot be entirely disentangled or dissociated.

Before we look at the history of the relation of the Church to the community, which has taken different forms at different times, there is one word to be said, of the first importance, in regard to the nature of the Church. The Christian Church is the custodian of a sacred scripture, or revealed Word, which its members are bound to obey as the ultimate standard of authority in all matters which it covers, and which they are bound to proclaim, not only to the other members (if there be other members who are not Christians) of the community in which they are set, but also to members of other communities all over the world, so far as they are still ignorant of the Word. A Christian Church is *sui generis* in its custody of the Word of God, and in the duty of mission—universal mission—incumbent upon it under the Word. One form of Church may differ from another in its interpretation of the Word; but all forms are agreed in their basic idea of a custody of the Word and of a mission imposed by that custody.

But the Christian conception of a Church goes farther than this. God has not simply left a Word in custody with a Church, which is thereby made unique, in virtue of the unique character of its common substance, among all other forms or varieties of community. He Himself remains in the Church, and His Spirit dwells perennially in its members. In the community of the Church, there *is* a Being which transcends the members, and yet is immanent in them. Here we may speak of an organism, as St. Paul did; for here we have 'the head, even Christ, from whom the whole body fitly joined together and compacted by that which every joint supplieth, according to the effectual working in the measure of every part, maketh increase of the body unto the edifying of itself in love'. Any organism has a life-purpose which is served by every part, and to which every part is instrumental. In the economy of God, and where He Himself is present, there can be a divine and eternal life-purpose which is served by every member of His Church, and to which every member is instrumental. Here, and here only, we can conceive of the soul of man as part of an organism, inspired and controlled by the life-purpose of that organism, but free in the service of that purpose by virtue of its own free love. Apart from the presence of

God, and in any system of human or secular economy, man can never be part of an organism, because the intrinsic and ultimate value of his personality—an end in itself, except before God—forbids him to be instrumental. St. Paul could conceive of man as growing in Christ—'in the unity of the faith and of the knowledge of the Son of God'—'up into him in all things'. He could speak, again, of the Christian life as 'hid with Christ in God'. But he could also warn the believer against being beguiled by those who intrude into the things which they have not seen, and are vainly puffed up by their fleshly mind, 'not holding the Head, from which the body by joints and bands having nourishment ministered, and knit together, increaseth with the increase of God'. . . . 'Not holding the Head', we cannot see any Being which transcends the members of a community, and yet is immanent in them; 'not holding the Head', we cannot rightly speak of a community as an organism, in which each part is an instrument.[1]

9. The Christian conception of a Church as unique among other forms or varieties of community, first in being the custodian and in being charged with the proclamation of a revealed Word which is the ultimate standard of authority in all matters which it covers, and secondly (and even more) in being permeated and made organic by the continuing and indwelling presence of a personal God in whose service all its members live and have their being—this was a conception new to the ancient world in which it appeared. The Stoics had some conception of a cosmopolitan but indefinite society in which all rational men, possessing their 'fragment' or $\dot{a}\pi\acute{o}\sigma\pi\alpha\sigma\mu\alpha$ of reason, were knit to the impersonal Reason of God (physically conceived as a sort of fiery ether); but that was a very different thing from the Christian conception of the Church. An impersonal God, who was fundamentally a fine and tenuous physical substance, could only constitute an equally impersonal society, united (if indeed it

[1] The metaphor of organism is still a metaphor, even when it is applied to the Church; and there is at most similarity—similarity over a wide area, but not a total identity—between the conception of organism and the conception of the Church. The argument of the text is simply that if the word 'organism' is used at all in reference to any group composed of human beings, it can best be applied to the Church, because the Church has a Head as well as members, and because it has a single life-purpose which every member must serve. But comparisons of a spiritual society to a physical system must always remain, at the best, approximations to truth.

could be called united) by a common physical sharing in the common physical substance of a mere fiery ether. What confronted the Christian Church, and challenged the Christian Church, was not the wraith of the Stoic cosmopolis, but the gigantic and visible fact of a universal empire united by the cement of a common worship of the emperor. This empire made no distinction, and allowed no distinction, between community and state—between the free partnership sharing in a common substance of civilization, and the legal association sharing in a common body of law intended to protect that substance. State and community were one in the Roman Empire, as they had been one in the Greek city-State. Everything hung on the one integrated body: religion was merely one of its departments: the conduct of worship was a legal duty of legal officials, and worship itself was a civic obligation.[1] When the Christian conception and practice of the Church emerged, a profound question—perhaps the profoundest in history—thus arose. What was to be the relation of this conception and practice of the Church to the community-State or State-community—the integrated body which was both these things in one?

It was not a possible answer to this question that the idea of community should be disengaged from that of the State, and that the Church should take its place in community as a part of its federal system and a vanguard and a leader in the play of its federal life. That might eventually be what the Church would do, and that might be its inward and ultimate trend; but many centuries were to elapse before that trend could become evident, and before the Church could attempt to take that place and act that part. In the conditions of the fourth century, when the Church took its place beside the old system, it could not become a part of community; there was no real community there of which it could become a part. Neither could it constitute itself as another world—a whole other world—over against the existing world of the community-State. That would have been an impossible dualism. What could be done, and what was done, was that the Church should, *formally*, permeate and Christianize the existing world of the community-State, and make it a single

---

[1] This is not to say that private worship, and private societies for its conduct, might not be added—subject to the State's consent—to the basic obligation of public worship.

integrated community-State-and-Church. In other words, the universal empire could, and did, become also, and at the same time, a universal or catholic Church. One body of men had henceforth two aspects: in one aspect it was a community-State, and in the other it was a Church. Or we may say, more exactly, that the community-State, becoming a community-State-and-Church, had henceforth two governments—a secular government in things temporal, and an ecclesiastical government in things spiritual. This was the way in which the matter was put by Gelasius I about A.D. 500, when he enunciated the theory of a dyarchy of two authorities, and of the parity of the two.

10. Identified with the community-State, the Church, in its outward form, ceased to be a pure body bearing the custody of the Word and knit organically to its Head; it became the *alter ego* of another body, subject to the fortunes and the historic vicissitudes of that other body. As the community-State altered, contracted, split, and showed fissures (by a sort of process analogous, in its way, to geological change), the outward form of the Church was correspondingly affected. Not that its own inner life, or the Word of which it was guardian, or the movement of its guiding Spirit, were ever, for a moment, inactive, or ever without effect in determining its outward form and order. The Church was never merely passive; but it is none the less true that, once identified with the community-State, and made conterminous with it, it was necessarily affected by the changes and contingencies of the life of that body.

First the community-State bifurcated: it developed an Eastern or Byzantine manifestation, as well as a Western or Roman; and there arose an Eastern or Orthodox Church as well as a Western or Catholic. Then, many centuries later, in the era of the Reformation, there came another historical fissure; and Protestantism emerged. This was partly produced by the working of the Word and the Spirit (we should be blind if we did not see that working); but it was also produced, in part, by a change of the community-State, and there is thus a sense in which we may say that once more the Church, in its outward form, 'bent with the remover to remove'. The general designation of Protestantism cannot conceal the fact of a plurality of Protestant Churches; and when we study this plurality, we have to remember not only the different doctrines (or different interpretations of the Word) on which it was based, but also the emergence of a new and plural conception and practice of the community-state.

The two things are tangled and intertwined; but following the thread of our argument we may concentrate our attention on the way in which the outward form of the Church was affected by the change of the community-State in western and northern Europe. Here there had emerged what we cannot yet generally call by the name of the 'nation' (though in some places it might be such), but what we may safely call by the more indeterminate name of the 'region'. Each region—whether it was a kingdom, or, as in Germany and Switzerland, a principality or a canton—had now begun to act as an autonomous community-State. If such a region seceded from Rome, and adopted the principle of a Reformed Church, it now ruled that this Church, in its outward form, must be identical and conterminous with itself. The old idea of the community-State-and-Church persisted: it only assumed a new, particular, and local form. Hooker states this new form when he writes that 'in a ... Christian state or kingdom ... one and the self-same people are the Church and the commonwealth'. In other words, three things are the same: a people, or community, is also a commonwealth or State, and it is also a Church. What was held by the Anglican Hooker was held also by Lutherans and Calvinists. It was the common—we might almost say the inevitable—belief of the sixteenth century. And it was inevitable because it was nothing new, but simply the accepted inheritance of the past, applied—and logically applied—to the new conditions of the present.

11. How was this identification of community, State, and Church to be ended? How was community to be separated from State, and how was the Church to find its place and its peace in the free partnership of community? The seed of the answer had always been present in the Church, and it was to germinate from the Church. The Church, as a society of the Word and a community in the Spirit, had always been in its essence distinct from the community-State with which, in its outward form, it had so long been identified. If it began to thrust upwards again, in its own nature, it would not only distinguish itself from the community-State; it would also help to distinguish the community from the State; it would form a nucleus of free community which

would encourage the general growth of such community. Men have often distinguished between the Church invisible and the Church visible, or the Church universal and the particular Church. Perhaps more important is the distinction between the Church as a society of the Word and a community in the Spirit, and the Church as conterminous and identified, in its outward form, with the range of the community-State. After the sixteenth century that distinction (never absent,[1] but never developed) began to assume new life, with consequent effects on the community-State itself.

On the one hand, the reformed Catholic Church of the counter-Reformation began to stand out distinct, not only from the new Protestant Churches, but also from the community-State. In the new order, or the new disorder, there was no community-State broad enough to be conterminous with its range. In the theory of Suarez the Church, as a *communitas politica vel mystica* of divine foundation, is distinguished from the communities of human invention, however 'perfect' (in the sense of having full capacity of political government) these may be. It is interesting also to notice that in his theory the category of 'perfect communities of human invention' not only includes the State, but also embraces local communities and even personal groups.

On the other hand, the Protestant area of Europe began also to develop, in the course of the seventeenth century (though the movement was already beginning in the sixteenth), the idea of the separate community of the Church. The regional (or, as it was commonly called, the 'territorial') principle began to be challenged by what has been called the 'collegial'. The 'collegial' principle appeared among the Calvinists; it may already be traced in the sixteenth century; but it is definitely enunciated by the Dutch Calvinist, Voetius, in the seventeenth, when he argues that the Church is based on its own contract of society, independent of the political, and is therefore a 'collegial' or corporate body with its own free membership and its own power over its own body. This is a doctrine like, and yet unlike, that of Andrew Melville, when he proclaimed to James VI of Scotland, in 1596, his theory of the two kings and the two kingdoms in Scotland. Melville was anxious to vindicate the claims of the

---

[1] The distinction is present in the argument of St. Augustine's *City of God*: see the previous essay, pp. 249 ff.

custodians and governors of the spiritual kingdom against those of the earthly king; but he still held that the two kingdoms were conterminous—or, in other words, that every subject of the Scottish king should also belong to the Presbyterian Church. Voetius goes farther, and his collegial Church is of a different pattern from Melville's spiritual kingdom. But it is not so much in Calvinism (even of the type of Voetius) as in the English Independents of the seventeenth century, and in English Nonconformity generally, that the doctrine of the collegial Church sinks deep and becomes the one foundation. The 'Free Churches' were firmly grounded as societies of the Word and communities in the Spirit, distinct from the community-State. So grounded, they not only rooted themselves, apart from and outside the 'integral' community-State: they also served as the nucleus of a further growth of free community; and they thus helped, as we have already had reason to notice, to disengage state and community and to foster the general growth of community (with themselves as part of it) in English thought and practice.

We must not over-emphasize the part played by the Christian Churches, during the course of modern history, in disengaging State and community. Other forces have also been at work; there has been, for example, the economic, from the voluntary companies which colonized in the seventeenth century to the trade unions of the nineteenth. Nor must we exaggerate the extent to which community has been actually disengaged from State. The French Revolution was a triumph, or a return, of the integrated community-State, anxious to absorb the Church and to make itself the one and only common ordering of human life. Only yesterday, in Nazi Germany, the same triumph was once more celebrated, with an even fiercer zeal. Under such conditions there have again appeared curious Erastianisms—or even, if we may use the word, Diocletianisms. None the less, we may say today—speaking of ourselves in England, and speaking of the matter as we see it with our own eyes—that the community is something which may be distinguished from the State; that the Churches have helped to make it distinct; that the Churches belong to the essence of community; but that they belong to it in a particular way, which depends on their own particular character.

12. A Church, as we have said, is a part of the federal nature

of community. But, as we have also said, it is a part which is *sui generis*. It is a custodian of the Word, according to its own interpretation; and it has a mission imposed by the Word of which it is a custodian. This conception of mission will carry a Church, in foreign missionary enterprise, outside the limits of the community in which it is set. But the cardinal question, when we are considering the relations of Church and community, is the question of the mission of the Church to its own immediate community.

Let us suppose that community to be (as it generally is) a nation—a single nation—a nation which lives and builds a general national tradition behind and beyond the legal association of the State, though if the State be a national State (as again it generally is) there will be sympathy and co-operation between the nation as such and the legal association as such. Upon this basis a Church, with its mission to the nation and with its duty of testimony to the nation, may be impelled to draw its adherents from the whole of the nation, and to draw the whole of the nation into itself. It is in this sense that the Presbyterian Church of Scotland seeks to be a 'national Church, representative of the Christian faith of the Scottish people', with 'a call and duty to bring the ordinances of religion to the people in every parish of Scotland'.[1] The Church thus widens itself to the width of the whole community; and in one sense it is the community. In another sense it is just a part, or an aspect, or a function of the community—an aspect accompanied by other aspects, a part co-operating with other parts (economic, for instance, or educational) which, though less extensive in their range of membership or the scope of their general endeavour, still have their own place, and their own function, in constituting the general community.[2]

That is one possibility. Still confining ourselves to the relation of Church and community, and still leaving the state out of account, we can also see other possibilities. The different Free Churches in England help to constitute the English community,

---

[1] The phrases are quoted from the Church of Scotland Act, 1921.

[2] It should be added that the Presbyterian Church of Scotland, broad as it is, does not, of course, include the whole of the Scottish people. Besides the Roman Catholic Church there are also, in the general field of Protestantism, (1) some independent Presbyterian bodies; (2) Free Churches of the English type; and (3) an Episcopal Church allied to, but independent of, the Church of England.

but none of them seeks to embrace the whole of it: each of them recruits its own circle of members; all of them acknowledge and respect one another's boundaries; and each and all can cooperate, through a federal council of the Free Churches, to defend and maintain, before the community, and for the benefit of the community, the common principles on which, in spite of their differences, they are all alike based. By their side stands the Church of England. Its relation to the English community is far from simple. In one sense it seeks, like the Presbyterian Church of Scotland, to be a national Church, embracing the whole community, and bringing the ordinances of religion to the people of England in every parish. In another sense, less formal and more real, it is content, like the Free Churches in England, to recruit its own particular circle of adherents; and like them it helps to constitute the English community without claiming (otherwise than in form) to cover the whole of it. In still a third sense—when we take the State into account as well as the community—the Church of England has a peculiar relation to the State. It is 'established' by it—that is to say, it is given certain legal rights and subjected to certain legal duties which may be regarded as the corollary of its rights. Here we must notice a peculiar and perplexing fact, which can only be explained by the accidents of historical development. The Church of England, which, as such, and as its name indicates, exists in and for the English community, is established by a State (and so far as establishment involves control, is controlled by a State) which is not the State of the English community, but a State including Scotland and Wales, and also Northern Ireland, as well as England.

The relation of Church and community in England is peculiar and peculiarly complicated. It is simpler in Wales. Here there exist Free Churches, as in England; and here, since 31 March 1920, there exists what is called 'the Church in Wales'—a body which is, in a sense, a branch of the Church of England, but a body which, having been 'disestablished' since 1920, is separate from the established Church of England and governs itself autonomously. The general result is that the community of Wales, in its relations to the Christian Churches, offers a simple pattern. Different Churches, on the same footing, help to constitute the community. None of them seeks to embrace or include the whole, in reality or in form; each of them brings its contribution to the whole.

In the course of the analysis of community, in the first part of this essay, something was said about the multiform and multi-coloured nature of the British conception and practice of community, and about the many concentric areas of operation in which that conception was active. Not only do we regard each community as in itself a federation of groups (religious, educational, economic, and the like); we are also prepared to see successive circles of community—from the circle in which Scotland, England, and Wales are separate communities to the circle in which all the United Kingdom is a community, and from that circle again to the circle in which the whole of the British Commonwealth is a community. When we consider this succession of circles we see that it is an artificial simplification of the relation of Church and community to discuss that relation only in regard to the circle in which Scotland, England, and Wales are communities.

We have also to think of the relation of the Christian Churches to the community of the United Kingdom. Since that community is organized as a State (while the Scottish, English, and Welsh communities are not), it is in this area that the problem of the relation of Church and State arises; and it is in this area that, as has just been noticed, the peculiarity exists of a Church being established by the State in only one part of its territory. But the community of the United Kingdom still remains a community, even if it is organized as a State, and even if we think of it largely as a State. Many of the Churches, like most of our trade unions, are constituted on the general basis of the community of the United Kingdom, and help to constitute that community. The Free Churches of England, though they may have originated in England, and though they may be particularly represented in England, have flowed over the United Kingdom. The Church of England may be peculiar to England, but it is also closely associated with the Church in Wales and with the Episcopal Church in Scotland.

Nor is the United Kingdom the full limit of the range either of the Free Churches or of the Church of England. We have also to think of the wider circle of the community of the Commonwealth. The one connexion in which we habitually use the dubious prefix 'Pan' is when we speak of the Pan-Anglican Synod which gathers together representatives from all the episcopalian Churches in the whole of the Commonwealth.[1] The Free Churches are similarly spread. The connexion which unites all the Episcopalian Churches of the Commonwealth, or all the different branches of the various Free Churches which are spread over it, may be loose. But there *is* a connexion; it is a part of the connexion and the general constitution of the community of the Commonwealth. It would be hard to say that the community of the Commonwealth is organized as a State—at any rate as a State of any ordinary type. It would be equally hard, when we remember that it has a common king, and a system of common co-operation between its various governments, to say that it is *not* a State. What is not hard is to say that it is a community, and that the Churches which ramify through it, and by their common life are part of its common life, help to constitute this community.

13. The theme of the relation between Church and State belongs to another inquiry. That inquiry turns on the point whether a community which is legally organized as a State should give, and whether a Church should receive, a special legal status involving special legal rights and their correlative special legal duties (whether it be by way of 'establishment' or by way of 'concordat'): it also turns on the point whether, apart from such giving of special legal status to a particular Church, the State has a general legal control over all Churches and, if so, to what extent and within what limits. The present inquiry, which is simply concerned with the relation between Church and community, has already dealt with the various *forms* which the Church may take within a community as one of its parts or aspects: it only remains, in conclusion, to say some word about its *function*.

In its essentials the function of any Church, in the community in which it is set and which it helps to constitute, is the simple function of mission—the proclamation of the Word of which it is custodian, under the guidance of the Spirit by which it is made one body. Unique among all other forms or parts of com-

[1] Since 1866 all the bishops of the Anglican Communion have been invited, at intervals of ten years, to a conference held in London at Lambeth Palace, under the presidency of the Archbishop of Canterbury. The Conference includes bishops not only from Great Britain, the Dominions, India, and the Colonies, but also from the Protestant Episcopal Church in the United States of America.

munity in the treasure of which it has custody, it has to diffuse that treasure, to the best of its power, among the whole community. No Church lives to itself alone: each has to give its message and its service to the entire community, so far as lies in its power; and each, in order to give, must take something from the community—something of its colour, something of its general stock of ideas, something of its general temper and habit of life. Not that the community has any right, or even claim, to assimilate the Churches which it contains to its own image. They are, in their essence, societies of a universal Word, and communities in a universal Spirit; and they shape themselves according to their essence—each according to its particular interpretation of the Word, and each according to its particular apprehension of the Spirit. But while they shape themselves according to their essence, they will also colour themselves freely and voluntarily—it may even be by an instinctive and unconscious spontaneity—with the colour and general character of the community in which they are set. This is a simple necessity if their message is to be understood by the people to which it is given. If a Church had no community colour, but were a simple neutral gray—still more if it took the colour of some other community—it would lose its appeal, forfeit its sympathy, and become a foreign body embedded in the community rather than a part of its life.

But it is one thing to say that a Church will assimilate itself to the general life of the community, in order to serve it better and with a better understanding. It is another thing, and a very different thing, to say that a community may, or can, assimilate a Church perforce to itself. The community as a community has neither the right nor the power to attempt such assimilation. All it can do as a community is to diffuse the general influence of its whole tradition among Churches, as it does among all the other parts of itself; and this it will do in any case, apart from any question of right or power, by the mere fact of being itself. Where right is claimed or power asserted, it is not the community as such which is acting. It is the community organized as a State: more simply, it is the State. It is only the State, and not the community, which can claim right or assert power.

In giving its message and service to the community a Church will act in many ways. It will not only preach the Word, within its walls and without: it will also seek to provide education and general guidance (in clubs and camps and otherwise) for the young: it will seek to provide social activities, and methods of using and enjoying leisure, for adults. Whatever can bring to it new adherents, or comfort and sustain existing members, will lie within its scope and be part of its duty of mission to the community. But here a problem arises which has become acute in our days, and which vitally concerns the general relation of Churches and the community. A Church, exalting its mission and widening its scope, may tend to become, at any rate in respect of its own members, a totalitarian body. It may seek to engulf the whole of their life in itself—providing them with societies, organized and directed by itself, for their every activity, and founding, for example, special trade unions for them which will keep them within its fold, or special political parties which will tend to the same effect. It is the danger of such a policy that it may tend to provoke a violent reaction. The State, claiming to represent the general community, may be led to exalt *its* mission and to widen *its* scope: going beyond its legal province, and assuming the function of general director and educator, it may claim for itself the whole guidance of youth and the whole provision of social activities to fill the leisure of adults. But there is a graver objection to the totalitarian Church than the danger that it may tend to provoke, by way of reaction, the totalitarian State. A Church which assumes such a form is defeating the general nature of community—and defeating also itself.

If, as has been argued, the community is by its nature federal —'a community of communities'—it is a part of the duty of Churches to act within the federal system. They must recognize that they coexist with other societies—trade unions, parties, and other groups—and that they have to live and to make their peace with these other societies. If each Church became a total society, and if the community became a community of total societies, it would be an irreparably divided community. Nor would the community only suffer. The individual would also suffer. It is part of his freedom that he should belong to more than one society within the community; it is part of his general education, and his general moral development, that he should learn to conciliate different loyalties, and to bring different duties, when they conflict, into harmony.

But above all—and this, from the point of view with which we are here concerned, is the final consideration—the Church itself must suffer if it seeks to be total, and if it fails to take its place and assume its station as one in the 'great array of differentiated social cohesions'. If the Church has a mission to the whole community, its members must take their place in groups other than the Church, and they must carry the mission of the Word into these other groups. If the whole Church has a mission, the best way of its discharge is that *each* Churchman should mix with the general community, and with the different groups of the community—not living the life withdrawn, but the life of varied fellowship. The Church which seeks to be total is barred by its very zeal from its own essential duty—the duty of 'total mission' in the other and truer sense of a mission to the *whole community*. It is a noble temptation of a Church to seek to include its members for every purpose, and to seek to deliver to them 'the message of the Church' on every issue, with the authentic voice of total direction. But if it is noble, it is also a temptation. That Church best discharges its mission which has many missionaries, all true to itself, but all, in their truth to it, true also to other societies, and true to the general community. The uniqueness of the Church, as a society among the other societies of the community, is not the uniqueness of a self-contained and total society, which peculiarly absorbs its members. It is the uniqueness of a society operating as a leader, *through its individual members*, in the service of other societies and of the whole community—a society which fulfils, *through its individual members*, in those other societies and in the whole community, the mission imposed upon it by its custody of the Word and the motion of the Spirit.

INDEX

Abelard, 237, 265.
Acton, Lord, 87, 225.
Aesthetics and politics (Burke's view of relation), 219, 224; *and see also* Sentiment.
Agreement and difference, both needed in parliamentary government, 65–6.
Allegiance, as a bond of the Commonwealth, 13, 16, 17, 18.
Althusius, 89, 91.
Amateur, in politics, 28, 33–4.
American Revolution, period of, 121 ff.; *and see also* Revolution.
Anglicanism, 36, 65, 293 ff.
Annual Register, 168.
Aristocracy, 25, 28–31, 37, 55; 171–2, 209.
Aristotle: influence of, on medieval political theory, 87–8; influence on Burke, 219, 221 n., 225 n.; quoted, 276.
Asquith (Lord Oxford), 26, 27, 52–4, 79.
Association: of countries of Commonwealth in recognition of the King as Head, 13, 15, 17, 18; relation of associations to Community, 281, 283, 297; *and see also* Federation.
Atheism, Burke's fears of, 208, 213.
Augustine, St., theory of Society, 234–69.
Aurelius, Marcus, 241.
Authority, regarded by St. Augustine as a mode of service, 259–60.

Balance, of the constitution, 10–11, 143, 209.
Bar and barristers, in British politics, 26.
Beaconsfield, Burke and his house at, 172, 193, 204.
Belgium, 60.
Bentham, Jeremy, 120, 121, 125, 129 n. 2, 135, 136 n. 2, 141, 155, 156.
Bible, used as a basis of political theory, 87.
Bill of Rights, 3, 140, 217.
Biology and politics, 218.
Blackstone, on the British Constitution, 120–53.
Bolingbroke, 25, 26, 27, 31, 113, 166, 168.
Bosanquet, Bernard, 104, 272, 282.
Brickdale, member for Bristol, 157, 178, 203, 204.

Bristol, 156–64, and Essay VI *passim*.
British Commonwealth: function of monarchy in, 13, 14–19; statesmen of, 45; parliaments of, 61, 64, 82–5; Blackstone's conception of, as it stood in the eighteenth century, 147–51; general view of its nature, 48, 273, 274, 275, 295.
British Empire, Colonial, 13–14, 19–20, 84–5.
Burke, Edmund: and his Bristol constituency, 154–204; on the French Revolution, 205–33; other references, 26, 27, 35, 50–1, 52, 113, 121, 122, 128, 150, 258, 278.
Burke, Jane, 176, 181, 204.
Burlamaqui, 105, 129 and n. 1, 135 and n. 1.
Business and politics, 29, 38–40, 53.

Cabinet system: in Great Britain, 3, 10, 70, 71; in France, 72.
Calvinism, 89, 93, 290–1.
Cambridge, British statesmen trained at, 26.
Canning, 40.
Carolina, Locke's constitution for, 95, 97.
Castlereagh, 36, 38.
Catholic Church: political theory of, in the Middle Ages, 88–9; its position in Ireland in the eighteenth century, 187–8; general view of its development, 286–8.
Cecil, Lord, 29, 36.
Ceremony: monarchy and, 6, 7, 8, 10, 11, 12; Burke on, 219.
Cession, colonies acquired by, 82, 149.
Chamberlain, Joseph, 25, 27, 29, 45, 52–3.
Champion, Richard, and Bristol, 160, 179, 195, 204.
Chivalry, Burke on, 215, 224.
Church and community, 270–98.
Church and State: Burke's view of their relation, 209, 225–7, 231; St. Augustine's conception of the Church, 245–6, 249–51, and his view of its relation to the State, 251–2, 266–8; general view of the relation of Church and State, 292–5; *and see also* Collegial.
Church of England, *see* Anglicanism.
Church of Rome, *see* Catholic Church.
Churchill, Winston, 9, 26, 54, 81.

INDEX

Cicero, 262, 263.
Circumstances, Burke on importance of, 184, 219–20.
City: St. Augustine's view of the city of God or heavenly city, 240–3, 245–6, 261; his view of the earthly city, 243, 246–7, 264.
City of God (De Civitate Dei), St. Augustine's summary of its argument, 239–40.
Civitas: St. Augustine's conception of, 240–1; St. Paul on, 242.
Classics, influence of, on British statesmen, 27–8.
Clifton, and Bristol, 164.
Collegial conception of Church, 290–1.
Colonies: North American, Blackstone's view of, 147–51; relations of Bristol with, 157–8, 159–61, 185. *See also* British Empire *and* French Union.
Commerce, influence of, on British statesmen, 29, 38–40, 43–4.
Commissions, discharge of, for constituents, 194–5, 196–7.
Common Law, English, Blackstone's view of, 126, 140–1.
Commons, House of, its origin, 63.
Commonwealth, *see* British Commonwealth.
Communications, influence of, on area of community, 277.
Community: its relation to government, 4, 73, 91, 198; its relation to the Church, 270–98; *and see also* Society.
Compromise, 64, 68.
Concordance, Burke on the 'divine concordance' of the Universe, 218 and n. 1, 232, 258.
Conference, Imperial, 13, 15.
Conquest, colonies acquired by, 14 n. 1, 149.
Conservatism: of Blackstone, 126; of Burke, 209–10, 215, 217–18, 222–4, 231–2.
Constitution: nature of, 92, 109, 270; Blackstone's description of the British, 137–46.
Continuity, principle of, in politics, 1, 4, 33, 217–18, 222, 231–2.
Contract: general theory of social contract, 86–119, 146, 270, 276; the particular theory of a 'contract of government', 90–3, 100, and Hume's criticism of that theory, 116–18; the particular theory of a 'contract of society', 90–3, and the expression of it in Locke, 98, and in Rousseau, 110; Burke's idea of the contract of the Universe, 258.

Coronation Oath, 88, 147.
Corporation: Locke's view of the people as a corporation, 102; Blackstone's view of the chartered North American colonies as corporations, 150–1.
Council, the Great (*Magnum Concilium*), 62–3.
Court, monarchy and, 7, 215.
Criminal law in England, Blackstone's view of, 132.
Cromwell, Oliver, 26, 35, 50, 81.
Crown: in relation to the British Commonwealth and Empire, 14–20; Blackstone on the rights of the Crown, 146.
Cruger, member for Bristol, 160, 179, 181–2, 203, 204.

Dante, 237, 265 and n. 1.
Declaration of Independence, American, 123, 136, 139 n. 2, 139–40.
Democracy: in Switzerland, 58; in the system of representative government, 67–74; in the theory of Locke, 103; in the theory of Rousseau, 110, 112–14; defects in Burke's appreciation of, 198.
Dicey, A. V., quoted, 130, 142.
Discussion, parliamentary system of, 31, 67–8, 198.
Disraeli, 27, 29, 37, 52.
Dissent, *see* Nonconformity.
Divine Right, theory of, 88, 116, 225.
Dominium, St. Augustine's theory of, 247, 257.
Dulany, Daniel, 123.

Ecclesiasticus, book of, 198, 229 n. 2.
Economics and statesmanship, 38–40.
Education: of British statesmen, 25–8; legal education, 128, 132, 152; the Church and education, 284, 297.
Electorate, function of, 69, 70, 189–90, 199–201.
Élite, recruitment of, 29–30, 55, 198.
Eloquence: its function in a parliamentary system of government, 31–2, 54; character of Burke's eloquence, 173.
Empire: British, Blackstone's view of, 147; the Roman Empire in relation to the Church, 287–8; *and see also* British Empire *and* French Union.
Establishment of Church: Burke's view of, 225–7; general view of, 293, 295.
États Généraux, 60.
Executive: Locke's view of the, 99; Rousseau's view, 111–12.
Experience, Burke on its value, 221–3.
Experiment in politics, 34–5, 43, 231–2.

INDEX

Federalist, the, 123.
Federation: Imperial, 85; Rousseau's suggestion of federal form of State, 114; the community regarded as a federation in its nature, 281, 287, 292, 294, 297.
Feudalism, 88.
Filmer, Sir Robert, 87, 89, 95–6.
Finances, public, and their control, 146–7.
Folkmoots, 58, 61–2, 63.
Foreign policy: monarchy and the conduct of, 11–12; influence of business interests on, 29, 43; influence of religion on, 36; general lines of its conduct by British statesmen, 40–4.
Fox, C. J., 51, 211, 213.
France, 56–7, 60, 66, 72, 75, 78, 80, 84–5; *and see also* 205–33.
Francis, Philip, 211, 215.
Free Churches, *see* Nonconformity.
Free Trade: policy of, 39–40; demand for, in Ireland in the eighteenth century, 166, 186–7.
French Empire, or Union, 84–5.
French Revolution, 56; Burke on, 205–33.
Friendship, St. Augustine on, 255.
Frontiers, influence of, 65.

Game laws, Blackstone on, 132.
General Will (*Volonté générale*) in the theory of Rousseau, 109–10, 112–14.
Geneva, Rousseau and, 104, 110.
Gibbon, Edmund, 121, 125.
Gierke, O., his views on the influence of St. Augustine's theory of Society, 266.
Gladstone, 25, 29, 36, 42, 43, 81.
Greek history and theory: influence of, on British statesmen, 27; on Rousseau, 110.
Gregory VII, 248, 266.

Hamilton, 'single speech', 168–9.
Harnack, on St. Augustine, 266, 268.
Harrington, author of *Oceana*, 28, 29.
Head: of State, 4, 6, 9, 10; of the Commonwealth, 13, 17–19; *and see also* Monarchy.
Head of government, Prime Minister as, 4, 6, 10.
Hegelianism, Rousseau and, 107, 108.
Heredity: monarchy and, 6, 9; Burke on principle of, 217–18, 223–4.
History, Burke on importance of, 209–10, 211, 217–18, 219, 220–4.
Hobbes, political theory of, 90, 91, 92 and n. 1, 97, 98, 101, 102, 104, 110, 111.

Holdsworth, Sir W., quoted, 127 n. 2, 128 n. 1, 152, 153.
Holland, Locke and, 93, 96; *see also* Netherlands.
Homogeneity, social, in England, 65.
Honours, political, 7.
Hooker, 88, 95, 209, 226, 263, 289.
Huguenots, political theory of, 86, 89, 93, 96.
Humanity, Burke's spirit of, 174, 202.
Hume, David, 115–19.
Hunton, Philip, *Treatise of Monarchy*, 95.
Hypocrisy, 8, 32.

India: Republic of, 16–18, 83 and n. 1; development of parliamentary institutions in India generally (after 1861), 83.
Indirect Rule, 20, 45, 84.
Individualism: of Locke's political theory, 96–7; how far present in theory of Rousseau, 106–7.
Institutionalism, 70–1.
Instructions, *see* Mandate.
Ireland, 147, 186–7.

Jefferson, Thomas, 123, 136.
Johnson, Samuel, 162, 164, 170.
Justice: value of, implied in theory of Social Contract, 87; St. Augustine's view of justice, 262–3; *and see also* Righteousness.

Kent, *Commentaries* of, 128, 152 n. 2.

Labour party, and its leaders, 30, 55.
Language as a basis of community, 275–6.
Law: of constitution as stated by Blackstone, 137–46; law and political theory, 86–7, 129–30; relation between law and the State, 270–1.
Lawyers, part played by, in the American Revolution, 128, 129.
Leadership in parliamentary states, 79–81.
Legislator, Rousseau's recourse to a, 109–10, 113–14.
Legislature: Locke's view of the, 98, 102, 103; Rousseau's view, 111–13.
Liberalism, 78–9.
Liberty: value of, implied in theory of social contract, 87; Blackstone's conception of, 138–9; Burke's view of, 174, 228–30.
Locke, John, 88, 89, 91, 93–104.

Macaulay, Mrs. Catharine, 163, 177.
Majority, Locke's view of rights of, 98.

Mandate of electorate, 70–1, 182, 184, 189 ff., 194–7.
Manegold, 87.
Mariana, 89.
Massachusetts, 150, 159.
Melville, Andrew, 290–1.
Mercantile system, 157–8.
Metaphysics, relation of, to politics, as conceived by Burke, 209–10, 211, 219, 232.
Methodists, 161.
Middle Ages, political theory of, 88–9.
Ministers, relation of, to the Crown, 8–9, 27.
Mission, churches and duty of, 285, 297–8.
Mixed constitution, 143, 217.
Monarchy: British constitutional, 1–22; Blackstone's view of, 143–6; Burke's attitude to, 217–18.
Monasticism, Burke on, 222 and n. 1.
Montesquieu, 99, 133 n. 1.
More, Hannah, 163, 180.
Multitude, Burke's conception of the, 199–201, 222, 230; *and see also* People.

Nation: conception of, 56, 271–2, 292; Burke's view of, 222.
Natural Law: and the theory of social contract, in Locke's view, 89, 90, 94, 103; Rousseau's attitude to, 105–7; Blackstone's view of, 129, 136–7; St. Augustine's conception of, 267–8 (cf. also 247–8).
Natural Rights, 89, 94; *and see also* Rights of Man.
Nature: State of, in Locke's view, 197–8; in the view of Rousseau, 108.
Netherlands, 60, *and see also* Holland.
Nominalists, the medieval, 268–9.
Nonconformity, 36, 50, 65, 97, 130, 207–8, 279, 291, 292–3, 294.

Oligarchy, Disraeli on English, 29.
Opinion, public, or national, 3, 4, 30–1, 38, 200–1.
Opposition, function of, 10.
Oratory, *see* Eloquence.
Ordo, St. Augustine's conception of, 245, 257–9.
Organism, Social, conception of, 283–4, 285–6.
Oxford: British statesmen trained at, 27; burns books on political theory (1683), 95.

Paine, Thomas, author of *Rights of Man*, 119, 121, 122–3, 156, 207, 212, 213, 214, 215, 223.
Paley, William, 122.

Palmerston, Lord, 42.
Parliament: the British, 56–8; Locke on need of reform of, 103; Rousseau's criticism of, 111–12 and 112 n. 1; Blackstone's description of, 130–1, 132–3, 137, 141, 143–5; Burke's view of, 189 ff.
Partnership (in Latin *societas*), *see* Society.
Party: system of, 6, 10, 31–2, 36, 47, 69, 71, 77; Rousseau's criticism of, 112–13; Burke's view of, 171–2, 175, 197.
Paul, St., 241 n. 1, 242.
Peace, St. Augustine on the nature of, 256–7, 258, 259.
Peel, Sir Robert, 25, 29, 31, 37, 42.
People: as determining the form and conferring the exercise of authority, 88; Burke's conception of the people, 199–201, 227, 229–30, *and see also* Multitude; St. Augustine's conception of the nature of a *Populus*, 253, 262–4; people and community, 271–2.
Persecution: Rousseau and, 114; of the early Church, 261–2.
Personality: sense of, in St. Augustine, 236; Nominalist view of, 269.
Pitt, the elder, 26, 31, 32, 46, 50, 54, 76, 81.
Pitt, the younger, 3, 24, 39, 41, 42, 51–2, 53, 81.
Plantations, North American, 147–51.
Plato, St. Augustine's debt to, 235, 243, 244–5, 252–3, 268.
Policy, moral, Burke's conception of, 220.
Politician, definition of, 20–1.
Poor Laws, Blackstone's criticism of, 133.
Portland, third Duke of, 171, 175.
Posidonius of Apamea, 240–1.
Powers of government: as defined by Locke, 99; separation of powers, 99–100, 143.
Prejudice, Burke's conception of, 223–4.
Prerogative, Blackstone on, 144–6.
Prescription, Burke's conception of, 217, 223–4.
Priestley, Joseph, dissenting minister and radical, 126, 130, 155, 207, 212, 214.
Prime Minister: office of, 2, 3, 9, 10; prime ministers of the Commonwealth, 15–16.
Private Bills, 196–7.
Professionalism in politics, 20–1, 33–4.
Progress, experimental British method of, 34, 37–8.
Property: Harrington's view of its rela-

INDEX

tion to political power, 28, 29; Locke's theory of its basis, 94, 96–7; Burke on property, 215, 217–18; St. Augustine's view of property, 247, 265.
Protection and Free Trade, 39–40, 157–8, 186–7.
Protectorates in British Colonial Empire, 19 and n. 1.
Protestantism, 288–9, 290–1.
Public, eighteenth-century conception of the, 102.
Punishment, Locke on the right of, 97–8.
Puritanism, Locke and, 96; *and see also* Nonconformity.

Quakers, of Bristol, Burke and, 156, 161, 179, 201.

Race, 274–5.
Radicalism, 189–90, 207, 212, 214.
Reason: basis of parliamentary democracy, 67–8, 71, 73; Burke on the sovereignty of collective reason operating in history, 231.
Reform Bill of 1832, 2, 78.
Region, church and *regio*, 289, 290.
Religion: politics and 35–6, 65–6; political theory and, 88, 89, 90; Burke's views on religion and politics, 155, 187–9, 209, 221, 224–7, 231–2; St. Augustine's view that a common religion is necessary to a true State, 262–3; general view of the place of religion in the community, 270–98.
Representation: monarchy and its function of, 4; parliamentary system of, 56, 62–3, 69; Rousseau's objection to, 111, 113; Blackstone on parliamentary representation, 130–1, 132–3; Burke's conception and practice of, 182–3, 189 ff., 196–201.
Republicanism, 21, 22.
Residence in constituency, 193–4.
Resistance, right of, 88, 89; Blackstone's views on, 137 n. 4, 142, 146; Burke on methods of, 200.
Responsibility, political, 2–3.
Revolution: American, 94, 120, 123, 185, 205, 210, 277; English (of 1688), 1, 2, 3, 29, 64, 116–17, 137 n. 4, 205–6, 208, 216–18; French, 3, 56, 60, 94, 155, 205–33, 291.
Revolution (of 1688) Societies in England, 205, 207, 212, 213.
Rhodes, Cecil, 25, 29, 45, 49.
Righteousness (*Justitia*), St. Augustine's conception of, 243–5, 262; distinction of absolute and relative, 247.

Rights of Man, Blackstone on, 136; Burke's view of, 217, 228.
Rights of subject, Blackstone on, 137–40; Burke's view of, 218, 228–9.
Rockingham party, 169, 170, 177, 183, 192.
Roman Law and political theory, 87, 100.
Romanticism: Rousseau a forerunner of, 107; Burke and, 219, 224.
Rome, fall of, to Alaric, 238.
Rousseau, political theory of, 90, 91, 103, 104–15.

Salisbury, third Marquis of, 36, 42.
Scotland, 147, 274, 290–1, 292.
Scriptures, in relation to Church, 285.
Seeking, principle of, in politics, 38, 50.
Sentiment: function of, in politics, 5, 6, 7, 10, 12; Burke on the importance of, 219–24.
Separation of powers, 99–100, 143.
Settlement, colonies acquired by, 147–8.
Shaftesbury, first Earl of, 27–8, 93, 95.
Shakespeare, use of the term 'politician', 23.
Slave-trade: abolition of, 36, 156, 162, 205; Bristol and, 160–1, 202.
Slavery, St. Augustine's view of, 260–1.
Smith, Adam, 21, 122, 157–8.
Smuts, Field-Marshal, 26, 27, 45.
Social Contract, *see* Contract.
Society: play of voluntary (as distinct from the action of the State), 48–9, 68, 270–1, 272–3, 277–80, 282; conception of Society in the theory of the Social Contract, 90–3; Rousseau's failure to distinguish between Society and State, 109 (cf. also Burke's identification of the two, 278); St. Augustine's theory of Society, Essay VIII *passim*, and particularly 240, 255, 258, 259–60; society in the sense of *le grand monde*, 7, 273.
Soil, how far community based on common, 275.
Sovereignty: national, 56; general nature of, 71; Locke's view of, 100, 102–3, 104; Rousseau's view, 107, 111, 112, 114; Blackstone's view, 135–7, 143–5.
Spain, parliamentary institutions in, 58–9.
Stage, Burke and the, 166, 169–70.
Standing Orders of the House of Commons, 145 and n. 3, 196.
State: nature of the, and the idea of contract, 92; Burke's view of the

nature of the State, 225, and especially of its relation to the Church, 225–7; St. Augustine's conception of the State, 246–8, and of its relation to the Church, 248 ff., 265–8; the relation between State and Community, 270–2, 279–80, 282, *and see also* Society.
Statesman: definition of, 23–4; British statesmen, 23–55; statesmen in parliamentary systems of government generally, 79–81.
Stoicism, 94, 240–1, 243, 254, 286–7.
Suarez, 89, 91, 290.
Sweden: parliamentary institutions in, 59; *coup d'état* (of 1772), 154.
Switzerland, parliamentary institutions in, 58.
Symbol, monarchy as a, 4, 5, 6, 15, 18.

Territorial, Church, 289, 290.
Theocracy, St. Augustine and, 266–7.
Thomas, St., political theory of, 87–8, 218 n. 1, 225, 226 n. 3.
Time, value of respecting, in politics, 198–9, 221–2.
Tolerance, in politics, 64.
Toleration: religious, Locke on, 93, 95, 96; Burke and, 188.
Totalitarianism, in the thought of Rousseau, 114.
Trade Unions, 7, 284, 297.
Trinity College, Dublin, 165, 198.
Troeltsch, Ernst, quoted (on St. Augustine), 267–8.
Trust: legal notion of, applied to politics and political theory, 56, 91, 94, 98–9, 100–2; trusteeship for colonial territories, 36, 51; trusts for Free Churches and trade unions, 284.
Tucker, Rev. Josiah, 158, 162–3.

Universities, training of statesmen in, 26–8.
United States of America, 9–10, 64, 76, 77, 120 ff., 205; *and see also* Colonies, North American, *and* Revolution, American.
Unwin, George, quoted, 279 and n. 1, 283.

Vattel, E., 105.
Vindiciae contra Tyrannos, 89, 260.
Vindiciae Gallicae (of James Mackintosh), 213.
Vinerian Chair of English Law at Oxford, 124, 153.
Virginia, 124, 139, 160.
Voetius, 290–1.
Volk, German conception of, 239–40.

Wales, 147, 274, 293–4.
War: statesmanship and, 40–1, 74–7; St. Augustine on, 255.
Wendover, Burke and his constituency of, 169, 177, 191–2.
Westminster: Statute of (1931), 15, 17, 45; School, Locke educated at, 95.
Whig Party, 32, 39, 86, 94, 95, 115, 126, 170–2, 206, 209.
Wilkes, John, 131, 178, 189–90.
Will: Burke on place of, in politics, 199, 227, 230; *and see also* General Will.
Witan, Anglo-Saxon, 62.
Wyclif, 265, 268, 269.